CIM
STUDY TEXT

New syllabus

Advanced Certificate

The Marketing Customer Interface

First edition September 1999

ISBN 0 7517 4084 5

British Library Cataloguing-in-Publication Data
A catalogue record for this book
is available from the British Library

Published by

BPP Publishing Limited
Aldine House, Aldine Place
London W12 8AW

http://www.bpp.co.uk

Printed in Great Britain by WM Print
Frederick Street
Walsall
West Midlands WS2 9NF

We would like to acknowledge the major contribution made to this text by Dr Ted Johns.

We are grateful to the Chartered Institute of Marketing for permission to reproduce in this text the syllabus and specimen examination paper of which the Institute holds the copyright.

We are also grateful to the Chartered Institute of Marketing for permission to reproduce past examination questions. The suggested solutions to past examination questions have been prepared by BPP Publishing Limited.

Contents

HOW TO USE THIS STUDY TEXT

Aims of this Study Text

To provide you with the knowledge and understanding, skills and applied techniques required for passing the exam

The Study Text has been written around the new CIM Syllabus and the CIM's Tutor's Support Manual.

- It is **comprehensive**. We do not omit sections of the syllabus as the examiner is liable to examine any angle of any part of the syllabus - and you do not want to be left high and dry.

- It is **on-target** - we do not include any material which is not examinable. You can therefore rely on the BPP Study Text as the stand-alone source of all your information for the exam, worrying that any of the material is irrelevant.

To allow you to study in the way that best suits your learning style and the time you have available, by following your personal Study Plan (see below)

You may be studying at home on your own until the date of the exam, or you may be attending a full-time course. You may like to (and have time to) read every word, or you may prefer to (or only have time to) skim-read and devote the remainder of your time to question practice. Wherever you fall in the spectrum, you will find the BPP Study Text meets your needs in designing and following your personal Study Plan.

To tie in with the other components of the BPP Effective Study Package to ensure you have the best possible chance of passing the exam

Recommended period of use	Elements of BPP Effective Study Package
3-12 months before exam	**Study Text** Acquisition of knowledge, understanding, skills and applied techniques
1-6 months before exam	**Practice and Revision Kit (9/99)** Tutorial questions and helpful checklists of the key points lead you into each area. There are then numerous Examination questions to try, graded by topic area, along with realistic suggested solutions prepared by marketing professionals in the light of the Examiner's Reports. The edition for the new syllabus will be published in September 1999.
last minute - 3 months before exam	**Passcards (in due course)** Short, memorable notes focused on what is most likely to come up in the exam you will be sitting
1-6 months before exam	**Success Tapes (9/99)** Audio cassettes covering the vital elements of your syllabus in less than 90 minutes per subject. Each tape also contains exam hints to help you fine tune your strategy.

Settling down to study

By this stage in your career you may be a very experienced learner and taker of exams. But have you ever thought about *how* you learn? Let's have a quick look at the key elements required for effective learning. You can then identify your learning style and go on to design your own approach to how you are going to study this text - your personal Study Plan.

Key element of learning	Using the BPP Study Text
Motivation	You can rely on the comprehensiveness and technical quality of BPP. You've chosen the right Study Text - so you're in pole position to pass your exam!
Clear objectives and standards	Do you want to be a prizewinner or simply achieve a moderate pass? Decide.
Feedback	Follow through the examples in this text and do the Action Programme and the Quick quizzes. Evaluate your efforts critically - how are you doing?
Study Plan	You need to be honest about your progress to yourself - do not be over-confident, but don't be negative either. Make your Study Plan (see below) and try to stick to it. Focus on the short-term objectives – completing two chapters a night, say - but beware of losing sight of your study objectives
Practice	Use the Quick quizzes and Chapter roundups to refresh your memory regularly after you have completed your initial study of each chapter

These introductory pages let you see exactly what you are up against. However you study, you should:

- **read through the syllabus and teaching guide** - this will help you to identify areas you have already covered, perhaps at a lower level of detail, and areas that are totally new to you

- **study the examination paper section**, where we show you the format of the exam (how many and what kind of questions etc)

Key study steps

The following steps are, in our experience, the ideal way to study for professional exams. You can of course adapt it for your particular learning style (see below).

Tackle the chapters in the order you find them in the Study Text. Taking into account your individual learning style, follow these key study steps for each chapter.

Key study steps	Activity
Step 1 *Chapter topic list*	Study the list. Each numbered topic denotes a **numbered section** in the chapter.
Step 2 *Setting the scene*	Read it through. It is designed to show you **why the topics in the chapter need to be studied** - how they lead on from previous topics, and how they lead into subsequent ones.
Step 3 *Explanations*	Proceed **methodically** through the chapter, reading each section thoroughly and making sure you understand.
Step 4 *Key concepts*	**Key concepts** can often earn you **easy marks** if you state them clearly and correctly in an appropriate exam.
Step 5 *Exam tips*	These give you a good idea of how the examiner tends to examine certain topics – pinpointing **easy marks** and highlighting **pitfalls**.
Step 6 *Note taking*	Take **brief notes** if you wish, avoiding the temptation to copy out too much.
Step 7 *Marketing at Work*	Study each one, and try if you can to add flesh to them from your **own experience** - they are designed to show how the topics you are studying come alive (and often come unstuck) in the **real world**.
Step 8 *Action Programme*	Make a very good attempt at each one in each chapter. These are designed to put your **knowledge into practice** in much the same way as you will be required to do in the exam. Check the answer at the end of the chapter in the **Action Programme review**, and make sure you understand the reasons why yours may be different.
Step 9 *Chapter roundup*	Check through it very carefully, to make sure you have grasped the **major points** it is highlighting
Step 10 *Quick quiz*	When you are happy that you have covered the chapter, use the **Quick quiz** to check your recall of the topics covered. The answers are in the paragraphs in the chapter that we refer you to.
Step 11 *Illustrative question(s)*	Either at this point, or later when you are thinking about revising, make a full attempt at the **illustrative question(s)**. You can find these at the end of the Study Text.

Developing your personal Study Plan

Preparing a Study Plan (and sticking closely to it) is one of the key elements in learning success.

First you need to be aware of your style of learning. There are four typical learning styles. Consider yourself in the light of the following descriptions. and work out which you fit most closely. You can then plan to follow the key study steps in the sequence suggested.

Learning styles	Characteristics	Sequence of key study steps in the BPP Study Text
Theorist	Seeks to understand principles before applying them in practice	1, 2, 3, 7, 4, 5, 8, 9, 10, 11 (6 continuous)
Reflector	Seeks to observe phenomena, thinks about them and then chooses to act	
Activist	Prefers to deal with practical, active problems; does not have much patience with theory	1, 2, 8 (read through), 7, 4, 5, 9, 3, 8 (full attempt), 10, 11 (6 continuous)
Pragmatist	Prefers to study only if a direct link to practical problems can be seen; not interested in theory for its own sake	8 (read through), 2, 4, 5, 7, 9, 1, 3, 8 (full attempt), 10, 11 (6 continuous)

Next you should complete the following checklist.

Am I motivated? (a) ⬜

Do I have an objective and a standard that I want to achieve? (b) ⬜

Am I a theorist, a reflector, an activist or a pragmatist? (c) ⬜

How much time do I have available per week, given: (d) ⬜

- the standard I have set myself

- the time I need to set aside later for work on the Practice and Revision Kit and Passcards

- the other exam(s) I am sitting, and (of course)

- practical matters such as work, travel, exercise, sleep and social life?

Now:

- take the time you have available per week for this Study Text (d), and multiply it by the number of weeks available to give (e). (e) ⬜

- divide (e) by the number of chapters to give (f) (f) ⬜

- set about studying each chapter in the time represented by (f), following the key study steps in the order suggested by your particular learning style.

This is your personal **Study Plan.**

Short of time?

Whatever your objectives, standards or style, you may find you simply do not have the time available to follow all the key study steps for each chapter, however you adapt them for your particular learning style. If this is the case, follow the Skim Study technique below (the icons in the Study Text will help you to do this).

Skim Study technique

Study the chapters in the order you find them in the Study Text. For each chapter, follow the key study steps 1-2, and then skim-read through step 3. Jump to step 9, and then go back to steps 4-5. Follow through step 7, and prepare outline Answers to the Action Programme (step 8). Try the Quick quiz (step 10), following up any items you can't answer, then do a plan for a question (step 11). You should probably still follow step 6 (note-taking), although you may decide simply to rely on the BPP Passcards for this.

Moving on...

However you study, when you are ready to embark on the practice and revision phase of the BPP Effective Study Package, you should still refer back to this Study Text:

- as a source of **reference** (you should find the list of key concepts and the index particularly helpful for this)

- as a **refresher** (the Chapter roundups and Quick quizzes help you here)

SYLLABUS

Aims and objectives

- To address the marketing opportunities presented through effective interaction between the organisation and its customers

- To equip students with a conceptual framework which enables them adequately to distinguish between different stakeholder groups across a variety of marketing environments

- To develop a sophisticated understanding of customer dynamics, in which customer behaviour is viewed as an interactive process influencing product/service innovation

- To acquaint students with the range of methodologies through which customer dynamics may be investigated, measured, analysed and interpreted

- To examine the strategic, managerial and operational implications of customer-focused marketing

- To explore trends in customer behaviour over the foreseeable future, both incremental and transformational

Learning outcomes

Students will be able to:

- Describe and interpret the significance of the differences between 'customers', 'users', 'consumers' and 'payers'.

- Critically appraise the relationship between customer dynamics and marketing

- Evaluate the effectiveness of the marketing/customer interface within specific product sectors, and propose cost-effective performance improvements where appropriate

- Understand the (psychological, social, cultural and economic) factors influencing customer dynamics in particular the marketing scenarios and the impact upon product/service improvement or innovation

- Analyse key issues in customer dynamics including segmentation, relationship marketing, and the behavioural patterns found within the Decision Making Unit

- Design and carry out operational investigations into customer dynamics, customer perceptions of product/service performance, and customer satisfaction/delight

- Develop visionary yet practical strategies for mobilising customer-focused marketing programmes within defined organisational settings

- Maximise returns from investments in IT and people within the arena of customer-focused marketing and customer service

- Comprehend the directions for customer dynamics in the foreseeable future and identify related marketing opportunities

Syllabus

Indicative content and weighting

3   Customer dynamics (25%)

4   Investigating customer dynamics (20%)

BPP PUBLISHING

TUTOR'S GUIDANCE NOTES

The Marketing Customer Interface

The following is BPP's summary of the Tutor Manual produced by the CIM for this subject.

This new subject in the CIM qualifications programme hinges on the marketing/customer relationship. The following elements are important:

- Virtually all companies (even those not currently operating in a competitive environment) believe that relating to and **understanding customers** presents major opportunities for ongoing **competitive advantage**.

- Customers themselves are **demanding more** (more access, better service, lower prices, resorting to legal sanctions, forming pressure groups).

- Companies must attain **performance standards** previously seen as unattainable if they are to remain competitive. They cannot confine themselves merely to what it suits them to provide.

- Customers have **precise requirements** and expect them to be fulfilled. They must be 'delighted' by the product offering if they are to come back – mere '**satisfaction**' is no longer enough.

- The **globalisation** of the world market place, influenced by factors such as communications and mass travel, has influenced customer tastes and preferences.

- **New competitors** are emerging and bringing with them new methods, systems, technology and innovative thinking. They are not hidebound by tradition.

- As competition accelerates, so does the pressure on the company to be **imaginative and resourceful** when devising customer-focused programmes. This has to be done without damaging overall **corporate viability**.

- Organisations must have greater concern with the **internal processes** which deliver value for customers. In other words, there must be enhanced 'customer priority' within organisations.

This new module therefore emphasises the strategic importance of getting close to customers and processes which enable organisations to communicate with and relate to their customers.

You should note that it is recommended that you supplement your studies with collection of up to date information from magazines, journals (such as *Marketing Week* and *Marketing Business*) and quality newspapers.

The following notes have been produced by the Senior Examiner.

For those studying *The Marketing Customer Interface*, it may be useful to rehearse once again what the subject is about, what students will be expected to achieve, and why the focus on customer dynamics has acquired such prominence in the revised CIM qualification framework.

In his 1996 book, *Customer-Driven Marketing*, John Frazer-Robinson bases his whole argument on a key point:

> **The object of a business is not to make money.**
> **The object of a business is to serve its customers.**
> **The result is to make money.**

Too often, this fundamental principle is forgotten. Sometimes marketers in practice operate more like sales people, seeing their role as trying to sell whatever their organisation has already decided to make. According to this perspective, customers are passive, receptive and reactive, influenced this way and that by economic, psychological and sociological factors, but at the same time capable of being manipulated into purchasing whatever is put in front of them. Ironically, too, marketers holding such views can often claim, simultaneously, that for them the customer is king.

Worldwide, the situation is changing. Organisations are gradually discovering that satisfying customers and, whenever possible, exceeding their expectations, is essential for long-term business success. In turn, customers themselves are more articulate, more prepared to complain (instead of simply taking their business elsewhere), more willing to collaborate in order to face down organisations which appear indifferent to their needs, more aggressive in pursuing litigation or in seeking media support if they believe that in doing so their grievances are more likely to be addressed.

At the same time, customers are the ultimate source of corporate prosperity and survival. Without customers - without someone who is prepared to pay, in other words - no organisation can exist for very long. And customer "loyalty", if properly activated, understood and sustained, is an asset which the best and more successful organisations cultivate carefully. Whilst they recognise that some customers may be very demanding, the creation of customer continuity offers a potential advantage which other organisations - coping incessantly with customer attrition - cannot enjoy.

To emphasise the significance of the customer for effective marketing, here are some contributions from recently published sources.

* According to Bill Gates (*Business at the Speed of Thought*, 1999), customer service will become the competitive differentiator for all organisations in the new digital age. Moreover, intermediaries like travel agents and insurance brokers will have to add value through service, or they will perish as customers increasingly buy products online.

* Customers now want more access time (typically 24 hours a day, seven days a week) and won't wait for telephones to be answered.

* Customers don't want choice, if the range of options doesn't include exactly what they want. Instead, they increasingly expect products and services to be customised to their specific requirements - generalised segmented offerings are no longer acceptable.

* It isn't enough to make your customers satisfied: customers now want to be delighted. Merely ensuring that products and services meet functionality performance criteria will not produce delight.

* Customers who rate an organisation as "very good", or who are "very satisfied" with the organisation's products, are up to six times more likely to recommend the organisation to others, unprompted, than customers who are simply "satisfied".

* Dissatisfied customers will actively recommend competitors.

* In the UK, more than 80 per cent of companies segment their customers, but only 40 per cent calculate annual profitability per segment and even fewer (22 per cent) measure lifetime profitability.

* For many organisations, methods of tracking customer satisfaction (and customer complaints) are questionable, and measures of customer loyalty even more so.

Against this background, therefore, *The Marketing Customer Interface* emphasises the strategic importance of getting close to the customer, the organisational processes which enable organisations to communicate with their customers, the mechanisms for sustaining product/service innovations which are genuinely customer-focused, methodologies for investigating customer dynamics, and (most important of all) the competitive implications for proactivity in sustaining organisation/customer dialogue.

The Senior Examiner for *The Marketing Customer Interface* was previously Senior Examiner for *Understanding Customers* at Certificate level. In order to pass the examination, it is necessary to demonstrate (not only possess) six competencies, as defined briefly below. Each of the competencies is as significant as the others, so it will not be acceptable for candidates to trade off inadequacy in one dimension against superior effort in another. The six competencies are:

(1)   *Subject-matter knowledge* - which has to be up-to-date. Textbooks are important, but not sufficient because, for example, they cannot report on developments which have occurred within, say, the past six months or so.

(2)   *Analytical skills* - the cerebral detachment which enables fact and hyperbole to be recognised and separated, plus the willingness to question such naive sentiments as "the customer is king" and "the customer is always right".

(3)   *Application capability* - the capacity to create and present solutions to broadly-stated situational scenarios. It is necessary to remember that the Chartered Institute of Marketing is a professional body, and the distinguishing feature of a professional is the capacity to 'make things happen'.

(4)   *A businesslike and commercial focus* - recognising that a customer-facing orientation is appropriate only if it generates an enhanced flow of profitable business; it is not desirable for its own sake.

(5)   *The readiness to cite supporting evidence* - through references to relevant literature, articles, textbooks and corporate marketing materials.

(6)   *Presentation and packaging skills* - producing answers which are coherent, legible, articulate, well-structured, and concise.

THE EXAM PAPER

Assessment methods and format of the paper

	Number of marks
Part A: compulsory question, mini-case	40
Part B: three questions from six (equal marks)	60
	100

Time allowed: 3 hours

Some illustrative questions and the specimen paper, along with some explanatory notes from the senior examiner, are reproduced at the back of the Study Text.

STUDY CHECKLIST

This page is designed to help you chart your progress through the Study Text and the Action Programme. You can tick off each topic as you study and try questions on it. Insert the dates you complete the Action Programme in the relevant boxes. You will thus ensure that you are on track to complete your study before the exam.

	Text chapters Date completed	Action Programme Number	Date completed

PART A: OVERVIEW, CONCEPTS AND BACKGROUND

	Text chapters Date completed	Number	Date completed
1 Terminology and definitions		1, 2	
2 Customer power in the new competitive climate		1	
3 Customer-focused marketing in specific economic sectors		-	

PART B: MANAGING THE MARKETING/CUSTOMER INTERFACE

4 The strategic dimension: vision and leadership		1, 2, 3, 4, 5, 6, 7	
5 The managerial dimension for mobilising performance		1, 2, 3, 4, 5, 6	
6 Creating positive relationships with customers		1	
7 Innovation and the culture of continuous improvement		1, 2	

PART C: CUSTOMER DYNAMICS

8 The holistic perspective of customer behaviour		1, 2, 3, 4, 5	
9 Classifying customers for competitive advantage		1, 2, 3, 4	
10 The individual customer: attitudes and behaviour		1, 2, 3	
11 Individual customers: external influences and personality profiling		1, 2, 3, 4	
12 Groups and organisations as customers		1, 2, 3, 4, 5, 6, 7	

PART D: INVESTIGATING CUSTOMER DYNAMICS

13 The basic principles		1, 2, 3, 4, 5	
14 Quantitative methodologies		1, 2	
15 Qualitative methodologies		1	
16 Secondary information sources		1, 2, 3, 4, 5	

PART E: CUSTOMER DYNAMICS AND THE FUTURE

17 Trends in customer behaviour and expectations		1	
18 Market trends with customer-facing implications		-	

BPP PUBLISHING

Part A
Overview, concepts and background

1 Terminology and definitions

Chapter Topic List	Syllabus reference
1 Setting the scene	1.1
2 Terminology and definitions	1.1
3 Assumptions, stereotypes and myths	1.1

Learning Outcomes

Upon completion of this chapter you will be able to:

- describe and interpret the significance of the differences between 'customers', 'users', 'consumers' and 'payers'

- understand the distinction between a sales orientation and a marketing orientation

- appreciate the changes in customer/marketing dynamics which are challenging old assumptions

Key Concepts Introduced

- Customer
- User
- Consumer
- Decision making unit (DMU)

Examples of Marketing at Work

- Sainsbury and Tesco
- Volkswagen Beetle & GM
- Eurostar

1 SETTING THE SCENE

1.1 Successful organisations in the late twentieth century focus on **marketing** rather than **selling**. They realise that the organisation as a whole needs to direct its effort at providing the customer with what is required (the product) at the right time (place), the right price and in the right manner (promotion). In this way the customer is likely to be satisfied: he will keep the product, pay his bill, buy again, and recommend to others. An organisation that thinks solely in terms of selling may find itself unable to compete in the marketplace.

3

1.2 It appears self-evident, then, that the organisation needs to focus on the customer above all else. But what do we mean by 'the customer' and how may he, she or it be identified? How are customers perceived by the organisations that they do business with, how has this changed in recent years, and what are the implications of these changes?

1.3 Ted Johns (*Perfect Customer Care*) makes the distinction between **customers** and **users**. The word 'customer' in its rigorous sense should refer to **someone who pays**.

> ### Key Concepts
> - **Customers** are people who use goods and services and **pay** for them.
> - **Users** are individuals who are affected by, or themselves affect, the product or service being supplied. Users are often people who use the product or service, but **do not pay** for it.

1.4 It therefore follows that some customers may not be users, and some users are not customers. This may be said to be true of the toy market - parents have traditionally been the customers and their children the users. However, with the growth of toy advertising, children are increasingly doing most of the choosing and so the **customer/user relationship** is shifting.

1.5 In an organisation, the **Decision Making Unit** (DMU) often takes the decision to purchase a product or service (it is the customer) without consulting eventual users. This is often the case with company car fleet arrangements.

1.6 Users have not bought the product, and may have had no direct say in the decision, but their satisfaction is vital if customer loyalty is to be maintained. It will be important therefore to profile the user of a product as much as the person or organisation that acquired it.

1.7 We can also distinguish between **customer** and **consumer** along the same lines.

> ### Key Concept
> A **consumer** is the end user of a product or service who may or may not be the customer. For example, the consumer of a tin of cat food will be the family pet, whilst it was the pet owner who was the customer.

1.8 Not all organisations accept this distinction between '**customer**' (the person who **pays**) and '**user**' (the person who **consumes**). In particular, **not-for-profit organisations** such as local authorities, libraries and schools often have a diversity of people and groups interested in the products and services they supply. These people and groups may be variously described as 'clients', 'users' or as 'customers'. As an example, Spennymoor School, a 740-pupil comprehensive in NE England, defines its 'customers' as children, parents, local industry and the community.

2 TERMINOLOGY AND DEFINITIONS

2.1 **What is a customer?** Simplistically, a customer is an **individual** or an **organisation**, who **buys a product** from the marketing organisation.

Users

2.2   It is crucial that you understand the importance of the **user** of the product from the marketing point of view. The user is the person who actually **uses** a product - a machine operator of a print press, for instance, or a salesman driving a fleet car - as opposed to the person who **pays for** the product, namely the customer (in our examples, the printing factory or the selling organisation).

Action Programme 1

Try to think of some more examples where the distinction between customer and user is significant.

Internal and external customers

2.3   We have seen how the **user** may be distinguished from the **buyer** or payer. A situation where there is a clear distinction between buyer and user is within an **organisation**, where some departments or sections are **internal customers** of other departments' products or, more normally, services. For instance, the sales division is an internal customer of the head office accounting or personnel function, and it is helpful for those **service departments** to perceive themselves as providing a service to a customer, that is to develop a '**marketing focus**', even though in fact the customer/user has no choice but to make the purchase.

2.4   Increasingly, these days, individual functions within organisations are being given the discretion to **obtain services from outside** if they wish. In local government there is now an obligation to consider the option of contracting out. Even if internal customers cannot go elsewhere they can still exercise the choice of **whether to use their colleagues' services or not** - they may prefer to do without them altogether.

The decision making unit (DMU)

2.5   Although it is often helpful to refer to 'the customer' as a **single, identifiable unit** at whom marketing efforts can be directed, in practice it is not that simple.

2.6   A surprisingly large number of purchases actually involve **more than one person**. In marketing we refer to the group of people who actually come together to influence a purchase decision (positively or negatively), at any stage in the buying process as the **Decision Making Unit** or DMU. We shall return to this concept frequently in this book.

Key Concept

The **decision making unit** (DMU) is the group of people in a business who decide whether to buy a product.

2.7   The complexity of the DMU in each market needs to be understood, and we need to be able to identify what role individuals are playing in the buying decision. Each of these people will have their own concerns, motivations and interests.

    (a)   A child (the **user**) may pick up a new breakfast cereal when in the supermarket - it looks new and exciting. Mum or Dad (the **customer**) is concerned to ensure that it contains no added sugar or colourings. Note the distinction between customer, the person responsible for the purchase decision, and user, the person or group who has ultimate enjoyment of the product purchased.

(b) The office manager (**adviser**) may recommend to the board of directors (**deciders**) the details of the new computer hardware she proposes be installed, and pass details of the required budget to accounts (**financiers**). In general terms, the **more expensive** the purchase and the **more infrequently** it is made, the **more complex** the DMU is likely to be.

2.8 A number of models of the DMU exist, but most identify the following roles.

(a) **Gatekeeper.** Controls the flow of information about the product or service, eg receptionists, secretaries.

(b) **Indicators or initiators.** These are the individuals who first suggest the idea of buying a particular product. They may be influenced by a *trigger* - an identifiable event or person which brings the need for the purchase to the fore.

(c) **Influencers.** These are people who stimulate, inform or persuade at any stage of the buying process. (An influencer could be a character in a TV advertisement.)

(d) **Deciders.** These are the people who make the decision that a product should be bought.

(e) **Buyers.** The people who actually go out and buy the product. They might not be the person who originally decided that it ought to be bought.

(f) **Users.** The ultimate users of the product might be neither the decider nor the buyer, although their perceptions of what the user needs is likely to influence the buying decision/purchase action.

(g) **Financiers.** These people set the budget.

Action Programme 2

Produce a schematic representation of the stages in a major purchase you have recently been involved with. This can be a purchase at work, or at home - a holiday, new car or electrical good, or a new office computer system etc.

Make sure that you identify all those who were involved in the purchase. Use the DMU as a framework for your model.

Reaching the DMU: DMU access

2.9 It is not always easy to gain access to the whole DMU. It takes **research** and well planned **sales activity** to get past the gatekeepers, particularly in industrial and public sector markets. Gatekeepers **control the flow of information** into an organisation and often restrict access to key individuals within it. Personal assistants, designated buyers and reception staff are the most common gatekeepers. Once the salesperson has got past the gatekeepers, there is still the problem of contacting everyone in the DMU.

Exam tip

In the old syllabus *Understanding Customers* June 1997 exam a major toy manufacturer provided the context for the three-part question, the first part of which covered segmentation, a topic which we will be looking at in a later chapter. Part (b) asked candidates to explain the relevance of the customer/user distinction to the toy manufacturer, while part (c) required an outline of the importance of understanding the other roles in the DMU and the way in which the organisation's marketing activities might be influenced by them.

In a solution to part (b) you would need to provide a definition of customers and users and provide examples of both with respect to the toy manufacturer. You would also need to explain how this distinction impacted on the toy manufacturer's marketing approach.

An answer to part (c) would need to set out who fulfils the various DMU roles (be it parent, child, relatives and so on), and describe how this knowledge could be used to the organisation's advantage.

So all that you need to be able to do to provide first-rate solutions to the second and third parts of this question is apply information from this chapter to a particular scenario.

3 ASSUMPTIONS, STEREOTYPES AND MYTHS

3.1 There are two basic **definitions of marketing**, which Winston Fletcher (*Financial Times*, 20 January 1997) has called the 'functional definition' and the 'fundamentalist definition'.

(a) The **functional definition** views marketing as a **job description**, like personnel or production. According to this approach, marketing's job is to **increase sales** via all forms of marketing communication - advertising, packaging, sponsorship, customer relations, sales promotion and the rest - and to be responsible for all **market research** and **market analysis**.

(b) The **fundamentalist definition,** by contrast, views marketing as a paramount **business philosophy**.

(i) This definition, taking its lead from Professor Theodore Levitt at Harvard, states that the **objective** of any business must be **long-term customer satisfaction**.

(ii) Further, this 'fundamentalist definition' states that, under the committed leadership of the chairman and CEO, any business hoping to thrive in the 21st century must **embrace marketing** wholeheartedly as a **central architectural process**. Such a view is endorsed by the (UK) Marketing Council, which has 'introduced a new definition of marketing' based on 'customer satisfaction', 'customer needs', 'customer focus', 'customer service', 'customer care' and 'a customer culture'.

3.2 All this talk of customers represents a **major shift in marketing emphasis** for many organisations which at one time did not realise (or act as if they realised) they had customers at all. Indeed, British Telecommunications plc (BT) used to call its customers 'subscribers', and kept them diligently **at arm's length**; many public-sector service operations were not in any sense 'customer-focused' simply because they were monopolies, supplying services like education, housing and refuse collection to 'ratepayers' **whether they wanted them or not**.

3.3 Nowadays, by contrast, many organisations have come to realise that customer satisfaction (or, better still, **customer 'delight'**) is the only route to long-term sustainable competitive advantage. Equally, customers themselves have begun to flex their muscles: they are **much less inclined to remain servile and silent** in the face of indifferent attention; they are much more willing to take their business elsewhere when presented with the opportunity to do so; attracting and retaining their **loyalty** has become a major issue in boardrooms everywhere.

3.4 **Despite all this effort**, however, customer service and customer care still remain **problematic** for many organisations and even within whole industry sectors. As Chris Daffy claims (in *Once a Customer, Always a Customer*, Oak Tree Press, 1996):

> 'The sorry fact is that service levels today in most industries are low (even lousy) to mediocre. Most people find it difficult to list five businesses where they get really good service. But when asked to list ten where they would describe the service as poor they usually have no problem.'

3.5 As well as a lack of explicit customer service strategies linked to overall mission and policy, many organisations are still **unclear about the role of customer service** and how to organise it in order to deliver added-value and enhanced profitability (which is, after all, the point of the exercise). If an organisation does not know how good it is at delivering customer service, then it will tend to become **complacent**, inhabiting a **self-enacted reality** which embodies these characteristics.

(a) **The use of vague, generalised statements** like 'quite good', 'getting better', 'world class' (without any comprehension of what being 'world class' might actually entail)

(b) **The counting of customer complaints** in the belief that the incidence of complaints is a direct measure of customer satisfaction (without realising that, in most cases, only between 10 and 20 per cent of customers actually complain: the rest simply take their business elsewhere)

(c) **Reliance on infrequent survey data about customer perceptions** and the selective application of the data thus acquired

(d) **So-called 'improvements' which only address front-line 'customer-care' features** like answering the telephone within three rings - when what really matters is how customers are handled once the telephone has been picked up

---

Marketing at Work

An example of the importance surrounding customer focus is the battle between the two UK supermarket companies, *Sainsbury* and *Tesco*. Tesco comfortably beats Sainsbury on loyalty, satisfaction, trust and awareness, according to independent research carried out by MORI in 1997.

3.6 Many organisations - not just in retailing - make their task harder by two failings.

(a) They concentrate on defending sales margins, but tend to think about reducing employment levels before they think about redesigning their **business processes**.

(b) Information about changing **customer tastes and opinions** is hidden from head office by a **culture** which emphasises top-down communication and **discourages feedback from below**.

In practice, the **front-line staff** of the organisation are the key to communication with (and from) customers.

3.7 **Service excellence**, in short, is a powerful ingredient to corporate survival and competitive advantage for the organisations of the future. Service excellence is about what it takes to build and sustain a customer-focused organisation; it is about everything an organisation does to **win, satisfy and keep customers**. Of course, it has to be done profitably (in commercial organisations) because it then becomes a source of investment and return to shareholders; it also has to be done **better than the competition**.

3.8 Excellent service providers understand the **needs** of their customers - they also understand the **future direction** of those needs. These organisations also know who their customers are, and how well their needs are being met. Sometimes choices have to be made about which customers should have priority, and which customers may be discarded: these are unenviable options, but may be compulsory if the organisation's resources do not enable all potential customers to be addressed.

The marketing concept

3.9 There are many definitions of marketing. Here we will consider two which will provide insight into how marketing is used in practice.

3.10 **Marketing is the management of exchange relationships**.

This emphasises the role of marketing in relating to the world outside the organisation. All **relationships which cross the boundary** between the organisation and the outside world, especially when they relate to customers, need to be managed. These contacts are vital in creating a positive image for the organisation with customers and the public.

3.11 **Marketing is concerned with meeting business objectives by providing customer satisfactions**.

This definition is important because it stresses the importance of the customer, and more particularly, **customer satisfaction**. Products and services help to solve a customer's problems. It is the solution to these problems that customers are buying.

3.12 A **market orientated organisation** will have:

(a) a **focus** on meeting the needs of customers; and

(b) **structures and processes** which are designed to achieve this aim. Rather than just employing a marketing manager or a market research department, **all of the company's activities must be co-ordinated around the needs of the customer** when making decisions.

3.13 In summary, the marketing concept has these elements:

(a) customer orientation;

(b) a co-ordination of market led activities;

(c) a profit orientation, but not-for-profit organisations often employ marketing too (for example, churches or organisations such as the Boy Scouts).

3.14 The activities and philosophy of market orientated companies contrast sharply with **production orientated** and **sales orientated** organisations.

Peter Doyle provides a useful distinction between these viewpoints.

(a) 'A **production orientation** may be defined as the management view that success is achieved through producing goods of optimum quality and cost, and that therefore, the major task of management is to pursue improved production and distribution efficiency.'

(b) 'A **sales orientation** is the management view that effective selling and promotion are the keys to success.'

BPP PUBLISHING

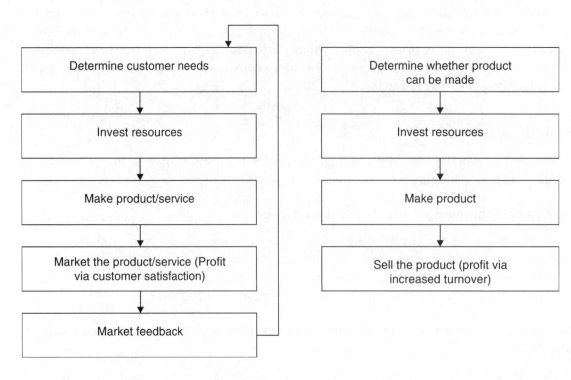

Market orientation — *Sales/production orientation*

Customer orientation

3.15 Theodore Levitt distinguishes between sales and marketing orientations in terms of **the place of the customer** in the marketing process.

> 'Selling focuses on the needs of the seller; marketing on the needs of the buyer. Selling is preoccupied with the seller's need to convert his product into cash; marketing with the idea of satisfying the needs of the customer by means of the product and the whole cluster of things associated with creating, delivering and finally consuming it.'

3.16 The marketing concept suggests that companies should focus their operations on their customers' needs rather than be driven solely by the organisation's technical competence to produce a particular range of products or services, or a belief in the sales force.

3.17 If new products and services are developed with an inadequate regard for customer requirements, the result will be the need for an expensive selling effort to persuade customers that they should purchase something from the company that does not quite fit their purpose. Repeat purchase is also less likely.

3.18 According to Peter Drucker: 'the aim of marketing is to make selling superfluous'. If the organisation has got its marketing right, it will have produced products and services that meet customers' requirements at a price that customers accept. Little or no sales effort will be needed - in theory!

The marketing concept in practice

3.19 Even though the marketing concept, and the attempt to match goods to consumer needs, is widely accepted, there will always be a need for an **effective sales force**. The need to convince the customers that they should buy the company's products arises because it is highly unlikely that their market needs can be exactly satisfied. Also, they may not be aware of the needs which the product satisfies. The sales force will therefore have to overcome the following problems.

(a) **The organisation is unlikely to be the only potential supplier**. It will therefore be necessary to convince customers to buy from the company and not from a competitor who may also have attempted to match the customer's needs and wants.

(b) **Customers may need to be reassured** about the benefits of owning or using the company's product or service. In industrial markets buyers will require evidence that technical specifications and appropriate industry standards are met.

(c) It may not be feasible to meet the **exact requirements** of each specific customer. When mass production techniques are targeted at the average customer's requirements, it may be that no individual's needs are actually satisfied.

(d) **Customers' requirements might have changed** since market-led production decisions were made. In markets for basic commodities, customer requirements are stable over considerable periods. Other markets are very dynamic and consumer needs change quickly.

3.20 All good sales presentations are customer orientated. Instead of merely cataloguing a series of product features, the intelligent salesperson concentrates on **promoting the benefits** that will be derived from the company's product or service. In industrial markets such benefits might include the cost reductions that can be gained using the company's products, the reliability of deliveries and product quality.

Marketing orientated strategy

3.21 Theodore Levitt's seminal article *Marketing Myopia* appeared in the Harvard Business Review in July-August 1960, arguing that a market orientation should determine the longer term **strategic direction** of companies. If managers perceive the company's business solely in technical and production terms, products will be perceived according to their physical properties, and everyone will appear to produce similar products.

A marketing orientation focuses on the needs of the customer. If these **needs change**, or a **better technology** emerges that more closely attends to these needs, the company will be responsive.

3.22 Even if the need to respond to change is accepted, adherence to a production orientation can produce costly mistakes.

Marketing at Work

In the late 1950s and early 1960s the American car market was under threat from import penetration, with the Volkswagen Beetle making the most significant inroads.

General Motors, the largest American motor manufacturer, reacted in a way which betrayed the production orientation followed by the company. GM's four main 'badges', used to segment the market place, are:

(a) Cadillac - the super luxury market
(b) Pontiac - the executive range
(c) Buick - middle range
(d) Chevrolet - value for money and young driver segment

The *physical* product characteristics of a VW Beetle might include:

(a) small (by US standards);
(b) rear engined;
(c) air cooled engine (therefore noisy);
(d) minimal instrumentation.

This was the product to which GM was losing sales. Chevrolet, the corresponding wing of the company, set about making just such a product. Naturally the new small car was to be powered by an air cooled rear engine and it would have very basic instrumentation. GM were ill-prepared for this venture. The company was under pressure from senior management to produce the new car quickly. The smallest available engine block was a flat six cylinder that was still very heavy for a relatively small car. The new engine also needed to be air cooled as that was what the customers were buying. To achieve this, Chevrolet mounted a large fan that sat on top of the engine driving air vertically down on to the cylinder heads. To drive this large fan a long fanbelt was added that took the power from the crankshaft via a right angle pulley.

The new car was launched as the Chevrolet Corvair. Its design caused a number of serious problems. The stresses on the fan belt frequently led to either the belt breaking or the bracket holding the right angle pulley fracturing. The car was so noisy that the sound of these mechanical failures could not be heard. Naturally, with minimal instruments the driver could not sense that the engine was now rapidly overheating until, as often happened, the engine either seized or caught fire. To compound these problems, the weight distribution on such a small car with a very heavy rear engine caused difficulties. For safe driving the rear tyres had to be pumped up rock hard whilst the front tyres were kept soft.

After a number of fatal accidents, the consumer activist Ralph Nader produced *Unsafe at Any Speed*, which recounted the story of the Chevy Corvair. The book made little impact until General Motors, unwisely, sued and lost. Nader was established as the leader of the American consumer movement.

3.23 What would have happened if GM had followed a marketing orientation and had attempted to find out why people were buying the Beetle rather than looking at the Beetle's product features? Key consumer benefits might have included:

- reliability
- economy
- affordability
- ease of parking

The marketing concept: a critical review

3.24 Not all commentators accept that the use of the term **marketing** rather than **selling** represents a real shift in basic philosophy. Some suggest that this simply reflects the fact that bringing in revenue is now more complex. It makes sense to use advanced techniques in advertising and market research that were previously unavailable. Others argue that today's 'sophisticated' consumers are more critical and more aware than their forefathers. So-called 'marketing techniques' are simply a continuation of the same old process of **persuasion in order to sell products**.

3.25 The most strident advocate of this view is the economist J K Galbraith who has summarised his views as follows.

> 'So called market orientated companies have merely adopted more sophisticated weapons for selling the product.'

3.26 The value of the marketing orientation is illustrated in the following case.

Marketing at Work

Eurostar is losing £180 million a year on its London to Paris and Brussels services. Passenger numbers are 40 per cent (about 3.5 million people) short on targets set by parent London & Continental Railways (LCR). And even the most optimistic assessment says it will not break even until 2001 – two years after it was scheduled.

The competing interests of LCR's eight shareholders has been criticised as contributing both to the over-inflated targets it used to secure the Eurostar contract, and to the inconsistency in its advertising and business strategies.

A fast link from central Paris to central London, without air travel delays, should surely be a winner. How could a company involved in this project so significantly fail to meet its targets? City sources, as well as people in the ad industry, have singled out a misguided marketing strategy as the crux of its woes.

"It gave away too many discounts," said one analyst. "Once it had done that it found it increasingly difficult to raise the price."

A senior ad agency source says that the price discounting worked against the message it was putting across in its advertising. "It was made into an aspirational brand through its advertising and marketing. But because it was most relevant to business class travellers it has forfeited everything that made it sexy and exciting in pursuit of passengers."

Personnel changes have also affected Eurostar's consistency. Mark Furlong was seconded from Virgin to be marketing director but moved back to Virgin last November. Commercial director Ian Brookes left to rejoin Virgin in October last year. The arrival of Hamish Taylor as managing director from British Airways 12 months ago was designed to bring more consistency to the marketing effort.

Taylor says the company will develop the leisure market, which makes up about 80 per cent of its business, through product enhancements such as special ski trains, and targeting new customers outside the South East where most of the advertising has run in the past. He is also looking to create a consistency over the business and leisure markets.

"It should have been more confident in marketing the success of Eurostar," says a source close to the company. "The whole Channel Tunnel rail link has been dominated by engineers and finance departments and nobody has ever worked out the potential and what was needed to meet targets. It sacrificed the brand advertising for the short-term need to fill trains cheaply," says the source.

(Adapted from The Economist, 10/6/96)

3.27 General Electric, one of Rolls Royce's major competitors, made its commitment to the marketing concept as long ago as 1952.

'(The marketing concept) ... introduces the marketing man at the beginning rather than at the end of the production cycle and integrates marketing in each phase of business. Thus, marketing, through its studies and research, will establish for the engineer, the design and manufacturing man, what the consumer wants in a given product, what price he is willing to pay, and where and when it will be wanted. Marketing will have authority in product planning, production scheduling, and inventory control, as well as in sales distribution and servicing of the product.'

(1952 Annual Report: US General Electric Company)

Customers' wants and needs

3.28 Critics of marketing have accused it of creating unnecessary wants and needs in customers, but a company which produced products and then tried to create a market for them would be in trouble very quickly. Marketing can, however, **influence buying behaviour**, which is complex in its motivations and outcomes.

Chapter roundup

- Because the decision-making unit comprises a number of individuals, and the decision-making process is often a lengthy and complex one, there is an important distinction to be made between *customers* - who buy the product/service - and *users*, who make use of its provision.

- Customers may be within an organisation as well as external to it.

- The Decision Making Unit is the group of people who come together to influence, positively or negatively, a purchase decision. They usually comprise gatekeepers, initiators, influencers, deciders, buyers, users and financiers. An individual may occupy, concurrently or consecutively, more than one role in the unit. Reaching the key figures in the DMU is a crucial role of the marketer.

- Central to the principle of marketing-led organisations is the process of getting to know our customers. They need first to be identified before they are understood.

- The marketing concept has three elements:
  - customer orientation
  - co-ordination of market-led activities
  - generally, a profit orientation.

BPP PUBLISHING

Quick Quiz

1   Distinguish between a customer and a user. (2.2)

2   What is an internal customer? (2.3)

3   Identify seven DMU roles. (2.8)

4   What concepts does the (UK) Marketing Council's definition of marketing embrace? (3.1)

5   What are the characteristics of a company that is complacent about customer service? (3.5)

6   Contrast a market orientation and a production or sales orientation. (3.14)

Action Programme Review

1   An excellent illustration is the market for children's toys where the 'customer' is the parent but (though not always) the 'user' is the child. Should toy-manufacturer marketing be targeted towards parents or towards children? Some companies focus on parents, stressing the educational benefits to be secured from purchasing their toys; others aim directly at children, on the argument, presumably, that children can exert powerful pressure on the buying habits of their parents.

There are many other legitimate examples. Perhaps you work for an organisation that provides membership of a gym for its employees. In this instance your employer is the customer and you are the user.

2   Our schematic representation of a holiday purchase is shown below.

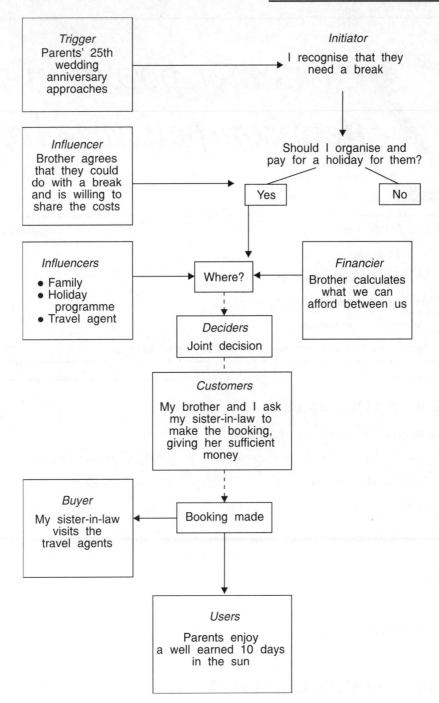

2 Customer power in the new competitive climate

Chapter Topic List	Syllabus reference
1 Setting the scene	1.2
2 The complacency of the past	1.2
3 The driving forces of competition	1.2
4 Customers who complain	1.2
5 Significance of trends for the marketing customer interface	1.2

Learning Outcomes

After studying this chapter you should be able to:

* critically appraise the relationship between customer dynamics and marketing

* understand the role of developments such as relationship marketing

* appreciate that customers have new power, and the effect on organisations

Key Concepts Introduced

* Customer care

* Relationship marketing

Examples of Marketing at Work

* GEC and Hitachi in South Wales

* In-flight magazines

* Range Rover launch

* Customer relationship management software

1 SETTING THE SCENE

1.1 As the examiner says in his introduction to the syllabus, marketers too often act like sales people, seeing their role as one of trying to sell whatever the organisation has to offer. Customers are seen as being **passive, receptive and reactive**, influenced this way and that by economic, psychological and sociological factors, but at the same time capable of being manipulated into purchasing whatever is put in front of them.

1.2 However, customers are becoming more articulate: they are more prepared to **complain**, more enthusiastic about taking their custom to a **competitor**, more willing to face down organisations which appear indifferent to their needs, and more aggressive in pursuing litigation or in seeking media and political support.

> **Exam tip**
> The issue of 'genuine consumer power' is an important one, and customer dynamics is a core part of the syllabus. The senior examiner is very concerned with it and you should always regard the customer in the marketing/customer relationship as someone who has greater expectations and a greater willingness to move to a competitor.

2   THE COMPLACENCY OF THE PAST

2.1 The **pattern of organisational life** has undergone a **massive transformation** in the past couple of decades. It cannot be handled purely through the incremental application of the solutions, strategies and management techniques used in the past.

2.2 At the same time we **don't want to exaggerate**. Many employees continue to hold to the belief that they have a **job for life,** or that if they do not, then the resultant insecurity does not apply to them; many organisations, especially in the public sector, can legitimately plan for the future by **extrapolating from current activities** and functions; in many fields of commercial endeavour, **technological change continues to operate selectively**; and many customers remain as they have always been: **passive, docile, uncomplaining** and **undemanding**.

2.3 Having got these caveats out of the way, let us turn to the reality with which most of us are already familiar.

   (a) Not that long ago, organisations offered products and services to customers in circumstances where, on the whole, **customers were eager to buy whatever was put in front of them,** they were tolerant of product inadequacies (after all, they knew no better) and they accepted poor, slow and expensive service.

   (b) Not surprisingly, organisations operating in this world were **uncompetitive**, although in fact many organisations, not just in the public sector, had no competition at all. No wonder they regarded their customers with indifference.

   (c) There is **no recorded case** in history of a **monopolistic organisation being customer-focused:** all monopolies become **self-serving** oligarchies. Despite the presence of good and altruistic intentions, those running monopolies inevitably find it more pleasurable to **make themselves comfortable first**.

2.4 Without energetic competition, without articulate customers, without the presence of the Japanese, without a free market in Europe, without real challenges about pricing and cost control, companies (and non-profit making organisations as well) could laze along, carrying **superfluous employees.** This was the price to be paid for what was thought to be life-long job security: for some, it may have been a price worth paying, but it did mean that as international markets became liberalised, high-cost operations were in jeopardy.

2.5 It also followed, in this world of the recent past, that **organisations themselves,** lacking customer focus but compensating through incestuous self-regard, had several **common features**.

(a) A belief in some **universal laws of management** like the 'span of control' principle, which guaranteed very tall structures and the capacity for close supervision at every level.

(b) **Command-and-control cultures** with very restricted scope for entrepreneurial decision-making at all levels.

(c) Work systems heavily dependent on **checking and monitoring performance** in detail. Typically, in financial services companies, for example, clerks would **do,** supervisors would **check** and managers would **scrutinise**. No wonder that employees had no incentive, in that famous quality phrase, to 'get it right first time'.

(d) Fragmented and mechanistic problem-solving which was consistently reactive.

(e) Employees were treated as **individuals,** not as **team members** or as contributors to corporate purposes. Payment and other recognition processes rewarded people for their individual contributions; **competitive behaviour** was encouraged.

(f) **Job descriptions** were written as **lists of tasks and responsibilities**, without any expectation that employees (except at very senior levels) might **add value**. Even when an over-arching 'Job Purpose' statement preceded the task list, this was seldom expressed in words which suggested that the job-holder might be required to **make a difference**. Think about that for a moment: no philosophy of continuous improvement, no constant pressures for change, no sequence of transformational initiatives, but instead an opportunity to stay in a rut.

3   THE DRIVING FORCES OF COMPETITION

3.1   In some ways analysing the **factors which precipitated change** is pointless because whether we like it or not, whether organisations like it or not, **the change has occurred** and it is most unlikely that it will be reversed.

COMPETITION – THE DRIVING FORCES AND CRITICAL SUCCESS FACTORS

(Adapted from: Institute of Personnel and

Development, 'People Make the Difference, 1995)

How this is affecting the way people are organised and managed

- Decentralisation and development of decision-making
- Slimmer and flatter management structures
- Total quality and 'lean organisation' initiatives
- Fewer specialists directly employed
- Developing a flexible workforce
- More project based and cross functional initiatives and team working
- Empowered rather than command structures
- Partnership approach to supplier links

The driving forces

- Customers demand products and services increasingly customised to their needs
- Customer satisfaction standards are increasingly established by global competition
- Reductions in international trade barriers
- Industrialisation of Pacific rim countries
- Slow growth in the mature economies
- New overseas competitors in mature production and service sectors
- Technology is rapidly changing and easily transferable
- Public sector financial constraints, political pressures for higher value for money and privatisation or market testing
- Communities are becoming more concerned about the effects of economic development on the environment and social well being

What this means for employees

- Customer-orientation to meet the needs of both internal and external customers
- Greater self-management and responsibility for individuals and teams
- Contributing to the continuous improvement of processes, products and services
- Commitment to personal training, development and adaptability

How organisations are responding

- Highly differentiated goods and services
- Customer-led organisations; relationships
- 'Step' change and continuous improvement of products, processes and services
- Quicker response times
- Lower costs and sustainable profits
- Flexibility from people and technology
- Investing in and developing the core competences of people

What this means for managers

- Facilitating, co-ordinating roles
- Greater interpersonal, team leadership and motivational skills
- Integrated management and communication systems
- Openness, fairness and a partnership in employment relations
- Managing constructively the interests of groups of employees and their collective and individual representation
- Ensuring part-time and temporary employees and those contracted to supply services are fully integrated

3.2   Of course, the IPD's portrayal is too simplistic. Arguably it hides or under-plays the pains of change.

BPP
PUBLISHING

Marketing at Work

As an example of these pains, take the consumer-electronics factory at Hirwaun in South Wales. In 1981, run as a joint venture between GEC and Hitachi, the factory achieved a one-day record output of 1,750 TV sets with 2,200 employees. This performance was accomplished on a so-called Zero Defects Day, often a feature of corporate quality-improvement programmes in the early days of the TQM movement. Employees promised to go to bed early on the day before the Zero Defects event and not to drink themselves into insensibility (a regular feature of the Hirwaun lifestyle); additionally - and note this carefully - they also promised that when they came to work on the Zero Defects Day, **they would concentrate on what they were doing.**

By 1986, all such pussy-footing around had been stopped. Hitachi was running the factory on its own. It was routinely churning out, **every day**, 2,400 TV sets, 500 hi-fi units and 500 VCRs, with a workforce of only 1,000 people. Many of these people were the same people who had worked there in 1981: they were now being managed properly, they now had the support of massive technological investment and, better still, they were now competitive.

Even more important is the need to recognise that the innovations wielded by Hitachi were not the result of some secret methods known only to them. Indeed, it is a popular misconception to suppose that the commercial success of the Japanese is attributable to some magic formula: if only we could tap into it, the argument goes, we could be equally successful ourselves. In the early days of the Japanese incursion into the UK's motor industry, a delegation visited various Japanese car manufacturers in an attempt to divine their secret. Their hosts appeared to be showing them everything, however, and the group became increasingly perplexed at a pattern of behaviour which would not have been theirs had the positions been reversed. Eventually they delicately raised the issue: 'Why are you not concealing things from us - or are you concealing things so well that we don't even know what is being concealed?' The Japanese response, at the time, was shattering and took two forms.

(a)   We aren't concealing anything because even if you went back to the UK and instantly implemented everything that we do here, it would take you five years to make it work and by that time we would be much further ahead.

(b)   In any case, we don't think you will apply what we do here. In practice, you seem to be seeking panaceas which you can graft onto your existing organisations without undergoing the kind of radical surgery which is actually necessary.

Painful though it may be, the Japanese verdict was correct. Like many other companies and businesses facing unprecedented competition - whether from Asia Pacific or elsewhere - the motor manufacturers were considering change under compulsion. No wonder they wanted to keep the quantity of change to a minimum: no wonder, then, that they seized eagerly on such peripheral devices as Quality Circles, creating the appearance of shop-floor involvement but without any of the inconvenience of managerial restructuring. Change under compulsion is rarely radical, seldom transformational, is minimalist in purpose, content and execution - whereas change inspired by strategic vision is impressively different.

4   CUSTOMERS WHO COMPLAIN

4.1   The propensity of customers to complain has changed radically over the past few years. Not only are customers much **more willing to make a noise** about their grievances, but they will also **tolerate much less** by way of restitution and delays - and, moreover, they will (as organisations see it) **fight dirty** more quickly, using threats of disclosure to television programmes and/or litigation in order to achieve their objectives.

(a)   Technically, one has to argue that if customers are more prepared to tell you about their dissatisfaction, then this means that the organisation will secure **more reliable, representative and comprehensive customer feedback** than it ever did when it relied on a situation where only 1 in 10 of the customers who were dissatisfied bothered to tell you about it. The remaining nine either quietly took their business elsewhere, or bided their time until the moment when they could do so.

(b)   Of course, **not all companies see the complaint process as an opportunity**.

(i)   Some still have **no proper complaint-handling mechanism** at all, which means that customers have some initial communication barriers to overcome; it may also mean that the **treatment of complaining customers is erratic**, with some receiving generous restitution whilst others are simply told to push off.

(ii) Some organisations **don't keep records of the complaints received** - indeed, they may have **no clear definition** of the term 'complaint' so that, for example, someone telephoning to ask for a copy of assembly instructions accidentally omitted from a flatpack furniture product may find that their call has been classified as 'information request' rather than 'complaint', especially if there is corporate pressure to minimise the number of 'complaint' items.

4.2 Yet more organisations, receiving complaints, will respond **defensively** and seek to imply, if they can, that there is **something wrong with the complainant**: they washed the product by hand when the instructions clearly said that it should only be dry-cleaned. Several will hope, apparently, that if they simply **ignore** complaints then most of them will go away: thus correspondence does not stimulate replies, telephone calls are not returned and customer service managers are mysteriously unavailable.

4.3 The continuation of these strategies is made more likely by the plain fact that, from some points of view, they are **effective**. If there is nobody to complain to, then complaining is made more difficult; if the complaint statistics are suitably massaged, then those employing the embrocation avoid criticism and may even receive some praise for their diligence; and if complainants are treated patronisingly or ignored, then many of them disappear through the sheer force of attrition.

4.4 It may be argued, of course, that such consequences will ultimately be damaging to the organisation, because customers who are already dissatisfied will be **even more dissatisfied** if their product/service supplier treats them with disdain; however, some companies enjoy such a generous flow of new customers that the **promise of repeat business holds no particular attraction** for them.

4.5 In this context, perhaps, appropriate examples may include **hotels near** major international **airports** or enterprises whose **likelihood of securing repeat business** is already **remote**. By the time the customer shows any intention of coming back for more, their recollections of the appalling treatment they received first time round may well have faded - and in any case they may entertain the optimistic belief that things have changed.

4.6 More enlightened organisations will recognise that **complaints are part of the marketing process**. If you actively **encourage** your customers to complain, you demonstrate **faith in your product/service** offer. **Analysing the nature of each complaint**, as well, will show where design, manufacturing, delivery and functionality resources need to be concentrated. If complaints are handled efficiently, expeditiously and sympathetically, then potentially defecting customers can be tied to you even more closely than before: they will rather **tell others about the wonderful way in which you handled their complaint** than tell them about what was wrong in the first place.

4.7 When customers walk into a shop, or phone the customer complaints line, they want the company's employees to **own the problem**. They do not want to be **passed around the houses** and they do not want to be told about the **organisation's difficulties** ('we're very short-staffed at the moment' or 'the computer's down' or 'she's at lunch').

4.8 Ownership of the problem needs to be reinforced by the ability to give an **immediate response**.

BPP
PUBLISHING

(a) **Front-line staff** must be **empowered** to deal with complaints quickly: for most customers, time is of the essence, and if they are kept waiting, or transferred through several departments, then the original complaint rapidly escalates into rage.

(b) **Managers** find empowerment very difficult: they **worry excessively** about what customer-facing people will do if **left to their own devices**, forgetting about their own frustrations when they were in similar positions themselves and had to comply with the rules which not only seemed nonsensical but which also had the effect of making customers more irritated than they were before. What seems to happen, in effect, is that organisations devote all their energies to designing **procedures** which will prevent recovery and restitution systems from being **abused**, by either customers or employees: they forget that 99 per cent of all complaints are genuine, and 99 per cent of all employees are trying to do their best.

4.9 The ability to **empathise** is a key component in the effective handling of customer complaints, yet, typically, organisations are **reluctant to look at 'problems' from the customer's perspective**. If they did then much more attention would be given to creating procedures which lean over backwards to ensure that the complaining customer is mollified.

Marketing at Work

A regular airline customer wrote to the company, complaining that its in-flight golf magazine catered only for Americans. His recommended solution was for the airline to supply equivalent golf magazines for British passengers. The airline wrote back to say that this was not practicable, but that as he was a regular flyer then they had arranged for him to have a year's subscription to the British magazine he'd mentioned. The subscription cost the airline around $30, but every time the magazine landed on the customer's doormat it would remind him positively of the company.

4.10 **Training staff** on how to deal with customers, then **letting them get on with it**, are two fundamental elements in the complaints management process.

4.11 Why should a business embrace **customer service** as a source of competitive advantage? The simple answer is that **if you don't, someone else will** - and, all other things (price, availability or whatever) being equal in the eyes of the consumer, better service or customer care will lead the consumer to choose your competitor's product.

Key Concept
Customer care emphasises the importance of **attitude** and covers every aspect of the organisation's relationship with its customers. It aims to **close the gap between customers' expectations and their experience**. Clutterbuck defines customer care as:

'a fundamental approach to the standards of service quality. It covers every aspect of a company's operations, from the design of a product or service to how it is packaged, delivered and serviced.'

Essentially, it is a guiding concept which can become a policy and a set of activities.

4.12 Ted Johns, in *Perfect Customer Care*, outlines the following excuses for bad customer service, and the scenarios whereby the organisation will fall on its face.

Excuse for bad customer service	Likely outcome
No organisations in the sector care about their customers	One will break ranks and compete successfully on the basis of customer care
The organisation competes on other factors, like price	Other factors, like service, have been shown to be more important
The organisation has no competitors	It won't stay a monopoly for ever, and privatisation hurts!
Demand for the organisation's output exceeds supply in the market	Success will only last as long as demand keeps up - and it is likely to go elsewhere once another provider arrives on the scene

---

Action Programme 1

Are factors like service and quality *really* more important to the consumer than price, or is this just a myth put about by clever marketing people?

Think about this in terms of purchases that you make regularly, on the one hand, and very seldom on the other.

---

5 SIGNIFICANCE OF TRENDS FOR THE MARKETING CUSTOMER INTERFACE

Relationship marketing

5.1 The twentieth century has been characterised by **mass media** (television, newspapers, radio) creating **mass marketing** and **mass consumption**, aided by production efficiencies. Products became nationally recognisable via distribution and advertising. Technology impacted dramatically on transportation, travel and communications, helping to create a **global market**. The emphasis on individual customer service became, to an extent, diluted.

5.2 This situation is now changing. For example, long-standardised products such as Coca Cola now have different variants (Diet, Cherry) to appeal to different customer segments. Now that there are more products to promote, companies need to **target the market** more carefully.

5.3 **Relationship marketing** helps them to do this. Technology is the key factor. Software developments have made **databases** flexible and powerful enough to hold large amounts of **customer specific data**. While the corner shop of old recognised customers visually, companies today can recognise them electronically.

Key Concept

Relationship marketing can be seen as the successor to mass marketing, and is the process by which information about the customer is consistently applied by the company when developing and delivering products and services. Developments are communicated to the customer, for example via specially targeted promotions and product launches, in order to build a 'partnership' with him and encourage a long term relationship by paying attention to his specific needs.

Marketing at Work

The Range Rover launch, 1995

Ten days before it launched the 1995 Range Rover, Rover let 10,000 of its most privileged customers into its secret. Each one of them received an invitation to a champagne breakfast or candle-lit dinner to see the new car privately - before the rest of the world got to hear about it. Those who came along were not expected to enter into any firm commitments; instead, the aim of the exercise was to turn these 10,000 people into 'brand ambassadors' for Rover. The aim of the preview, said John Russell, Managing Director of Rover International, was 'to achieve the intimacy of a dinner party among friends where our launch messages would be passed on by word of mouth - overheard, not overhyped. We set out not to launch a product but to achieve a breakthrough in the quality of our customer relationships'.

5.4 The underpinning idea behind Rover's approach was relationship marketing, turning 'ordinary' customers into 'brand advocates'. The rewards from effective relationship marketing are potentially impressive (and are linked to the whole exercise of **customer retention**).

(a) One credit card company calculated that a 5% increase in customer retention would create a 125% increase in profits.

(b) American Express believes that by extending customer lifecycles by five years, it could treble its profits per customer.

(c) According to Coca-Cola, a 10% increase in retailer retention should translate to a 20% increase in sales.

5.5 In a **relationship approach**, 'smart marketers try to build up long-term, trusting, win-win relations with valued customers, distributors, dealers and suppliers ... it is accomplished by building strong economic, technical and social ties with the other parties.'

5.6 The justification for relationship marketing comes from the **need to retain customers**. There are five different levels of customer relationship.

(a) **Basic**. The salesperson sells the product without any further contact with the customer.

(b) **Reactive**. The customer is encouraged to call the salesperson if there are any problems.

(c) **Accountable**. The salesperson phones the customer to see if there are any problems and to elicit ideas for product improvements.

(d) **Proactive**. The salesperson contacts the customer on a regular basis.

(e) **Partnership**. The salesperson and customer work together to effect customer savings. Partnership sourcing implies that the commercial buyer works more closely with the supplier to ensure that all aspects of the deal suit the needs of both parties, not just for this deal, but those which can be expected in the future.

5.7 Broadly speaking, the greater the number of customers and the smaller the profit per unit sold, the greater the likelihood that the type of marketing will be **basic**. At the other extreme, where a firm has few customers, but where profits are high, the **partnership** approach is most likely.

(a) Customers are in long-term relationship with their banks. Banks try and satisfy many of customers' financial needs over a customer's lifetime (eg current accounts, overdrafts, secured lending, pensions advice, investment advice, insurance).

(b) On the other hand, there is no-long term relationship between a consumer of chocolate bars and the chocolate manufacturer.

5.8   Some firms are trying to **convert** a basic approach into relationship marketing. Many car dealerships, for example, seek to generate additional profits by servicing the cars they sell, and by keeping in touch with their customers so that they can earn repeat business.

Relationship marketing and competition

5.9   In terms of the competitive forces, relationship marketing attempts to make it harder, or less desirable, for a customer to switch. It raises **switching costs** (emotional, if not financial). The advantages to the supplier can be made more apparent if we estimate the potential profit made from a customer over the customer's lifetime. For example, when a customer changes bank, the deserted bank loses potential commission on products such as pensions, as well as loss of profits on loans the customer will need in future.

5.10   To work, relationship marketing has to operate in three ways.

   (a) **Borrow the idea of customer/supplier partnerships from industry**: by sharing information and supporting each other's shared objectives, marketers and their customers can create real mutual benefit.

   (b) **Recreate the personal feel** that characterised the old-fashioned corner shop or Edwardian department store: make customers feel valued as individuals, and (using modern IT systems) convince them that their individual needs are being recognised and catered for.

   (c) **Continually deepen and improve the relationship** by making sure that everything which impinges on the customer's experience of the brand delights them.

5.11   The value of relationship marketing lies in the fact that customers, consumers, retailers, distributors and agents may be spread all over the world, but they will still look for the familiar features when deciding whether or not to do business: product or service performance, enhancements and reliability of supply. If these business partners are looked after, market share will be of better quality because a greater proportion of sales will be derived from repeat business.

Marketing at Work

From *Computer Business Review,* March 1999:

Customer relationship management (CRM) software is an industry in its own right. California-based Siebel Systems is market leader and its chief executive, Tom Siebel, says: 'I think now we have entered an era where the most precious resource is being recognised as the customer relationship. 'A customer in Paris, London or New York ordering on the Internet or by telephone does not care where the supplier is based, he just wants good service and quick delivery. 'There is a huge feeling, even in formerly not-so-service-oriented economies, that companies need to reach, serve and embrace customers. And the game they are playing is absolutely economic survival'.

Another CRM company boss says 'Think of any industry - telecoms, high tech, consumer packaged goods, financial services. There is no time for building relationships ... a system has to be implemented immediately. Loyalty and retention equal revenue ... [and] ... it is the level of service that will keep customers coming back'.

In many industries, mass globalisation has diluted the significance of product features and functionality. Customers are clamouring for a more personalised service, and companies have to satisfy highly individualised markets - ultimately a target market of one customer. Companies like One 2 One, BAT and the Prudential are all using CRM software to build databases and customer information profiles.

BPP
PUBLISHING

Chapter roundup

- Until relatively recently many organisations were able to regard their customers with indifference.

- Command-and-control cultures thrived; there was no expectation that employees could make a difference.

- Increasing competition has meant that organisations have to change.

- Customers are much less tolerant and are willing to complain if they have a grievance.

- When customers walk into a shop, or phone the customer complaints line, they want the company's employees to **own the problem**. They do not want to be **passed around the houses**; they do not want to be told about the **organisation's difficulties** ('we're very short-staffed at the moment' or 'the computer's down' or 'she's at lunch'); even less do they want to hear the employee adding some **complaints of his own** about the way he is treated.

- Customer care is 'a fundamental approach to the standards of service quality. It covers every aspect of a company's operations, from the design of a product or service to how it is packaged, delivered and serviced.'

- Relationship marketing is one development that reflects growing customer power.

Quick quiz

1   Name a monopolistic organisation that is customer-focused. (see para 2.3)

2   List six common features of organisations of the recent past. (2.5)

3   What does increasing competition mean for employees? (3.1 diagram)

4   Why are many organisations indifferent to complaints? (4.1 - 4.3)

5   Why are complaints valuable to an organisation? (4.6)

6   Define customer care. (4.11)

7   What is relationship marketing? (5.3)

8   What are the five different levels of customer relationship? (5.6)

3 Customer-focused marketing in specific economic sectors

Chapter Topic List	Syllabus reference
1 Setting the scene	1.3
2 Financial services	1.3
3 Leisure and tourism	1.3
4 Local government	1.3
5 The retail sector	1.3
6 Manufacturing	1.3

Learning Outcomes

- After studying this chapter you will be able to evaluate the effectiveness of the marketing/customer interface within specific product sectors including public service and not-for-profit organisations, and propose cost-effective performance improvements where appropriate.

Examples of Marketing at Work

- Kevin Smith
- First Direct
- British Telecom
- The Borough of Basingstoke & Dean

- The Borough of Spelthorne
- The London Borough of Brent
- Tesco and Sainsbury
- Streamline

1   SETTING THE SCENE

1.1   In this chapter we glance at some of the **activity sectors in the UK economy** which often feature in discussions about customer service.

1.2   Some sectors excite attention because their service reputation is so (comparatively, at least) **outstanding**, either across the sector as a whole or within specific organisations; other sectors gain publicity for precisely opposite reasons, because their perceived service standards are so **poor** and, conceivably, there are no businesses which might even constitute an oasis of achievement within these arenas.

BPP PUBLISHING

1.3 Before we delve into the detail, here's the big picture. According to 1997 figures, **32 of the top UK companies are service industries**, and 13 of these 32 employ over one million people each: BT (135,200), HSBC (109,093), NatWest (96,800), J Sainsbury (95,519), Barclays Bank (92,044), Lloyds TSB Group (91,044), Tesco (84,895), Boots (77,475), Bass (76,919), Grand Metropolitan (57,538), British Airways (55,296), Allied Domecq (54,975) and British Gas (54,754).

1.4 The 32 organisations as a whole employ 1.5 million people. Of these 32, just over one-third are in **financial services**, 27% in **retail**, 19% in **entertainment** (including the breweries), 15% are **utilities** (gas, electricity, water), whilst the remaining four per cent constitute a **miscellaneous** collection.

1.5 Despite the apparent domination in the service sector as a whole by a few large companies, in reality **most service organisations are very small** (as our normal experience would suggest): 98% of all service enterprises, for instance, have a turnover of less than £5 million. So we are talking of a very large number of organisations, many of them quite small, but collectively accounting for a powerful proportion of the workforce: in 1996, the number of **people employed in the service sector** was more than **four times as large** as the numbers employed in **manufacturing**.

2 FINANCIAL SERVICES

2.1 The traditional banks are walking embodiments of Richard Pascale's 1990 observation that:

> 'Winning organisations ... are locked in the embrace of a potentially deadly paradox. This is because great strengths are inevitably the root of weakness.'

2.2 In the **past**, banks operated in a world which they **took for granted**. That world had the following features.

(a) If there was **competition** between the banks, it was **muted**, since their interest rates were identical, their ways of operating were the same, their charges did not vary, even their premises were built to conventional design principles.

(b) Their **customers were kept in their place** by bank managers who ruthlessly exploited their position of power and superiority. They could give or withhold overdrafts without fear that account-holders could go elsewhere. Customers inevitably became eager to please and docile when castigated for incompetent account management. They were above all characterised by **inertia** - a reluctance to take their business elsewhere. Indeed, the banks made it very difficult for customers to contemplate moving somewhere else: there were standing orders to unravel, new cheque books to be printed, forms to be filled in; no wonder that most customers gritted their teeth and stayed where they were. This inertia was reinforced by the (probably accurate) belief that if they did go to another bank, things would be no better.

(c) There was no cross-bank fertilisation so far as staff were concerned, and **no injection of new blood** from other industries at more senior levels. Boards of directors for banks were composed of bankers; anything else would have been viewed as indefensible.

(d) The **rate of technological change was slow** and, therefore, easily manageable.

(e) Bank **employees** were attracted, retained and motivated through a combination of job **security**, appeals to **loyalty**, and **golden handcuffs** (low-interest mortgages and the like). Such incentives encouraged people to remain with the organisation, but did not stimulate innovation, originality, or any desire to rock the boat by questioning the way things were done.

2.3 Some years ago, Ashridge Management College research yielded a list of **factors associated with poor-performing organisations**. The list has general relevance to most sectors in the UK economy, but has special poignancy for banking, since virtually all of these factors were present in the traditional banking environment (resistance to change has ensured that some of them are still there today).

(a) **Hierarchical relationships** which emphasise status differences and seniority rather than, say, contribution and ability.

(b) **Insularity and complacency**, including a reluctance to believe that anything can be learned from studying the external world.

(c) A **masculine culture** with the vast majority of senior people being male except, conceivably, in functions like HR or marketing.

(d) A **secretive approach to information**, with sharing founded on the 'need to know' principle.

(e) A strong preference for functionalism in structural design, breeding lateral **communication barriers**, **stereotyping**, **defensiveness** and **limited breadth of perspective** among senior people reared from a single functional area.

(f) Orientations strongly focused on **production and tasks**, rather than on the performance of people.

(g) **Bureaucratic** reliance on deeply-embedded **rules and procedures**, rigidly applied and intended to embrace every conceivable scenario encountered in the organisation.

(h) Highly **centralised decision-making**, with lower-level staff viewed as non-discretionary implementers.

(i) A **toleration of incompetence**, with poor performers being shunted into peripheral roles.

2.4 Possession of these features was **fine so long as the customers** continued to **put up with the consequences** and the **competitors** (if that is how they can be described) exhibited all the **same features themselves**. The overall economic environment was characterised by **slow growth and change**, and would-be entrants to the market place were deterred by the **domination of** the **existing key players**. Once things began to change, then the banks began to look increasingly anachronistic.

(a) The financial services market was **deregulated**.

(b) New **competitors** appeared on the scene, especially Virgin, Tesco, Sainsbury.

(c) **Technological change** made possible the appearance of First Direct and a realisation that no longer was it necessary for people to visit their banks in person.

(d) New technology also means that many bank **staff do not need** to be personally equipped with highly-developed **knowledge about banking and finance** - instead, their competency frameworks dwell more cogently on **customer relationships, customer service, selling skills and IT comprehension.** Banks nowadays do not require their people to become professionally qualified in banking as a necessary prelude to career advancement; nor do they, any more, expect their staff to remain with them for life.

2.5 So, what does all this mean? For all their talk about customers and customer service, the vast majority of traditional banks have **some way to go.** In some ways their problem lies with their **historical baggage.** Their sheer size, the weight of their past momentum, the continued presence of bankers at the top rather than marketers, can mean that these banks are less proactive and less responsive than the newcomers (like Virgin), which can establish a **more flexible culture from the start.** Not only that, but new entrants can also **cherry-pick for customers,** seeking clients from the potentially more profitable segments and, if possible, leaving the established banks to cope with more problematic groups.

Branches

2.6 The traditional banks, as Richard Pascale would doubtless point out, are saddled with the **enormous costs of their branch networks.** At the time of writing, for example, Lloyds TSB has around 2,800 branches, but this number can be expected to fall quite rapidly.

2.7 Some people still regard going to the bank as an opportunity for social contact and will resist change. The vast majority of these people are in the upper age ranges, and their **resistance to telephone banking** may be associated with **technophobia**; it is easily possible to imagine that within the next few years the retired population will be entirely IT-literate and that the numbers needing face-to-face dialogue with a bank branch official will decline more rapidly once again.

Image

2.8 Yet another hurdle for the traditional banks is their **image.** Survey after survey has revealed that they are generally **distrusted** (whereas the Virgin organisation, for example, deliberately exploits the squeaky-clean image of its chief executive, and communicates with its clients in a **language** which appears remarkably **straightforward** compared with that often used by more conventional companies). Not only are the banks distrusted, but their efforts to scrub their image clean are repeatedly undermined by occasional **lapses** - which invariably receive high-profile press publicity - and by their determined resistance to the possibility of cash-dispenser error.

Mergers

2.9 Some of the banks have addressed all these formidable barriers to their commercial continuity. The Lloyds/TSB merger will help to solve some branch network and other fixed-cost difficulties, and more mergers - or, as they should more properly described, acquisitions - are in the pipeline.

Marketing at Work

Who is Kevin Smith? This is the question on the lips of thousands of Halifax mortgage borrowers who have tried to call him over the past few months. His is the name at the bottom of routine letters such as notification of interest changes. But you will not be able to talk to him.

Barbara Ball, a Halifax customer with mortgage problems, tried to do just that when she received a letter from him recently.

'Oh,' said the woman at the other end of the phone, when Barbara asked to speak to him, 'Kevin Smith doesn't exist. It's just a name we put at the bottom of letters.'

'That's ridiculous,' said Barbara. 'We know,' said the woman. 'We've had several complaints.'

Source: *Sunday Telegraph, 17 May 1998*

In the same issue, the *Telegraph* reported that it had suddenly started to receive complaints from readers about inexperienced and overworked staff subjecting them to severe delays and giving them conflicting or inaccurate information. They say that phone calls are never returned, promised documents never arrive and they rarely get to speak to the same person twice.

In one particular incident a Ruislip couple had been trying to find out whether they still owed money on their repayment mortgage. Eventually, on 2 December 1997, they wrote to the Halifax chief executive, Mike Blackburn, listing an 'alarming catalogue of errors and incompetence' experienced at the hands of his organisation. They received a reply three months later. In apologising for the delay, the 'complaints officer' revealed that the customer relations department had been swamped by a 'significant and sustained' volume of 'enquiries'.

Marketing at Work

It is interesting to note that First Direct does not normally figure in these depressing scenarios.

First Direct claims to enjoy the highest level of customer satisfaction in its field, whilst admitting that this is not much of an accolade because the competition is so poor. Independent surveys of First Direct customers by NOP regularly show around 90% to be 'extremely' or 'very' satisfied. Bear in mind that customers who are extremely or very satisfied are likely to remain with the organisation, will recommend it spontaneously to others, and will forgive it whenever it makes mistakes (up to a point, anyway). The company's achievement is especially remarkable when one remembers that it only started in 1988 but was already profitable from 1993 onwards. The secrets of its success are by no means secret, yet several of its recipe ingredients are not easily or immediately replicable.

(a)   Whereas the ordinary, traditional banks have a parent/child relationship with their customers, First Direct claims that its approach is adult/adult.

(b)   Its culture is firmly antithetical to the more conventional approaches to be found in the 'other' banks, and reveals the influence from Japanese theories about quality management. Thus the Leeds headquarters is more like a factory than an office: breezeblock walls, productivity slogans hung from the ceiling, noticeboards urging teamwork, creativity and self-improvement.

(c)   First Direct's single-minded focus - its ability to concentrate on one tight-knit operation - creates consistency of service response among staff who can therefore become authoritative and experienced within a relatively short period of time.

(d)   The absence of hierarchies and the paraphernalia of branch banking have allowed First Direct to develop an ethos and attitude to customers which imitators and competitors find hard to emulate.

(e)   The company is characterised by consistent and continuous leadership over time, with constant reiteration of a set of principles and values.

  • Respect - individuals are valued
  • Openness - team-building to build trust
  • Contribution - 'non-status' approach
  • Ownership and pride - so that individuals identify with First Direct
  • Culture - spoken, not mechanistic

(f)   Of course, the company has also been helped by the fact of its appearance at the right moment, when technology was able to deliver the means through which First Direct could communicate with its customers.

(g)   Finally, First Direct's competitive advantage partially stems from the fact that it has not piggy-backed onto the branches of Midland Bank (now HSBC), but has kept itself separate (whilst still having access to group services).

(h)   It may be appropriate, as a footnote, to refer to the cleverness with which First Direct has aimed itself at its target clientele, namely, individuals aged between 25 and 54, in the ABC1 socio-economic groups. In

BPP PUBLISHING

many ways its advertising is sensitively Freudian, too ('Do you really want to bank at the same bank as your father and mother?')

Exam tip

The examples given in this chapter are a good illustration of customer issues in different sectors. They have been provided for this text by the senior examiner himself!

3 LEISURE AND TOURISM

3.1 Television consumer programmes in the UK have concentrated with particular relish on the hotel, travel, leisure and tourism industries. *Watchdog* and its sister programme, *Weekend Watchdog,* have transformed customer relations in several industries, but it is questionable whether it has yielded significant improvements in so far as **travel** is concerned; instead, it may have turned holidaymakers into serial complainers, **raising their expectations very significantly** about acceptable levels of performance and even about equitable degrees of compensation when things go wrong. If Mr and Mrs Jones win £3,000 for a noisy apartment, cockroach-infested kitchen and a delayed flight, then viewers everywhere legitimately think they can try their luck as well. Unfortunately it may be less easy for them, if there are no television cameras in the vicinity and no *Watchdog* journalists to make notes.

3.2 In 1998, *Watchdog* launched its **'Holiday Rescue' package**. The formula for this kangaroo court is simple: if you are having a terrible holiday, you ring a telephone number and ask to be rescued. Over a shot of what looks like your rescue plane taking off, the song *Rescue Me* is played, the holidaymakers are brought back to Britain and the travel company brought to book. Viewers may then vote on whether the holidaymakers should receive a partial refund, a full refund, or nothing at all. All of this, of course, is very watchable: bad holidays make good television.

3.3 Anyone defending the travel companies is likely to be accused of taking their side, possibly for financial reasons. Yet there are suggestions that programmes like *Watchdog* do encourage holidaymakers to complain by offering them inducements (flights, overnight hotels); on the other hand, *Watchdog* itself claims that it receives 5,000 letters and e-mails a week from people who have been unable to get satisfaction by complaining down conventional routes - and in 1997 it won £1 million in compensation on behalf of 600 people.

3.4 The **holiday companies** say that **too many people complain about little things** which could have been settled locally; they are more inclined to take their complaints into the public domain or into litigation; their expectations are steadily escalating; in some instances they **complain automatically** in the hope of extracting some compensation which will help **defray the costs of the holiday** (quite often, people returning from holiday are in a black mood anyway, and their sunniness is not helped when they reflect on how much they have spent: if they can retrieve some, with an insurance claim or a grievance against the travel firm, then they will feel much better).

3.5 At the same time, the holiday companies themselves complain too much about being **victimised. If they sold better holidays,** then *Watchdog* would soon find itself out of business, or find itself turning to other themes, like whether or not viewers receive value for money from their licence fees.

4 LOCAL GOVERNMENT

4.1 Textbooks on managerial economics will invariably include sections which discuss the (economic) advantages and disadvantages of **monopolies**.

(a) Economies of scale shift the monopolist's cost curves to the right, which means that it has **greater opportunities to benefit from economies of scale**, and can quite possibly offer its products or services at a lower selling price than would otherwise be the case.

(b) Monopolies can afford to **spend more on research and development**, and are therefore able to exploit innovation and technical progress much better than small organisations.

4.2 There are of course many other arguments in favour of monopolies, but not all of them are strictly relevant here. Most of the **counter-arguments**, however, do make sense.

(a) The **profit-maximising aspirations** of the monopolist are likely to lead to prices and production levels which enable the monopoly to enjoy large profits or even 'superprofits' at the expense of the customer.

(b) The resultant profit-maximisation process will operate at a level where **total output is lower, and prices are higher**, than would have been the case in a competitive market.

(c) Monopolies **do not use resources in the most efficient way** possible, ie so as to minimise average unit costs.

(d) If there are no economies of scale, then a monopoly will **produce less and sell at a higher price** than the combination of firms in a competitive market.

(e) Monopolists can operate **restrictive practices**, such as price discrimination.

(f) Because they are not threatened by **competition**, monopolies may become **slack about cost control**, and **complacent about innovation**.

4.3 It may seem to be **begging the question** by starting this section about local government with a list of the economic consequence of monopolies, and in some sense it is. Not everything undertaken by local government is an expression of monopoly power.

(a) If local authorise run leisure and sports centre, theatres and so forth, they characteristically compete with the private sector.

(b) They are subject to external regulation and benchmarking of one sort or another, through political initiatives like CCT (compulsory competitive tendering) and 'best value'.

(c) They may well be led by dynamic chief executives and/or elected members devoted to a combination of good housekeeping and added-value.

4.4 Nonetheless, it remains true that in great segments of local authority (and, in a wider context, public sector) activity, there **is not (nor could there be) competition**: and where there is no competition, then a number of consequences become much more probable.

(a) The major **disadvantages of monopolies** are translated into reality.

(b) The interests of **consumers or customers are not placed first** in the list of priorities so far as tangible action is concerned. Consumers, customers, clients, council-tax payers may appear first in the corporate rhetoric, of course, but that is not allowable as genuine evidence of behaviour.

(c) Resources are devoted to the process of **'managing' consumer expectations** so that, for example, expectations do not exceed what the organisation is prepared to deliver.

BPP PUBLISHING

4.5   To find justification for these claims, one has only to contemplate the transformation of organisational performance typically experienced when a previously public operation is **privatised** and suddenly finds itself exposed to competition.

Marketing at Work

BT now employs 'only' around 150,000 people; it is possible to have a telephone installed within a couple of days; virtually all telephone call boxes function all the time; there are impressive response times and service standards even for 'POT' (plain old telephone) customers; customers can have any telephone they like (except the Trimphone); and, most important of all, we are now actually called 'customers' rather than 'subscribers'. Much the same can be said - eventually - of the utility suppliers, with the exception of water, where one type of corporate monopoly has been simply replaced by another.

4.6   In many instances, therefore, a **competitive philosophy** has been implemented in previously single-supplier public-sector operations, either through direct **exposure to competition** or through **outsourcing**. The result, generally, has been **reduced costs and improved service**. In other scenarios, genuine attempts have been made to convert local government structures into customer-focused cultures.

Marketing at Work

Since 1993, the chief executive at Basingstoke and her immediate team have worked assiduously to promote customer service as the key differentiator both for internal and for external customers. This has proved to be easier in some parts of the organisation (like leisure services) than in others (like planning); as with other local authorities, the position is made more complex by the difficulties of defining precisely what is meant by the term 'customer'.

*   Are you a 'customer' if you submit a planning application to build a garage on the side of your house?

*   Are you a 'customer' if you file some objections to your neighbour's application to build a garage on the side of his house?

*   Are you a 'customer' if you apply for housing benefit?

*   Are you a 'customer' if you fraudulently apply for housing benefit?

If your answer to all of these questions is 'yes', then think what it might mean if your organisation's mission is to maximise 'customer' satisfaction. To satisfy the first customer, you grant his application; to satisfy the second, you refuse it. To satisfy the third and fourth customers, you give them both housing benefit - and in the case of the fourth one, you don't allow your suspicions to get the better of you.

Basingstoke has not allowed itself to be deflected from its purpose by such definitional ambiguities. It has an overall mission statement ('To serve with excellence') which is customer-focused; it has eight corporate goals or objectives, five of which mention customers; several of its staff have achieved customer-service qualifications.

Marketing at Work

Spelthorne (which covers Staines in Middlesex) has clear customer-service priorities and goals, largely concerned with the achievement of customer 'delight'. In the public sector this is an ambitious vision, since the attitude of many council-tax payers to the services provided by the local authority is frequently founded on the fact that they are involuntary customers - in other words, they are customers whether they like it or not, and the 'price' they pay (in the form of council tax) is a 'distress' purchase, ie one which they would prefer to avoid and from which they expect to derive little benefit.

Such customers are content with experiencing 'satisfaction', namely, a state of taken-for-granted indifference, when they contemplate their experience with local government services. If their refuse is collected on the expected day, they are satisfied; if it isn't, they are dissatisfied, and will respond accordingly. As with more overtly commercial organisations, the Borough of Spelthorne can stimulate customer 'delight' - it may supply separate wheely-bins for biodegradable rubbish, for example, or undertake to print identifying marks on each bin, or supply householders with garden refuse sacks - but there is still no clear-cut evidence that the investment in such service innovations will reap worthwhile customer-perception rewards.

Marketing at Work

In an article entitled 'The Brent Conversion' (*Management Today,* March 1994), Anita van der Vliet describes the council's One Stop Shop (where residents may obtain information on local matters) as 'a place of spacious and carpeted calm, where knowledgeable staff in pleasant uniforms will deal with any query or complaint. Here there are no queues, no overflowing ashtrays, no scruffy noticeboards, none of the normal signs of a municipal domain. Instead, you see neatly arranged customer charter leaflets making quite specific promises - from answering phone calls within five rings to paying out refunds if dustbins are not collected - and even, astonishingly, offering apologies for service that has not been good in the past.'

The most fundamental change at Brent since 1988 is that the needs and wishes of 'customers' have been made paramount. This change of terminology is significant, away from the amorphous concept of 'the public', the derogatory references to 'punters', or the patronising talk of 'clients'; moreover, it reflects a major philosophical shift for a type of organisation where, as Brent's chief executive cheerfully admits, 'The customer imperative is not immediately apparent.'

There are several mechanisms which have enabled Brent to deliver its customer-service vision into operational systems.

(a) The providers of the services are separated from those who commission them. Quoted directly in the *Management Today* article, Brent's chief executive says, 'The belief that lies behind this is that if the same people are responsible for commissioning a service and for providing it, human nature dictates that purchasing policy will be influenced by the providers at the expense of the customer or the community.'

(b) Traditionally, local government has been structured both hierarchically and functionally with, say, the finance department being isolated from leisure services or environmental health - and with entirely separate career structures in each of these sectors until, that is, people reach very senior levels indeed. This inevitably creates empires, which become self-enclosed, self-perpetuating, remote from customers, arrogant and conservative. Conformance to process becomes an important criterion for supposed effectiveness, rather than added-value or innovation. In Brent, cheques used to pass through 33 pairs of hands, because (in the words of the chief executive) 'it was only by passing bits of paper up the system that people could justify their jobs.'

(c) Territorial protectionism is quite inappropriate to local government in principle, since services such as housing, care in the community and nursery education overlap; this being so, interdisciplinary and cross-functional teamwork should be relevant, but are often inhibited because of stereotyping and the usual obstacles placed in the way of effective group dynamics.

(d) In traditional local government organisations, administrative detail is sucked up the organisation. Senior managers are allowed to feel that they are performing a vital role when in fact their real (but more difficult) task should be leadership and strategic thinking. Indeed, one of the reasons why senior managers allow themselves to remain immersed in details is precisely that the alternative - thinking - is so painful.

(e) In 1991, Brent Council launched its Total Quality Programme, with three core values (quality, efficiency, and putting the customer first, to which has subsequently been added a fourth priority, 'valuing and empowering staff'). The number of Council departments was cut from 10 to 5; the number of senior managers was cut by a third; new fixed-term contracts and performance-related pay were introduced. In order to measure effectiveness, the Council has instituted focus groups, a rigorous complaints procedure, and a regular programme of customer surveys.

The Brent Revenues and Benefits Service (BRBS) shows in more detail what can be done. The service had a culture conditioned to failure; even serial reorganisation achieved little, until the changeover to council tax meant that fewer staff were required. All 350 staff were made redundant and were able to re-apply for jobs in a new structure with around 250 positions. After team-building and the involvement of customers in document design, the BRBS unveiled its 'charter' which specified clearly-understood service standards. Here are a few examples.

- To deal with letters within five days of receiving them, answering queries in plain English
- To see all customers in 30 minutes
- To send out all bills within 10 days of receiving information from the customer

Monitoring figures are displayed publicly and published annually; a ticket waiting system tells customers how long their wait is likely to be (the average is less than 15 minutes); when customers phone, 'conditional routing' measures the amount of time it will take for the call to be answered, and if the wait exceeds four minutes then the caller is invited to leave a message, with a guaranteed response within one day. Virtually speaking, BRBS is a self-contained business unit: in the words of Steve Simpson, its director, 'We now have our own bank

BPP
PUBLISHING

account, we employ contractors directly, we manage IT, premises - we even manage the caretaker. ... We may not be serving M&S sandwiches yet, but we're fairly confident we'll well on the way to giving our customers what they want.' ('Top of the League!', *Municipal Journal*, November 1994)

4.7 As these examples illustrate, **customer service in a local government context is not a contradiction in terms**. Indeed, the Brent achievement in particular is one from which many so-called commercial organisations can learn, even companies which already claim that they put the customer first.

5 THE RETAIL SECTOR

5.1 For the retail industry in particular, another convulsive development is in the offing, according to Professor Gary Hamel (*Financial Times*, 22 October 1998). The main threat to companies in the retail sector is that prices will be driven down by consumers' ability to shop around using the **Internet**. This phenomenon - dubbed 'frictionless capitalism' by Bill Gates of Microsoft - will make it harder for companies to make money using traditional business models.

5.2 The advent of **electronic commerce**, moreover, compels retail companies to shift their thinking. Until now, they have generally focused on improving the efficiency of their **distribution systems**: sophisticated supply chains have allowed retailers to bring an enormous range of goods under a single roof, thereby passing on distribution economies to their customers.

5.3 Hamel claims that we are moving from this type of **distribution economy** to a **search economy**: customers will want to purchase over the Internet and will pay a premium in order to have their goods delivered. Further, the customers selecting this option will not merely be the affluent who can afford the delivery charges. In practice, Internet shopping will be particularly attractive for ordinary dual-income families, especially when they have children.

5.4 All these changes - some **technological**, some **customer-driven**, some inspired by **competitive action** in other business fields altogether - will force companies to build **new competences**, like the ability to deal with consumer queries online.

5.5 At the same time, **such transactions do not appeal to some customers**. Some prefer to have a relationship with the retailer, and those who enjoy browsing. One of the reasons why Charles Schwab, the leading online stocks/shares broker, can charge bigger fees than some of its rivals is that it combines its online service with a low-cost branch network and a personalised telephone capability. As Hamel points out, 'They have recognised the web has certain virtues and weaknesses. The web is lousy if you have complex question. Likewise, it does not allow for people's need for relationships.'

5.6 In a warning note, Hamel argues that the current leaders in retailing will struggle to adapt to the new ways of doing business. He claims that every time there has been a significant change in the retail industry - such as the growth in out-of-town shopping or the arrival of the megastores - the arrivals have undermined the leaders.

5.7 Hamel's argument does not seem to apply, so far at least, to Tesco, which sets the pace for electronic commerce in supermarket retailing. For all we know, however, such established concerns as Sainsbury, Marks & Spencer, and even Tesco, may one day disappear. After all:

- From the 100 largest US companies in 1900, only 16 are still in existence.

- Only 32 of the 100 organisations featuring in *The Times* first list of Britain's 300 biggest companies were still there by 1995.

- During the decade of the 1980s, a total of 230 companies - 46 per cent - disappeared from the Fortune 500 group.

5.8 Plenty of companies have dipped their toes into the waters of electronic commerce, but so far few have made any money. One obvious reason derives from the still limited number of households with a personal computer. In 1998, only around five per cent of UK households were connected to the Internet. The numbers and proportions have risen impressively, but even so we should be cautious about the implications. It is sometimes assumed that households with PCs are likely to have above-average disposable incomes, but many Internet-wired PCs are 'owned' by children.

Marketing at Work

Tesco Direct was launched in 1996, and by 1998 was operating through 15 stores, mainly within the M25 London orbital road. Customers can contact the Tesco website and order goods for delivery the next day; in 1998, only around 5,000 customers were using the system weekly, compared with the average of 30,000 who visit a single Tesco store in an average week. However, Tesco intend to persist with their initiative, which in some respects they regard as a pre-emptive strike, and the pace has accelerated since they introduced a 'free' Internet capability system.

One of Tesco's principal competitors, Sainsburys, had introduced home shopping to 32 stores by September 1998, giving it a potential market of around 4 million people. Sainsburys customers can choose from personal shopping catalogues made up of items they are particularly interested in, and built up when they first register; this avoids them having to select between thousands of line items each time they use the service. All Sainsburys 'Orderline' enquiries are handled by an outsourced call centre, and delivery is handled by a national distribution company.

In mid-1999 it was disclosed that Sainsburys have gone further in their attempts to gain insights into shopper habits and preferences. They have created 'SimStore', which is a computer replica of one of the company's north London supermarkets. SimStore's artificial shoppers are programmed to behave just like their real-life counterparts; their movements help the supermarket to match what is on the shelves to the actual needs of their genuine customers. The simulated store also allows Sainsburys to try out new store layouts without inconveniencing real shoppers. The artificial people react just like ordinary humans - they spend more time browsing for wine than they do picking up milk - and if a particular arrangement of shelves and displays causes congestion in the simulation then it is likely to do so in the real world as well.

5.9 One further dimension of the retail sector concerns the impact of changes in **domestic lifestyles**. Almost everybody nowadays spends less time on housework than did their parents or grandparents. According to the 'Americans' Use of Time Project', a US census directed by John Robinson from the University of Maryland, the time allocated to housework, child care and shopping has dropped from over 27 hours a week in 1965 to around 22 in 1996.

5.10 **Changing attitudes to work and leisure,** plus the opportunities supplied by new technology, are helping to commercialise chores that people at one time expected to do for themselves. In 1997 too, for the first time, Americans spent more money eating out than at home; even when shopping for food to eat indoors, customers are increasingly looking for 'meal solutions' - convenience foods rather than ingredients. One of the best-selling products for the Marks & Spencer food department is its ready-to-eat chicken tikka masala; Sainsburys even sells ready-peeled oranges for those who want to protect their fingernails.

5.11 **On-line shopping** permits a growing number of people to avoid personal shopping altogether, although growth in this field has been restrained by the need to create delivery systems. Some UK operators, like Sainsburys, use specialised contractors.

Marketing at Work

Portents for the future are suggested by the **Streamline** initiative in Boston, Massachusetts. For $30 a month, the company places a refrigerator, freezer and shelves in the customer's garage or basement. Using an electronic keypad, Streamline staff can get in to deliver shopping once a week at a time which suits Streamline, without anybody having to be at home to receive them. Further, Streamline has taken some of the thinking out of shopping. On its website, customers can create a list of 'Don't Run Outs' (DROs), such as toilet paper and orange juice, which are automatically replenished. Customers can also receive relevant advertising and promotional offers; they can even compare nutritional values by a mere mouse-click, something that would take ages in a supermarket.

The Streamline service, already impressively customer-focused, does not end there. It can pick up and return dry cleaning and videos, post letters, and develop camera film. It delivers firewood in the winter, collects deposits on empty bottles and offers monthly menus of prepared meals and recipes. In effect, Streamline offers the same single-source supply facility to the domestic consumer as many commercial companies do for their corporate clients, thus simplifying all transactions into a unified framework.

One particularly clever feature of the Streamline operation is the way in which it targets its Internet advertising. A customer browsing the Streamline virtual supermarket for popcorn, for example, may see an ad for a John Travolta film, which can be rented from Blockbuster Video, a Streamline partner. Precision marketing of this sort has helped to generate response rates of up to 15 per cent - a vast improvement on the two per cent return typically achieved by conventional direct advertising.

Streamline's system has yet another attraction. It combines real-time information from the Internet with ads stored on a CD-ROM, so that customers can receive tantalising images far too complex to be sent down a normal Internet connection. Thus Procter & Gamble has created a 'training video' for customers who are sceptical about dry-cleaning at home, and Gillette's audience can rotate a 3-D image of its 'Mach 3' razor. By creating interactive opportunities of this kind, advertising becomes more customer-friendly and, in turn, more likely to generate purchases.

---

6 MANUFACTURING

6.1 The case of General Electric demonstrates some of the problems and opportunities arising from the unavoidable application of **information technology** to commerce and business. In recent years, GE has changed is core competencies completely and has transformed itself through a vision of 'more and more services, driven by providing useful information to customers'. This presupposes that GE is able to discover what information its customers will find useful, and will then be able to invent some means through which the information can be collected, analysed, assessed and subsequently delivered to the customer in a useable form. Undoubtedly, too, one of the risks with GE's strategy is that, by giving customers more information, power shifts away from the seller. On the other hand:

(a) For **complex products or services** - including the locomotives or insurance policies sold by GE - customers still want a direct, face-to-face relationship with a sales person.

(b) At least so far as GE is concerned, the Internet's application in electronic commerce is likely to remain limited. Although most GE businesses will accept customer orders posted over the Net, it still represents no more than around two per cent of the company's revenue. In GE's view, the sort of **business-to-business** contracts in which it specialises are likely to be less affected by the Internet, and even the impact on consumer markets may be more restricted that is commonly visualised. Gary Reiner, GE's chief technology officer, says: 'I can see where bookstores get hurt. I can see where some kinds of clothing stores get hurt. But I just don't see it in our business. Ten years from now, I'd be surprised if many lightbulbs are sold over the Internet.'

(c) Business-to-business transactions now rely heavily on **electronic data interchange**, a market which GE estimates will grow at 20 per cent a year. Much of that is driven by an attempt to squeeze out the costs caused by order processing errors - a field within which many companies are intensely vulnerable.

(d) **Relationships with suppliers** have been similarly affected. Through a web-based catalogue posted on GE's own intranet, buyers anywhere in the group can order indirect materials.

6.2 Also significant for General Electric has been the way in which **information processing and dissemination** has helped to turn a collection of old-fashioned manufacturing companies into a conglomerate whose growth and profitability are dependent on **services**. For example:

(a) **Remote monitoring** (sensors planted inside machines or engines to glean information about how the equipment is functioning) means that more than 10,000 scanners and other hospital equipment can be monitored by GE engineers in Tokyo, Paris and Milwaukee. The same method has been applied to aircraft engines and locomotives. It has helped to detect some equipment failures before they have occurred, but its main benefit has been to cut repair and technician visit costs. This is very important for GE, given that so much of its profitability now originates with service rather than manufacturing itself.

(b) GE can provide services to help customers use their assets better: the locomotive division, for instance, sells software that enables customers to manage the routing on their railways more efficiently.

(c) GE plans to develop a capability which will allow it to keep track of all the modifications and changes made to every one of its heavy-engineering products, so that it can assemble a **complete history of each item**. This in turn permits the company to offer more knowledgeable and expert advice when required; it too ties the customer more closely to GE, especially if it turns out that GE knows more about the customer's equipment than the customer does.

Chapter roundup

- Banks are hampered by highly traditional structures and cultures, resistance to change, and large investment in branch networks.

- Holiday companies find themselves at the mercy of consumer power.

- Many public sector organisations have benefited from implementing a competitive philosophy.

- Electronic commerce is having a profound effect on the retail sector.

- Domestic lifestyles have changed, as have attitudes to work and leisure. This has affected the retailing environment and purchasing habits.

- IT has also had an effect on the manufacturing sector but it remains true that many business-to-business customers for complex products value the face-to-face approach.

Quick quiz

1   List nine factors associated with poor-performing organisations. (2.3)

2   Why is image a problem for traditional banks? (2.8)

3   Who is Kevin Smith? (2.9)

4   How do holiday companies respond to criticism? (3.4, 3.5)

5   What are the disadvantages of monopolies? (4.2)

6   What are the consequences of not having competition? (4.4)

7   What is a possible reason for the failure of some companies to have made any money from e-commerce? (5.8)

Part B
Managing the marketing/ customer interface

4 The strategic dimension: vision and leadership

Chapter Topic List	Syllabus reference
1 Setting the scene	2.1
2 Corporate strategy, culture and structure	2.1
3 Vision and leadership	2.1
4 Stimulating customer-focused behaviour	2.1
5 The drive for sustainable competitive advantage	2.1
6 Organisational aspects and accountability	2.1
7 Outsourcing	2.1
8 The corporate scorecard	2.1

Learning Outcomes

- After studying this chapter you will be in a position to develop strategies for mobilising customer-focused marketing programmes within defined organisational settings.

- It will be clear that customer focus should be created and led by senior management.

- Customer focus is central to an organisation's structure and systems.

Key Concepts Introduced

- Organisation
- Societal marketing concept
- Vision
- Customer loyalty
- Consumerism
- Empowerment

- Business process re-engineering
- Competitive advantage
- Value chain
- Total quality management
- Internal marketing
- Balanced scorecard

Examples of Marketing at Work

- Elida Gibbs
- TNT and the Lands End Clothing Company
- British Airways, Kwik Fit, Eurocamp
- Leicester Royal Infirmary
- Product innovation

- Charities
- Coutts
- The Automobile Association, Cigna Services, Hamilton Acorn
- Birmingham & Midshires Building Society, TNT Express

- British Airways
- Mercedes
- Human resource management policies
- Philip Morris

- Rover cars
- Privatisation of public utilities
- Digital Equipment
- The balanced scorecard

1 SETTING THE SCENE

1.1 Marketers are effectively the bridge between the organisation and its customers. Marketers need to understand certain basic facts about organisational life in order to understand:

(a) how they can be effective in championing the customer's concerns and getting other people to do so

(b) the constraints over what they themselves can achieve

(c) how best to organise the deployment of marketing resources

1.2 As well as these technical issues of structure, there is the issue of corporate culture which involves the basic assumptions people have about what the business is and what they should do. Marketing orientation and corporate culture are related strongly to each other. In service industries the underlying attitude towards satisfying customers can offer success or failure.

1.3 The most effective way of achieving customer focused behaviour is through the commitment of top management. In Sections 3, 4 and 5 we look at some measures that can be taken to encourage customer care and secure competitive advantage, including some key models, such as Reichheld's service/profit cycle.

1.4 A lot of the material on vision and leadership in this chapter has been specifically provided by the senior examiner.

1.5 This chapter also considers the benefits of outsourcing and the balanced scorecard in providing customer focus.

2 CORPORATE STRATEGY, CULTURE AND STRUCTURE

2.1 As organisations are made up of people, how these people are brought together and organised has a profound effect on how efficiently they perform. Managers today are very aware of the need to understand both formal and informal relationships within an organisation when preparing and implementing plans.

Key Concept

Organisation is a mechanism or structure that enables living things to work effectively together. There are three basic elements of organisation.

- Division of labour, ie specialisation ('who does what?').
- A source of authority, ('who is responsible for seeing that they do it?').
- Relationships ('how does it fit in with what everyone else is doing?').

Organisation design or 'structure'

2.2 Organisational design or structure implies a framework or mechanism intended to do the following.

    (a) **Link individuals** in an established network of relationships so that authority, responsibility and communications can be controlled.

    (b) **Group together** (in any appropriate way) the tasks required to fulfil the objectives of the organisation, and allocate them to suitable individuals or groups.

    (c) Give each individual or group the **authority** required to perform the allocated functions, while controlling behaviour and resources in the interests of the organisation as a whole.

    (d) Co-ordinate the **objectives and activities** of separate units, so that overall aims are achieved.

    (e) Facilitate the **flow of work,** information and other resources required, through planning, control and other systems.

2.3 Many factors influence the structural design of the organisation.

    (a) **Size**. As an organisation gets larger, its structure gets more complex: specialisation and subdivision are required.

    (b) **Nature of its work**. An organisation's structure is shaped by the division of work into functions and individual tasks, and how these tasks relate to each other.

    (c) **The nature of the market** will dictate the way in which tasks are grouped together: into functions, or sales territories, or types of customer etc.

    (d) **Staff**. The skills and abilities and aspirations of staff will determine how the work is structured and the degree of autonomy or supervision required.

    (e) **Legal, commercial, technical and social environment**. Examples include: economic recession necessitating staff 'streamlining' especially at middle management level; new technology reducing staff requirements but increasing specialisation.

    (f) **Age**: ie the time it has had to develop and grow, or decline, whether it is very set in its ways and traditional or experimenting with new ways of doing things and making decisions.

    (g) **Culture and management style**: how willing management is to delegate authority at all levels, how skilled they are in organisation and communication (for example in handling a wider span of control), whether teamwork is favoured, or large, impersonal structures accepted by the staff etc, whether the company is product or market oriented and what the driving force for change is, for example research and development, increased market share or profit.

Structural departmentation by customer

2.4 Departmentation by customer is commonly associated with marketing departments and selling effort, but it might also be used at the product development stage. Such an approach encourages **cross selling** across the whole product range and the orientation of activities to meet the needs of client groups.

BPP
PUBLISHING

Exam tip

Structure has an impact on the culture of the organisation. Attempts to reposition the 'culture' say from product to a market orientation, are often best tackled with a new structure, after re-organisation. This need for a new structure is often implicit in major CIM case studies and is something you should look out for.

Recent trends in marketing organisation

Team-based working

2.5 Teams and groups will become increasingly popular in a marketing context. In *Marketing Business* (December 1995/January 1996), Anthony Freeling suggests that teams from a number of business functions will carry out most marketing tasks.

(a) 'When an entire organisation is focused on marketing, the need for a separate [marketing] department may disappear'.

(b) 'Successful companies will in future rely primarily on - and organise themselves around - integrators and functional specialists.'

    (i) **'Integrators** are responsible for serving each distinct consumer, channel or product.' They will pool and co-ordinate the organisation's resources for the customers' benefit. They will lead teams which will contain people with a variety of skills.

    (ii) **'Specialists** will create competitive advantage by helping the company build world class skills in the two or three most important areas of marketing.' A team might contain a pricing specialist, a specialist in database marketing, to name but two.

(c) 'Successful companies will link these integrators and specialists together through teams and processes rather than through functional or business unit structures.'

'The teams will be organised around key cross-functional business processes like building brand unity and ensuring superior customer service.'

Customer service departments: who is in charge?

2.6 Many firms are setting up **customer service departments**, particularly in relation to building up relationships with customers. To build loyalty, customer service is regarded as an important competitive tool. For service companies, obviously, good 'customer service' is essential to success.

2.7 *Marketing Business* reported (March 1997) that many customer service departments are no longer under the control of the marketing director.

A changing role for brand management

2.8 Within the marketing department, there have been two contrasting roles.

(a) A **product manager** may be responsible to the marketing director for the effective sales, distribution and marketing of a product or line. In fact, the marketing director may delegate responsibility to a number of product managers.

(b) A **brand manager's role** is responsible for competing, within and outside the company, for brand leadership: in other words the brand manager will be heavily involved in advertising and creative work to build **consumer awareness**.

2.9   Many FMCG are redesigning marketing activities along the lines of **business processes**.

Marketing at Work

Elida Gibbs (now Fabergé) is a subsidiary of Unilever, and sells brands such as Lynx.

A process redesign aimed at creating a more natural flow for the company's work prompted chairman Helmut Ganser to [remove] day to day operating and tactical marketing from longer term issues of brand development, creating three separate centres of expertise along the way: one each for the *consumer/brand*, the *category* and the *retailer/customer*.

The *category manager* took over those operational marketing activities that flow through the retailer, such as pricing and promotions. Category managers also had the responsibility of feeding retailers' views back into the company's thinking about its brands.

The process of *brand development* was internationalised. As part of a global reorganisation, parent company Unilever reapportioned responsibility for marketing strategy and innovation to regional innovation centres. London became Unilever's European strategy and NPD leader for deodorants, while Milan took up the baton for haircare, for example.

That further changed the brand manager's role. In marketing departments which had ceded strategic responsibility to an innovation centre in another country, brand managers were effectively reduced to implementing other people's strategy, tweaking the brand proposition for their local conditions. Innovation centre responsibility became so big that the brand management job split into two. A brand like Lynx has a *brand manager* responsible for *consumer directed marketing communications* and short term innovations such as new fragrances and an *innovation manager developing the longer-term brand proposition*. (Extracts from *Marketing Business,* February 1997.)

The societal marketing concept

2.10   Critics of the marketing concept suggest that true marketing is rarely practised, and the **proper wants of the consumer** are ignored. Not only are customers' wants inadequately considered, but also there is much reason for fearing that the goods and services of many organisations are against the long-term interests of customers' and society as a whole (eg the polluting of the environment by cars, chemicals etc; the waste of raw materials as non-returnable, non-biodegradable packaging, the sale of non-nutritious or harmful food and drugs etc).

2.11   Kotler suggested that a **societal marketing concept** should replace the marketing concept as a philosophy for the future.

> ### Key Concept
> 'The **societal marketing concept** is a management orientation that holds that the key task of the organisation is to determine the **needs and wants of target markets** and to adapt the organisation to delivering the desired satisfactions more effectively and efficiently than its competitors in a way that preserves or enhances the consumers' and society's well-being.'

Ethics

2.12   As an extension of this view, we can identify increasing concern with issues of ethics. This affects companies directly and indirectly.

2.13   In general, ethical issues - how companies behave - have become of more importance recently. Many companies are exploiting new found public concern with ethical concern. The Co-operative Bank has developed a whole advertising campaign around avoiding investment in countries with oppressive regimes. As Alexander Garrett (*Marketing Business*

July/August 1996) reports, 'marketing poses its own set of ethical questions'. For some companies, copying Body Shop and the Co-operative Bank is not really an option (eg tobacco firms, drinks firms).

2.14 Responses to ethical concerns include the following.

(a) Introducing codes of conduct (eg to help and guide employees in difficult situations).

(b) Inviting outsiders to review ethical performance in some way.

Ethical issues and marketing

2.15 In the August 1996 edition of *Marketing Success*, the senior examiner briefly covered some issues of ethics which might be of relevance to marketers, using the 4Ps of the marketing mix as a framework.

(a) **Product/service**

(i) Failure to inform customers about risks associated with the use of the product: **dishonesty**. Currently, there is a lawsuit in the US in which people are suggesting that the tobacco companies, despite their denials, have known for some time that nicotine is addictive.

(ii) Using materials of a poorer quality in a bid to cut costs.

(iii) Does manufacture involve an unacceptable environmental cost?

(b) **Pricing**. In economic terms, price is a matter of supply and demand and, in the pursuit of profit, prices are 'what the market will bear'. Ethics come into the discussion when:

(i) cartels attempt to 'fix' prices by rigging the market.

(ii) consumers are sometimes charged extras, not officially disclosed.

(c) **Promotion**

(i) Advertising: honest, legal, decent and truthful.

(ii) Tastefulness of imagery (eg violence, sexual stereotyping).

(d) **Place**. Ethical concerns regarding relationships with intermediaries can involve the use of power, delays in payment to give two examples.

2.16 Marketing is a company-wide commitment to providing customer satisfaction. It is also a managerial process involving the regular analysis of the firm's competitive situation, leading to the development of marketing objectives, and the formulation and implementation of strategies, tactics, organisations and controls for their achievement.

2.17 A **strategic marketing orientation** is a combination of marketing and organisational factors which contribute to improving effectiveness and form the basis of sound organisational performance.

2.18 A number of steps need to be undertaken when trying to change what is essentially the culture of the organisation.

(a) **Understand the existing orientation** (eg production or selling)

(b) **Identify the level of marketing effectiveness**

(i) **Customer philosophy**. To what extent does the firm acknowledge the importance of the market-place and customer needs in shaping company plans?

(ii) **Integrated marketing organisation**. To what extent is the company staffed for marketing planning and control?

(iii) **Adequate marketing information.** Does management receive the quality of information necessary to conduct an effective planning process?

(iv) **Strategic orientation.** Does the company's management generate innovative strategies for long term growth and profitability, and to what extent have these plans proved successful?

(v) **Operational efficiency.** Is marketing implemented in a cost-efficient manner and are results monitored to ensure necessary corrective action is taken?

(c) **Identify a marketing champion.** Without top management support, the programme can degenerate into a token management-training exercise.

(d) **Conduct a needs analysis**

The next step is to conduct a management-development needs analysis based on interviews with appropriate managers and staff. The sorts of knowledge, skills and attitudes that can be developed through training include competitive strengths and weaknesses, clients' motivations, planning, motivating and communication skills and customer focused attitudes.

(e) **The management development programme**

Appropriate courses can be developed to include different types and levels of staff to explain the knowledge, skills and attitudes necessary for the development of a strategic marketing orientation.

(f) **Key support activities**

(i) Establish a **marketing task force** to oversee the development of marketing activities

(ii) **Organise for marketing.**

(iii) **Acquire and develop marketing talent.**

(iv) **Use external consultants.** Marketing research, customer care training and communication agencies seem appropriate areas.

(v) **Promote marketing-orientated lawyers.** This will aid in developing an appropriate culture which clearly sees customer service, planning and innovation as important.

(vi) **Develop a marketing-information system.** In particular regular studies of clients and competition. A greater awareness of sales potential and profitability of different markets and the measurement of the cost effectiveness of different types of marketing expenditure.

(vii) **Install an effective marketing planning system.** The planning process, including feedback mechanisms should be formalised. The time spent and people involved in developing the marketing strategy needs to be improved. Thought should be given to contingency planning and a more strategic use made of the elements of the marketing mix.

(viii) **Recognise the long term nature of the task.** Developing a strategic marketing orientation represents a major change in attitudes and a fundamental shift in core values. Change can take from three to six years and will be gradual in nature.

BPP PUBLISHING

The key phases for service delivery

2.19 For 'customer service' and 'customer care' to be sources of **competitive advantage**, then, several key aspects of organisational functioning have to work together. This necessity for **corporate integration** is illustrated in the following diagram (taken from *Once a Customer, Always a Customer* by Chris Daffy, 1997).

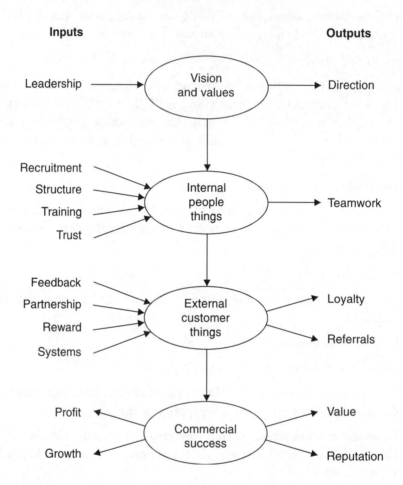

The key phases for service delivery

Phase one - vision and values

2.20 One of the seven habits of highly effective people, according to Stephen Covey, is to '**begin with the end in mind**'. In fact, virtually all organisations which are good at developing relationships with their customers are organisations which have a clear vision of what they are trying to create.

> ### Key Concept
> A **vision** constitutes a view of the future which is different and better than the present; they are often shared with colleagues (who may have indeed helped create the vision). Therefore the people leading these organisations all **know what goal they are aiming for**, and what is expected from them at work to help achieve it.

Phase two - internal 'people things'

2.21 If employees are to give good service to customers, they first have to **receive good service from their managers and colleagues**. In fact there are many organisations that expect their customers to be treated like gold - by employees who are treated like dirt. This never works. At best the service that employees give to customers will only mirror the service they get from their colleagues: so it follows that **good customer care must start internally** if it is to have any chance of working externally.

2.22 Key factors in managing the quality of internal service operations include the **recruitment** of customer-facing people, the supply of appropriate (and generous) **training,** and the ability to **take decisions which will attract and keep customers,** especially when their future loyalty is threatened.

Marketing at Work

(a) 'Empowerment' in action at TNT

One member of staff at the Atherstone location for TNT, the delivery company, has responsibility for ensuring that the team has the vehicles they need, where and when they need them, in order to make the deliveries on time, as promised to customers. In his words, 'The deliveries must get there as promised. So if a truck breaks down, I get another. If that breaks down I find another one. And if necessary, I get an aeroplane!'

(b) The Lands End Clothing Company

If you receive a catalogue from this (US) mail-order clothing firm, study the eight principles for doing business which have been developed by the company's founder, Gary Comer. All the eight principles can be distilled into one simple, driving sentence which is internalised by all Lands End employees: 'Don't worry about what's good for the company, worry about what's good for the customer'.

Phase three - external 'customer things'

2.23 **Feedback** is the way that organisations try to ensure that customers' views can be used to trigger and drive any necessary changes and improvements.

2.24 It is salutary to recognise that in the UK several **forms of measuring customer satisfaction** are not as prevalent as in Japan. A survey by the Digital Equipment Company (reported in *Customer Care* by Sarah Cook, Kogan Page, 1992) contrasted experiences and attitudes in the UK and Japan, by asking the question, 'To measure customer satisfaction, which of the following methods does your company use?' The following table summarises the results.

Measuring customer satisfaction	Respondents replying (%)	
	Japan	*UK*
Personal visits by management	99	91
Personal visits by sales people	99	98
Analysis of complaints received	98	86
Questionnaires	98	68
Observations and assessments by independent professionals	99	64
Focus meetings with groups of customers	99	62
Toll-free telephones	99	27

Marketing at Work

Organisations with distinctive reputations in the customer service field have established many ways of gathering, analysing, communicating and then acting upon customer feedback.

(a) *British Airways* has a Market Place Performance Unit, employing 10 people who have the job of measuring, analysing and reporting on 350 items that affect the customer's perception of an airline.

(b)   *Kwik Fit* makes 5,000 to 10,000 telephone calls each weekday evening to gather customer feedback.

(c)   *Eurocamp* holds focus group sessions with customers and telephones them after their holidays in order to assess their views.

2.25   The **partnership approach** to relationships with customers (and suppliers) is also common among organisations with a strong reputation for customer focus. Moreover, it is important to **reward staff** for delivering customer service (and for rectifying the situation when it goes wrong).

2.26   The final key element of this phase is the creation of efficient, customer-friendly **systems**. It is no good expecting staff to give great service to customers if the systems they need to support them are not capable of doing so.

Marketing at Work

Leicester Royal Infirmary

In one area of women's health, the process used to take on average 79 hours of the patient's time, with 90 minutes of waiting in the hospital seeing 16 different people with about 650 yards of walking around the hospital.

As a result of customer-focused re-engineering, the process takes just 36 minutes, with only 8 minutes of waiting, 3 different people to see and 90 yards of walking around the hospital.

Phase four - commercial success

2.27   It must always be remembered that the point of the exercise (at least for commercial organisations) is **profitability, survival and (usually) growth**. Good customer care, in other words, is **not an end in itself**: theoretically, it would be possible to create an organisation which delivers superb customer service but which does so at such a cost that eventually it goes out of business. However, such an outcome is (thankfully) very rare and unlikely because:

(a)   competent customer care implies a differentiating advantage from which the organisation benefits through acquiring **new customers**; and

(b)   competent customer care is a powerful mechanism for sustaining **customer loyalty** - and attracting new customers is normally far more costly than keeping the current ones.

3   VISION AND LEADERSHIP

Strategy and transformation

3.1   For some organisations, customer service is nothing more than a **back office function**, driven exclusively by customer feedback, returns and complaints. For others, there is no customer service at all - perhaps because the organisation is indifferent to its customers, or because the customers are themselves **passive**, willing to accept whatever is offered without argument, provided, perhaps, that the price is low. It has to be understood that where the organisation is a **monopoly**, too, then there is no incentive to service customers efficiently, because these customers cannot go elsewhere.

3.2   Increasingly, however, inertia is being replaced by activity and by a consciousness that things can be changed. Customers are now prepared to combine for **collective action**; they often have **media opportunities** to exploit (principally through television consumer-affairs programmes), and will even threaten **litigation**; customers are prepared to **take their business elsewhere**, and have enhanced avenues for doing so as new organisations present a more entrepreneurial face to the world and operate through different distribution channels such as the Internet.

3.3 Corporate ideas about **competitive strategy** are also changing as it comes to be realised that incremental performance improvement is not a particularly strategic way to operate. Strategy, if it is anything, is about **transformation**: about creating new products, about developing new services on the back of existing products, about reaching out to actual and potential customers in entirely new ways, about innovative approaches to customer segmentation, and the like.

Gary Hamel ('*Strategy as Revolution*', Harvard Business Review, July/August 1996) is one of the principal advocates of the view that organisations cannot succeed if they simply imitate what has gone before.

3.4 In essence, he defines three principal types of company:

(a) The **rule makers** - who dominate their respective marketplaces and who (try to) set the competitive conditions under which they and others will operate. The rule makers in today's environment include Microsoft, Hertz, General Electric and McDonalds.

(b) The **rule takers** - the companies who, in effect, imitate the rule makers, who accept the competitive framework which has been established by the dominant players, and who try to beat the rule makers at their own game. Rule takers include Avis and Burger King.

(c) The **rule breakers** - organisations which refuse to accept the implicit assumptions made by existing competitors, and which therefore seek to establish a new paradigm. Companies in the rule breaker category include Body Shop (Anita Roddick once said that she watches what the conventional perfume/toiletry companies are doing, and then deliberately goes in the opposite direction), IKEA, Dell, Amazon.com, and First Direct. Eventually, if a rule breaker becomes highly successful, it dominates its market place and can fall into the trap of turning into a rule maker, ie, it believes that it has an enduring formula for success which needs nothing more than incremental tweaking.

3.5 A similar framework is offered in another Harvard Business Review article (Jan-Feb 1997). This is expanded upon below.

CREATING VALUE THROUGH INNOVATION

The five dimensions of strategy	*Conventional logic*	*Value innovation logic*
Industry assumptions	Industry's conditions are given.	Industry's conditions can be shaped.
Strategic focus	Competitive advantages to beat the competition.	Competition not the benchmark. A company should pursue a quantum leap in value to dominate the market.
Customers	Further segmentation and customisation, focussing on the differences in what customers value.	A value innovator targets the mass of buyers and willingly lets some existing customers go. It focuses on the key commonalities in what customers value.

The five dimensions of strategy	Conventional logic	Value innovation logic
Assets and capabilities	A company should leverage its existing capabilities.	A company must not be constrained by what it already has. It must ask, 'What would we do if we were starting anew?'.
Product and service offerings	An industry's traditional boundaries determine the products and services a company offers. The goal is to maximise the value of those offerings.	A value innovator thinks in terms of the total solution customers seek, even if that takes the company beyond its industry's traditional offerings.

Industry assumptions

3.6 The conventional logic, especially for a new entrant, is that in any competitive framework the market conditions are given. Yet in practice many of these conditions are derived from logic which was faulty from the start or which has become faulty as customer aspirations have changed. **Value innovation logic** suggests that competitive conditions can be shaped by new entrants precisely because they do not have the cultural baggage of those already there. Not surprisingly, for instance, electronic commerce is dominated by emergent companies, such as Amazon.com.

3.7 It used to be thought, for example, that companies would be more profitable if they had a **few large customers** rather than a **large number of small ones**. While this may be true for some fields of commercial activity, there are others where it is not: thus BOC, for instance, has found that when it investigates profitability-per-customer, its small customers generate much more added-value for BOC. This is because large customers tend to pay their bills more slowly and use their size in order to force down prices (through discounts, rebates or other forms of special deal).

3.8 Equally, think about estate agents. They are all much the same, aren't they? They all have coloured photographs in their windows; they all charge their customers on the basis of a percentage of the agreed selling price; they even use similar words and phrases when describing the properties which they are trying to sell. It is as if they were each hypnotised into believing that there is no other way to function. Yet (apart from laws regulating financial transactions, and the disciplinary rules of the relevant professional bodies) nobody compels estate agents to be the same as each other and they could break out from the mould. One way to encourage it could be as follows:

3.9 Require the partners to **articulate and write down all the 'rules'** under which they do business, whether these rules are legally/professionally enforced or not. Writing down such rules is quite difficult, because many of the rules are taken for granted, never challenged, and never seriously discussed. One of them will be the rule that all clients are charged a fee which is conventionally a percentage of the agreed sale price of the property.

3.10 **All the rules must now be challenged**: what would happen were they to be discarded? Would the sky fall in? Very often it turns out that many of the so-called rules are nothing more than conventions, justifying the Hamel argument that competition is dominated by rule makers and rule takers.

3.11 Develop new products and services through abandonment of rules. In this way the company begins to think 'outside the box'. Thus a firm of estate agents could create new pricing offers, such as a standard-fee 'Gold Package' which includes the sale commission, legal charges, and the cleaning of either the new property or the old one.

Strategic focus

3.12 The traditional way to approach strategy is to think of it as a means through which the company seeks to create and exploit one or more **competitive advantages**. But the lessons from Value Innovation Logic on pages 53 and 54 suggest that organisations should not simply watch other companies in the same business as themselves: if they do, they engage in destructive 'me-too' rivalries with price as the major competitive discriminator. Think about the supermarket price wars, for example, or the price competition in mobile telephony, package holiday tours and airline travel.

3.13 Instead, organisations will be more successful if they spend less time looking over their shoulders and more time peering into the future. It is this visionary thinking which has produced spectacular success for First Direct, Body Shop, and Tesco, among others.

Customers

3.14 Conventional organisations devote a lot of time to clever **segmentation** (new ways of classifying their customers) and to **customisation** (tailoring the product/service to individual requirements). Nobody is suggesting that such activities are fruitless, but what they sometimes ignore is whether some customers represent greater profit opportunities than others. In a headlong search for market share (normally a feature of mature market places), companies may not notice that they are acquiring customers from whom they make no money at all.

3.15 This is why the value innovator may willingly let some customers go, on the argument that

(a) we are not deriving any profit from such customers or customer categories,

(b) there is no feasible prospect of deriving profit from them,

(c) their continued existence in our customer portfolio may even make it more difficult for us to acquire customers from elsewhere,

(d) if these customers were to go elsewhere, then our overall performance would be enhanced.

3.16 Increasingly, in the UK, for example, we see banks introducing account charges for customers who previously paid nothing at all (provided they maintained a credit balance), and also introducing fees for services previously supplied free (e.g., the £5-per-transaction payment at Abbey National for over-the-counter business).

Assets and capabilities

3.17 Assets are what the organisation has (capital, people, land, intellectual property and so forth), and capabilities reflect what the organisation does with what it has. Many corporate strategies concentrate on maximising the yield from organisational assets but value innovation logic suggests that the proper question to ask is: 'What would we do if we were starting anew?'

3.18 For example, would a retail bank nowadays deliberately set out to create a UK branch network with over 2000 offices? Would an insurance company consciously recruit a direct sales force to sell pensions in people's homes? Would a consumer electronics company establish its manufacturing operations in the UK?

3.19 Most companies concede that they would not operate the way they do now if they had their chances all over again. Stephen Covey (*The Seven Habits of Highly Effective People*) points out that one of the distinguishing features of highly effective people is that they start from where they want to be, rather than from where they are now.

Product and service offerings

3.20 The organisations of today and tomorrow are unlikely to succeed if they allow themselves to be governed by **traditional boundaries**. Already some companies have broken through these boundaries with conspicuous success - one thinks of Tesco entering financial services, or bookshops offering cafe/restaurant facilities for their customers. The value innovator visualises the **total customer solution** and acts accordingly, even if it does mean that some cherished assumptions are being challenged.

Marketing at Work

The domestic video-recorder supplies an excellent illustration of this process. The first recorders were so complicated that only technologically-literate children could operate them; the second generation deployed Video-Plus technology enabling customers simply to key in a multi-digit number in order to activate the recording process; the third generation, launched in 1999, includes a 'Habitwatch' neural-network circuitry and digital capability (not constrained, in other words, by the three or four hour limitation of a videotape). These video-recorders 'learn' about the programmes typically enjoyed by the customer and will automatically record such programmes (e.g., soap operas) whether instructed to do so or not.

Yet another illustration is the book vending pattern promoted by Amazon.com over the Internet. Anyone showing interest in a specific book is invited to study extracts from reviews (not all of them favourable), and will also be shown details of other books on the same subject and additional books which recent purchasers of the book in question have often bought at the same time.

Strategic advantage through service

3.21 All authorities agree that when organisations seek strategic advantage through customer service, they can only succeed if their external service delivery is integrated with a strong service ethos inside the organisation.

Customer service: critical factors

Leadership	People	Results
Suppliers Values Quality Market acuity	Empowerment Circle of virtue	Service quality Customer growth Business performance Productivity Altruism
	Performance management Balanced scorecard	

The service process

Moments of truth - Continuous Improvements - Innovation

(*Source: Adapted from Professor Chris Voss, International Service Study, 1997 (LBS)*)

3.22 The International Service Study has shown a strong positive correlation between customer service performance (as perceived by customers themselves), on the one hand, and the existence in the organisation of customer-focused practices, on the other.

Customer service: practices and performance

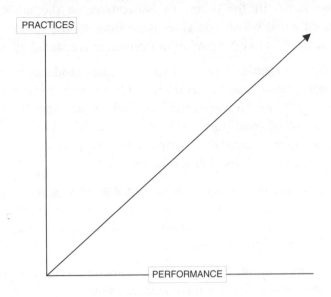

These practices can be subdivided into five principal areas, as follows:

(a) **Leadership**. Echoing Daffy, the ISS believes top-down direction-setting to be the essential first step: the specification of positive, **customer-related values**; the emergence of **partner arrangements with suppliers**; a strong **quality message**; and the promotion of **market acuity**, ie, the selection of priorities based on business (and profit) potential rather than on any other criteria.

Marketing at Work

Early in 1999, a British Airways jumbo jet, carrying around 400 (mainly Economy Class) passengers from Los Angeles to London, had just entered Atlantic airspace. The passengers were horrified to hear a taped announcement that because of engine problems, the aircraft was about to ditch into the sea; they were instructed to adopt the crash position and prepare themselves for the descent. The announcement was repeated a few moments later; it was only later that the Captain (who had been unaware of the panic which ensued after the first message) reassured everyone about the flight and told the passengers that broadcasting the announcement had been a ghastly mistake, possibly even a practical joke. A month after the aircraft landed safely at London, the passengers received letters of apology from BA and offers of restitution: a bottle of wine, a bouquet of flowers or a box of chocolates. At about the same time, a British Airways Concorde had flown from Washington to Heathrow, but because of technical difficulties it could not fly at its normal supersonic speed. The journey took an hour or so longer than timetabled. As passengers disembarked, they were given vouchers entitling them to free return flights on Concorde in the future.

British Airways was clearly treating these two different groups of passengers in different ways. However, different treatment can be justified against the company's declared strategy (published in its 1999 Annual Report) of concentrating its efforts on business-class and First-Class passengers, ie, those where the profit margins are greater.

(b) **People**. The ISS investigators promote the benefits of **empowerment** defined as the freedom of (in particular, the front-line service) employees to use their initiative when dealing with customers, provided they act in ways which are consistent with the broad corporate direction. In Barclays Bank, front-line bank branch employees can offer restitution to customers of up to £2,000 without reference to any higher authority (provided, of course, they feel that such restitution is justified).

(i) Graham Clark of the Cranfield School of Management, writing in the School's own magazine, *Management Focus* (July 1999), points out that certain organisations and people are not as suited to empowerment as others. His argument is expressed as a 2x2 matrix, with **compliant organisations** (allowing their staff little discretion) in one corner, and **adaptive organisations** (practising empowerment) in the other. In between come the **anxious zone** and the **frustrated zone**, which you enter depending on the direction you are moving and whether you like having lots of freedom or are scared by it.

(ii) **Compliant organisations** - such as mass-production systems, fast-food restaurants, retail financial services, and businesses involving risk like airlines - cannot empower their workforces too much or their standardised products could turn out wrong and upset the customers. In addition, attempts to move employees from compliant to adaptive behaviour could be a bad thing if those employees happen to like being told what to do.

(c) **Results**. The ISS group stresses such measures as service quality, customer growth (and retention, if appropriate), overall business performance measured by financial out-turns, employee and resource productivity, and altruism (which simply means the appearance of being concerned about others).

(d) **Performance management**. From the start, customer service has to be integrated into the organisation's balanced scorecard of key indicators.

(e) **The service process**. Relationships with customers derive from sustained positive experiences through each transaction when the customer interacts with the organisation: a telephone enquiry, a website 'hit', receipt of a bank statement, behaviour of the waitress, attitude of the hotel receptionist, and so forth. A single negative experience can offset hundreds of favourable ones; moreover, because competitor organisations continue to deliver enhancements, continuous **improvement and innovation** must be built into the service process as a whole.

3.23 The presence of service **practices** inside the organisation can be correlated with the perception of service **performance** by customers themselves, in order to produce a 2x2 matrix.

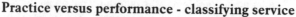

Practice versus performance - classifying service

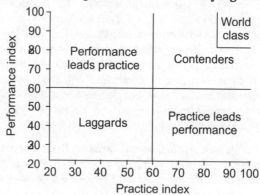

(a) **World class** organisations are those where superb performance is linked to first-class practices. Only a few companies have reached this point (and the number is smaller than the number of companies who think they are world class): examples include Disney and Marriott Hotels.

(b) **Contenders** are companies with enviable reputations for service and whose continued devotion to improvement and change will probably mean their entry into the world class category.

(c) **Laggards** consist of service suppliers who deliver indifferent or poor levels of customer service and whose internal support mechanisms do not endorse service and customer relationships as priorities. One would like to think that laggard organisations would eventually go out of business, but this is by no means inevitable: they may be **monopolies**, whose customers cannot defect even if they wanted to; they may have **undemanding customers** who are prepared to tolerate indifferent service; or they may operate in a competitive field where historically service levels are low despite prolonged customer dissatisfaction.

(d) The other two categories represent very interesting and even bizarre alternatives. **Performance leads practice** in organisations where front-line service is delivered by highly committed people despite the absence of any supportive infrastructure. Examples may include school-teachers, hospital nurses, social work, or even customer service activities in commercial organisations if the relevant positions happen to be occupied by caring, altruistic individuals. Where **practice leads performance**, by contrast, the existence of the infrastructure is not aligned to the achievement of results - perhaps because messages about the importance of customers and customer service are not reflected in an appropriate reward system for managers and front-line personnel.

The service profit cycle

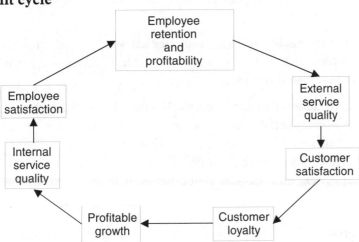

Source: *The Loyalty Effect*, (Reichheld), Harvard Business Review, Bain & Company

3.24 Reichheld's highly influential model establishes beyond doubt the linkages between external service performance and internal strategic instruments in a sequence which operates as a 'circle of virtue'.

(a) If the organisation has a respectable level of **profitability**, then it can more easily afford to produce **external service quality**.

(b) **External service quality** generates **customer satisfaction** - though we have to remember that it is not enough to produce customers who are merely 'satisfied'. 'Satisfied' customers (even those who give their supplier a score of 8 out of 10 in a customer-satisfaction survey) are just as prone to defect as customers who are 'dissatisfied'. The goal has to be **customer delight** - that sense of elation which goes well beyond the taken-for-granted.

(c) If customers are satisfied, they will display **customer loyalty**. Again we need to be quite explicit about what we mean.

> **Key Concep**
> Ted Johns, CIM Senior Examiner for the marketing customer interface, defines **customer loyalty** as: **voluntary repurchasing or referral**. It is voluntary in the sense that it has not been 'bought' through a discount or 'loyalty card' (which is nothing more than a sales discount offer); and it involves the external expression of customer support of some kind, typically articulated through repurchasing or referral to others.

    (d) **Customer loyalty** leads to (more) **profitable growth**. This is because it is always more economical for an organisation to service its existing customers than to acquire new ones. Convention dictates that it can cost between 5 and 15 times more to find new customers compared with the costs of customer retention - and in some fields of activity, where the frequency of purchase is low (eg cars, double glazing, house-buying), the costs of customer acquisition are significantly greater. It is always a source of amazement that many companies spend little on **relationship marketing** and **key account management**; the result is that these companies make things much harder for themselves.

    (e) **Profitable growth** is likely to be correlated with **internal service quality** because retained customers enable service providers to move more rapidly up the experience or learning curve.

    (f) If **internal service quality** is high, **employee satisfaction** will increase: staff feel good about themselves, they receive a lot of favourable feedback about their performance, and they are rewarded accordingly.

    (g) **Employee satisfaction** will almost certainly mean that **employee retention** accelerates - again with consequential benefits so far as service standards are concerned. Where staff remain, customers can experience continuity; the organisation spends less on recruitment, selection, training and product familiarisation; **profitability** benefits and the results spill over into the start of another cycle so far as **external service quality** is concerned.

3.25   We have here presented the service/profit cycle as constantly spiralling upwards as each element leads seamlessly into the next. It does not have to be like this: not only may there be some interruptions, gaps and inadequacies but, even more significantly, the whole cycle can be reversed and become **progressive decline**:

    (a) When **profitability** drops, the organisation may cut costs. As it does so, **external service quality** deteriorates (and the perceived deterioration may be even faster, since customers with high expectations will notice any drop in standards).

    (b) A decline in **external service quality** means that **customer satisfaction** falls.

    (c) Lower levels of **customer satisfaction** signify a larger number of customer defections and a reduction in **customer loyalty**.

    (d) If customers are less loyal, the organisation will have to devote more resources to attracting new customers, and it may have to compete vigorously (through introductory offers, price discounts, and so forth) in order to do so. As a result, **profitable growth** is endangered.

    (e) **Internal service quality** suffers as the people in the organisation struggle to meet the expectations and demands of new (and unfamiliar) customers.

    (f) Not surprisingly, **employee satisfaction** reaches a new low.

    (g) When **employee satisfaction** collapses, no wonder that **employee retention** caves in as well. The organisation has to recruit newcomers, many of whom will be inexperienced;

its recruitment, training and familiarisation costs rise, and **external service quality** falls still further.

It is much easier to destroy capabilities than it is to create them. A capability like customer confidence can be eradicated overnight; building it up again may take a decade.

4 STIMULATING CUSTOMER FOCUSED BEHAVIOUR

Top management commitment

4.1 The most effective way of achieving customer focused behaviour is through the **commitment of top management**. The chief executive in particular needs to be convinced of the appropriateness of the new thinking and be enthusiastic about its implementation throughout the organisation.

4.2 All managers wear essentially two hats:

- their role as managers
- their specialist skills and responsibilities.

4.3 The marketing manager acts as the bridge between the company and its external audiences, particularly customers.

(a) The marketing managers takes on the responsibility of representing the **customer's needs and interests** within the organisation. The marketing manager is the customer's champion.

(b) Sales and marketing managers often have the ambassadorial or figurehead role in the organisation because of their activities outside the company. Moreover, the marketing department generally creates relationships with customers, and controls the firm's communications with them. This added dimension means that the people skills of the marketing manager must be particularly strong.

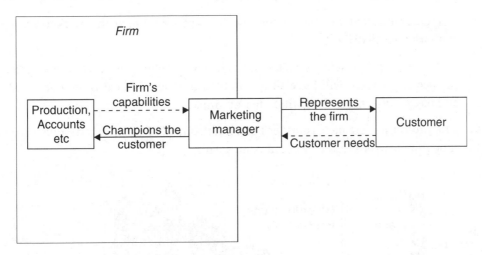

Embedding the market orientated culture

4.4 Marketing managers have not been very effective at playing the role of catalyst for culture change within the organisation. Whilst the marketing concept clearly indicates that, if a marketing approach is to be effective, 'organisational integration' is critical, marketers have generally been poor at spreading the gospel of customer orientation. Too many of their colleagues perceive marketing as being the same as advertising, selling or promotion and have **operational**, but no **strategic**, expectations of the marketing expert.

4.5 In many sectors, marketers have even reinforced the product focus of the business with their system of **brand management** in which managers are given responsibility for individual brands, rather than the needs of customers. It is only now that a number of FMCG manufacturers are re-assessing the value of the traditional brand manager, replacing them with the more market-orientated manager.

4.6 Much of the marketing philosophy has, however, been picked up by the **Total Quality Management** (TQM) movement, with the concepts of **internal customers, relationship marketing** and quantification of **value added** at each stage of the production process. Whether these developments are called marketing or something else is relatively unimportant, as long as the philosophy of customer satisfaction is effected within the business. An important role will remain for the managers responsible for external liaison, and for identifying and anticipating the changing needs of their customer base.

Marketing at Work

For many years Mercedes cars have been sold on the basis of their technical excellence. Recently the firm has decided to expand to smaller models, perhaps because it was felt that the firm's cars were 'over-engineered' and that this could no longer justify the price premium. It was rumoured that when a prototype of one of the new smaller models was introduced, it had to be withdrawn as the boot could not fit a baby buggy, or a set of golf clubs.

Influencing the mix

4.7 The degree of freedom the marketing department has to determine the mix elements varies, because of required financial targets, existing production equipment and distribution systems. The marketing department probably has most control over promotion.

(a) The **product** element will be affected by the degree to which the marketing department has an influence over production and R&D.

(b) The **place** element will be affected by the degree to which the marketing department can influence distribution.

(c) The type of **price** demanded for a product will reflect the cost to a degree, and the finance department will have an inevitable influence. This also includes credit offered and payment terms each of which has an impact.

(d) The **promotion** element is under the direct control of the marketing department, even though many activities will be subcontracted.

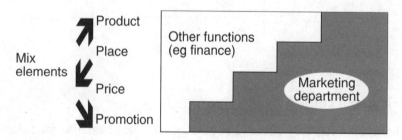

Degree of influence

Arguably although the personnel in the marketing department may have limited influence in some cases, the **marketing orientation** should have been adopted by all in the organisation.

4.8   Embedding the marketing orientation means convincing other departments that for long-term success they should place the customer at the focus of their decision-making, and use their specialist expertise with this in mind.

Marketing at Work

Recently as part of its series on Mastering Management, the Financial Times highlighted the ways in which companies in direct competition with each other differ significantly in their human resource management policies.

For instance Boston Consulting Group and McKinsey and Company are two leading strategic management consultants. Boston prefers to hire candidates with varying business experience and also academics as consultants. The formal training that they receive is likely to be provided outside the company. By contrast McKinsey tends to hire candidates straight from university and rarely from other organisations. McKinsey provides extensive training in the company's methods, which are regarded as very much the McKinsey ways and are not widely publicised.

Two top courier services Federal Express and Courier have very different management practices. Federal Express uses the most up-to-date human resource management techniques such as pay for suggestion in order to increase empowerment and encourage staff to develop the work organisation and technology. In Courier working practices are imposed, based on time and motion studies. Incentives there include the best wage and benefit package in the industry, and also excellent prospects, based on filling senior positions from within.

Perhaps the best example of why businesses in the same sector may use different human resource practices is provided by Coca Cola and Pepsi. With Coca Cola, maintaining the position of Coke is the top priority, and the business lacks diversity compared with others of similar size. The emphasis is on gaining understanding of the product, and rewards are given to long-term career managers who are steeped in the company's ways. With Pepsi the emphasis is on gaining new markets, and hence on innovation to be able to exploit gaps. People are hired with advanced degrees and significant business experience, and the atmosphere is competitive, with the prospect (for the most successful) of much quicker advancement than at Coca Cola. This is reinforced by a decentralised system which gives individual divisions a great deal of independence. These practices result in a great deal of innovation, and the means to exploit market opportunities.

You may be able to think of other examples. From the viewpoint of the exam you need to take account of company policies like those outlined above, if your advice is to be realistic. Advice to Pepsi for example might concentrate on practices that would maintain the company's record of innovation.

Consumerism

4.9   **Ethical responsibilities** towards customers are mainly those of providing a product or service of a quality that customers expect, and of dealing honestly and fairly with customers. To some extent these responsibilities coincide with the organisation's marketing objectives. The guidelines of United Biscuits plc provide a good example of how these responsibilities might be expressed.

> 'UB's reputation for integrity is the foundation on which the mutual trust between the company and its customers is based. That relationship is the key to our trading success.
>
> Both employees and customers need to know that products sold by any of our operating companies will always meet their highest expectations. The integrity of our products is sacrosanct and implicit in the commitment is an absolute and uncompromising dedication to quality. We will never compromise on recipes or specification of products in order to save costs. Quality improvement must always be our goal.
>
> No employee may give money or any gift of significant value to a customer if it could reasonably be viewed as being done to gain a business advantage. Winning an order by violating this policy or by providing free or extra services, or unauthorised contract terms, is contrary to our trading policy.'
>
> *United Biscuits plc*

4.10   Social responsibility, which is desirable in theory, is not easily achieved in practice, because managers are commonly judged by a different set of results - profits, sales growth, market share, earnings per share etc - and not in terms of achievements for society. After all, why should company A incur high costs on improving the safety standards of its product when a competitor, company B, does not spend any money on such improvements, and would therefore be able to undercut company A's prices on the market?

4.11   Managers are unlikely to act with proper responsibility unless they are made accountable for what they do. Social and ethical responsibilities are unlikely to be anything more than fine words and phrases unless managers are judged according to their achievements.

4.12   If an organisation sets its own social and ethical guidelines, managers should be given objectives to achieve, and actual performance should be measured against those objectives in a formal system of control reporting. For example, any manager found guilty of a breach of the code of ethical conduct should be reprimanded, or other such disciplinary measures should be taken against him.

4.13   Social responsibility is to some extent forced on managers by the wishes of consumers.

> ### Key Concept
> **Consumerism** has been defined (by Mann and Thornton) as a 'social movement seeking to augment the rights and powers of buyers in relation to sellers up to the point where the consumer is able to defend his interests'.

4.14   Aspects of business activity on which consumer organisations have focused include the following.

(a)   Dangerous products (such as cigarettes, the content of car exhaust emissions).

(b)   Dishonest marketing or promotion. In the UK there is legislation designed to deal with this kind of abuse.

(c)   The abuse of power by organisations which are large enough to disregard external constraints and even government pressure.

(d)   The availability of information. For example, consumers are anxious to be informed of any artificial additives in foodstuffs.

Marketing at Work

The US tobacco company Philip Morris took out a series of advertisements in which it claims that certain scientific studies reveal that the dangers of passive smoking (ie inhaling other people's cigarette smoke) have been much exaggerated.

This campaign is very controversial. Allegedly, the tobacco industry funded the research, and as importantly, other research studies contradict these conclusions. The general public is probably imperfectly aware of scientific procedure and much of the literature on the topic.

The accountability of managers

4.15   Managers might only feel socially responsible, in the long run, if they are held accountable.

4.16   However, by what means can managers be made accountable to the public? For private companies, we have seen that accountability can be achieved through the exercise of law, or adverse public reaction and the threat of lost customer demand. For public sector organisations, however, where social responsibility ought to be strong, management might choose to escape their responsibility by passing the blame on to someone else. Responsibility does not lie with just one department, nor even just one organisation.

Action Programme 1

A company manufacturing baby food, in a very competitive market, has received in private a disturbing phone call. Some cartons of its product have been tampered with, and contain shards of broken glass. The affected cartons are already for sale in chemists and supermarkets. What would be the most ethical approach to deal with this problem? What do you think would be in the best interests of the company?

(a) Withdraw all goods from sale?

(b) Take out warning advertisements in newspapers?

(c) Assume a hoax, but offer substantial compensation to people whose children were affected, in return for their silence if the threats turn out to be true?

4.17 As issues of accountability in social and ethical terms are often concerned with consumer's image and perception of the organisation the marketing manager is likely to be at the forefront of such issues and will be relied upon:

(a) to provide market views and feedback to inform management decision making;

(b) to communicate policy and strategy to the market through public relations and other communication options;

(c) to help direct the company towards satisfying all the customers' needs, including those driven by ethical or environmental concerns.

Marketing at Work

Charities are a good example of organisations which have refocused their marketing strategy. Forecasts suggest that charitable income from legacies and private donations is likely to fall over the next few years. Many charities also face the problem of differentiating themselves from their 'rivals'; how, for example, does the prospective donor tell the difference between the different cancer charities.

Some charities also wish to educate as well as obtain funds. An environmental charity for example would be trying to show people how to look after the environment as well as obtain money.

Two major ways that charities have tried to enhance their position are by more arresting poster campaigns and increasingly sophisticated direct mailing. An example highlighted in an article in *Marketing Business,* June 1997 of a shocking poster was the poster campaign by the NSPCC of children about to be hit. The choice of subject was influenced by the fact that there has recently been significantly more press coverage about sexual abuse of children than there has been about violence against children.

The second element of enhancing of development of strategy has been an increase in direct marketing. A survey by the Charities Aid Foundation found that a quarter of charities always use direct mail for their publicity campaigns. This research also shows that charities are using targeting techniques to an increased extent, using segmented databases, donor profiling, response rate measurement and information about rivals. These targeting techniques feed through to charity advertising since for example it appears that younger donors are more likely to give more as a result of seeing disturbing images than older donors are.

Results of new tactics have varied. Many charities still face problems differentiating themselves from other charities. People's perceptions of charities are often outdated- 95% of people questioned in a 1995 survey still believe that Barnardo's still ran orphanages despite the fact that the last orphanage closed in 1981.

The solution lies in making advertising part of an integrated marketing approach. In the case of Barnardo's this meant consultation through focus groups of Barnardo's members, workers and other stakeholders to come up with 'brand' messages emphasising hope for the future. Charities must also select the right overall approach.

There is for example a distinction between charities with an audience-based marketing strategy such as medical charities and those charities with a product-based approach. An obvious example of a charity with a product-based approach is the National Trust offering membership. However this approach is being used more widely. Haven, the breast cancer charity, is launching a credit card on the grounds that people may use a product in preference to another if they feel that product will raise money for a good cause, even if they do not give a direct donation.

A further problem charities may face is the perception that they are advertising too aggressively. A recent survey by Audience Selection found that 42% of respondents felt that charities were over-hyping their message, and of those 63% said that it made them less inclined to give. Underlying this may be a feeling that charities are spending too much money on administration and marketing. However in today's climate more effective marketing is not an *optional* extra.

Activities to establish and build customer relationships

4.18 As with staff, customers are expensive to recruit. The cost of attracting new customers is considerable and servicing a new account may not be 'profitable' for a year or two. On the other hand it is usually relatively inexpensive to retain an existing customer, so marketing strategy has tended to favour:

(a) increasing sales to existing customers (of related products, or by increased usage);

(b) reducing the proportion of 'lost' customers through the development of customer loyalty schemes and the increased emphasis on customer loyalty.

4.19

(a) As can be seen above, to turn a non-user into a light or infrequent customer is very expensive in promotional and marketing costs. The non-user has to be taken through the whole decision making process from unawareness to awareness to interest, to desire and final action. In practical terms converting non-users to light users can involve several techniques such as general advertising, building mailing lists, and general mailshots which are expensive and the direct impact of which is uncertain.

(b) On the other hand, the loss of an established heavy user it may require three or more new customers to replace the value of that business in the short run. In the long run of course, you would hope new customers will become committed heavy users.

(c) It is much cheaper in marketing terms to convert 'light' to 'medium' and 'medium' to 'heavy' users. Improved database management enables companies to segment their own customer base in this way, and to develop loyalty and promotional strategies designed to increase usage and retain these customers who represent a considerable marketing investment. Techniques may include business meetings, seminars, client entertainment and customer care programmes (see below).

(d) Databases should provide information about product range bought, staff on both sides responsible for the relationship, and the current position with the customer, including client satisfaction (or otherwise) with the goods or services provided. More detailed systems will have information about the background of the customer and how financially significant the customer's business is to the organisation. The database should also include information about the long-term relationship with the customer and whether more business is likely to be obtained in the future.

Marketing at Work

Coutts Bank announced that it was changing its operations. Over 90% of its customers use it for simple account maintenance facilities, and are not terribly profitable. The bulk of its profits come from 10%: the very wealthy, who use the bank's investment advice services. Coutts has decided to withdraw from the higher volume business to concentrate on the very wealthy and profitable 10%.

4.20 In the past, managers perhaps have tended to focus mainly on winning new business, and they have been somewhat guilty of taking existing customers for granted. This is certainly changing.

4.21 Building customer loyalty has two aspects:

(a) delivering customer satisfaction ie providing a quality product which meets the customer's expectations;

(b) customer care to ensure customers are valued and looked after effectively.

4.22 We will be considering the impact of quality in more detail in the next section, but what is important to emphasise here is that quality has to be defined from the customer's perspective. Quality does not mean best, or even 'fit for the purpose', but means it **satisfies the needs of the customers**.

4.23 Marketers have to avoid falling into the trap of raising a customer's expectations through glamorous promotion and fancy packaging, because if the product fails to meet these expectations, a disappointed and dissatisfied customer may choose alternative suppliers.

4.24 Losing customers is bad news for any business; not only are **today's sales lost**, but **future potential earnings** are also sacrificed.

(a) A woman in her mid 20's spends an estimated £100 a year on cosmetics. Dissatisfied by her current brand she switches to a competitor. She remains loyal for over 20 years to the new product. Cash revenue from the lost client is worth £2,000 before the time value of money is taken into account.

(b) The car manufacturer who estimates an average driver will buy seven cars in his or her lifetime is looking at perhaps £140,000 in lost custom if the salesperson fails to provide the service or approach needed to convert the buyer into a driver loyal to the brand.

4.25 But besides the lost value from that customer, bad service or products will generate bad word of mouth publicity. This can be very persuasive and can cost the company even more in lost customers or potential customers.

Action Programme 2

Over the next 2 weeks keep listening for word of mouth publicity about products or services. Keep a note of the relative proportions of good and bad messages. How much credibility do they have? Do they influence your behaviour?

You will find they come up in many forms.

- Have you tried that new restaurant?
- Did you see the latest film?
- What is the service like?

Try actively eliciting comments by asking for advice on a new car purchase or holiday destination.

4.26 So marketers must work hard to ensure customers' needs are:

(a) identified; and

(b) satisfied

by the organisation's offering.

Auditing fulfilment of customer needs

4.27 In their book *The Success Culture - how to build an organisation with vision and purpose* Lesley and Malcolm Munro-Faure list the following ways in which organisations can identify whether customer needs are being identified and satisfied and whether the quality of service can be improved.

- Customer satisfaction surveys
- Mystery shopper surveys
- Work won and lost
- Changes in market share
- Monthly ratings from major customers
- Revenue from newly released products
- Sales backlog
- Quality control reviews
- Rework and warranties
- Assessment of needs of non-customers
- Time spent with prospective customers

Customer care

4.28 Inevitably things will go wrong from time to time. Most customers, however, are less concerned with the mishap than how the issue is rectified. This is where **customer care** is relevant. Customer care has been very much in the forefront of management thinking in both the public sector (with the citizen's charter etc) and private sector over recent years. Whilst it is easy to scoff, the Citizen's Charter, Patient's Charter, Rail User's Charter and so on have all tried to specify the level of service users are entitled to expect and compensation if this is not delivered. This start at quantification is an excellent beginning. From these benchmarks improvements can be developed, implemented and monitored.

4.29 In *Perfect Customer Care*, Dr Ted Johns argues that 'The majority of customer complaints will not directly relate to the quality of the service/product, but to the peripheral issues. Quality in the eyes of the customer is always supposedly much more than the quality of the product or basic service offered'.

Action Programme 3

Assume that you have ordered two fencing panels from a local DIY store. For a small extra charge, the panels will be delivered (as they are too big to fit into your car). On the appointed day, a delivery is made - but only one of the panels you purchased, not two. You phone up; delivery is promised the following day, but fails to arrive. You phone up again and speak to a senior manager, who apologises for his staff. Delivery is made, and you are given a third extra panel to compensate for the inconvenience. The fencing panels themselves are fine. What customer care lessons can you learn from this example?

4.30 Most complaints are apparently peripheral to the actual product/service offered, and relate to telephone courtesy, delivery, availability of product, user instructions and so forth.

4.31 **Customer care programmes** are devoted to maximising the benefits a customer receives within the operating constraints of the business. This means, effectively, that the operations staff who deliver service should do so with a **marketing philosophy** in mind.

4.32 In other words, the service should be designed as far as possible with the customer in mind, rather than the procedural conveniences of the company. Although the old adage 'you can't please all of the people all of the time' may still be true, it is still important to put in place systems, procedures and practices to minimise customer dissatisfaction.

Empowerment

Key Concept

Empowerment allows individuals in the organisation, particularly front-line sales staff in the context of customer care, to decide how to do the necessary work, using the skills they possess and acquiring new skills as necessary.

4.33 With power comes responsibility, so individuals become **personally responsible** for what they do. This increases motivation.

Business process re-engineering

Key Concept

Business process re-engineering is a very grand term for a particular method of organisational structure whereby a business is organised according to the **processes** it performs (a sale involves production people, sales people, the warehouse, the accounts department) rather than the **function** performed (separate departments for production, sales, warehousing, accounts).

4.34 For organisations, one of the key components of service excellence is **process alignment**, ie making sure that the organisation serves the customer rather than the other way round. In the words of Arthur Andersen (the global management consultants), it is 'deliberately designing and modifying business processes so that **every activity is geared to meeting the customer's wants**'.

4.35 Chris Daffy in his book, *Once a Customer, Always a Customer*, argues that an organisation structure that is totally customer-focused would have just two layers.

The Customer-Focused Company

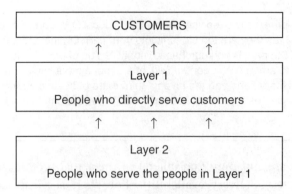

Certainly the organisations which are **most effective** at dealing with customers are typically those which have **radically changed their structures** in order to make them **less hierarchical**.

Marketing at Work

(a) The Automobile Association

The AA has gone through a major delayering exercise, cutting the number of levels between its front-line employees (the patrolmen) and the Chief Executive from 12 to 5, and delegating much more responsibility at lower levels.

(b) Cigna Services UK (health insurance)

Cigna now operates almost totally on the basis of multi-functional teams. The customer is assigned to a team and that team, rather than separate functional groups within the organisation, deals with very aspect of that customer's business with Cigna.

(c) Hamilton Acorn (paintbrush manufacturer)

Acorn's customer services department now draws together in a single unit a number of functions that had previously been done separately: warehousing and distribution, customer queries, data input, sales administration and export. The company has also reorganised the factory floor into cells or small teams, each with its own supervisor, and each responsible for a product form start to finish. This manufacturing re-organisation was vital if the improvements demanded by customers were actually going to happen: as the company's Operations Director has said, 'You can't just put a sign up and say, 'Hooray, now we've got a customer services department, now we're going to be great', because they can't do a damned thing unless they've got the back-up from the manufacturing side all the way through.'

Get it right, first time

4.36 One of the basic principles of TQM is that the **cost of preventing mistakes is less than the cost of correcting them** once they occur. The aim should therefore be to **get things right first time**.

> 'Every mistake, every delay and misunderstanding, directly costs a company money through wasted time and effort, including time taken in pacifying customers. Whilst this cost is important, the impact of poor customer service in terms of lost potential for future sales has also to be taken into account.' (Robin Bellis-Jones and Max Hand, *Management Accounting,* May 1989)

4.37 For instance, a 1:3:8 ratio is used in shipbuilding. A defect corrected when it occurs only costs 1 unit; if it has to be corrected at a subsequent inspection it costs 3 units; but if it has to be corrected after delivery to the customer it costs 8 units. Arguably the figure of 8 units should be even higher.

Marketing at Work

Birmingham Midshires Building Society

Until recently, a major source of complaint from the customers of the Birmingham Midshires Building Society concerned delays and errors. In response, the Society has adopted a 'right first time' philosophy throughout the organisation. They recognise, in the words of their director of customer services, Jon Gresham, that 'Re-work is costly, complaints are costly, and to recover properly from complaints about errors is a drain on business resources. Therefore we need to make sure that we've got the right measures and mechanisms in place to start providing a timely, high quality service'.

TNT Express (deliveries and distribution)

According to Alan Jones, Managing Director of TNT Express UK Limited: 'Some people believe that quality actually adds to cost. We do not agree. Our experience in the recession (of the early 1990s) reinforced our view that quality reduces costs. A get-it-right-first-time approach is reducing the often significant cost of correcting mistakes in our business.'

The Ted Johns blueprint for customer service excellence: the 12 pillars of performance

4.38 Ted Johns, CIM Senior Examiner for *The Marketing Customer Interface*, has created the following framework for

(a) specifying the desirable mix of internal, external and strategic components needed by an organisation which majors on service as a source of competitive advantage,

(b) evaluating the actions needed by organisations if they seek to establish themselves as 'contenders' or 'world class' players.

4.39 The framework involves three major dimensions: your **strategy**, your **people** and your **customers**. Each in turn has four sub-dimensions. None of the 12 factors is optional, and none is more important than the others (though without the **strategy** impetus, it is very unlikely that anything significant will happen).

4.40 **Dimension 1: Your strategy**

(a) **Commitment.** Customer service is a key corporate scorecard indicator.

The example of Xerox illustrates the pay-off from integrating top-level vision with managerial action, recognition for accomplishment and progress, and a restless, continuous search for further improvement. These are the key factors in the Xerox repertoire:

(i) **A clear and shared vision** from the top, rooted in the customer. Xerox seeks customer delight, satisfaction and retention as key parameters for progress, arguing that profitability will follow from the achievement of these measures.

(ii) Sustained top-management **commitment** to change.

(iii) Visible **role-modelling** by senior managers, who set a positive example for others.

(iv) Employee **involvement and engagement** - through quality improvement teams, customer-based focus groups, and many other activities.

(v) Motivation via customer-linked **rewards and recognition** systems. A significant proportion of the executive bonus system is conditional upon the achievement of (externally-measured) customer-satisfaction objectives.

(vi) **Training** for change management so that people can understand what they have to do in order to make it happen within their accountabilities.

(vii) Bold goals for **performance improvement** - not merely incremental targets which simply require minor efficiency enhancements.

(viii) **Benchmarking**. Xerox is always prepared to **learn from other organisations**, whatever their field of business.

(b) **Credibility**.

Your customers must have good grounds for believing your promises. As Charles Handy once famously claimed, trust is as fragile as a pane of glass: easy to smash, but hard to re-assemble. Even when an organisation is trusted by its customers, it must continue to work hard to ensure that its reputation remains intact.

(c) **Classification**. You segment your customers, periodically review your segmentation profiles and vary your product/service offer across segment boundaries.

One of the most significant findings in the Bain & Co study, The Future Of Customer Service (Institute of Customer Service, 1998) was that few organisations currently differentiate their service offering by segment; equally, not enough companies track customer loyalty or repurchasing, and very few organisations understand the concept of segment profitability.

(d) **Concentration**. You focus your marketing efforts on your most profitable customers. This may seem trite, but many companies disseminate their marketing efforts without any regard to **customer profitability potential**, **segment profitability potential**, or even **product/service profitability potential**.

4.41 **Dimension 2: Your people**

(a) **Capability**. All your people, whether in the front line or not, are recruited and trained against a customer service competency blueprint. Many of the most successful Japanese companies are successful precisely because they pay so much attention, when recruiting people, to possession of the right attitudes (ie customer focus, flexibility, enthusiasm for change, teamworking readiness).

(b) **Continuity**. You have **retention, reward and recognition** strategies which encourage your people to remain. The **Reichheld service/profit cycle** shows the enormous benefits which are likely to accrue from employee retention.

(c) **Courtesy**. Your people are polite, considerate, tolerant and friendly when dealing with customers.

(d) **Creativity**. Your people produce ideas for service **innovations and improvements**. After all, employees at the front line are often the first to notice that customers are asking for different things and are beginning to complain about elements in the product/service package.

4.42 **Dimension 3: Your customers**

(a) **Consistency**. Your customers always know what to expect from you. Virtually all the research into corporate effectiveness has supported the view that **customers like to know what to expect** from what Nelson and Winter have called organisational routines, ie various predictable ways of operating that ultimately help to create customer confidence through familiarity and experience. This does not mean, however, that customer expectations remain static: they are constantly rising, fuelled by experiences in other fields of commercial activity, reinforced by experiences in other countries, and enhanced by the media.

(b) **Communication**. Your customers understand what you say to them; equally, you actively promote opportunities for two-way dialogue. Note the two-way emphasis on listening as well as talking here: and some of the new Internet-based companies have proved extremely successful at facilitating customer feedback in one form or another.

(c) **Comfort**. Your customers feel comfortable with everything which collectively comprises the **company reputation**. Recent surveys on **electronic commerce** have strongly endorsed the argument that customers are much more willing to enter into transactions if they feel they are dealing with a reputable brand or organisation.

(d) **Contact**. You offer customer service at times to suit your customers. Increasingly, as the 1998 Bain study shows, customers expect service to be available 24 hours a day, seven days a week. They also expect the person on the other end of the telephone to be able to give them information and solutions.

Exam tip

These 12 Pillars of Customer-Service Performance have been devised by the senior examiner and supply a useful framework for analysing the performance of any organisation, and in particular for approaching any case-study questions. The model is included in this text on his specific recommendation.

5 THE DRIVE FOR SUSTAINABLE COMPETITIVE ADVANTAGE

Key Concept

Competitive advantage comes about as a result of those factors which enable firms to compete successfully on a sustained basis.

5.1 Porter (in *Competitive Advantage*) grouped the various activities of an organisation into a **value chain**. He identified nine **value-adding** activities. As you can see from the diagram below, marketing and sales is one of the activities which adds value for the customer and is a key source of competitive advantage. The **margin** is the excess the customer is prepared to pay above the **cost** to the firm of obtaining resource inputs and providing value activities.

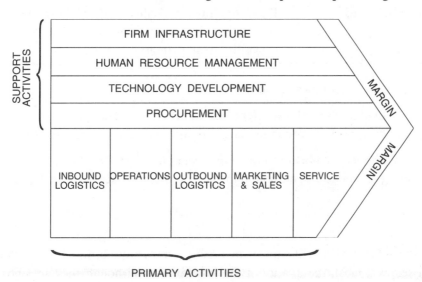

> **Key Concept**
>
> The **value chain** is the sequence of business activities by which, in the perspective of the end user, value is added to the products or services produced by an organisation.

Activity

5.2   **Primary activities** are directly related to production, sales, marketing, delivery and service.

	Comment
Inbound logistics	Receiving, handling and storing inputs to the production system (ie warehousing, transport, stock control etc).
Operations	Convert resource inputs into a final product. Resource inputs are not only materials. 'People' are a 'resource' especially in service industries.
Outbound logistics	Storing the product and its distribution to customers: packaging, warehousing, testing etc.
Marketing and sales	Informing customers about the product, persuading them to buy it, and enabling them to do so: advertising, promotion etc.
After sales service	Installing products, repairing them, upgrading them, providing spare parts and so forth.

5.3   **Support activities** provide purchased inputs, human resources, technology and infrastructural functions to support the primary activities.

Activity	Comment
Procurement	Acquire the resource inputs to the primary activities (eg purchase of materials, subcomponents equipment).
Technology development	Product design, improving processes and/or resource utilisation.
Human resource management	Recruiting, training, developing and rewarding people.
Management planning	Planning, finance, quality control: Porter believes they are crucially important to an organisation's strategic capability in all primary activities.

5.4   **Linkages** connect the activities of the value chain.

(a)   **Activities in the value chain affect one another**. For example, more costly product design or better quality production might reduce the need for after-sales service.

(b)   **Linkages require co-ordination**. For example, Just In Time requires smooth functioning of operations, outbound logistics and service activities such as installation.

Value system

5.5   Activities that add value do not stop at the organisation's **boundaries**. For example, when a restaurant serves a meal, the quality of the ingredients - although they are chosen by the cook - is determined by the grower. The grower has added value, and the grower's success in growing produce of good quality is as important to the customer's ultimate satisfaction as the skills of the chef. A firm's value chain is connected to what Porter calls a **value system**.

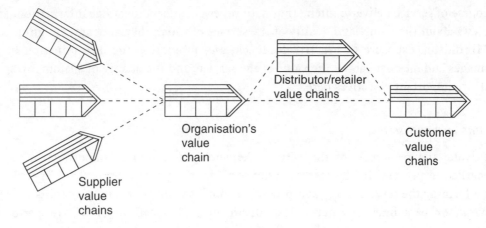

5.6 **Using the value chain.** A firm can secure competitive advantage by:

- Inventing new or better ways to do activities
- Combining activities in new or better ways
- Managing the linkages in its own value chain
- Managing the linkages in the value system

Action Programme 4

Sana Sounds is a small record company. Representatives from Sana Sounds scour music clubs for new bands to promote. Once a band has signed a contract (with Sana Sounds) it makes a recording. The recording process is subcontracted to one of a number of recording studio firms which Sana Sounds uses regularly. (At the moment Sana Sounds is not large enough to invest in its own equipment and studios.) Sana Sounds also subcontracts the production of records and CDs to a number of manufacturing companies. Sana Sounds then distributes the disks to selected stores, and engages in any promotional activities required.

What would you say were the activities in Sana Sounds' value chain?

5.7 The value chain is an important analytical tool because it helps people:

- to see the **business as a whole**
- to identify potential **sources of competitive advantage**
- to suggest **strategies**
- to analyse **competitors**

5.8 The level, and also the quality, of service which is available to the customer is especially sensitive to the efficient organisation of the processes by which services are delivered. Problems with regulating the supply make this a key factor in competitive advantage - a company which 'gets it right' is likely to be **clearly differentiated** from competitors. Key factors are:

(a) **capacity utilisation,** matching demand sequences to staff utilisation to avoid unprofitable underprovision and problematic understaffing;

(b) **managing customer contact,** to avoid crowding and customer disruption, meet needs as they arise, and increase employee control over interactions;

(c) **establishing objectives within the not-for-profit sector,** for example, standards for teachers or medical staff.

5.9 For marketing service managers, the 'quality control' and 'engineering' of the interactions which take place between customers is a key strategic issue. Customers are often, in the course of service delivery, interacting with other customers to gather information, and form views about the nature and quality of the service of which they are contemplating purchase. Minimising exposure to negative feedback, and promoting the dissemination of positive images and messages about the value of the service, and the quality of customer responses to it, are important objectives here.

People and customer service

5.10 **People**, the personnel of the service deliverer, are uniquely important in the service marketing process. In the case of some services, the physical presence of people actually performing the service is a vital aspect of customer satisfaction. You may think of clerks in a bank, or personnel in catering establishments. The staff involved are performing or producing a service, selling the service and also liaising with the customer to promote the service, gather information and respond to customer needs.

Action Programme 5

The role of people in services marketing is especially important. What human characteristics improve the quality of client service?

5.11 A key strategic issue for the service marketing mix then is the way in which personnel are involved in implementing the marketing concept, and measures need to be established which will institute a customer orientation in all sectors of organisational activity.

5.12 Customers who lack security and confidence in an intangible service will tend to use cues from the demeanour and behaviour of staff to establish a view about the image and efficiency of the organisation.

5.13 The higher the level of customer contact involved in the delivery of a service, the more crucial is staff role in generating customer service and adding value. In many cases the delivery of the service and the physical presence of the personnel involved are completely inseparable - technical competence and skill in handling people are of equal importance in effective delivery of a service since quality is in the eye of the (consuming) beholder!

Action Programme 6

All levels of staff must be involved in customer service. To achieve this end, it is vital for senior management consciously to promulgate values of customer service constantly, in order to create and build a culture of customer service within the company. How do you think that this might be achieved?

5.14 Juran, author of the *Quality Control Handbook*, believes that it is the neglect and low priority given to quality planning and quality improvement which are the major weaknesses in western companies. Japanese companies have succeeded by implementing quality improvement programmes supported by massive management training and the enthusiastic commitment of top leadership. As a consequence, the Japanese experience demonstrates the value of this investment in terms of competitive advantage, reduced failure costs, higher productivity, smaller inventories and better delivery performance.

5.15 P H Crosby developed his ideas during a successful career at International Telephone and Telegraph (ITT), where he moved from line inspector to corporate vice-president over a period of 14 years. He describes his system in two sets of principles, the 'absolutes of quality management' and the 'basic elements of improvement'.

5.16 The 'absolutes of quality management' are as follows.

(a) **Quality means conformance to requirements, not elegance**

Crosby insists that quality is a series of requirements which must be clearly stated. It can then be communicated and measured to see if it has been achieved. These measurements will establish the presence or absence of quality. Absence of quality is a nonconformance problem or an output problem. How requirements are set is a managerial issue.

(b) **There is no such thing as a quality problem**

Problems arise in specific departments and must be identified by those departments. Quality, as well as a problem, is created in a specific department and is not the province of a specific 'quality' department within the organisation.

(c) **There is no such thing as the economics of quality; it is always cheaper to do the job right first time**

Quality is free. Nonconformance costs money.

(d) **The only performance measurement is the cost of quality**

The cost of quality is the expense of nonconformance. While most companies spend almost 20% of their revenue on quality costs, a well run quality management programme can reduce this to less than 3%. A major part of the programme involves measuring and publicising the costs of poor quality, to focus managerial attention on this problem.

(e) **The only performance standard is zero defects**

Zero defects is a performance standard, with the theme 'do it right the first time'. This means concentrating on the prevention of defects rather than finding and fixing them.

5.17 This is, Crosby argues, a matter of concentrating, of applying the same standards we have in our private life to the way in which we approach the workplace. He asserts:

'Most human error is caused by lack of attention rather than lack of knowledge. Lack of attention is created when we assume that error is inevitable. If we consider this condition carefully and pledge ourselves to make a constant effort to do our jobs right the first time, we will take a giant leap towards eliminating the waste of rework, scrap and repair that increases cost and reduces individual opportunity.' (Philip Crosby, *Quality is Free,* 1979)

5.18 This is quite clearly different from the ideas of Juran and Deming, neither of whom would have placed this emphasis on the responsibility of the line worker when the majority of imperfections in the system of production are due to poorly designed equipment and systems which are beyond the control of the individual.

5.19 'Basic elements of improvement', the other aspect of his system, includes three themes:

(a) **determination,** or the commitment of management to this process;

(b) **education,** which involves transmitting the absolutes to the members of the organisation; and

(c) **implementation,** which should clearly specify the process whereby quality is to be established within the organisation.

5.20 This has proved a popular approach because it emphasises behaviour processes within organisations rather than simply the use of statistical techniques. At the same time, it does not stipulate what a programme will involve in fine detail. As a consequence, it can be fitted alongside existing corporate strategies with minimal disruption and tailored to the enterprise involved to accommodate all kinds of idiosyncrasies.

Total quality and total customer orientation

5.21 A **customer orientation,** seeking to satisfy the customer, is pursued in marketing by recognising that customers buy 'the sizzle, not the steak' - products are bought for the benefits they deliver; how customers can use the product to accomplish the things they want to do.

5.22 Feigenbaum (1983) identifies Total Quality Management (TQM) directly with the customer.

> ### Key Concept
> **Total quality management** is defined as:
> '... the total composite product and service characteristics of marketing, engineering, manufacture and maintenance, through which the product and service in use will meet the expectations by the customer.'

5.23 What constitutes a 'quality product or service' must, it seems, be related to what the customer wants. Indeed, quality would have no commercial value unless it delivered customer benefit, since the key reason for aiming to produce quality products is to derive extra sales, to establish competitive advantage through tangible and generally perceived superiority in particular product or service features. All the gurus would agree that the customer must be the final arbiter of the quality which a product possesses.

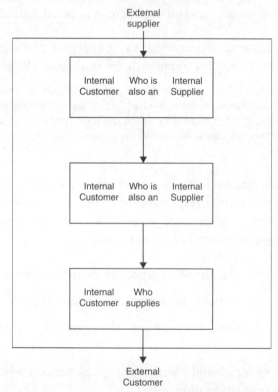

5.24 John Oakland argues that **meeting customer requirements** is the main focus in a **search for quality**. While these requirements would typically include aspects such as availability, delivery, reliability, maintainability and cost effectiveness, in fact the first priority is to establish what customer requirements **actually are**.

(a) If the customer is outside the organisation, then the supplier must seek to set up a marketing activity to gather this information, and to relate the output of their organisation to the needs of the customer.

(b) **Internal customers** for services are equally important, but seldom are their requirements investigated. The quality implementation process requires that all the supplier/customer relationships within the 'quality chain' should be treated as marketing exercises, and that each customer should be carefully consulted as to their precise requirements from the product or service with which they are to be provided. Each link in the chain should prompt the following questions.

Of customers

- Who are my immediate customers?
- What are their true requirements?
- How do or can I find out what the requirements are?
- How can I measure my ability to meet the requirements?
- Do I have the necessary capability to meet the requirements? (If not, then what must change to improve the capability?)
- Do I continually meet the requirements? (If not, then what prevents this from happening, when the capability exists?)
- How do I monitor changes in the requirements?

Of suppliers

- Who are my immediate suppliers?
- What are my true requirements?
- How do I communicate my requirements?
- Do my suppliers have the capability to measure and meet the requirements?
- How do I inform them of changes in the requirements?

Internal marketing

5.25 The nature of marketing has traditionally been focused upon the relationship between an organisation and its customers. The role of **internal marketing** recognises the **importance of employees** and the significant and often vital role which they can play in implementing the marketing plan effectively.

5.26 Employees are a vital asset in **increasing sales**, improving **profitability** and delivering **service** to the customer. It is therefore important that all employees throughout the organisation are able to identify with its **objectives**, but more importantly are allowed access to the necessary resources to accomplish these objectives.

> **Key Concept**
> **Internal marketing** attempts to smooth the working relationship between functional areas of the organisation and in so doing to establish the organisation as an integrated whole, rather than an aggregation of disparate and opposing units.

5.27 It is not uncommon for departments and individuals to pursue their objectives in isolation. The sales people will promise anything to close the deal and achieve their targets, leaving the customer service department to worry about placating the customer when his product arrives three weeks late and is the wrong colour.

5.28 In practice, internal marketing is concerned with exactly the same issues as the overall marketing strategy. However, in addition it ensures that through active **involvement and participation** in the marketing plan the organisation is able to **satisfy the needs of its customer**. By doing so, it is able to develop for itself a **discernible competitive advantage.**

5.29 Drucker points out that efficiency or productivity is now less related to the productivity of manual labour or machinery, and more related to the increasing role of '**knowledge work**', ie the work of managers, researchers, planners, designers and innovators. Many managers today believe that the only opportunity left for competitive advantage lies in their **human resources**.

5.30 **Business-to-business marketers** must strive to achieve a distinct competitive advantage and where this is not price, the battleground moves to a variety of **add-on services** which can be classed as pre-sale and after sale. Technical advice is a valuable pre-sale service and rapid spares availability is an after sales service that may tip the balance on who gets the order.

5.31 It is worth emphasising some key lessons underlying customer care and customer retention, as they directly affect relationship marketing and quality.

(a) Putting things right is fine, but it would be better had they not gone wrong in the first place. Effectiveness in customer care 'happens before the product/service even reaches the customer'.

(b) Most customer complaints relate to 'peripheral' issues: but the customer buys the package.

(c) The problems of the producer are not those of the consumer; in other words if things break down, this is not the customer's problem. (However, many customers do appreciate an explanation of why things have gone wrong, especially users of public transport.)

(d) It is the customer who decides ultimately, what quality is. Quality is 'fitness for use'.

(e) Market research is limited in that customers do not always know what they want.

(f) Quality information is often hidden from senior decision-makers.

(g) Better customer service has to be driven from the top, and managers need training as well as customer service staff.

(h) Good customer service is not something that is achieved once only, but requires constant reinforcement.

6 ORGANISATIONAL ASPECTS AND ACCOUNTABILITY

6.1 We can examine the type of relationship between customer and supplier as being of two types.

(a) In a **transaction**, a supplier gives the customer a good or service in exchange for money. The marketer, in offering the good or service, is looking for a response. Transaction-based marketing is based on such transactions and little else, such as when you buy a bar of chocolate.

(b) In a **relationship approach,** 'smart marketers try to build up long-term, trusting, win-win relations with valued customers, distributors, dealers and suppliers ... it is accomplished by building strong economic, technical and social ties with the other parties.'

6.2 The justification for relationship marketing comes from the need to retain customers. Companies lose money unnecessarily. Kotler estimates that 'the cost of attracting a new customer may be five times the cost of keeping a current customer happy.' There are five different levels of customer relationship.

(a) **Basic**. The salesperson sells the product without any further contact with the customer.

(b) **Reactive**. The customer is encouraged to call the salesperson if there are any problems.

(c) **Accountable**. The salesperson phones the customer to see if there are any problems and to elicit ideas for product improvements.

(d) **Proactive**. The salesperson contacts the customer on a regular basis.

(e) **Partnership**. The salesperson and customer work together to effect customer savings. Partnership sourcing implies that the commercial buyer works more closely with the supplier to ensure that all aspects of the deal suit the needs of both parties, not just for this deal, but those which can be expected in the future.

6.3 Broadly speaking, the greater the number of customers and the smaller the profit per unit sold, the greater the likelihood that the type of marketing will be basic. At the other extreme, where a firm has few customers, but where profits are high, the partnership approach is most likely.

(a) Customers are in long-term relationship with their banks. Banks try and satisfy many of customers' financial needs over a customer's lifetime (eg current accounts, overdrafts, secured lending, pensions advice, investment advice, insurance).

(b) On the other hand, there is no-long term relationship between a consumer of chocolate bars and the chocolate manufacturer.

6.4 Some firms are trying to convert a 'basic' transaction based approach into relationship marketing. Many car dealerships, for example, seek to generate additional profits by servicing the cars they sell, and by keeping in touch with their customers so that they can earn repeat business.

6.5 The salesperson must think of his or her role as being that of the spokesperson for the rest of the organisation, with a clear responsibility to provide feedback to the company.

6.6 The salesforce can make an important contribution to the management information system. Feedback and market intelligence gathered by the sales team are a valuable by-product of the sales process.

6.7 Management must provide systems and opportunities to encourage this information. The members of the sales team on their part need to recognise their contribution in providing such market knowledge and take a positive and proactive approach to it. A proactive approach involves not only taking positive steps to bring information to management's attention, but also actively to look out for changes and developments in the market place.

6.8 Management are likely to be particularly interested in customer feedback covering a number of key areas.

- The product/service
- Promotional activities
- Pricing and credit
- Delivery and service queries
- The sales activity

7 OUTSOURCING

7.1 The decision about whether to produce components or services in-house, or to sub-contract work to external suppliers, is referred to as **outsourcing**. In-house provision can be cheaper than buying them, because an external supplier will charge a price which must cover his fixed costs and give him a profit, but the direct comparison of in-house costs with suppliers' prices is only one factor. Other issues to consider are the following.

(a) **Resource usage**. When a company makes products in-house it is tying up resources (management and labour, working capital, fixed assets, space in buildings etc) which could be used for other more profitable purposes (ie there is an opportunity cost).

(b) **Supplier commitment**. If a company cannot produce all the output it needs in-house, it will be forced to use external suppliers to some extent. This might oblige the company to offer a supply contract to a supplier which guarantees a minimum supply quantity over a period of time.

(c) **Control**. In-house production should be easier to control in terms of product quality and the reliability of delivery.

(d) **Quality assurance**. External suppliers need to be reliable in terms of product quality and reliability of delivery times, and alternative sources of supply should be sought, in case one supplier becomes too unreliable or too expensive. One way of vetting suppliers is to check to see if they have BS EN ISO 9000 (formerly BS 5750) certification.

(e) **Compulsion**. Certain areas of the public sector are required to consider outsourcing.

(f) **Vulnerability**. If the outsourcing arrangement goes wrong a firm can suffer if it loses the expertise.

(g) **Contract compliance**. The outsourcing arrangement requires strict attention to contracts. This *can* be a source of operational inflexibility, if the contract has to be laboriously renegotiated when circumstances change.

Marketing at Work

Rover Cars had a long-standing arrangement with Unipart – the components and logistics group – whereby Unipart distributed parts for Rover cars.

Early in 1998, BMW, Rover's owner, decided to take back control of the parts division. BMW wanted strategic control of its parts distribution and the profits stream stemming from it. Rover now has to set up its own distribution infrastructure.

Unipart has expanded into other components businesses, working for Jaguar, Volkswagen and Daihatsu. It has parts distribution contracts with non-car firms such as Hewlett-Packard and various railway companies. It is also working with the UK government's buying agency to improve services and goods supply chains.

7.2 The growth of 'facilities management', the name given to one very important aspect of outsourced externally supplied services has been very rapid - faster, in fact, than any other aspect of middle management. The main reasons for this are as follows.

(a) There has been a large scale re-sourcing of support services.

(b) The extension of highly professional standards to the management of the key physical resources upon which the basic performance of company business depends.

(c) Changing circumstances and the nature of markets has forced change upon those in charge of organisations.

7.3 Services upon which organisations depend to function properly must be well managed, so that the outside suppliers who are called upon to carry out these tasks are a key aspect of the overall functioning of the organisation.

Briefing

7.4 Good briefing ensures good working relationships. Bad briefing will lead to misunderstandings between client and supplier to the detriment of the ultimate customer.

7.5 In the event of a dispute, a full brief will leave less room for doubt as to the requirements of the contract agreed to.

7.6 Typical matters to consider in briefing outside suppliers include the following.

- To what extent do we take outside suppliers into our confidence?
- What do they need to know?
- Who will draw up the briefs?
- How often should the brief be reviewed?

Management of externally sourced factors

7.7 Increasingly, companies have begun to 'farm out' their non-essential activities, in order to concentrate on what they see as the core activities of their business. This has been a spur to the growth of 'facilities management', since it has led to the contracting out of *key* services.

7.8 'Downsizing' has the same consequences. During the shakeouts and privatisations which took place in the UK during the 1980s, many sections or functions within large companies were encouraged to set up as separate external enterprises, providing what were often intermittently needed functions (for example, maintenance of plant, or market research information) on a contract basis.

7.9 The costs of staffing, training and manning such functions on a long term basis were removed, and the function could be fulfilled on a competitive basis. Other sorts of services, such as cleaning, catering and security began to be fulfilled under the same conditions.

7.10 This practice has been widely extended, and simple sub-contracting has been supplemented by the 'outsourcing' of the management function too.

The degree of outsourcing varies from business to business

7.11 Companies vary in what they see as their **core business**. In smaller companies, many of the functions associated with marketing may actually be sourced from outside the company. Obvious examples would be market research services, advertising, design of packaging, and specialist aspects of product testing (for example, sensory testing of new food products, or safety tests on new electrical goods). Other aspects of organisational function upon which marketing activity depends are also typically subcontracted. For example, when promotional campaigns are being mounted, 'leafleting' is typically the province of small subcontractors. So too would be the teams of promotional staff who dispense free samples during in-store promotional exercises.

BPP
PUBLISHING

Marketing at Work

The privatising of public utilities within the UK provides a useful illustration of one of the dangers involved in working with external suppliers. The major managerial problems associated with management of, for example, the National Health Service has led to massive increases in the number of managers employed by the new 'Hospital Trusts', coupled with a reclassification and redeployment of health services. Yet, as a recent report revealed, there was also huge expenditure on the employment of management consultants in order to make recommendations concerning the most efficient deployment of the new management within the organisation.

Given the large scale of outsourcing, the newly developed structures, and a remit to develop efficient and competitive units based on competition within internal markets, this might seem like a logical move. However, a report suggested that there were a number of mistakes involved.

(a) Consultants were not briefed adequately. Too often, consultants would be called into 'fix' an organisation without real guidance as to the areas which needed to be addressed, and without any limits on the scope of the problem with which they were involved. As a consequence, the reports they produced were often inappropriate, unrealistic or ineffective.

(b) Consultants were given too much power. Managers employing consultants in these circumstances were inclined to delegate too wide a range of decisions to them.

(c) Public perceptions were not considered sufficiently.

Total outsourcing

7.12 In the case of facilities management, the general change within the 'enterprise culture' has generated a movement towards downsizing in which functions have been shed or hived off and given over to the control of independent managers. For companies involved in 'core' activities, this means that they can subcontract virtually every other function which they need in order to operate, from catering, cleaning and building security to IT and the plant and fittings which they use from day to day - all will be maintained in the most appropriate and cost effective way by subjection to 'market discipline'.

Action Programme 7

What are the main advantages of outsourcing?

8 THE CORPORATE SCORECARD

8.1 Financial measurements do not capture all the strategic realities of a business. A technique which has been developed to integrate the various features of corporate success is the **balanced scorecard**, developed by Robert Kaplan and publicised in the *Harvard Business Review* in 1992. One aspect of the scorecard is customer-related measures, and these are discussed here.

Key Concept

The **balanced scorecard** is a way of providing information to management to assist strategic policy decisions. It emphasises the need to provide the user with information addressing all relevant areas of performance. The information may include both financial and non-financial elements, and covers the customer perspective (outlined below), the financial perspective, the internal business perspective and the innovation and learning perspective.

Customer perspective

8.2 'How do customers see us?' Given that many company mission statements identify customer satisfaction as a key corporate goal, the balanced scorecard translates this into specific measures.

(a) **Time**. Lead time is the time it takes a firm to meet customer needs from receiving an order to delivering the product.

(b) **Quality**. Quality measures not only include defect levels but accuracy in forecasting.

(c) **Performance** of the product. (How often does the photocopier break down?)

(d) **Service**. How long will it take a problem to be rectified? (If the photocopier breaks down, how long will it take the maintenance engineer to arrive?)

Internal business perspective

8.3 Findings from the customer's perspective need to be translated into the actions the firm must take to meet these expectations.

(a) The **internal business perspective** identifies the business processes that have the greatest impact on customer satisfaction, such as quality and employee skills and behaviour.

(b) Companies should also attempt to identify and measure their distinctive **competences**. Which processes should they excel at?

(c) An information system is necessary to enable executives to measure performance. An **executive information system** enables managers to drill down into lower level information.

Innovation and learning perspective

8.4 The question is 'Can we continue to improve and create value?' Whilst the customer and internal process perspectives identify the **current** parameters for competitive success, the company needs to learn and to innovate to satisfy **future** needs. This might be one of the hardest items to measure. Examples of measures might be these.

(a) How long does it take to develop and manufacture new products?

(b) What percentage of revenue comes from new products?

(c) How many suggestions are made by staff and are acted upon?

(d) What are staff attitudes? Some firms believe that employee motivation and successful communication are necessary for organisational learning.

Financial perspective

8.5 Some still consider that financial issues take care of themselves, and that they are only the result of the customer, internal process, and innovation and learning issues discussed above. An extreme example of this approach was the chief executive of a silicon-chip manufacturing firm. At each monthly meeting to review performance, the figures for quality were attended to in great detail, but profit figures did not interest him so he would leave the meeting early.

8.6 This view is rather naive for a number of obvious reasons.

(a) Money is a **resource** which needs to be properly controlled

(b) Financial control systems can assist in marketing programmes (eg by identifying where actual results vary from those that were expected).

Marketing at Work

The fall from grace of Digital Equipment, in the past second only to IBM in the world computer rankings, was examined in a *Financial Times* article in June 1998. It is long way from its 1987 peak.

The downfall is blamed on Digital's failure to keep up with the development of the PC, but also on the company's culture. The company was founded on brilliant creativity, but was insufficiently focused on the bottom line. Outside the finance department, monetary issues were considered vulgar and organisational structure was chaotic. Costs were not a core part of important decisions - 'if expenditure was higher than budget, the problem was simply a bad budget'. Ultimately the low-price world of lean competitors took its toll, leading to losses of more than $2 billion in 1992 and 1994.

8.7 An example of how a balanced scorecard might appear is offered below.

Balanced Scorecard

Financial Perspective

GOALS	MEASURES
Survive	Cash flow
Succeed	Monthly sales growth and operating income by division
Prosper	Increase market share and ROI

Customer Perspective

GOALS	MEASURES
New products	Percentage of sales from new products
Responsive supply	On-time delivery (defined by customer)
Preferred supplier	Share of key accounts' purchases
	Ranking by key accounts
Customer partnership	Number of cooperative engineering efforts

Internal Business Perspective

GOALS	MEASURES
Technology capability	Manufacturing configuration vs competition
Manufacturing excellence	Cycle time
	Unit cost
	Yield
Design productivity	Silicon efficiency
	Engineering efficiency
New product introduction	Actual introduction schedule vs plan

Innovation and Learning Perspective

GOALS	MEASURES
Technology leadership	Time to develop next generation of products
Manufacturing learning	Process time to maturity
Product focus	Percentage of products that equal 80% sales
Time to market	New product introduction vs competition

8.8 To apply the scorecard successfully, it must be clearly applicable to the operations involved, and be clearly communicated. A study by the consultants KPMG came up with the conclusion that the balanced scorecard is a very useful tool, as long as the organisation implementing it is very clear as to what it wants to achieve!

Marketing at Work

An oil company (quoted by Kaplan and Norton, Harvard Business Review) ties:

(a) 60% of its executives' bonuses to their achievement of ambitious financial targets on return on investment, profitability, cash flow and operating cost;

(b) 40% on indicators of customer satisfaction, retailer satisfaction, employee satisfaction and environmental responsibility.

Chapter roundup

- Structure has an impact on the culture of the organisation.

- Recent trends in marketing organisation include team-based working and the setting up of customer service departments.

- The societal marketing concept believes that the key task of the organisation is to determine the needs and wants of target markets. There is also increasing concern with ethical issues.

- Chris Daffy (1997) devised a model of the key phases for service delivery, built around vision and values, internal people, external customers and commercial success. External service delivery needs to be integrated with a strong service ethos inside the organisation.

- Reichheld's Service Profit Cycle demonstrates the linkages between external service performance and internal strategy.

- Embedding a customer focused culture requires top management commitment. The senior examiner reinforces this with his model 'The 12 Pillars of Performance'.

- The value chain devised by Michael Porter highlights the marketing and sales function as an activity which can add value for the customer and be a key source of competitive advantage.

- John Oakland argues that meeting customer requirements is a key focus of quality management.

- The role of internal marketing recognises the importance of employees and the significant and often vital role they play in implementing the marketing plan.

- The general change within organisational culture has generated a movement towards shedding or hiving off activities and giving them over to the control of independent managers. This is the process known as outsourcing.

- The balanced scorecard emphasises the need to provide information addressing all relevant areas of performance.

Quick quiz

1   What are the three basic elements of organisation? (see para 2.1)

2   What are the key phases for service delivery? (2.19)

3   What are the three types of company defined by Hamel? (3.3)

4   Explain Reichheld's Service Profit Cycle. (3.24)

5   What are customer care programmes designed to achieve? (4.31, 4.32)

6   Outline Ted Johns' 12 Pillars of Performance. (4.39 - 4.42)

7   How is the value chain relevant to achieving competitive advantage? (5.1)

8   What is Total Quality Management? (5.22)

9   What are the five different levels of customer relationship? (6.2)

10   What are the four perspectives associated with the balanced scorecard? (8.1)

Action Programme Review

1   This is similar to a case in the USA. The affected company withdrew all its products for sale, and better security procedures were installed at the factory. An advertising campaign was instituted to reach people who had purchased the product. This draconian approach earned the company public goodwill.

2   Just do it!

3   The customer care lessons from this example are these.

(a)   Offering delivery is good customer care, focused around the customer's needs.

(b)   The failure to deliver was a mistake, which should have been rectified immediately together with an apology. It should not have been compounded.

(c)   The extra fencing panel, whilst symbolic of the company's contrition, is not really appropriate if there is no use for it. Similarly, if a manager has to apologise for his staff, it means they are not properly trained.

(d)   It is far better to get things *right first time*, a key belief of the quality movement.

4   Sana Sounds is involved in the record industry from start to finish. Although recording and CD manufacture are contracted out to external suppliers, this makes no difference to the fact that these activities are part of Sana Sounds' own value chain. Sana Sounds earns its money by managing the whole set of activities. If the company grows then perhaps it will acquire its own recording studios.

5   The following are all dimensions of client service quality.

(a)   Problem solving creativity: looking beyond the obvious and not being bound by accepted professional and technical approaches

(b)   Initiative: includes anticipating problems and opportunities and not just reacting

(c)   Efficiency: keeping client costs down through effective work planning and control

(d)   Fast response: responding to enquiries, questions, problems as quickly as possible

(e)   Timeliness: starting and finishing service work to agreed deadlines

(f)   Open-mindedness: professionals not being 'blinkered' by their technical approach

(g)   Sound judgement: clients want business advice not just accounting advice

(h)   Functional expertise: need to bring together all the functional skills necessary from whatever sources to work on a client project

(i)   Industry expertise: clients expect professionals to be thoroughly familiar with their industry and recent changes in it

(j)   Managerial effectiveness: maintaining a focus upon the use of both the firm's and the client's resources

(k)   Orderly work approach: clients expect salient issues to be identified early and do not want last minute surprises before deadlines

(l)   Commitment: clients evaluate the calibre of the accountant and the individual attention given

(m)   Long-range focus: clients prefer long-term relationships rather than 'projects' or 'jobs'

(n)   Qualitative approach: accountants should not be seen as simple number crunchers

(o)   Continuity: clients do not like firms who constantly change the staff that work with them - they will evaluate staff continuity as part of ongoing relationship

(p)   Personality: clients will also evaluate the friendliness, understanding and co-operation of the service provider

Source: *Marketing News*, 28 May 1990

6   This means concrete policies and the continuous development of the following.

- Policies of selection.
- Programmes of training.
- Standard, consistent operational practices ('MacDonaldisation').
- Standardised operational rules.
- Effective motivational programmes.
- Managerial appointments.
- The attractiveness and appropriateness of the service offer.
- Effective policies of staff reward and remuneration.

7 • Cost savings

   • Specialism of the company and ability of outsourcing company to concentrate on core activities

   • Accountability is tied to specific performance

   • Introduction of desirable outside qualities (such as imagination, fresh ideas etc) into particular sorts of activities

   • Risk shedding

BPP
PUBLISHING

5

The managerial dimension for mobilising performance

Chapter Topic List	Syllabus reference
1 Setting the scene	2.2
2 Maximising the corporate benefits	2.2
3 People management	2.2
4 Motivational issues and job design	2.2
5 Internal service level agreements	2.2
6 Assessing customer/segment profitability	2.2

Learning Outcomes

- After studying this chapter you will understand the importance of investments in IT and people within the arena of customer-focused marketing and customer service.

Key Concepts Introduced

- Internet
- Management
- Supervisor
- Power, authority and responsibility
- Team
- Development and training

- Reward and incentive
- Morale
- Job enrichment
- Job enlargement
- Transfer price
- Customer profitability analysis

Examples of Marketing at Work

- Thrift Drug
- CACI
- Hallmark and Compaq
- Peapod.com
- Harvester Restaurants
- Customer related competency model

- BP Express
- Doing and achieving
- General Electric
- Post Office
- Siemens
- ABC analysis

1 SETTING THE SCENE

1.1 This chapter examiners the management of people involved in customer service.

1.2 Information technology is examined (Section 2) for the customer focused advantages that it can bring.

1.3 Motivational issues and job design (Section 4) are evolving to take account of the importance of customer service. Within this, customer related competency models are increasingly being used.

1.4 Dedicated customer service and a customer focus are designed to generate repeat business and increase profitability. The final section of this chapter looks at methods of assessing customer profitability.

2 MAXIMISING THE CORPORATE BENEFITS

Information technology

2.1 A recent major survey actually found that 70 per cent of users thought their IT systems were not providing a return on investment, partly because staff using IT systems are left to learn 'on the job' instead of being properly trained.

2.2 A marketing information system (MkIS) does not have to be expensive in order to add value. It can actually be a powerful source for competitive advantage. Already many organisations are reaping the benefits from a sophisticated MkIS.

Technology providing information for competitive advantage

Marketing at Work

'One retailer, Thrift Drug, estimates that it had paid back its $1.3 million investment in a new information analysis system within six months. Thrift believes that the system has made profound changes to the way it goes about organising promotions, cross-selling and pricing. For example, it found that its assumptions about how to display confectionery for Valentine's Day had been quite wrong. For years it had been clearing its shelves of everything but specially-packaged products in the run-up to 14 February; by analysing its sales data, it found that it could dramatically increase its profits by displaying a mixture of ordinary and specially-packaged products.'
Marketing Business

2.3 A major impact of new technology is that firms are becoming increasingly aware of the competitive advantage that may be achieved. Information systems can affect the way the firm approaches customer service and can provide advantages over competitor approaches. Airlines, insurance companies, banks and travel companies are amongst the leading industries that have developed on-line enquiry and information systems to enhance customer service. In order to meet this objective, information which is **up-to-date**, **accurate, relevant** and **timely** is essential.

2.4 Information systems may alter the way business is done and may provide organisations with **new opportunities**. Let us take the example of a theatre which is in a tourist city and which wants to use new technology to build a **database**. The types of data it may wish to have are as follows.

(a) Analysis of theatregoers by specific **characteristics**: age, sex, home address

(b)   How many **performances** each theatre customer sees in the year

(c)   How many day visitors stay in the city and how they chose a day or night at the theatre

(d)   **Types of production** customers like to watch

(e)   **Factors** important to their decision to visit the theatre, such as price, location, play, cast, facilities

(f)   Where they obtained **information** on the theatre and its productions: press, hotel, leaflets, mailings and so on

(g)   **Other purchases** customers make when visiting the theatre

(h)   **Other entertainment** theatregoers choose to spend their money on

This data could then be used by the theatre marketing management to build relationships with customers and to exploit sales and promotional opportunities.

2.5   Information may be viewed as a **marketing asset** since it impacts on performance as follows.

- It helps to increase **responsiveness** to customer demands.
- It helps to identify **new customer opportunities** and new product/service demands.
- It helps to **anticipate competitive attacks** and threats.

2.6   Information technology has created new **marketing techniques** and new **marketing channels. Database marketing** allows vast amounts of customer data to be stored cheaply and to be used to produce more accurate mailshots as well as other marketing tactics. This is important if a firm is able to gain an advantage over competitors by accessing and applying technologies that a competitor is unable to develop.

2.7   **Computer links to suppliers and customers** are common in some industries; a firm is able to place orders regularly via a computer link to replenish stock from a supplier; a customer is able to order from a firm directly. For example, in the motor-vehicle industry some distributing garages for particular makes are able to satisfy customer demand by entering the precise specification of the vehicle and placing the order via computer link to the factory where the vehicle will be manufactured. On placing the order the manufacturer is able to provide the distributor with a production schedule and advise a firm delivery date which can be communicated to the customer.

Database information

2.8   A management information system or **database** should provide managers with a useful flow of relevant information which is easy to use and easy to access.

2.9   In theory, a database is simply a coherent structure for the storage and use of data. It involves the centralised storage of information, which provides:

(a)   **common data** for all users to share;

(b)   avoidance of **data duplication** in files kept by different users;

(c)   **consistency** in the organisation's use of data, and in the accuracy and up-to-dateness of data accessed by different users, because all records are centrally maintained and updated;

(d)   **flexibility** in the way in which shared data can be queried, analysed and formatted by individual users for specific purposes, without altering the store of data itself.

2.10 This could be achieved by a centralised file registry or library, or a self-contained data record like a master index card file. In practice, however, large scale databases are created and stored on **computer systems,** using **database application packages** such as **Microsoft Access**.

2.11 Basic features of database packages allow you to:

(a) **find particular records,** using any data item you know;

(b) **sort records alphabetically,** numerically or by date, in ascending or descending order;

(c) **filer records,** so that you 'pull out' and view a selection of records based on specified criteria (all addresses in a certain postcode, for example, or all purchasers of a particular product);

(d) **interrogate records,** generating the selection of records based on a complex set of criteria, from one or more linked tables. (For example, you might specify that you want all customer records where the field 'City' equals London or Birmingham and where the field 'Product' equals Widget and where the field 'Purchase Date' is between January 1999 and January 2000. The query would generate a table consisting of customers in London and Birmingham who purchased Widgets in 1999;

(e) **calculate and count** data entries, (for example if you wanted to find out how many customers had purchased each product, you could run a query that asked the database to group the data by the field 'product' and then count by field 'customer ID' or 'last name': it would count the number of customer ID numbers or names linked to each product. You could also ask to 'sum' or add up all the values in a field: total number of purchases, or total purchase value).

(f) **format** selected data for a variety of uses, as reports, forms, mailing labels, charts and diagrams.

2.12 Benefits of database systems might include:

(a) increased **sales and/or market share** (due to enhanced lead follow-up, cross-selling, customer contact);

(b) increased **customer retention** (through better targeting);

(c) better use of **resources** (targeting, less duplication of information handling);

(d) better **decision-making** (from quality management information).

Marketing at Work

CACI is a company which provides market analysis, information systems and other data products to clients. It advertises itself as "the winning combination of marketing and technology".

As an illustration of the information available to the marketing manager through today's technology, here is an overview of some of their products.

Paycheck: this provides income data for all 1.6 million individual post codes across the UK. This enables companies to see how mean income distribution varies from area to area.

People UK: this is a mix of geodemographics, life stage and lifestyle data. It is person rather than household specific and is designed for those companies requiring highly targeted campaigns.

InSite: this is a geographic information system (GIS). It is designed to assist with local market planning, customers and product segmentation, direct marketing and service distribution.

BPP PUBLISHING

Acorn:	this stands for A Classification of Residential Neighbourhoods, and has been used to profile residential neighbourhoods by post code since 1976. ACORN classifies people in any trading area or on any customer database into 54 types.
Lifestyles UK:	this database offers over 300 lifestyle selections on 44 million consumers in the UK. It helps with cross selling and customer retention strategies.
Monica:	this can help a company to identify the age of people on its database by giving the likely age profile of their first names. It uses a combination of census data and real birth registrations.

Identifying the most profitable customers

2.13   The Italian economist Vilfredo Pareto was the first to observe that in human affairs, 20% of the events result in 80% of the outcomes. This has become known as Pareto's law, or the 80/20 principle. It shows up quite often in marketing. For example, twenty percent of the effort you put into promotion may generate eighty percent of the sales revenue. Whatever the precise proportions, it is true that in general a small number of existing customers are 'heavy users' of a product or service and generate a high proportion of sales revenue, buying perhaps four times as much as a 'light user'.

2.14   A customer database which allows purchase frequency and value per customer to be calculated indicates to the marketer who the potential heavy users are, and therefore where the promotional budget can most profitably be spent.

Identifying buying trends

2.15   By tracking purchases per customer (or customer group) you may be able to identify:

(a)   **loyal repeat customers** (who cost less to retain than new customers cost to find and attract, and who therefore need to be retained.

(b)   **'backsliding'** or lost customers, who have reduced or ceased the frequency or volume of their purchases. (These may be a useful diagnostic sample for market research into declining sales or failing customer care);

(c)   **seasonal** or local purchase patterns (heavier consumption of soup in England in winter, for example);

(d)   **demographic purchase patterns**. These may be quite unexpected. Grey Advertising carried out studies in the US in 1987 which showed that many consumers behave inconsistently to the patterns assumed for their socio-economic groups. Lower income consumers buy top-of-the-range products, which they value and save for. Prestige and luxury goods, which marketers promote largely to affluent white-collar consumers, are also purchased by students, secretaries and young families, which have been dubbed 'Ultra Consumers' because they transcend demographic clusters;

(e)   purchase patterns in response to **promotional campaigns**. (Increased sales volume or frequency following promotions is an important measurement of their effectiveness).

Identifying marketing opportunities

2.16   More detailed information (where available) on customer likes and dislikes, complaints, feedback and lifestyle values may offer useful information for:

(a)   **product** improvement;

(b)   **customer care** and quality programmes;

(c)   new **product development**; and

(d) **decision-making** across the marketing mix: on prices, product specifications, distribution channels, promotional messages and so on.

2.17 Simple data fields such as 'contact type' will help to evaluate how contact is made with customers, of what types and in what numbers. Business leads may be generated most often by trade conferences and exhibitions, light users by promotional competitions and incentives, and loyal customers by personal contact through representatives.

2.18 Customers can be investigated using any data field included in the database: How many are on e-mail or the Internet? How many have spouses or children? Essentially, these parameters allow the marketer to **segment** the customer base for marketing purposes.

Marketing at Work

Hallmark salespeople in the US have laptop computers which allow them to analyse the mix of greeting cards sold at individual stores, in order to create a merchandising package tailored to capitalise on the strengths of each store customer.

Compaq Computers has a similar program, with sales people linked by computer to the headquarters' databases providing information on every product and every client. In the first two years of the programme, it reduced its sales force by a third - and doubled its sales volume.

Using database information

2.19 The following is a summary of the main ways in which database information can be used.

(a) **Direct mail** used to:

- maintain customer contact between (or instead of) sales calls;
- generate leads and 'warmed' prospects for sales calls;
- promote and/or sell products and services direct to customers;
- distribute product or service information.

(b) **Transaction processing**. Databases can be linked to programmes which generate order confirmations, despatch notes, invoices, statements and receipts.

(c) **Marketing research and planning**. The database can be used to send out market surveys, and may itself be investigated to show purchasing patterns and trends.

(d) **Contacts planning**. The database can indicate what customers need to be contacted or given incentives to maintain their level of purchase and commitment. A separate database may similarly be used to track planned and on-going contacts at conferences and trade shows and invitation lists to marketing events.

(e) **Product development and improvement**. Product purchases can be tracked through the product life cycle, and weaknesses and opportunities identified from records of customer feedback, complaints and warranty/guarantee claims.

Technological developments

Electronic point of sale (EPOS)

2.20 Retailing businesses have been revolutionised by **EPOS systems**. Next time you enter a supermarket or visit the high street stores observe the way in which your purchasing transactions are dealt with. Goods will usually have a barcode on them and that barcode is passed under or over a scanner by the sales assistant. The barcode holds information on stock item identification, price and store location, amongst other things. When your purchase is complete the stock account for the store will be updated, the difference between the selling price and cost price will be recorded to furnish profit on the item and if needs be the item will automatically be replenished by the EPOS system triggering a re-order.

Action Programme 1

What types of marketing and sales information can such systems provide instantly?

2.21 Using EPOS and EFTPOS (Electronic Funds Transfer at Point of Sale) enables individual transactions and individual purchasers to be tracked, identified and linked. This allows retailers to build up a very detailed picture of the buying habits of individual customers.

2.22 In addition to product data, customer **loyalty cards** or membership cards can be linked to the EPOS system to provide detailed information on customer buying habits. Specific customer data captured includes the following.

- Number of **visits** per month
- Average **spend** per visit
- Customer **basket** analysis

Television shopping

2.23 Television shopping is in embryonic form, but nevertheless many investors consider that TV shopping presents them with an opportunity to use the medium to sell a variety of products and services. Just as high street retailing developed from street markets, so too might the new technologies provide **convenience shopping** to future generations of customers.

Home banking

2.24 Several major banks have already developed **home banking services** for customers whereby access is gained to your bank 24 hours a day to execute simple transactions. These systems work in utilising communication technology via a modem, telephone link and/or a video/computer terminal link depending on which options you choose and which banking system you connect to. Bank balances, standing orders, direct debits and the issue of cheques are all possible within home banking systems.

2.25 Home banking offers increased levels of **customer service** and presents the banks with an opportunity to provide to customers (for example, insurance, mortgages, loans, brokerage, taxation). This may reduce the necessity to invest in high street retailing branches and to produce the numerous paper communications for offering services to customers. Promotional efforts could be carefully targeted using home banking systems, providing a higher return for a given promotional spend.

Global technologies and communication networks

2.26 **Global technologies** mean that it is possible to exchange data across geographical areas in a matter of seconds. Speed of transmission opens up vast possibilities for firms wanting to trade globally. The speed of data exchange also poses threats in the shape of corporate fraud which could also be perpetrated in a matter of seconds. Global communication technology has no boundaries.

Multimedia

2.27 Combining telecommunications and computers has enabled the development of a new global industry, **multimedia**.

2.28 BT expects the market for multimedia to increase to £20 billion worldwide by the year 2000. Of that, £13 billion will be for network operation and £7 billion for capital equipment. Multimedia is expected to **transform consumer markets**, first by using video kiosks in major shopping centres and thoroughfares and later by entering the home. Using a combination of phone, television and personal computer, people will be able to (and in some cases can already) access directly everything from groceries to holiday bookings.

E-commerce and the Internet

Key Concept
The **internet** is the sum of all the separate networks (or stand-alone computers) run by organisations and individuals alike. (It has been described as an **international telephone service** for computers.)

'The internet offers efficient, fast and cost effective email, massive information search and retrieval facilities. There is a great deal of financial information available and users can also access publications and news releases issued by the Treasury and other Government departments.

To access the internet you require a microcomputer, a modem and the services of an internet provider.

One of the main uses of the internet is for the sending and receiving of email. This has become a popular method of communication for companies of all sizes.

The main advantage of email is the speed of delivery; messages are delivered within a few seconds and take no longer to travel to Moscow than to Manchester. Messages can be sent to multiple addresses, they can contain images, sound and computer files in addition to the text.'

Certified Accountant, August 1997

Electronic commerce and the internet

2.29 The Internet allows businesses to reach potentially millions of **consumers** worldwide and extends trading time to seven days, around the clock. Electronic commerce worldwide is valued at US$12 billion, and is set to **reach US$350-500 billion by 2002**. The OECD forecasts global e-commerce to be worth $1 trillion by 2003-05.

2.30 E-commerce can reduce expensive **sales and distribution** workforces, and offers new **marketing** opportunities.

Distribution

2.31 The Internet can be used to get certain products **directly into people's homes**. Anything that can be converted into **digital form** can simply be uploaded onto the seller's site and then **downloaded** onto the customer's PC at home.

Marketing

2.32 Besides its usefulness for tapping into worldwide information resources businesses are also using it to **provide information** about their own products and services.

2.33 For **customers** the Internet offers a **speedy and impersonal** way of getting to know about the services that a company provides. For **businesses** the advantage is that it is much cheaper to provide the information in electronic form than it would be to employ staff to man the phones on an enquiry desk, and much more effective than sending out mailshots that people would either throw away or forget about when they needed the information.

2.34   For many companies this will involve a **rethink of current promotional activity**.

Marketing at Work

Peapod.com is an online supermarket and one of the more sophisticated recorders and users of customers' personal data and shopping behaviour. With over 100,000 customers in eight US cities, Peapod's website sells groceries that are then delivered to customer's homes. a list of previous purchases (including brand, pack size and quantity purchased) is kept on the site, so the customer can make minor changes from week to week, saving time and effort.

Peapod creates a database on each shopper that includes their purchase history (what they bought), their online shopping patterns (how they bought it), questionnaires about their attitudes and opinions, and demographic data (which Peapod buys from third parties). A shopper's profile is used by the company to determine which advertisement to show and which promotions/electronic coupons to offer. Demographically identical neighbours are thus treated differently based on what Peapod has learned about their preferences and behaviours over time.

Shoppers seem to like this high-tech relationship marketing, with 94% of all sales coming from repeat customers. Manufacturers like it too. the more detailed customer information enables them to target promotions at customers who have repeatedly bought another brand, thereby not giving away promotion dollars to loyal customers.

Collecting information about customers

2.35   People who visit a site for the first time are asked to **register**, which typically involves giving a name, physical address and post code, e-mail address and possibly other demographic data such as age, job title and income bracket.

2.36   From the initial registration details the user record may show, say, that the user is male, aged 20 to 30 and British. The **website can respond** to this by displaying products or services likely to appeal to this segment of the market.

Possible strategies

2.37   There are four possible strategies that a company may adopt towards e-commerce.

(a)   **Do not sell products through the internet at all,** and prohibit resellers from doing so. Provide only product information on the internet. This may be an appropriate strategy where products are **large, complex and highly customised,** such as aircraft manufacturing.

(b)   **Leave the internet business to resellers** and do not sell directly through the internet (ie do not compete with resellers). This can be appropriate, for instance, where manufacturers have already assigned exclusive territories to resellers.

(c)   The manufacturer can **restrict internet sales exclusively to itself.** The problem with this is that most large manufacturers do not have systems that are geared to dealing with sales to end users who place numerous, irregular small orders.

(d)   Open up internet sales to everybody and **let the market decide** who it prefers to buy from.

2.38 If the decision is made to enter into e-commerce a new e-business needs **support and long-term commitment from high-level management**. Ideally such a project should be 'sponsored' by the chief executive or a board-level director.

Value chain efficiencies

2.39 To get a bird's-eye view of an organisation's operations is the purpose of the **value chain** model of corporate activities, developed by Michael Porter. One model of the organisation is that it is a system which transforms inputs from the environment into outputs to the environment. **Competitive advantage**, says Porter, arises out of the way in which firms organise and perform **activities**.

2.40 The needs of the customer are affected by all the activities in the value chain. A customer does not only encounter sales and marketing staff, but accounts staff, warehouse people etc. The value chain as a model shows how satisfying the customer profitably can exert pressure throughout the value chain.

2.41 **Activities** are the means by which a firm creates value in its products. (They are sometimes referred to as **value activities**.) Activities incur costs and, in combination with other activities, provide a product or service which earns revenue. 'Firms create value for their buyers by performing these activities'. Let us explain this point by using the example of a restaurant. A restaurant's activities can be divided into buying food, cooking it, and serving it (to customers). There is no reason, in theory, why the customers should not do all these things themselves, at home. The customer however, is prepared to pay for someone else to do all this. The customer also pays more than the cost of the food, wages etc. The ultimate value a firm creates is measured by the amount customers are willing to pay for its products or services above the cost of carrying out value activities. A firm is profitable if the realised value to customers exceeds the collective cost of performing the activities.

2.42 The restaurant has a number of choices as to how to create value.

(a) It can become **more efficient**, by automating the production of food, as in a fast food chain.

(b) The chef can develop **commercial relationships** with growers, so he or she can obtain the best quality fresh produce.

(c) The chef can **specialise** in a particular type of cuisine (eg Nepalese, Korean).

(d) The restaurant can be sumptuously decorated for those customers who value **'atmosphere'** and a sense of occasion, in addition to the restaurant's purely gastronomic pleasures.

(e) The restaurant can serve a **particular type of customer** (eg celebrities).

2.43 Activities that add value do not stop at the organisation's **boundaries**. For example, when a restaurant serves a meal, the quality of the ingredients - although they are chosen by the cook - is determined by the grower. The grower has also added value, and the grower's success in growing produce of good quality is as important to the customer's ultimate satisfaction as the skills of the chef.

BPP
PUBLISHING

The importance of leadership

2.44 **Leadership** is the process of influencing others to work **willingly** towards a goal, and to the best of their capabilities. 'The essence of leadership is **followership**. In other words it is the willingness of people to follow that makes a person a leader' (Koontz, O'Donnell, Weihrich).

2.45 Leadership comes about in a number of different ways.

(a) A manager is **appointed to a position of authority** within the organisation. He or she relies mainly on the (legitimate) authority of that position.

(b) Some leaders (eg in politics or in trade unions) might be **elected**.

(c) Other leaders might **emerge by popular choice** or through their personal drive and qualities.

2.46 If a manager has indifferent or poor leadership qualities then the team would still do the job, but not effectively or efficiently. A good leader can ensure more than simply a compliance with orders. Leadership and management are different.

(a) Managing might involve the following.

(i) **Planning and budgeting** - target-setting, establishing procedures for reaching the targets, and allocating the resources necessary to meet the plans.

(ii) **Organising and staffing** - designing the organisation structure, hiring the right people and establishing incentives.

(iii) **Controlling and problem-solving** - monitoring results against the plan, identifying problems, producing solutions and implementing them.

(b) Everything above is concerned with logic, structure, analysis and control. If done well, it produces predictable results on time. **Leadership** requires a different set of actions and, indeed, a completely different mind set.

(i) **Creating a sense of direction** - usually borne out of dissatisfaction with the *status quo*. Out of this challenge a vision for something different is created.

(ii) **Communicating the vision** - which must meet the realised or unconscious needs of other people and the leader must work to give it credibility.

(iii) **Energising, inspiring and motivating** - in order to stimulate others to translate the vision into achievement.

2.47 Managers have an important role to play in creating and maintaining a positive corporate culture. Such a culture will help in the process of planning and influence the success of the business through the following.

(a) The **motivation and satisfaction** of employees (and possibly therefore their performance) by encouraging commitment to the organisation's values and objectives, making employees feel valued and trusted, fostering satisfying team relationships, and using 'guiding values' instead of rules and controls.

(b) The **adaptability** of the organisation, by encouraging innovation, risk-taking, sensitivity to the environment, customer care, willingness to embrace new methods and technologies etc.

(c) The **image of the organisation** ('physical evidence' in service marketing). The cultural attributes of an organisation (attractive or unattractive) will affect its appeal to customers and potential employees.

Action Programme 2

Charles Hampden-Turner describes British Airways in the years before it become the 'World's favourite airline'.

(a)   People's job titles, not their names, were on their office doors.

(b)   Late one evening, one of the senior directors was overlooking the airport. 'They're all here,' he said. 'The whole fleet, apart from one which is due back from Switzerland in half an hour.' 'What if you wish to fly to Switzerland *tonight?'* you ask. 'Go by Swiss Airways. None of this lot are leaving until tomorrow morning.'

What does the above tell you about the culture of BA before it changed?

2.48   Not all organisations are fortunate enough to enjoy a positive culture, but it is possible to 'turn around' a negative culture. Cultural change involves people and their attitudes, and it is often a slower and more painful process than you might at first think.

2.49   A number of actions which will help to bring about organisational change.

(a)   The **overt beliefs** expressed by managers and staff can be used to 'condition' people, to sell a new culture to the organisation, for example by promoting a new sense of corporate mission, or a new image. Slogans, mottos ('we're getting there'), myths etc can be used to energise people and to promote particular values which the organisation wishes to instil in its members.

(b)   **Leadership** provides an impetus for cultural change: attitudes to trust, control, formality or informality, participation, innovation etc will have to come from the top - especially where changes in structure, authority relationships or work methods are also involved. The first step in deliberate cultural change will need to be a 'vision' and a sense of 'mission' on the part of a powerful individual or group in the organisation.

(c)   The **reward system** can be used to encourage and reinforce new attitudes and behaviour, while those who do not commit themselves to the change miss out or are punished, or pressured to 'buy in or get out'.

(d)   The **recruitment, selection and training** policies should reflect the qualities desired of employees in the new culture.

(e)   **Visible emblems** of the culture, for example design of the work place and public areas, dress code, status symbols etc, can be used to reflect the new 'style'.

3   PEOPLE MANAGEMENT

Key Concept
Management can be defined as: 'getting things done through other people'.

General management functions

3.1   **Fayol** listed the functions of **management**.

Function	Comment
Planning for the future	Selecting objectives and the strategies, policies, programmes and procedures for achieving them.
Organising the work	Establishing a **structure of tasks** to be performed to achieve the goals, **grouping these tasks into jobs** for individuals, creating **groups of jobs** within departments, **delegating authority** to carry out the jobs, providing **systems of information,** and co-ordinating activities.
Commanding	Giving instructions to subordinates to carry out tasks over which the manager has authority for decisions and responsibility for performance.
Co-ordinating	**Harmonising** the activities of individuals and groups within the organisation, reconciling differences of resources.
Controlling	**Measuring** the activities of individuals and groups, to ensure that their performance is in accordance with plans. Deviations from plan are identified and corrected.

Action Programme 3

Using Fayol's functions of management, indicate under which of the five headings the activities below fall.

1   Ensuring that the sales department does not exceed its budget.
2   Deciding which products will form the main thrust of advertising during the next financial year.
3   Ensuring that the sales department liaises with production on delivery dates.

Managerial roles: modern theories

3.2   Managerial **functions** are those activities necessary for the **organisation** to be managed. A manager will do a number of **tasks** in each day. Mintzberg suggests that in their daily working lives, managers fulfil three **types** of managerial role.

Role category	Role	Comment
Interpersonal, from formal authority and position	**Figurehead** (or ceremonial)	Representing the company at dinners, conferences etc
	Leader	Hiring, firing and training staff, motivating employees, and reconciling individual needs with the requirements of the organisation
	Liaison	Making contacts with people in other departments

Role category	Role	Comment
Informational Managers have: • Access to all their staff • Many external contracts	**Monitor**	The manager *monitors* the environment, and receives information from subordinates, superiors and peers in other departments. It might be gossip or speculation.
	Spokesperson	The manager provides information to interested parties either within or outside the organisation
	Disseminator	The manager *disseminates* this information to subordinates
Decisional The manager's formal authority and access to information mean that no one else is in a position to take decisions relating to the work of the department as a whole.	**Entrepreneur**	A manager initiates projects, a number of which may be on the go at any one time.
	Disturbance handler	A manager has to respond to pressures over which the department has no control, taking decisions in unusual or unexpected situations.
	Resource allocator	A manager takes decisions relating to the allocation of scarce resources. The manager determines the department's direction and authorises decisions taken by subordinates.
	Negotiator	Both inside and outside the organisation takes up a great deal of management time.

3.3 Mintzberg states that general management is, in practice, a matter of **judgement and intuition**, gained from **experience** in **particular situations** rather than from abstract principles. 'Fragmentation and verbal communication' characterise the manager's work.

3.4 A manager will play some roles more than others: senior officials, for example, are more likely to be called upon to at as figureheads than team leaders, who will be more concerned with resource allocation and disturbance handling.

The supervisor

3.5 The supervisor is the lowest level of management.

> **Key Concept**
> 'A **supervisor** is a person selected by middle management to take charge of a group of people, or special task, to ensure that work is carried out satisfactorily ... the job is largely reactive dealing with situations as they arise, allocating and reporting back to higher management.' (Savedra and Hawthorn).

3.6 Features of supervision

(a) A supervisor is usually a 'front-line' manager, dealing with the levels of the organisation where the bread-and-butter work is done. The supervisor's **subordinates are non-managerial employees**.

(b) A supervisor does not spend all his or her time on the managerial aspects of his job. Much of the time will be spent doing **technical/operational work** himself.

(c) A supervisor is a '**gatekeeper**' or filter for communication in the organisation.

(d) The supervisor monitors and controls work by means of **day-to-day, frequent and detailed information:** higher levels of management plan and control using longer-term, less frequent and less detailed information, which must be 'edited' or selected and reported by the supervisor.

What do supervisors do?

3.7 As a supervisor's job is a junior management job, the tasks of supervision in a customer facing department can be listed under similar headings to the tasks of management.

3.8 **Planning for better customer service**

- Planning **work** so as to **meet work targets** or schedules set by more senior management
- Planning the **work for each employee;** making estimates of overtime required
- Planning the total **resources** required by the section to meet the total work-load
- Planning work **methods and procedures**
- Planning **staff training** and staff development

3.9 **Organising and overseeing the work of others**

- **Interviewing** and selecting staff
- **Allocating work** to staff
- Reorganising work (for example when urgent jobs come in)
- Establishing **performance standards** for staff
- Deciding **job priorities**
- Maintaining **liaison** with more senior management

3.10 **Controlling: making sure the work is done properly**

- **Keeping records** of total time worked on the section
- Disciplining and counselling staff
- Ensuring that work procedures are followed
- Ensuring that the quality of work is sustained to the required levels
- Checking the progress of new staff/staff training, on-the-job training
- Co-ordinating the work of the section with the work of other sections
- Ensuring that work targets are achieved, and explaining the cause to senior management of any failure to achieve these targets

3.11 **Motivating employees, and dealing with others**

- Dealing with staff problems
- Reporting to a senior manager
- Dealing directly with customers
- Motivating staff to improve work performance
- Helping staff to understand the organisation's goals and targets
- Training staff, and identifying the need for more training

3.12 **Communicating**

- Telling employees about plans, targets and work schedules
- Telling managers about the work that has been done

- Passing information between employees and managers, and between sections

3.13 'Doing'

- Doing operations work
- Giving advice to others to help solve problems

Work planning

3.14 Authority, responsibility and delegation

> **Key Concepts**
> **Power** is the ability to do something, or to get others to do it.
> **Authority** is the right to do something, or to get others to do it.
> **Responsibility** is the liability of a person to be called to account for the way he/she has exercised the authority given to him/her. It is an obligation to do something, or to get others to do it.

3.15 A **manager** or supervisor is usually given authority from above, by virtue of the position in the **organisation hierarchy** to which he/she has been appointed. (On the other hand, an elected team leader, for example, is given authority from below.) Authority is, in effect, 'passed' down the organisation structure, by **delegation**. The delegated authority of a manager of a subordinate in a direct line down the chain of command is sometimes called **line authority**.

Individuals, groups and teams

3.16 As an employee your relationship with the organisation is as an individual: after all, the employment contract is with you as an individual, and you are recruited as an individual. In your working life, though, you will generally find yourself working as part of a group or **team**; or, if you are a supervisor or a manager, you may direct a team.

3.17 Any organisation is composed of many groups, with such attributes of their own. People in organisations will be drawn together into groups by:

- A **preference for small groups**, where closer relationships can develop
- The **need to belong** and to make a contribution that will be noticed and appreciated
- **Familiarity:** a shared office or canteen
- **Common** rank, specialisms, objectives and interests
- The attractiveness of a particular group **activity** (joining an interesting club, say)
- **Resources** offered to groups (for example sports facilities)
- '**Power**' greater than the individuals could muster (trade union, pressure group)
- **Formal** directives: a department may be split up into small work teams in order to facilitate supervision.

3.18 **Informal** groups will invariably be present in any organisation. Informal groups include workplace 'cliques', and networks of people who regularly get together to exchange information, groups of 'mates' who socialise outside work and so on. They have a constantly fluctuating membership and structure.

3.19 **Formal** groups will be consciously organised by the organisation, for a task which they are held responsible - they are task oriented, and become **teams**. Although many people enjoy working in teams, their popularity in the work place arises because of their effectiveness in fulfilling the organisation's work.

Teams

> ### Key Concept
> A **team** is a 'small number of people with complementary skills who are committed to a common purpose, performance goals and approach for which they hold themselves basically accountable'.

3.20 **Roles of teams**

Type of role	Comments
Work organisation	Combine skills of different individuals.
	Avoids complex communication between different business functions.
Control	Fear of letting down the team can be a powerful motivator - teams can be used to control the performance and behaviour of individuals.
	Teams can be used to resolve conflict
Knowledge generation	Teams can generate ideas.
Decision-making	Decisions can be evaluated from more than one viewpoint.
	Teams can be set up to investigate new developments.

Teamworking

3.21 The basic work units of organisations have traditionally been specialised **functional departments**. In more recent times, organisations are adopting small, flexible teams. Teamworking allows work to be shared among a number of individuals, so it get done faster than by individuals working alone, without people:

- Losing sight of their 'whole' tasks; or
- Having to co-ordinate their efforts through lengthy channels of communication.

3.22 A team may be called together temporarily, to achieve specific task objectives (**project team**), or may be more or less permanent, with responsibilities for a particular product, product group or stage of the production process (a **product or process team**).

There are two basic approaches to the organisation of team work: multi-skilled teams and multi-disciplinary teams.

Multi-disciplinary teams

3.23 **Multi-disciplinary teams** bring together individuals with **different skills and specialisms**, so that their skills, experience and knowledge can be **pooled** or exchanged.

3.24 Multi-disciplinary teams:

(a) Increase workers' **awareness of their overall objectives** and targets.

(b) **Aid co-ordination** between different areas of the business.

(c) **Help to generate solutions to problems,** and suggestions for improvements, since a multi-disciplinary team has access to more 'pieces of the jigsaw'.

Multi skilled teams

3.25 A multi-skilled team brings together a number of individuals who can **perform any of the** group's tasks. These tasks can then be shared out in a more flexible way between group members, according to who is available and best placed to do a given job at the time it is required.

3.26 The recognition that greater autonomy can - and perhaps should - be given to work teams is reflected clearly in the comparatively recent concept of **empowerment,** which is discussed in the next chapter.

3.27 Teams and teamworking are very much in fashion, but there are potential drawbacks.

- Teamworking is **not suitable for all jobs** - some managers do not like to admit this.

- Teamwork should be introduced because it leads to better performance, not because people feel better or more secure.

- The teams can delay good decision-making. The team might produce the compromise decision, not the right decision.

- Social relationships might be maintained at the expense of other aspects of performance.

- **Group norms** may **restrict individual personality** and flair.

- **Group think.** The cosy consensus prevents consideration of alternatives or constructive criticism.

- Personality clashes and political behaviour can get in the way of decision making.

3.28 If employees are to give good service to customers, they first have to receive good service from their managers and colleagues. In fact there are many organisations that expect their customers to be treated like gold - by employees who are treated like dirt. This never works. At best the service that employees give to customers will only mirror the service they get from their colleagues: so it follows that good customer care must start internally if it is to have any chance of working externally.

3.29 Key factors in managing the quality of internal service operations include the recruitment of customer-facing people, the supply of appropriate (and generous) training, and the ability to take decisions which will attract and keep customers, especially when their future loyalty is threatened.

Expanding the team: the importance of search and selection

3.30 It will often be necessary to bring new people into the team, for a number of reasons.

- To fill an identified skills gap.
- To replace staff who have been promoted or who have left.
- Because the work of the team has expanded.

3.31 Whatever the reason for requiring new staff, the importance of the process should never be underestimated. Getting the wrong person can cause problems within the existing group, and the person will require either extensive training and development, or will require replacing with all the attendant disruption.

3.32 As a marketing manager, you may have the help and support of the **human resources (HR) specialists** but the responsibility for your team and its members will be yours. You know the skills, characteristics and approach which will fit in with the team and which are needed to fulfil the task. You will need to be directly involved throughout the process.

(a) Most large organisations have a human resource department.

(b) In smaller organisations, the marketing manager may have no help from HR specialists and will be responsible for all aspects of the search and selection process.

(c) Many firms outsource the early stages of the process to consultants or agencies.

3.33 The overall aim of the recruitment and selection process in an organisation is to obtain the quantity and quality of employees required by the human resource plan, with maximum efficiency (at the least cost consistent with fulfilment of the plan's objectives). Careful recruitment and selection can ensure that those employed in the customer service front line are those who enjoy dealing with customers. This process can be broken down into three main stages.

(a) The **definition of requirements**, including the preparation of job descriptions and specifications. It is the part of the process concerned with finding the applicants: it is a 'positive' action by management, going out into the labour market, communicating opportunities and information, generating interest.

(b) **Recruitment**. The attraction of potential employees, including the evaluation and use of various methods of reaching sources of applicants, inside and outside the organisation.

(c) **Selection** of candidates. Selection is the part of the employee resourcing process which involves choosing between applicants for jobs: it is largely a 'negative' process, eliminating unsuitable applicants.

An approach to recruitment and selection

3.34 If not approached systematically, the process of recruitment and selection can become costly and time-consuming. The organisation needs a very clear plan of:

- what resources it needs;
- what resources are available; and
- where and how those resources are to be found.

3.35 This methodical approach will therefore involve the following stages.

(a) Detailed **human resource planning**, defining what resources the organisation needs to meet its objectives - at marketing team level, this activity would require an analysis of the future marketing skills needed.

(b) **Job analysis**, so that for any given job there is:

- **a job description** (the job's component tasks, duties, objectives and standards);
- **a job specification** (of the skills, knowledge and qualities needed to do the job);
- **a personnel specification** (describing the person for the job).

(c) An identification of **vacancies,** from the requirements of the human resources plan or by a **job requisition** from the section needing a new post holder.

(d) Evaluation of the **sources of labour,** which again should be forecast and in the HR plan. Internal and external sources, and media for reaching both, will be considered.

(e) **Advertising.** Preparation and publication of information, which will:

   (i) attract the attention and interest of potentially suitable candidates;

   (ii) give a favourable (but accurate) impression of the job and the organisation;

   (iii) equip those interested to make an attractive and relevant application (how and to whom to apply, desired skills, qualifications etc).

(f) **Processing applications** and assessing candidates.

(g) **Notifying applicants** of the results of the selection process.

Action Programme 4

Find out what the recruitment and selection procedures are in your organisation and who is responsible for each stage. A procedures manual might set this out, or you may need to ask someone - perhaps in the Personnel or Human Resources department. In your own experience, what part does the manager play in these procedures? Get hold of some of the documentation your company uses. We show specimens in this chapter, but practice and terminology varies, so your own 'house style' will be invaluable. Try to find:

(a) the job description for your job;
(b) the personnel specification (if any) for your job;
(c) if your firm is currently recruiting, a full set of the paperwork including the job ad.

3.36 The diagram on the next page indicates clearly all the stages in the process which need to be completed. None can be ignored or taken lightly, if the best candidate for the post is to be found.

3.37 As you can see, before the search process can begin management have a great deal to do. When the need for a new member of the team is recognised the manager must firstly be sure that it is a post which should be made or filled. A careful review of what the team needs should be undertaken to ensure:

• there is a full time post available;
• to identify the contribution that person is expected to make.

3.38 Particular care is needed when the vacancy is due to a team member leaving. Simple replacement is not always the most appropriate. During the job holder's time in the job, the task itself may have changed, or the individual may have shaped the role from that which was advertised originally.

Recent trends

3.39 Recent trends towards flexibility and multi-skilling have encouraged a slightly different approach, which is oriented more towards 'fitting the job to the person' than 'fitting the person to the job'.

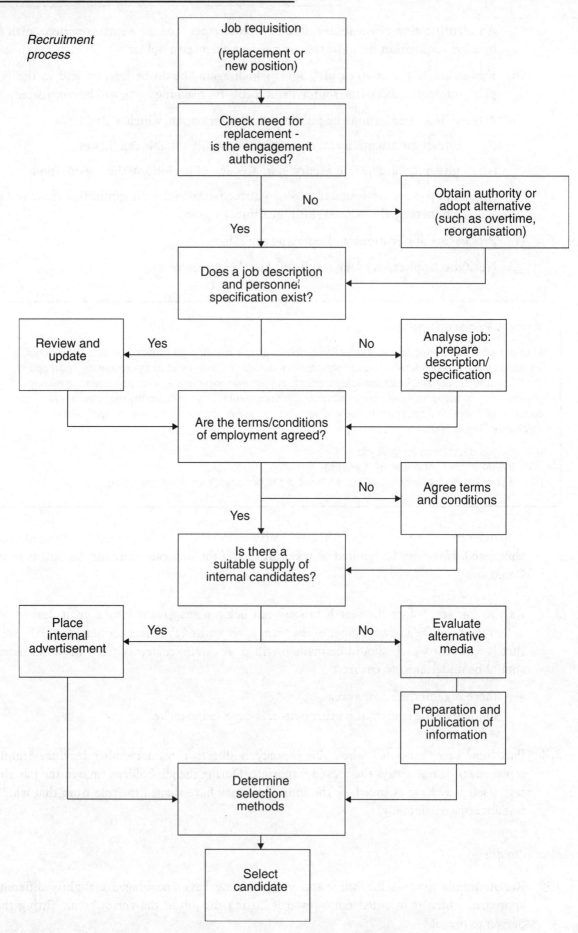

Recruitment process

Job requisition
(replacement or new position)

Check need for replacement - is the engagement authorised?

No → Obtain authority or adopt alternative (such as overtime, reorganisation)

Yes

Does a job description and personnel specification exist?

Review and update ← Yes — No → Analyse job: prepare description/ specification

Are the terms/conditions of employment agreed?

No → Agree terms and conditions

Yes

Is there a suitable supply of internal candidates?

Place internal advertisement ← Yes — No → Evaluate alternative media

Preparation and publication of information

Determine selection methods

Select candidate

(a) In a highly innovative market, technological environment or organisational culture, for example, rigid job descriptions would not be suitable. In order to 'thrive on chaos' (in Tom Peters' well-known phrase), organisations should be able to look at the skills and attributes of the people they employ, and gifted outsiders, and ask: 'What needs doing that this person would do best?'

(b) In a relatively informal environment, where all-round knowledge/skills/ experience are highly valued and suitable external labour resources scarce (say, in management consultancy), this approach would give much-needed flexibility. The organisation would try to recruit 'excellent', flexible, motivated and multi-skilled personnel, without reference to any specific job, as defined by a job description. They would form an available 'resource' for any tasks or requirement that arose.

3.40 However, the 'selection' approach ('fitting the person to the job') is still by far the most common, and is suitable to most organisations with fairly defined goals and structures.

Development and the role of training

Factors affecting job performance

3.41 There are many factors affecting a person's performance at work, as shown in the diagram below. Training and development are the ways by which organisations seek to improve the performance of their staff and, it is hoped, of the organisation.

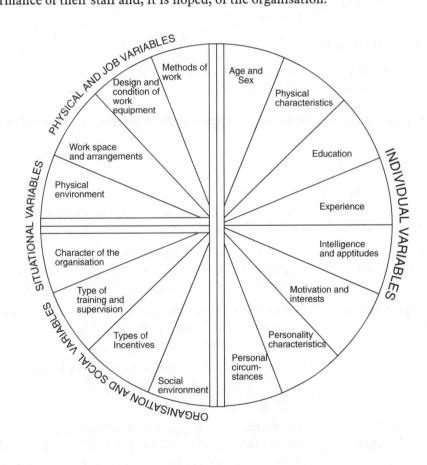

What is development?

Key Concepts

Development is 'the growth or realisation of a person's ability and potential through the provision of learning and educational experiences'.

Training is 'the planned and systematic modification of behaviour through learning events, programmes and instruction which enable individuals to achieve the level of knowledge, skills and competence to carry out their work effectively'.

(Armstrong, *Handbook of Personnel Management Practice*)

3.42 Overall purpose of employee and management development

- **Ensure** the firm meets current and future performance objectives by...
- **Continuous improvement** of the performance of individuals and teams, and...
- **Maximising people's** potential for growth (and promotion).

3.43 **Development activities**
- Training, both on and off the job
- Career planning
- Job rotation
- Appraisal
- Other learning opportunities

Training and the organisation

3.44 **Benefits for the organisation of training and development programmes**

Benefit	Comment
Minimise the learning costs of obtaining the skills the organisation needs	Training supports the business strategy.
Lower costs and **increased productivity**, thereby improving performance	Some people suggest that higher levels of training explain the higher productivity of German as opposed to many British manufacturers
Fewer accidents, and better health and safety	EU health and safety directives require a certain level of training. Employees can take employers to court if accidents occur or if unhealthy work practices persist.
Less need for detailed supervision	If people are trained they can get on with the job, and managers can concentrate on other things. Training is an aspect of **empowerment**.
Flexibility	Training ensures that people have the **variety** of skills needed – multi-skilling is only possible if people are properly trained.
Recruitment and succession planning	Training and development attracts new recruits and ensures that the organisation has a supply of suitable managerial and technical staff to take over when people retire.
Change management	Training helps organisations manage change by letting people know why the change is happening and giving them the skills to cope with it.

3.45 **Training cannot improve performance problems** arising out of:

- Bad management

- Poor job design

- Poor equipment, factory layout and work organisation

- Other characteristics of the employee (eg intelligence)

- Motivation – training gives a person the ability but not necessarily the willingness to improve

- Poor recruitment

Training and the individual

3.46 For the individual employee, the benefits of training and development are more clear-cut, and few refuse it if it is offered.

Benefit	Comment
Enhances portfolio of **skills**	Even if not specifically related to the current job, training can be useful in other contexts, and the employee becomes more attractive to employers and more promotable
Psychological benefits	The trainee might feel reassured that he/she is of continuing value to the organisation
Social benefit	People's social needs can be met by training courses – they can also develop networks of contacts
The job	Training can help people do their job better, thereby increasing job satisfaction

Rewards and incentives

Key Concepts

A **reward** is a token (monetary or otherwise) given to an individual or team in recognition of some contribution or success.

An **incentive** is the offer or promise of a reward for contribution or success, designed to motivate the individual or team to behave in such a way as to earn it. (In other words, the 'carrot' dangled in front of the donkey!)

3.47 Not all the incentives that an organisation can offer its employees are directly related to **monetary** rewards. The satisfaction of **any** of the employee's wants or needs maybe seen as a reward for past of incentive for future performance.

3.48 **Different individuals have different goals,** and get different things out of their working life: in other words they have different **orientations** to work. There are any number of reasons why a person works, or is motivated to work well.

(a) The 'human relations' school of management theorists regarded **work relationships** as the main source of satisfaction and reward offered to the worker.

(b) Later writers suggested a range of 'higher' motivations, notably:

BPP
PUBLISHING

(i) **Job satisfaction**, interest and challenge in the job itself - rewarding work; and

(ii) **Participation** in decision-making - responsibility and involvement.

(c) **Pay** has always occupied a rather ambiguous position, but since people need money to live, it well certainly be part of the reward 'package' an individual gets from his work.

Why is motivation important for managers?

3.49 You may be wondering whether motivation is really so important. It could be argued that if a person is employed to do a job, he will do that job and no question of motivation arises. If he person doesn't want to do the work, he can resign. So why try to motivate people?

(a) Motivation is about getting *extra* levels of commitment and performance from employees, over and above mere compliance with rules and procedures. If individuals can be motivated, by one means or another, they might work more efficiently (and productivity will rise) or they will produce a better quality of work.

(b) The case for **job satisfaction** as a factor in improved performance is not proven.

(c) The key is to work 'smarter'.

3.50 Motivation can be a negative process (appealing to an individual's need to **avoid** unpleasantness, pain, fear etc) as well as a positive one (appealing to the individual's need to attain certain goals).

(a) **Negative motivation** is wielding the big stick: threatening dismissal or demotion, reprimand etc - it is negative reinforcement.

(b) **Positive motivation** is dangling the carrot, and may be achieved by:

(i) The offer of extrinsic rewards, such as pay incentives, promotion, better working conditions etc

(ii) Internal or psychological satisfaction for the individual ('virtue is its own reward'), a sense of achievement, a sense of responsibility and value etc.

Intrinsic and extrinsic factors

3.51 The **rewards offered to the individual** at work may be these.

(a) **Extrinsic rewards**

These are not within the control of the individual but are at the disposal of others, such as wage or salary, bonuses and prizes, working conditions, a car, training opportunities.

(b) **Intrinsic rewards**

There are within the control of the individual himself: feelings of companionship, comfort, sense of achievement, enjoyment of status and recognition, interest in the job, responsibility, pride in the organisation's success etc.

3.52 The system of rewards used in an organisation or in the department will largely depend on:

(a) The **assumptions the managers make** about their subordinates' working life.

(b) The **employees' goals**.

Participation

3.53 People want more interesting work and to have a say in decision-making. These expectations are a basic part of the movement towards greater **participation** at work.

3.54 The methods of achieving increased involvement have largely crystallised into two main streams.

 (a) **Immediate participation** is used to refer to the involvement of employees in the **day-to-day** decisions of their work group.

 (b) **Distant participation** refers to the process of including company employees at the top levels of the organisation which deal with long-term policy issues including investment and employment.

3.55 Motivation through **employee satisfaction** is not a useful concept because employee satisfaction is such a **vague idea**. Drucker suggested that employee satisfaction comes about through encouraging - if need be, by pushing - employees to accept responsibility. There are four ingredients to this.

 (a) **Careful placement of people in jobs** so that an individual is suited to the role.

 (b) **High standards of performance in the job,** so that the employee should know what to aim for.

 (c) **Providing the worker with feedback control information.** The employee should receive routine information about how well or badly he or she is doing without having to be told by his boss.

 (d) **Opportunities for participation** in decisions that will give the employee managerial vision.

Morale

> **Key Concept**
> **Morale** is a term drawn primarily from a military context, to denote the state of mind or spirit of a group, particularly regarding discipline and confidence. It can be related to 'satisfaction', since 'low morale' implies a state of dissatisfaction.
> Morale relates to how a group feels.

3.56 The 'signs' by which morale is often gauged are by no means clear cut.

 (a) **Low productivity** is not invariably a sign of low morale. In fact there may be **little correlation between morale and output**.

 (b) **High labour turnover** is not a reliable indicator of low morale: the age structure of the workforce and other factors in natural wastage will need to be taken into account. Low turnover, likewise, is no evidence of high morale: people may be staying because of lack of other opportunities in the local job market, for example.

 (c) There is some evidence that satisfaction correlates with mental health - so that symptoms of **stress or psychological failure** may be a signal to management that all is not well, although again, a range of non-work factors may be contributing.

 (d) **Attitude surveys** may indicate workers' perception of their job satisfaction, by way of interview or questionnaire.

The reward system

3.57 Child has outlined six management **criteria for a reward system**. It should:

BPP
PUBLISHING

(a) Encourage people to **fill job vacancies** and to stay in their job (ie not leave).

(b) Increase the **predictability of employees' behaviour**, so that employees can be depended on to carry out their duties consistently and to a reasonable standard.

(c) Increase **willingness to accept change** and flexibility. (Changes in work practices are often 'bought' from trade unions with higher pay.)

(d) Foster and **encourage innovative behaviour**.

(e) **Reflect the nature of jobs** in the organisation and the skills or experience required. The reward system should therefore be consistent with seniority of position in the organisation structure, and should be thought fair by all employees.

(f) **Motivate** (increase commitment and effort).

What do people want from pay?

3.58 **Pay has a central - but ambiguous - role in motivation theory**. It is not mentioned explicitly in any need list, but it **offers the satisfaction of many of the various needs**.

(a) Physiological - pay for food, shelter.

(b) Security.

(c) Esteem needs - pay might be a mark of status, but also a level of pay may be a sign of fairness.

(d) Self-actualisation - pay gives people resources to pursue self-actualisation outside the working environment.

3.59 Individuals may also have needs unrelated to money, however, which money cannot satisfy, or which the pay system of the organisation actively denies. So to what extent is pay an inducement to better performance: a motivator or incentive?

3.60 Although the size of their income will affect their standard of living, most people tend not to be concerned to **maximise** their earnings. They may like to earn more but are probably more concerned to:

(a) Earn **enough**.

(b) Know that their pay is **fair** in comparison with the pay of others both inside and outside the organisation.

Rewarding the team

Group bonus schemes

3.61 **Group incentive schemes** typically offer a bonus for a performance which achieves or exceeds specified targets. Offering bonuses to a **whole team** may be appropriate for tasks where individual contributions cannot be isolated, workers have little control over their individual output because tasks depend on each other, or where team-building is particularly required. It may enhance team-spirit and co-operation as well as provide performance incentives, but it may also create pressures within the group if some individuals are seen to be 'not pulling their weight'.

Profit-sharing schemes

3.62 Profit-sharing schemes offer employees (or selected groups of them) bonuses, directly on profits or 'value added'. Profit sharing is based on the belief that all employees can contribute to profitability, and that that contribution should be recognised. The effects may include profit-consciousness and motivation in employees, commitment to the future prosperity of the organisation etc.

3.63 The actual incentive value and effect on productivity may be wasted, however, if the scheme is badly designed.

  (a) The sum should be **significant**.

  (b) There should be a **clear and timely link** between effort/performance and reward. Profit shares should be distributed as frequently as possible with the need for reliable information on profit forecasts, targets etc and the need to amass significant amounts for distribution.

  (c) The scheme should only be introduced if profit forecasts indicate a **reasonable chance of achieving** the above: profit sharing is welcome when profits are high, but the potential for disappointment is great.

  (d) The greatest effect on productivity arising from the scheme may in fact arise from its use as a focal point for discussion with employees, about the relationship between their performance and results, areas and targets for improvement etc. Management must be seen to be **committed** to the principle.

Share schemes

3.64 Some firms choose to reward employees and managers by way of shares, again allowing them to participate in the success of the company as measured by the share price. In effect, the employee is allowed to purchase, at a future date, shares in the firm at the current price or perhaps at a discount. If the share price has risen the employee can sell the shares and make a profit.

  (a) This is used often in the remuneration of chief executives; there has been some criticism especially with regard to rewarding executives of privatised utilities.

  (b) Many firms have introduced such schemes for all their staff. There have been some tax incentives also.

4 MOTIVATIONAL ISSUES AND JOB DESIGN

From the old employment charter to the new: the womb to the piranha tank

4.1 Although not written down anywhere quite so explicitly as expressed here, the **tacit employment contract** at one time in force between organisations and their staff could have been expressed something along these lines:

  > If you put in a decent day's work and keep your nose clean, then you can expect to stay with us either until you want to leave or until you choose to retire.

4.2 Nobody mentioned the need to **get customers, serve customers** and **keep them happy**. Nothing was said about the requirement for **continuous improvement** and change (arising from the permanently increasing expectations of customers). There was no expectation about **adding value**, about making a difference, about '**going the extra mile**'.

117 *BPP*

4.3   For most people at work today, such apparently halcyon days have departed, presumably for ever. As *Business Week* once put it:

> 'The organisation man is dead ... He thrived when airlines, banks and telephones were highly regulated. When Japan built shoddy cars. When computers were huge and an apple was something you ate.'

4.4   In the **new employment contract,** radically different obligations apply to both employer and employee:

(a) We will contract for your services, says the organisation. In return we ask you to **perform to the best of your ability,** so long as the relationship is **mutually beneficial**.

(b) Your **job may be in jeopardy** if circumstances change, because the organisation will be in jeopardy. Should that happen, we may ask you to **do something different,** or **move somewhere else**; and if neither of those escape routes is possible, then our paths may have to diverge.

(c) It isn't enough simply to fulfil the basic requirements of the job. You must 'add value' through **continuous improvement** linked to business purposes.

(d) You must **grow and develop** as the organisation grows and develops. We will **provide opportunities** - so that you can enhance your value both to us and to yourself through raising your employability quotient - but ultimately the **responsibility for your development is yours**.

(e) You must expect to be **paid for performance,** even if, in some roles, performance is difficult to assess and measure. Paying simply for turning up is a much less attractive option for the employer, and paying by the hour is not attractive at all - because it suggests that you are being paid for your presence rather than for your contribution.

(f) **Nobody** can automatically expect to **enjoy a lifetime connection** with one employer any more.

4.5   What all this means is that most working people now live in a dangerous world, with **no guarantee of lifelong job security** and no way of protecting themselves against change other than constant attention to their employability credentials.

4.6   On the other hand, most organisations now pay much more attention to the task of **securing commitment** from people, they're now more likely to **share information** about strategy, and they commonly stress the benefits of **teamworking**. Even when such efforts are halting, misjudged, incompetently implemented, cynically manipulative or embarrassingly patronising, they sound better than the previous regime, where:

(a) People joining organisations were not asked or expected to add value, but were **simply given tasks to perform,** without necessarily understanding what those tasks were for.

(b) **Training and development were non-existent** or, at the other extreme, were built around the employee's personal aspirations (if any), so that substantial sums of money were spent on acquiring qualifications and competencies that did not benefit the organisation at all, though they did look good on the recipient's CV.

(c) Payment systems **rewarded people for endurance** rather than achievement, if found on annual increments, and actually encouraged high-cost efficiency when structured around institutional overtime.

4.7   Nowadays, everyone in the organisation has to be **measured against the extent to which they add value** by making a contribution to the attainment of the corporate goals and vision. 'Adding value', by the way, does not necessarily signify any direct financial outcome.

The Norton/Kaplan 'balanced scorecard' approach, the European business excellence model, and the RSA 'Tomorrow's Company' programme, all make it clear that there are **several indices against which corporate 'success' may be evaluated**. Profit is only one of those indices - and not even a meaningful one for many public-sector and not-for-profit organisations; other measures might include customer value, productivity, ethical compliance, societal impact, product/service innovation, market standing or reputational advantage.

4.8 The concept of 'adding value' is now critical to the effective performance of people in tomorrow's organisations. It is still not well understood, or even accepted either within organisations themselves or by their employees.

4.9 Strictly speaking, nobody at work is paid to **do** anything: we're paid to **achieve** something. So what, for example, is 'customer service' meant to achieve? What's it all for? The question is fundamental, it's not new, but it's still a good one - and it's a question which applies to all jobs, whether in customer service or elsewhere.

Job design

4.10 The following classification of the roles performed by people in organisations suggests that their activities (yours too) fall into four groups.

Maintenance	Fire fighting or 'crisis' management
Crisis prevention	Proactively preventing problems or minimising their damage when they do occur
Continuous improvement	Doing things better, faster and cheaper against 'customer' aspirations
Innovation and change	Creating new and different things to do

Maintenance

4.11 Dealing with customer complaints and putting them right is part of the **maintenance** role. In most organisations it is essential work but all it does is to make sure that the organisation's **performance at the end of the day is no worse than it was at the beginning**. Concentrating exclusively on the maintenance aspects of corporate life means that people keep doing the same things to the same performance standards, and the organisation as a whole (being the collective output of all the people who work for it) continues to function at its established level of effectiveness.

4.12 Yet if the Bain research on *The Future of Customer Service* (Institute of Customer Service, 1998) is right about the accelerating expectations of customers, then organisations which do not improve will ultimately go out of business. The only ones which will not are those which:

- **do not have any competition**

- **do not have any customers** in the first place, but can continue to function without them

- have **customers who will put up with anything**

- have customers who for one reason or another are **tied to them**

119

Crisis prevention

4.13 **Crisis prevention** is significantly **more proactive** and interventionist, but although it keeps (potential) losses down, it still **does not add value** in the genuine sense of the term. Crisis prevention tries to create an environment with the minimum of surprise, by

(a) preventing **previous** crises from happening again, and

(b) anticipating **future** crises so that they can be avoided or their consequential damage contained.

4.14 In customer service terms, this means not only dealing with each complaint as it happens, but also looking for patterns so that **future complaints can be pre-empted**; it means supplying customers with a 'fault-handling' guide in their instruction booklets; it means the use of foolproof (though not necessarily customer-proof) components and controls; it means telephoning customers to ask about problems rather than simply waiting for problems to happen.

Continuous improvement

4.15 **Continuous improvement** is about doing things better in one or more of the only **three ways** in which things can be done to a higher standard: **quality, speed and cost**. 'Quality' in this context means **perceived** quality, not just 'fitness for purpose' or compliance with some quality certification standard. The only quality performance which matters is the quality that is perceived by the customer, so if performance improvements in this arena are introduced, the customer has to be sensitised to their existence and has to believe that the improvements are worthwhile - without that sensitivity and belief, quality is meaningless.

4.16 It is worth exploring this argument a little further. Many organisations have failed precisely because they have improved product/service quality in ways which are **invisible to customers** or **irrelevant** to customer aspirations. Think about Volvo's daylight lights, for example, which weren't introduced at all in France but were tolerated in the UK marketplace despite their nuisance value - which probably says something about the docility of the UK consumer.

Innovation and change

4.17 **Innovation and change** requires the introduction of new ideas, new methods, new services, new service extensions, new ways of relating to customers, new ways of attracting customers, new methods for retaining them. Innovation can come literally from anywhere, and its fertilisation will be explored in a later chapter. Suffice to say, here, that for most organisations the problem is not innovation, but the willingness to welcome innovation and make it work; stimulating that willingness is an exercise in innovation itself.

Efficiency and effectiveness

4.18 **Maintenance** and **crisis prevention** are about efficiency (**doing things right**) whereas **continuous improvement** and **innovation/change** are about effectiveness (**doing the right things**).

4.19 If adding value is the significant measure for evaluating the performance for individual employees, it is even more vital for the organisation which must add value to itself if it is to survive. **Only if people and terms add value to their organisation can they justify taking more rewards from it**: if rewards increase, but value is not added, then the organisation lurches towards extinction.

4.20 To some extent value is added **automatically** over time because of the so-called **experience or learning curve,** but even here one has to be careful. According to Peter Drucker, people who claim they've had twenty years' experience in, say, customer service, may be telling the truth, or they may simply have had **one year's experience repeated twenty times**.

4.21 There is no particular mystique about **job design**: it is merely the way in which tasks are fragmented or grouped to form a given job, and what decisions are made about specialisation, discretion, autonomy, variety and other job elements.

4.22 Employees working in customer service areas should have their jobs designed so that they have some autonomy over the decisions to be made and responses and level of service to be given to customers. Not only does this improve **customer service,** but it improves **employee motivation**. Stress has been specifically related to high workload and low discretion jobs. Its symptoms, including low morale, will invariably affect performance unless particular efforts are made to compensate the workers or make their jobs more interesting.

4.23 A customer service representative who has the **authority and autonomy** to offer solutions to a customer and follow a complaint through to its resolution is likely to both give better service and find the job more rewarding than a worker who simply takes down the details of the complaint and then hands responsibility for its resolution to someone higher up the chain.

4.24 To make the worker capable of higher levels of customer service may inevitably require training and some restructuring of the organisation, but customers will benefit from getting their queries and complaints dealt with by a single point of contact.

On the job training

4.25 On the job training has been the preferred method of training for decades in the UK. Managers learn by progressing from supervisory levels, through middle management and eventually to senior positions. They learn by mistakes and from other older and more experienced managers.

4.26 Different methods of on the job training include the following.

(a) **Coaching:** the trainee is put under the guidance of an experienced employee who shows the trainee how to do the job. The length of the coaching period will depend on the complexity of the job and the previous experience of the trainee.

    (i) **Establish learning targets.** The areas to be learnt should be identified, and specific, realistic goals (eg completion dates, performance standards) stated by agreement with the trainee.

    (ii) **Plan a systematic learning and development programme.** This will ensure regular progress, appropriate stages for consolidation and practice.

    (iii) **Identify opportunities for broadening the trainee's knowledge and experience** (eg by involvement in new projects, placement on inter-departmental committees, suggesting new contacts, or simply extending the job, adding more tasks, greater responsibility etc).

    (iv) **Take into account the strengths and limitations of the trainee** in learning, and take advantage of learning opportunities that suit the trainee's ability, preferred style and goals.

BPP PUBLISHING

(v) **Exchange feedback**. The supervisor will want to know how the trainee sees his or her progress and future. He or she will also need performance information in order to monitor the trainee's progress, adjust the learning programme if necessary, identify further needs which may emerge and plan future development for the trainee.

(b) **Mentoring:** where a senior staff member can provide advice and coaching support. This member need not be the line manager. Mentors can pass on practical skills and tips derived from their experience, and possibly in return receive new ideas or techniques from their pupil. Mentors need to be selected with care (not everyone will be suited) and trained appropriately. The mentor's workload needs to allow time for the mentoring, and regular discussions should take place to review progress.

(c) **Job rotation:** the trainee is given several jobs in succession, to gain experience of a wide range of activities. (Even experienced managers may rotate their jobs, to gain wider experience; this philosophy of job education is commonly applied in the Civil Service, where an employee may expect to move on to another job after a few years).

(d) **Temporary promotion:** an individual is promoted into his/her superior's position whilst the superior is absent owing to illness. This gives the individual a chance to experience the demands of a more senior position.

(e) **'Assistant to' positions:** a junior manager with good potential may be appointed as assistant to the managing director or another executive director. In this way, the individual gains experience of how the organisation is managed at the top.

(f) **Committees:** trainees might be included in the membership of committees, in order to gain an understanding of inter-departmental relationships.

(g) **Project teams:** a person's management skills and experience may be tested and enhanced by membership or leadership of a project team delegated to carry out a particular task. The trainee is responsible for a defined set of results and management skills, such as planning and leadership, can be exercised on a project.

(h) **Internal secondment:** experience can be given by giving someone a few months' experience in a different department or different office.

4.27 Essential steps in the **coaching** process are as follows.

(a) **Establish learning targets**. The areas to be learnt should be identified, and specific, realistic goals stated. These will refer not only to the 'timetable' for acquiring necessary skills and knowledge, but to standards of performance to be attained, which should if possible be formulated by agreement with the trainee.

(b) **Plan a systematic learning and development programme.** This will ensure regular progress, appropriate stages for consolidation and practice. It will ensure that all stages of learning are relevant to the trainee and the task he will be asked to perform.

(c) **Identify opportunities for broadening the trainee's knowledge and experience** - eg by involving him in new projects, encouraging him/her to serve on interdepartmental committees, giving him new contacts, or simply extending the job, giving more tasks, greater responsibility etc.

(d) **Take into account the strengths and limitations of the trainee**, and take advantage of learning opportunities that suit his ability, preferred style and goals.

(e) **Exchange feedback**. The manager will want to know how the trainee sees his/her progress and his future. He will also need performance information in order to monitor the trainee's progress, adjust the learning programme if necessary, identify further needs which may emerge and plan future development for the trainee.

Job design for job satisfaction

4.28 Herzberg suggested that the job itself can be a source of satisfaction, offering various ways of meeting the individual's needs for personal growth. Concepts such as combining tasks, forming natural work units, establishing client relationships, vertical loading (ie increased delegation, reduced controls) and feedback were said to result in enhancement of work experience in five **core job dimensions**:

- skill variety
- task identity
- task significance
- autonomy
- feedback

> **Key Concept**
> **Job enrichment** is planned, deliberate action to build greater responsibility, breadth and challenge of work into a job.

4.29 Job enrichment is thus a 'vertical' extension of the job design, which might include:

- removing controls
- increasing accountability
- creating natural work units
- providing direct feedback
- introducing new tasks or
- allocating special assignments

It would be wrong, however, to suppose that job enrichment alone will automatically make employees more productive.

> **Key Concept**
> **Job enlargement** is frequently confused with job enrichment, though it should be clearly defined as a separate technique. Job enlargement, as the name suggests, is the attempt to widen jobs by increasing the number of operations in which a job holder is involved. By reducing the number of repetitions of the same work, the dullness of the job should also be reduced. Job enlargement is therefore a 'horizontal' extension of an individual's work.

Empowerment

4.30 Recessionary pressures have encouraged processes such as **delayering** (cutting out levels of mainly middle-management) and **downsizing**, leading to 'flatter hierarchies', with more delegation and more **decentralisation of authority**. All this involves shifting responsibility to employees further 'down' the management hierarchy, a process recently given the broad name of **empowerment**.

4.31 'Empowerment' has been variously defined: like HRM, it means different things to different people. For example, an article in *Personnel Management* in November 1993 included definitions from a number of leading figures and personnel practitioners.

(a) 'What (companies) mean by empowerment varies dramatically ... many of them are really talking about firing middle management. But companies which are really serious are talking about the orderly distribution of power and authority.'

(b) 'To me it means people using their own judgement in the interests of the organisation and the customer within a disciplined context.'

(c) 'The purpose of empowerment is to free someone from rigorous control by instructions and orders and giving them freedom to take responsibility for their ideas and actions, to release hidden resources which would otherwise remain inaccessible.'

4.32 The argument, in a nutshell, is that by empowering workers (or 'decentralising' control of business units, or devolving/delegating responsibility, or removing levels in hierarchies that restrict freedom), not only will the job be done more effectively but the people who do the job will get more out of it.

Marketing at Work

The validity of this view and its relevance to modern trends appears to be borne out by the approach to empowerment adopted by Harvester restaurants, as described in *Personnel Management*. The management structure comprises a branch manager and a 'coach', while everyone else is a team member. Everyone within a team has one or more 'accountabilities' (these include recruitment, drawing up rotas, keeping track of sales targets and so on) which are shared out by the team members at their weekly team meetings. All the team members at different times act as 'co-ordinator' - the person responsible for taking the snap decisions that are frequently necessary in a busy restaurant. Apparently all of the staff involved agree that empowerment has made their jobs more interesting and has hugely increased their motivation and sense of involvement.

Customer related competency models

4.33 Increasingly popular in organisations - not always connected to the requirement for improved customer service - are competency frameworks which list the standard of behaviour required in any given job.

4.34 Competency frameworks can be used for many purposes: human resource planning, recruitment, selection, induction, training, development, performance appraisal, and promotion. They may consist simply of a collection of **defined and classified behaviours,** or they may be prioritised between the 'Essential' and the 'Desirable'.

4.35 It cannot be expected that the precise behaviours associated with any given competency will be the same at all levels of the organisation and within all functions. Look at the following example, which can be visualised as part of the competency framework for people working in a retail or financial services operation.

4.36 **Key result areas** are the following.

- Creating value through customers
- Creating value for the business
- Working with others
- Working smarter
- Managing change

We expand upon the result area of 'creating value through customers' in the box below.

Marketing at Work

Competences linked to creating value through customers

- Providing excellent customer service
- Managing the customer relationship

Core behaviours linked to providing excellent customer service

- Always keeps promises
- Develops excellent understanding of customer needs and concerns
- Takes personal responsibility for resolving all customer issues
- Strives to exceed customer expectations
- Consults regularly with customers to secure performance feedback
- Tries to anticipate customer needs and act accordingly

Role-specific behaviours linked to providing excellent customer service

Directors and senior executives

- Establishes clear criteria to measure customer satisfaction

- Identifies new opportunities to create competitive advantage through customer service

- Reinforces a commitment to customer service excellence in self and others

- Seeks to understand trends and developments elsewhere, with a view to adopting them for the company's use

- Takes 'best practice' ideas/solutions and makes them work for the company.

People managers and team leaders

- Reinforces key messages about customer service to all staff and team members

- Assists staff and team members to meet/exceed customer service standards by creating the right working environment

- Encourages, motivates, trains and coaches others in the assimilation of a customer-focused culture

Front-line customer service

- Treats each contact with customers as an opportunity to impress them with the service offered by the business

- Acts as the key ambassadorial interface between the business and its customers

Core behaviours linked to managing the customer relationship

- Builds rapport by taking a real interest in customers
- Builds customer trust by meeting their needs and fulfilling all promises
- Regularly seeks customer feedback and takes action accordingly
- Presents a positive image of the company to customers
- Listens sensitively to customer communications
- Remains polite, tactful, courteous and friendly towards customers

Role-specific behaviours linked to managing the customer relationship

Directors and senior executives

- Defines policies which enable all staff to understand the value of individual customer relationships

- Differentiates the services and products offered by the business from those of competitors

- Influences the external perception of the organisation and its brand(s) by raising the profile of the company

People managers and team leaders

- Makes the management of customer relationships a regular agenda item for team meetings, coaching session, and performance reviews

- Focuses attention on those customer relationships which are especially crucial in terms of their commercial significance

125

- Personally makes periodic contact with selected customers in order to retain expertise in the management of customer relationships

- Seeks out customers' views to establish realistic service level agreements (principally so far as internal customers are concerned)

Front-line customer service

- Collects and disseminates relevant information about customers
- Sensitively reacts to customer concerns and responds accordingly, with restitution if necessary
- Takes the heat out of what might otherwise be confrontational scenarios involving customers

4.37 Producing a list of **key result areas, competences,** and **core/specific behaviours** may seem a lengthy exercise. However the framework is a positive mechanism for promoting a **customer-focused culture,** if only because it emphasises the importance of customers for everyone, even those employees who never come into direct contact with customers at all. Also, the framework is invaluable when applied to staff recruitment, selection, induction, training, development, performance review, promotion, and reward/ recognition, because it supplies a common set of criteria against which suitability and/or achievement can be evaluated.

Marketing at Work

BP Express Shopping, in recruiting people to work in its retail outlets, seeks four Competences which are defined and amplified below.

- **Customer Service** - aware of what the customer wants, enjoys dealing with people, courteous, helpful and friendly.

- **Initiative** - acts on issues quickly, generates ideas and implements them to improve a situation, does more than the minimum.

- **Capability** - keen to learn, receptive to new ideas, sets high standards and is accurate and thorough in his/her work.

- **Teamwork** - puts the team first, offers help without being asked, co-operative, flexible and supportive.

Then, in a recruitment guide issued to its managers, BP Express Shopping suggests some questions which could be used when interviewing applicants and assessing their possession of the four competences. Here are the specimen questions relating to customer service:

* *Give me an example of when you have provided excellent customer service. What did you do?*
* *Tell me about a time when you had to deal with a customer complaint. How did you cope?*

Accountability profiles and the position of customer service

4.38 Many organisations now use **competency frameworks** in preference to person specifications, and **accountability profiles** in preference to job descriptions.

4.39 Whereas job descriptions conventionally consist of a comprehensive list of the various **tasks** and **activities** to be performed by the job-holder, accountability profiles focus on **results** and **outcomes.** The performance of tasks and activities is meant to contribute to the achievement of some desired result or other, so tasks and activities are not ends in themselves.

Marketing at Work

The significant difference between **doing** and **achieving** can be illustrated in the following (imaginary) conversation between a supermarket manager and one of his customer checkout staff.

Manager: What are you paid for?

Checkout operator: I'm a checkout operator

Manager: That's your title. What are you paid for?

Checkout operator: I'm paid to pass customer purchases in front of the barcode scanner, and then take the customer's money.

Manager: Those are activities - the things you do. I still want to know what you're paid for.

Checkout operator: Now that you mention it, I haven't a clue

It would be relatively straightforward to say to the checkout operator (as one UK supermarket company has already done) that her **principal accountability**, her key role is:

To make the customer want to come back

Against this principal accountability, everything the checkout operator does has a meaningful purpose.

4.40 All jobs can be outlined in this way, with a principal accountability defined as an **added-value output**, not simply as a summary of some key activities. It is important, too, that the principal accountability is kept simple, brief and straightforward.

4.41 **Subsidiary accountabilities** can include areas like personal efficiency, accuracy and customer relationship; these in turn can be linked to a relevant competency framework.

The position of customer service

4.42 If, strictly speaking, people in organisations are not employed to **do** anything, but are employed in order to **achieve** something, then what is customer service meant to achieve?

4.43 Customer service used to be something done by reactive people who waited for complaints, were shouted at, then put things right and organised compensation. In many organisations, service is still like that: it's seen as a ragbag, poorly-resourced residual department, an unpleasant necessity, an overhead, a refuge for staff whose performance is only marginally acceptable, rather than a marketing tool and an investment.

4.44 The Bain research (*The Future of Customer Service*, published by the Institute of Customer Service, 1998) shows that in the opinion of the major service-industry players, customer service will be a powerful ingredient for **competitive advantage** and **corporate survival** in the years ahead. This view is echoed by Bill Gates in *Business at The Speed of Thought* (1999): 'Customer service will become the primary added-value function in every business. Human involvement in service will shift from routine, low value tasks to a high value, personal consultancy on important issues, problems or desires of the customer.' Bill Gates goes on to say that 'Most transactions ... will become self-service **digital transactions. Intermediaries** will evolve to add value or perish.'

So the writing is on the wall for such intermediaries as travel agents, estate agents, insurance brokers and even retail outlets like bookshops or music stores: they mind find some way to compete successfully against the increasing opportunity to make purchases through the Internet - and the only way they can do it is to supply **superior service**.

4.45 If customers continue to want more, and competitors continue to offer more, and as new competitors emerge with innovative packages, then all organisations will want more from their people. People in front-line service roles are uniquely placed to deliver advance warning about the directions for **changing customer expectations.**

4.46 Andy Grove's 1996 book, *Only the Paranoid Survive*, argues that **strategic leaders are often remote** from their customers: in some organisations the people at the top may not have encountered customers for more than ten years. Their ideas about customers may not have kept up to date, and they may be out of touch with customer aspirations. Such companies have a particular need to encourage added-value behaviour from the people they employ in front-line service roles, because these people are generally the first to know when customers start demanding new things. As Grove points out, 'snow melts first at the periphery' - in other words, a company begins to fail at the point where it **interfaces** with the customer.

Competency frameworks for personal learning and development

4.47 We have already discussed the benefits of competency profiling for recruitment, selection and appraisal. Several organisations majoring on customer service as a source of competitive advantage have begun to use competencies for purposes of **self-appraisal, self-learning** and **self-development.**

4.48 Once a competency framework has been developed, individual employees may score themselves against each element within the system; they can also assess the relative importance of each competency.

4.49 The competencies which deserve attention will be those

- where current achievement is unsatisfactory
- where improvement is essential if the individual is likely to achieve career progression.

The questions to be asked in the self-evaluation process should include:

- Which competencies within the competency framework do I already display, and in what measure?

- Which of the components do I really need in order to do my present job satisfactorily?

- Which of the competencies do I need to concentrate on in order to prepare myself for predicted changes to my current role?

- Which of the competencies do I need to concentrate on in order to prepare myself for a career move?

- Which of the competencies do I need to address in relation to my current performance?

4.50 Here is an example of some learning activities linked to a customer focus competency.

- Select up to five named individuals as customers for your services.

- Consciously initiate a customer feedback programme in which you seek assessments from each of these five customers about their perceptions of what you supply for them, which areas could be improved, and which aspects are perceived to be either particularly important or relatively insignificant.

- Produce an action plan for personal customer-service improvement, with a timetable for measuring progress.

- Identify a 'benchmark' customer-service performance comparison, and seek to apply the lessons to be learned.

5 INTERNAL SERVICE LEVEL AGREEMENTS

5.1 **Service levels** and the pursuit of **quality** are closely related to each other. **Customer care programmes**, which seek to promote the achievement of service levels both internally and externally, focus on gaining deep knowledge of customers, and aim to identify their needs and improve care provided for them. Satisfied customers are likely to be loyal customers.

5.2 When it comes to internal communication and service, many organisations are still their own worst enemies. Many employees are ill- informed and unenthusiastic about their organisation's products or services; many are ignorant of the role that their colleagues play and how their own work impacts upon other departments. Employees are often more concerned with job preservation and adherence to procedures.

5.3 This may be understandable but needs to change. As Sun Tzu, the Chinese General, said: 'He will win whose army is animated by the same spirit throughout all its ranks.' This is what **internal marketing and internal communications** are all about.

5.4 Internal marketing can be separated into two distinct elements.

   (a) Internal marketing is concerned with all individuals within an organisation working to the **achievement of common aims and objectives**.

   (b) Internal marketing is a recognition that people who work together stand in exactly the same relationship to each other as do **customers and suppliers**.

5.5 Internal communications can be described as the process through which organisations share information, build commitment to achieve objectives and assist in the management and acceptance of change. Communication plays a vital role in maintaining company competitiveness through employee motivation.

5.6 The danger is that this process is seen as no more than a tactical move, which is restricted primarily to the operational level. Consequently, should such programmes receive little or no senior management backing, then the operational perspective will also eventually break down: internal marketing programmes will be seen as nothing more than a glossy veneer.

Elements of an internal service level agreement

5.7 This can be categorised in much the same way as the external marketing plan, in terms of product, price, place and promotion.

5.8 The **product** in this case is the agreement itself and the details of the agreement which are to be 'sold' to the organisation. This will possibly involve the organisation in creating new structures, positions of power and reporting responsibilities. The current trend towards flatter management structures has facilitated greater acceptance of these principals, by cutting through previous negative attitudes towards marketing orientation.

5.9 The **price** can be measured in terms of the time and effort in accepting, developing and implementing the agreement. It can also be interpreted as the longer-term cost of lost revenues involved in not retaining customers and remaining competitive.

5.10 **Distribution** (place) refers to the methods by which the strategies and plans are incorporated by individuals, groups and the systems of the organisation. This will involve, lectures, workshops, seminars, in-house training and informal meetings. Distribution is inextricably linked into the arena of human resource management, where retraining, reward and incentive schemes assist in creating the positive environment within which the marketing philosophy can thrive.

5.11 **Communication** (promotion) is concerned with the messages and form of media which are to be adopted in informing the organisation of the aims and objectives which are to be pursued.

Vision

5.12 In order for any internal service level agreement to be successful then the organisation needs to have a clear vision for the future. The diagram on the next page illustrates how British Petroleum articulate their vision for the future through their employees, customers, suppliers, the community and shareholders alike.

Marketing at Work

General Electric have an internal communications plan which attempts to deal with five major issues.

- Satisfying customers
- Surpassing the competition
- Minimising costs
- Responding to change
- Devising employee-specific communications

The programme emphasises the importance of communicating these themes by reporting and interpreting specific events which illustrate them. This will include orders won, orders lost, the names of competitors and how they are faring within the worldwide environment. The employee-specific information constantly builds up a picture of what the company is doing, so that in the event of any changes which need to be implemented, they can be achieved within an environment of understanding and willingness to accept and adopt change. The emphasis is upon open information and honesty. Information is provided on the immediate goals and related problems involved, attempting simultaneously to achieve business goals and to satisfy employee concerns.

Transfer pricing

Key Concept

A **transfer price** is the price at which a product component or service is passed, internally, from one company division to another. There are various methods of setting a transfer price but one of the key concerns is that it reflect commercial reality.

5.13 Where there are **internal transfers of goods or services**, the transfers could be made 'free' to the division receiving the benefit. For example, if a garage and car showroom has two divisions, one for car repairs and servicing and the other for sales, the servicing division will be required to service cars before they are sold. The servicing division could do its work for the car sales division without making any record of the work done.

BP VALUES

The principles and values to which we are committed and which underpin our vision are reflected in our responsibilities to all our stakeholders:

Our Employees:

For every employee our values mean a trusting, equal opportunity, non-discriminatory working environment. Our company offers challenging and exciting work. We will vigorously promote career development and we will aim to offer all employees a challenging career. We will seek to recognise both individual contribution and collective teamwork. We encourage our employees to strike a balance between their responsibilities to BP and to their home life.

Our Customers:

We are committed at all times to integrity and fairness; to quality products and services which give our customers good value; and to technological and innovative skills to develop new products. We seek to achieve customer satisfaction and to build long-lasting beneficial partnerships with them.

Our Shareholders:

It is only by achieving these values that our shareholders will benefit from a more productive and competitive BP which, in comparison with our competitors, will yield an attractive return in terms of dividend and long-term growth.

Our Suppliers:

We seek mutually beneficial relationships with suppliers, contractors and service industries. We offer to treat them as we wish to be treated by our customers.

The Community:

In all our operations we will act as responsible corporate citizens. Wherever we operate we strive to be an industry leader in safety practices and in environmental standards. We expect to involve ourselves in and to contribute to local communities and education. We will conduct our relationships with governments and statutory bodies not only within the law but also with exemplary standards of ethics.

BP VISION, VALUES AND THEMES

BP VISION

BP is a family of businesses principally in oil and gas exploration and production, refining and marketing, chemicals and nutrition. In everything we do we are committed to creating wealth, always with integrity, to reward the stakeholders in BP - our shareholders, our employees, our customers and suppliers and the community.

We believe in continually developing a style and climate which liberates the talents, enthusiasm and commitment of all our people. We can then respond positively to the increasing pace of change in a rapid and flexible way to achieve real competitive advantage. With our bold, innovative strategic agenda BP will be the world's most successful oil company in the 1990s and beyond.

5.14 However, if the cost or value of such work is not recorded, management cannot keep a check on the amount of resources (such as labour time) being used up on new car servicing. It is necessary for control purposes that some record of the inter-divisional services should be kept. Inter-divisional work can be given a cost or charge: a **transfer price**.

5.15 Since **profit centre performance** is measured according to the profit they earn, no profit centre will want to do work for another and incur costs without being paid for it. But, because the size of the transfer price will affect the costs of one profit centre and the revenues of another, profit centre managers are likely to dispute the size of transfer prices.

5.16 A transfer price should be set as part of any internal service level agreement at a level that overcomes such disputes.

(a) The transfer price should provide an **'artificial' selling price** that enables the transferring division to earn a return for its efforts, and the receiving division to incur a cost for benefits received.

(b) The transfer price should be set at a level that enables profit centre performance to be measured 'commercially'. This means that the transfer price should be a **fair commercial price**.

6 ASSESSING CUSTOMER/SEGMENT PROFITABILITY

Exam Tip

Assessing customer profitability is an important area, and you may be asked about the setting of appropriate selling prices for various types of customer, bringing in issues such as the giving of discounts. Remember always that you are going to be required to apply your knowledge to given contexts.

6.1 **Key customer analysis** calls for six main areas of investigation into customers. A firm might wish to identify which customers offer most profit.

(a) Key **customer identity**.

(b) **Customer history**

(c) **Relationship of customer to product**

• What does the customer use the product for?
• Do the products form part of the customer's own service/product?

(d) **Relationship of customer to potential market**

(e) **Customer attitudes and behaviour**

(f) The financial performance of the customer.

(g) **The profitability of selling to the customer.** This is the area we will expand on below.

Such an evaluation would be a part of research into potential market opportunities. Smaller customers should not be ignored and there should be a similar analysis of the organisation's other customers, although a separate analysis for each individual customer may not be worthwhile, and customers may be grouped - ie on the basis of order sizes or another such characteristic (ie geographical basis).

Customer profitability analysis (customer account profitability)

6.2 'An immediate impact of introducing any level of strategic management accounting into virtually every organisation is to destroy totally any illusion that the same level of profit is derived from all customers'. (Ward, *Strategic Management Accounting*)

Marketing at Work

As a basic example, take the Post Office. A uniform price is paid for a first class stamp irrespective of whether it is to be delivered to an address five miles away or five hundred (in the UK), despite the significant differences in transport costs. Of course, the advantages of a uniform price are that there are savings on the costs of administering a wide range of prices and that people are encouraged to use the postal services.

6.3 The total costs of servicing customers can vary depending on how customers are serviced.

(a) **Volume discounts**. A customer who places one large order is given a discount, presumably because it benefits the supplier to do so (eg savings on administrative overhead is processing the orders - as identified by an ABC system).

(b) **Different rates** charged by power companies to domestic as opposed to business users. This in part reflects the administrative overhead of dealing with individual customers. In practice, many domestic consumers benefit from cross-subsidy.

6.4 **Customer profitability** is the 'total sales revenue generated from a customer or customer group, less all the costs that are incurred in servicing that customer or customer group.'

Action Programme 5

Seth Ltd supplies shoes to Narayan Ltd and Kipling Ltd. Each pair of shoes has a list price of £50 each; as Kipling buys in bulk, Kipling receives a 10% trade discount for every order over 100 shoes. It costs £1,000 to deliver each order. In the year so far, Kipling has made five orders of 100 shoes each. Narayan Ltd receives a 15% discount irrespective of order size, because Narayan Ltd collects the shoes, thereby saving Seth Ltd any distribution costs. The cost of administering each order is £50. Narayan makes ten orders in the year, totalling 420 pairs of shoes. Which relationship is the most profitable for Seth?

Key Concept

Customer profitability analysis (CPA) focuses on profits generated by customers and suggests that profit does not automatically increase with sales revenue. With CPA a company:
(a) can focus its efforts on customers who promise the highest profit;
(b) can rationalise its approach to those which do not.

6.5 An important area in marketing strategy is **retaining customers,** so as to generate new business from them.

(a) This is especially true of a market which is declining or static, in which case retention is necessary to increase or maintain profitability.

(b) If the business has a **high fixed cost base,** then new business from existing customers creates **additional contribution**. For example, a bookshop might sell greetings cards or compact discs. Building an image of quality helped Marks and Spencer diversify from clothing into food. A danger, of course, is that all these products must fit into the same set of customer expectations as the original, or else the brand image will be contaminated.

Identifying profitable customers/segments

6.6 But how do you identify which customers, or customer groups generate the most profit?

   (a) This is a consideration that must be brought into the design of marketing information systems.

   (b) The firm's existing customer groupings, may reflect administrative measures rather than their strategic value. We explore this in the exercise below.

Action Programme 6

Busqueros Ltd has 1,000 business customers spread fairly evenly over the UK. The sales force is organised into ten regions, each with 100 customers to be serviced. There are sales force offices at the heart of each region. Information is collected on a regional basis. The marketing director has recently carried out an analysis of the major customers by sales revenue. There are five significant customers, who between them account for 20% of the sales revenue of the firm. They do not get special treatment. What does this say about customer profitability analysis in Busqueros Ltd?

6.7 To analyse customer profitability successfully it may be necessary to structure **information systems** to take account of the many factors by which customers can be analysed. A **relational database**, whereby information can be structured in many different ways, offers a useful approach.

6.8 How do you **apportion costs** to customer segments? Assume you have a customer base of 15,000 people. You have just spent £20,000 on an advertising campaign in part to attract new customers, and 5,000 new customers have been found. How do you allocate the cost of the campaign?

   (a) You do not know if the advertising campaign has also encouraged **existing** customers to spend more.

   (b) You do not know, on an **individual** basis, whether each new customer was attracted by the campaign, by word-of-mouth, or whatever.

6.9 To analyse **comparative** customer profitability, it is necessary to focus on the **right costs for comparison**, avoiding common costs and unavoidable overhead.

6.10 Different customer costs can arise out of the following.

   - Order size
   - Sales mix
   - Order processing
   - Transport costs
   - Management time
   - Cash flow problems (eg increased overdraft interest) caused by slow payers
   - Order complexity (eg if the order has to be sent out in several stages)
   - Stockholding costs can relate to specify customers
   - A key customer might demand lower prices/service.

6.11 Ward suggests the following format for a **statement of customer profitability**.

	£'000
Sales revenue	X
Less direct product cost	(X)
	X
Customer-specific variable costs:	
- distribution	X
- rebates and discounts	X
- promotion etc	X
	(X)
	X
Other costs	
- sales force	X
- customer service	X
- management cost	X
	(X)
	X
Financing cost	
- credit period	X
- customer-specific inventory	X
	(X)
	X

6.12 Such a report can highlight the differences between the cost of servicing different individuals or firms which can then be applied as follows.

(a) **Directing effort to cutting customer specific costs**. Installing an electric data interchange system (EDI) can save the costs of paperwork and data input.

(b) **Identifying those customers who are expensive to service**, thereby suggesting action to increase profitability. They might have a high level of complaints because the quality of the service they receive is poor.

(c) **Using CPA as part of a comparison with competitors' costs**. A firm which services a customer more cheaply than a competitor can use this cost advantage to offer extra benefits to the customer.

(d) Indicating cases where **profitability might be endangered**, for example by servicing customers for whom the firm's core competence is not especially relevant.

6.13 CPA might provide answers to the following questions.

(a) What **profit/contribution** is the organisation making on sales to the customer, after discounts and selling and delivery costs?

(b) What would be the **financial consequences** of losing the customer?

(c) Is the customer buying in order sizes that are **unprofitable** to supply?

(d) What is **return on investment** on plant used? (See Chapter 12 for discussion of financial ratios.)

(e) What is the level of **inventory** required specifically to supply these customers?

(f) Are there any other **specific costs** involved in supplying this customer, eg technical and test facilities, R & D facilities, special design staff?

(g) What is the ratio of net **contribution per customer** to **total investment**?

6.14 Cost drivers may be applied to achieve a product cost, product and customer profitability analysis and market segment profitability analysis.

Cost Driver

1   Set-up time in minutes
2   Time in minutes for total operations
3   Number of batches
4   Material value as a percentage of product cost
5   Quality control testing time
6   Number of sales orders
7   Number of sales quotes
8   Number of sales visits
9   Number of customers served
10   Marketing support time

6.15   Activity based costing often confirms that some products and customers are profitable, but are **subsidising** those which make a loss. Not understanding customer and product profitability lays companies open to attack from competitors.

Marketing at Work

Siemens had a product range varying from simple toasters to complex tailor made machines. Overhead costs were allocated with little regard for these varying degrees of complexity, making some products overpriced. New entrants (especially from the Far East) were able to spot these niches and undercut Siemens. With ABC, Siemens could eventually see that some products were overpriced (thereby subsiding other products) and uncompetitive.

6.16   ABC gives marketing strategists a clear picture of where to compete and encourages them to look at customers as a portfolio. Consider the diagram below.

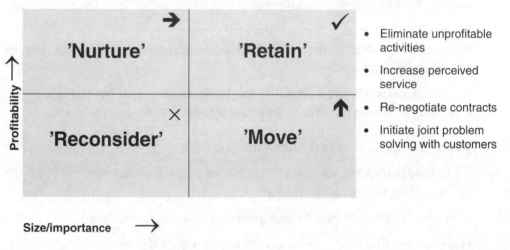

Adapted from 'Activity Based Costing: focusing on what counts' by Michael Gering (Management Accounting, February 1999).

6.17   We can see from the diagram that customers and products that are both important and profitable must be retained. Those that are neither must be reconsidered, and possibly axed. Those that are small in size or importance, but very profitable, should be investigated and nurtured, possibly with cross-selling or other enhanced promotional techniques. Those that are big and unprofitable are typically being invested in for very little return to the company, but it may be possible to make them profitable by moving them.

Marketing at Work

Adapted from Management Accounting, February 1999:

A large German grocery wholesaler undertook ABC analysis of customer profitability and found that nearly half of its customers (retail outlets) were unprofitable. Many of them had negotiated deals that were costing the wholesaler dear. Senior management took a series of steps, including renegotiation of terms and listening to customers to find out what they valued most.

Frequency of deliveries was both a significant cost driver and keystone of customers service perceptions. The challenge was to improve the service without a proportional increase in cost. Problem solving teams were set up.

BPP PUBLISHING

Chapter roundup

- A major impact of new technology is that firms are becoming increasingly aware of the competitive advantage that may be achieved. Information systems can affect the way the firm approaches customer service and can provide advantages over competitor approaches.

- Information can be viewed as a marketing asset. Database marketing allows vast amounts of customer data to be stored.

- A database is a coherent structure for the storage and use of data. Benefits of such systems might include:
    - increased **sales and/or market share**
    - increased **customer retention**
    - better use of **resources**
    - better **decision-making**

- E-commerce can reduce expensive **sales and distribution** workforces, and offers new **marketing** opportunities.

- To get a bird's-eye view of an organisation's operations is the purpose of the **value chain** model of corporate activities, developed by Michael Porter. The needs of the customer are affected by all the activities in the value chain.

- Leadership and people management have an important role to play in creating and maintaining a positive corporate culture, which will lead to success in such areas as customer focus and service.

- This chapter has also examined teamworking, recruitment and selection, development and training, rewards and incentives, and motivational issues.

- Nowadays, everyone in the organisation has to be **measured against the extent to which they add value** by making a contribution to the attainment of the corporate goals and vision.

- Customer service involves dealing with each complaint as it happens, and trying to pre-empt future complaints.

- Employees working in customer service areas should have their jobs designed so that they have some autonomy over the decisions to be made and responses and level of service to be given to customers.

- Recessionary pressures have encouraged processes such as **delayering** (cutting out levels of mainly middle-management) and **downsizing**, leading to 'flatter hierarchies', with more delegation and more **decentralisation of authority**.

- Increasingly popular in organisations - not always connected to the requirement for improved customer service - are competency frameworks which list the standard of behaviour required in any given job.

- Whereas job descriptions conventionally consist of a comprehensive list of the various **tasks** and **activities** to be performed by the job-holder, accountability profiles focus on **results** and **outcomes**.

- If customers continue to want more, and competitors continue to offer more, and as new competitors emerge with innovative packages, then all organisations will want more from their people.

- Internal marketing is a recognition that people who work together stand in exactly the same relationship to each other as do **customers and suppliers**.

- **Customer profitability** is the 'total sales revenue generated from a customer or customer group, less all the costs that are incurred in servicing that customer or customer group.' Businesses need to identify which of their customers generate the most profit.

- Activity based costing often confirms that some products and customers are profitable, but are **subsidising** those which make a loss.

Quick quiz

1. What features should information have in order to be useful in enhancing customer service? (see para 2.3)

2. How can information be viewed as a marketing asset? (2.5)

3. What are four possible strategies that may be adopted towards e-commerce? (2.37)

4. Define power, authority and responsibility. (3.14)

5. What criteria should a reward system fulfil? (3.57)

6. How could you classify the roles performed by people in organisations? (4.10)

7. What are competency frameworks? (4.33)

8. What do accountability profiles focus on? (4.39)

9. What is internal marketing? (5.4)

10. What costs are associated with servicing customers? (6.10)

Action Programme Review

1. (a) *Speed.* Computers can process data much more quickly than a human. This means that a computer has a much higher productivity and so ought to be cheaper for large volumes of data processing than doing the work manually. As computer costs have fallen, this cost advantage of the computer has become more accentuated. The ability to process data more quickly means that a computer can produce more timely information, when information is needed as soon as possible.

   (b) *Accuracy.* Computers are generally accurate, whereas human beings are prone to error. The errors in computer data processing are normally human errors (errors in the input of data) although there can be software errors (errors in the programs) and hardware errors (faults or breakdowns in the equipment itself).

   (c) *Volume and complexity.* As businesses grow and become more complex, the data processing requirements increase in volume and complexity too. More managers need greater amounts of information. More transactions have to be processed. The volume of DP work is often beyond the capability of even the largest clerical workforce to do manually.

   (d) *Human judgement.* Although a computer can handle data in greater volumes, and do more complex processing, the 'manual' or 'human' method of data processing is more suitable when human judgement is involved in the work. When human judgement is involved in making a decision, computer-processed information can help the decision maker but the final part of processing (making and communicating the decision) remains a human aspect of data processing.

2. This was not so much a commercial airline, but a military airforce. Hence, the concentration on rank, and the 'I counted them all out, and I've counted them in' mentality. A corporate culture which delighted in, or was relieved by, assets *not* used and more importantly, potential customers *not* served, is hardly a *business* operation at all.

3. Fayol's functions would define the activities

   1 = controlling
   2 = planning
   3 = co-ordinating

4. Just do it!

5. You can see that the profit earned by Seth in servicing Narayan is greater, despite the increased discount.

BPP PUBLISHING

	Kipling	Narayan
Number of shoes	500	420
	£	£
Revenue (after discount)	22,500	17,850
Transport	(5,000)	-
Administration	(250)	(500)
Net profit	17,250	17,350

6   The information reflects sales force administration and convenience. However, it might obscure an analysis of customer profitability, in which case presenting information by customer size might be more important than geography.

6 Creating positive relationships with customers

Chapter Topic List	Syllabus reference
1 Setting the scene	2.3
2 Customer loyalty, mass customisation and relationship marketing	2.3
3 Communicating with customers	2.3
4 Customer/supplier partnerships and agreements	2.3

Learning Outcomes

- After studying this chapter you will have an appreciation of the importance of creating positive relationships with customers and some of the ways in which this can be achieved.

Key Concepts Introduced

- Loyalty
- Relationship marketing

- Partnership sourcing
- Partnership marketing

Examples of Marketing at Work

- Zeneca Pharma UK
- Lloyds TSB
- TNT Express Delivery Services
- First Direct
- National Bicycle Company of Japan
- Levi Strauss and Co

- Coca Cola
- Customer service on the telephone
- Land Rover
- Safeway
- Mustang Industrial
- Magnetti Marelli

1   SETTING THE SCENE

1.1   Long-term relationships with customers are generally more profitable than one-off transactions, for the following reasons:

(a)   The **cost of acquiring** new customers can be high - especially where repeat purchasing is very infrequent (eg cars, double-glazing, houses).

141

(b) Loyal customers tend to **spend more** and cost less to serve.

(c) Satisfied customers are more likely to **recommend** your products and services to others.

(d) Advocates of a company are more likely to accept **premium prices** from a supplier whom they know and trust.

1.2 Retaining existing customers prevents competitors from gaining **market share**.

1.3 This chapter explores the issues surrounding customer relationships and loyalty.

2 CUSTOMER LOYALTY, MASS CUSTOMISATION AND RELATIONSHIP MARKETING

Customer loyalty

2.1 The customer is the basic reason for the existence of any business since without customers to sell to, a business cannot operate. **Meeting the needs of those customers more effectively than competitors** is the key to continued profitable existence for any business. Each customer who deals with an organisation should leave with a feeling of satisfaction. This outcome is important since it can lead to increased sales and/or a willingness to pay higher prices and thus lead to higher profits. If customers are satisfied they may:

- buy again from the same supplier;
- buy more of the same item, or more expensive items;
- advise their friends to buy from the supplier.

Key Concept

Ted Johns, CIM Senior Examiner for *The Marketing Customer Interface*, says that **loyalty** should properly be defined as: **voluntary repurchasing and referral**.

Action Programme 1

Why is customer loyalty important?

2.2 So-called 'loyalty cards' and similar schemes which use the word **loyalty** are nothing to do with loyalty: they are simply **sales promotion initiatives**.

2.3 Further, reward and loyalty schemes may change the way that customers think about the product, but not necessarily in a positive way. For example, they may come to expect rewards on an ongoing basis.

2.4 Frederick Reichheld, writing in the Harvard Business Review, says: "Creating a loyalty based system requires a radical departure from traditional thinking. It puts creating **customer value** rather than maximising profits and shareholder value **at the centre of business strategy** and demands significant changes in business practice."

2.5 Satisfaction with the product/service provider, and with its brands, is only one of the factors which determines the customer's purchasing behaviour. Other key elements include:

(a) The customer's **affinity to the organisation** and to its brands.

(b) The customer's affection or animosity towards **actual or would-be substitutes** and alternatives.

(c) The customer's **degree of involvement** in the relationship.

(d) The customer's **perceptions** concerning how difficult it might be to **sever the links** - in financial, practical and psychological terms.

2.6 Marketers are increasingly classifying customers according to their level of commitment to brands, using terminology such as **'entrenched'**, **'average'**, **'shallow'** or **'convertible'**. Tests over time have proved that this classification process does help marketers to predict future behaviour. For example, in one study of beverage brands in Canada, 54 per cent of those identified as convertible defected to a rival brand within a year, compared with just four per cent among the entrenched.

2.7 Lloyds TSB has reduced its marketing efforts aimed at customers whose commitment codes indicate that they are shallow or convertible. Experience indicates that the cost effectiveness of such efforts is poor when compared with initiatives aimed at customers noted for their loyalty and their commitment.

Marketing at Work

Developing Customer Intimacy (1): Zeneca Pharma UK

As its title suggests, Zeneca Pharma is a pharmaceutical company with a very varied customer base: patients, their families, patient associations, care groups, self-help associations, nurses, pharmacists, NHS trust contract managers, clinical directors, health economists, and doctors.

The company pursues a strategy of customer immersion, including both its internal and external customers. Various techniques enable the firm to get close to its customers: through internal liaison roles, a 24-hour medical information department, educational materials, focus groups, advisory boards, market research and customer questionnaires, 'work exchanges' between Zeneca and its customers, and 'organisational raids' in which business skills, information and best practice are swapped with chosen customers.

Patients themselves can be involved, too. During the development of a new schizophrenia drug, Zeneca Pharma invited a group of patients to help design the packaging. They said it was important not to have red packaging, which is very upsetting to those with schizophrenia.

The evidence of real improvement is available through the statistics: more than 60 per cent of Zeneca Pharma's customers now provide feedback (compared with ten per cent in 1997), and the percentage of repeat customers has grown to 98 per cent.

Commitment to staff training and development is impressive. Staff now receive an average of 20 days training each year; more than 90 per cent of staff state that they know and understand the vision and strategy of Zeneca Pharma.

Developing Customer Intimacy (2): Lloyds TSB

Lloyds TSB, product of a merger between Lloyds Bank and the Trustee Savings Bank, has around 2800 bank branches in the UK. Its financial performance is impressive in itself (in terms of profitability, growth, shareholder value), and even more impressive when evaluated against the typical returns found in the financial services sector.

The company aims single-mindedly to recruit and retain **profitable** customers. The rate of customer attrition has fallen consistently and now (in 1999) stands at only 1.5 per cent (0.5 per cent among high-value customers). The profitability from new customers has more than doubled; more than 90 per cent of Lloyds TSB customers state that they would recommend the bank to others in the future.

Lloyds TSB has introduced 30 customer-focused initiatives in the past year or so, including a streamlined complaints procedure, a new staff suggestion scheme, revised operational standards, extended customer service training, new employee recognition and incentive schemes, a new partnership with the Post Office enabling customers to do their banking at local post offices, and creation of the largest branch and ATM (Automated Teller Machine) network in the UK.

BPP PUBLISHING

In 1990, Lloyds Bank (before the merger with TSB) had a very poor reputation for customer service, but by 1997 Lloyds TSB was sufficiently confident to claim that it could be "first choice for customers by understanding and meeting their needs better than any other competitor."

Details of each customer are stored on an extensive database, which enables the overall customer base and individual customer segments to be analysed against a series of variables, such as propensity to purchase, attrition rates (ie the probability that customers may take their business elsewhere), satisfaction levels, key customer service priorities and customer characteristics. The integrated IT network means that staff can access details of any customer at any time, in order to look at (for example) transactional customer information and relationship details, correspondence and complaints.

Feedback from customers is systematically, frequently and regularly collected: focus groups, informal meetings, a free customer relations phone line, managerial call backs, customer suggestion forms, mystery shopping, questionnaires, monthly surveys for specific segments (eg new customers, recently-defected customers, and so forth).

Through a training programme, Delivering Service Excellence, staff are encouraged to resolve complaints as they arise. They have authority to make ex-gratia payments of up to £250 without reference to higher levels in the structure; they can refund charges; and all customers receive replies to their complaints within 48 hours.

Developing Customer Intimacy (3): TNT Express Delivery Services

In 1997, TNT Express had around 5000 employees, 1600 trucks, and moved just under a quarter of a million parcels for 26,500 customers every week.

With over 4000 parcel courier currently operating in the UK, customer focus has become a vital differentiator. For TNT Express, this emerged by 1993, when the company's customers said that, to them, customer care was a much more important factor than it had been two years earlier in helping them to determine the selection of one parcel carrier over another. Similar judgments were being made by industry experts, namely, that only the most customer-focused, flexible and fast-moving parcel carriers were likely to increase margins without sacrificing market share.

The 'Expressing Excellence' customer care training programme, initiated in 1993, had as its objective the aim of "Exceeding our customer expectations in all aspects of the business". Overall, the programme had two ingredients - "Ask our customers what they want and ask our people what they need" - and it was the second which began to be implemented in 1996 under the title 'Expressionism', whose purpose was to equip people with the necessary skills to get the job done right first time, every time.

Customer feedback drives all TNT Express customer initiatives, including its 13-point Customer Care Charter. Instant confirmation of delivery information is provided 24 hours a day, 365 days a year, via 'TNT Tracker' - an automatic telephone response system (now upgraded to Internet) which enables callers to establish where their parcel is at any time.

Customer delight doesn't arise merely from call-handling and tracking expertise: reliable collection and delivery of parcels is what customers regard as more important than anything. IN 1995, TNT Express introduced its Perfect Transaction Process, incorporating six elements:

- Collect the consignment on time
- Deliver it in perfect condition
- Deliver it on time
- Include a fully completed delivery note
- Send an accurate invoice to the customer
- Receive payment on time

The proportion of transactions meeting all six performance criteria is now in excess of 90 per cent. Almost 99 per cent of customers receive their consignments on time - and this applies even for circumstances beyond TNT's control, such as bad weather or incorrectly addressed parcels.

IT investment has helped TNT Express to stay ahead. A central computer system has been replaced by a distributed network, with full customer contact details logged on to the customer service management database, including type of business, company contact, hours of business, competitors used, trading frequency, and a full history of every telephone and face-to-face interaction.

Developing Customer Intimacy (4): First Direct

First Direct, originally a division of Midland Bank (now HSBC), targets its banking customers exclusively through the telephone system and, more recently, the Internet. It began operations in 1988 and became profitable from 1993 onwards - a remarkable performance for a company which incurred such high initial, IT-driven costs.

In the words of Moira Clark (Cranfield School of Management, quoted in Management Today, October 1998), "First Direct is a truly customer-centric organisation, which means ... placing the customer at the centre of the organisation and revolving everything around the customer. First Direct not only has a unique understanding of what their customers need now but also of what their customers desire for tomorrow. They are constantly striving to ensure that they recruit, train and develop the right kind of staff to be able to offer service excellence. Finally, a customer-centric organisation means having the vision, values and leadership which inspire customers, staff and stakeholders to want to be part of something very special."

First Direct has a powerful mission - to be "tomorrow's bank today" - and this is supplemented by three vision statements describing how the company will try to exceed the expectations of three sets of stakeholders:

- Customers - the mission is to ensure that they see First Direct as "my bank".
- Employees - the mission is that they see First Direct as "a great place for me to work".
- Shareholders - the mission is "to sustain profitable growth"

The key to understanding the nature and quality of service required by First Direct's customers is development of a comprehensive profile of their past activities, needs, expectations, and future intentions. First Direct knows a great deal about its customers, with dialogue initiated through quarterly surveys, annual focus groups, and independent research carried out through third-party market research companies. Here are just three of the things that First Direct knows:

- 70 per cent of its customers are aged between 25 and 44.
- 38 per cent live in households with annual incomes exceeding £35,000
- 82 per cent are in the ABC1 socio-economic categories

In cultural terms, First Direct is permanently restless and never complacent. As customer expectations rise and change, so organisations like First Direct must not only get better at what they do already, but they must also undergo rebirth: they must relaunch and revitalise themselves in order to keep up with the aspirations of their customers.

Some of the embedded systems and practices to be found in First Direct, to assist in creating a permanent climate of change involving interaction with customers, are as follows:

Customers are involved in the design of new products and services, eg 2000 First Direct customers helped to pilot the 12-month project for the introduction of PC banking.

To avoid repeated transferring between departments, First Direct telephone staff are trained to handle over 80 per cent of calls without the need to switch the caller elsewhere, and they are supported by a fully-integrated IT system.

The company regularly tracks competitors and measures itself against them.

Mass customisation as a route to customer intimacy

2.8 The argument continues to rage about whether it is still legitimate to segment customers into large groups unified against only one dimension or whether segmentation is now dead and has been superseded by the ultimate **segment of one**: the individual customer.

2.9 In some businesses, the individual customer is the only one who matters. If the range of product/service choice on offer doesn't include the specific alternative or combination that the customer seeks, then the customer is as dissatisfied as if he hadn't been offered any choice at all.

2.10 Recent developments in IT have made it possible to direct tailor-made marketing messages to individual customers, and to design specifically-manufactured products for them.

2.11 Once the customer has taught the company what he or she wants, the company must mass customise the product or service to meet the individually expressed need. Organisations, in other words, must recreate the age of the Victorian tailor, who made each item to measure and delivered it to order: this time around, however, the individually-structured products and services must also be **mass-produced** if the approach is to be cost-effective.

2.12 It is claimed that companies which combine **one-to-one marketing** with **mass customisation** can achieve new levels of customer satisfaction, loyalty, and profitability.

Mass customisation

2.13 In some respects, mass customisation is merely the next stage in the development of new manufacturing technologies. In other ways, however, mass customisation is revolutionary rather than incremental: it requires change throughout the company, much more rigorous and focused marketing strategies, a close identification with current (and predicted) customer tastes, highly developed distribution systems and, indeed, a fresh appraisal of the key components within the new value chain.

2.14 There are many areas where mass customisation is already well developed: PCs, insurance policies, cars, shampoo, vitamins, men's suits, bicycles, lighting, and refrigeration equipment. Equally, there are others where acceptance of the need for mass customisation has still some way to go: furniture is a classic instance where customers are frequently told that their preferred choices are unavailable or incapable of being supplied because they are not in the catalogue.

2.15 It has to be understood that **mass customisation is customer-led**, not technology-driven: it enables companies to respond to (and sometimes to anticipate) the changing fragmentation of the market place and the ever-increasing demands of customers.

2.16 Many successful companies have come into existence and prospered precisely because they have challenged conventional beliefs about customer preferences. When First Direct first appeared on the scene and stole competitive thunder from the traditional - and complacent - banking industry, many customers jumped ship and joined up.

Marketing at Work

The National Bicycle Company Of Japan

In this famous example of customisation in action, the company offers bicycles built to the customer's exact measurements. Each bicycle is ready for delivery in a few days, but the National Bicycle Co deliberately delays delivery by a couple of weeks because, if it is any quicker, customers don't believe that the bicycle has actually been customised!

Levi Strauss & Co

The Levi Personal Pair service enables customers to pay a surcharge and have jeans made to order from 4,224 permutations of different measurements. In the sewing plant, the denim is cut by computer numerically controlled machines and then shipped back to the store or direct to the customer. It is relevant to note that the clothes industry was one of the last to be industrialised, and has been one of the first to adopt mass customisation.

2.17 On the negative side, one-to-one marketing is very difficult to **initiate and achieve**. The examples that do exist have generally built themselves around the concept from scratch, like Dell (made-to-order computers), Custom Foot (personalised shoes) and Streamline (home deliveries). It is not always obvious that customers welcome being identified as individuals:

for many, anonymity is preferable, if it means that they are less likely (as they see it) to be pestered by pseudo-personalised communications through E-mail, telephone, the postal system, or even face-to-face meetings. According to one US study led by Harvard Business School assistant professor Susan Fournier, "the very things that marketers are doing to build relationships with customers are often the things that are destroying those relationships."

2.18 For mass customisation to work, says Don Peppers, organisations have to go through four key processes:

- **Identify** individual customers
- **Differentiate** those customers
- **Interact** with the customers; and
- **Redesign the product** or service to reflect each customer's specific needs and wants

2.19 This is easier said than done. Identifying individual customers is easy if you sell aero-engines, but a massive task if you make nails or jars of instant coffee.

2.20 Differentiating between individual customers can also present difficulties. In some markets, such as airlines, a tiny proportion of customers account for a huge percentage of revenue and profits. In other markets, such as bookselling, the value of each customer tends to be more equal. Virtually every bookshop customer's needs are different, and few of them want the same books. But the needs of airline customers, by comparison, tend to be pretty similar. Which means that some industries, where a few customers account for a high proportion of total profit and where the product or service is easily customised, lend themselves more readily to one-to-one marketing.

2.21 Pepper's third step, interaction, is even more difficult than the first two. Companies have to communicate with each of their customers in a way that

- recognises their specific needs and characteristics; and

- persuades them to respond, so that organisational perceptions of the customer can be fine-tuned.

2.22 The problem is further complicated by the variety of ways in which customers can communicate with organisations: phone calls, complaint letters to the Chief Executive, interactive Website connections, faxes, focus groups, questionnaires, surveys, and so forth. If companies are genuinely to claim that they know everything about each customer, they must have enterprise-wide information systems which enable them to assemble a comprehensive history of all customers and their interactions.

Relationship marketing

2.23 Before the evolution of mass markets, the natural approach to marketing was through building a relationship with **individual customers**. The traditional corner shop in the UK, now driven almost to extinction by the power of the big supermarkets, provides an example of a business based on understanding individual customer needs. A good relationship with the customer was essential for repeat business.

2.24 During the twentieth century, **mass media** (television, newspapers, radio) created **mass marketing** and **mass consumption**, aided by production efficiencies. Products became nationally recognisable via distribution and advertising. Technology impacted dramatically

BPP PUBLISHING

on transportation, travel and communications, helping to create a **global market**. The emphasis on individual customer service became, to an extent, diluted.

2.25 This situation is now changing. For example, long-standardised products such as Coca Cola now have different variants (Diet, Cherry) to appeal to different customer segments. Now that there are more products to promote, companies need to **target the market** more carefully.

2.26 Relationship marketing changes the focus away from **getting customers** (which is still seen as vital) towards **keeping customers**. This **change in emphasis** is the most fundamental distinction.

> **Key Concept**
> **Relationship marketing** can be seen as the successor to mass marketing, and is the process by which information about the customer is consistently applied by the company when developing and delivering products and services. Developments are communicated to the customer, for example via specially targeted promotions and product launches, in order to build a 'partnership' with him and encourage a long term relationship by paying attention to his specific needs.

2.27 The term relationship marketing, or relationship management, is used to communicate the idea that a major objective of marketing is to build long-term relationships with the parties who contribute to the organisation's success. Therefore a sale is not the end of the process but distinctively the start of an organisation's relationship with a customer.

2.28 Because service and industrial companies have direct, regular and often multiple contacts with their customers, for example the regular hotel guest who interacts with reception, restaurant and cleaning staff and the sales person who visits the equipment buyer every month and often brings along the technical specialist to meet production personnel, the importance of what Gummerson calls 'part-time' marketers is increased. Customer contact with all employees is vital. The need for **internal marketing** and cross-functional co-ordination increases, and hence the preference for the term **relationship management** (which takes away the functional emphasis on marketing).

2.29 The greater multi-disciplinary perspective of relationship marketing is emphasised by Christopher, Payne and Ballantyne (1992) when they suggest that successful relationship marketing requires the integration of customer service, quality and marketing.

ARE YOU CUSTOMERISED?

1. Do you have <u>as many</u> customers as you want?

☐ Yes   ☐ No

Can a bottom line be too healthy? Of course not. And neither can a growth oriented company have too many customers. They're the engine that generates revenue.

2. Are your customers <u>as loyal</u> as you want?

☐ Yes   ☐ No

It's one thing to gain customers. It's another to keep them. The strength of your business depends largely upon your ability to sustain a relationship with customers.

3. Do you generate <u>as much</u> business from each customer as you want?

☐ Yes   ☐ No

A critical component or business growth is increased sales content. To maximise each business opportunity, you need a way to leverage your entire organisation - to bring it totally to bear at the point of customer contact.

4. Do you <u>really</u> know what your customer want?

☐ Yes   ☐ No

Are you alert to *every* product your customers could use? *Every* service that might interest them? *Every* transaction they're prepared to make? *Every* sale they'd allow you to follow through? Are you thoroughly plugged into your market?

5. Does your <u>entire</u> organisation know what your customers want?

☐ Yes   ☐ No

A customer orientation has limited value unless it's embedded in the very heart of an enterprise - at all levels and at every place that directly or indirectly involves the customer/

6. Is your information strategy <u>focused</u> on helping you hear what customers and markets are trying to tell you?

☐ Yes   ☐ No

The next best thing to reading your customers' minds is listening to what they're saying. But unless you're constantly tuned in to customers' signals, you're missing messages that could guide you to greater results for your business.

7. Can your organisation respond <u>quickly</u> to what customers and markets are telling you?

☐ Yes   ☐ No

When the flow lines of your information system are not within your customer's reach, you won't always sense when opportunity knocks. But even if you do, getting the message is not enough. If you can't reply rapidly to market signals with information, products and services, revenue opportunities are lost.

8. Does your information strategy enable the pro-active delivery of information to your customers?

☐ Yes   ☐ No

Many business plans underestimate the power of information to build customer relationships. But imagine the advantage of an information technology strategy that transforms information into customer-generating, revenue-generating fuel.

9. Are the <u>full</u> capabilities of your organisation accessible to your customers at all your field locations.

☐ Yes   ☐ No

An office. A branch. A retail site. To a customer, that's your company. One small part of the whole. Which is why you need to leverage your entire organisation by extending its capabilities to each point of customer contact.

10. Does your information strategy reflect the <u>bottom-line importance</u> of customer service?

☐ Yes   ☐ No

Business is built on customers. Without them, there is no bottom line. Government is also built on customers, the public. And whether you're in the business of commerce or the business of government, no objective of an information strategy is more fundamental than enhanced customer service.

The bottom line. *If you answered No to any of these questions, you're not yet customerised. But you might well agree that this simple test suggests the enormous advantages of becoming customerised. And as the leader at customerising business and government, Unisys will work with you to provide the answers you need.*

2.30   The notion of trust and keeping promises is also important. To have an ongoing relationship, both parties need to trust each other and keep the promises they make. Marketing moves from one-off potentially manipulative exchanges towards **co-operative relationships** built on financial, social and structural benefits.

2.31   Another characteristic of relationship marketing that distinguishes it from traditional marketing is the idea of **multiple parties,** or a **network** of exchange partners. Customer relationships are important but so too are the relationships which organisations have with other parties such as suppliers, distributors, professional bodies, banks, trade associations etc.

2.32   The distinguishing characteristics of relationship marketing are as follows.

(a)   A focus on **customer retention** rather than attraction.

(b)   The development of an **on-going relationship** as opposed to a one-off transaction.

(c) A **long time scale** rather than short time scale.

(d) **Direct and regular** customer contact rather than impersonal, discrete sales.

(e) **Multiple** employee/customer contacts hence the increased importance of part-time marketers and internal marketing.

(f) **Quality** and customer satisfaction being the concern of all employees rather than just those who work in the marketing department.

(g) Emphasis on **key account relationship management**, service quality and buyer (partner) behaviour rather than the marketing mix.

(h) Importance of **trust** and keeping promises rather than making the sale.

(i) **Multiple exchanges** with a number of parties, network relationships, rather than a single focus on customers.

2.33 Relationship marketing's emphasis on high customer commitment is in keeping with the TQM approach being taken by many British companies in the 1990s. There is increasing recognition that internal customers and indirect customer contacts play crucial roles in the quality of external customer service. Put quite simply, if someone in the despatch department drops a case rather too heavily on the pallet, a subsequent customer complaint of damaged goods is likely to result. Failure of the works office to respond quickly to a sales office telephone enquiry on the progress of a job means a customer is let down and an expensively built-up relationship is tarnished.

'Customers are assets'

2.34 You might already be familiar with the concept of the customer as a current asset - a customer is a debtor. Goodwill - or a company's reputation - is also considered an asset. If you are looking for repeat business, you will expect future benefits from customers.

Marketing at Work

(a) *Coca-Cola* paid $200m to *Pernod* of France, which, under contract, had effectively built a customer base for Coca Cola, as well as building up a distribution network. Coca-Cola wanted to take charge of the marketing of Coke in France.

(b) Many supermarkets have introduced 'loyalty cards' whereby customers are awarded with bonus points, saving them money.

(c) Many banks lose money on student accounts, in the hope that they will earn it back over the customer's life cycle later, as part of a lifetime relationship.

2.35 Technology is the key factor. Software developments have made **databases** flexible and powerful enough to hold large amounts of **customer specific data**. While the corner shop of old recognised customers visually, companies today can recognise them electronically.

2.36 Relationship marketing is particularly relevant in business-to-business contexts. Many suppliers will share joint development with key customers. We illustrate some of the approaches taken in section 4 of this chapter.

2.37 Recently there has been a backlash against relationship marketing especially as applied to the consumer sector. Not all customers want a relationship and resent the potential intrusion. Furthermore, many firms practise relationship marketing purely as an information gathering exercise. Does the customer benefit?

Customer care

2.38 Customer care is not just the responsibility of the sales and marketing team. It involves all personnel whose actions have an impact on the customer. But marketing and sales staff, who have a direct involvement with the client, are those employees most obviously charged with the customer care responsibilities.

2.39 As we have established, **customer care is fundamental to a marketing orientation**. It is a direct statement that the customer matters and it is the organisation's intention to look after the needs of the customer (ie care about what the customer thinks and wants).

2.40 The quality of service offered by a company or a salesperson can be considered in two distinct parts:

- what they do (**technical** expertise)
- how they do it (**functional** expertise)

2.41 Those coming from a product orientated organisation are frequently expert technically (eg engineers and other specialists,) but are much weaker at client relations.

2.42 Good sales and marketing people have to wear both hats. In other words they must be knowledgeable about their products, but they must also 'care' about their customers.

2.43 Such an approach results in a change in the salesperson's role from:

- selling more goods (product orientated approach); to
- solving the customer's problems (customer orientated approach).

This change in positioning requires management support and commitment as well. Emphasis on short term sales targets instead of long term customer relationships is likely to produce a 'task orientated' sales force.

2.44 Future business relationships might become more 'people based'. Increasingly, companies are looking to develop **long term relationships with suppliers** they can trust and with whom they can tackle problems and develop opportunities. This symbiotic approach, advocated by those pursuing a total quality approach to management, is the basis of relationship marketing.

2.45 Customer care has to be inspired by the **culture** of the business. It has to be supported by **management actions** which facilitate problem solving for the customer. It can only be implemented when staff are trained, so they have the skills necessary to ensure they provide a quality service. This often means encouraging others in the business to see their role as supporting those spearheading the organisation.

2.46 It is increasingly being recognised that the satisfaction of **external customers** is the result of a sum of **internal transactions** between colleagues and departments. Encouraging staff to consider the needs of their internal customers, defined as, 'the next person to handle your work', will help ensure quality and excellence in the business. Customer care:

- is part of the purchase benefits that a product provides
- can be a source of differentiation
- can be a valuable source of information

BPP PUBLISHING

3 COMMUNICATING WITH CUSTOMERS

3.1 In the UK and elsewhere, **customers now expect consumer durables to function effectively**, irrespective of whichever brand or manufacturer's products are being purchased. As a result, **perceived quality is less significant** as a brand discriminator than once was the case when (for example) the reports of the Consumers Association were assiduously studied in order to isolate the 'best buy' in any given product field. In many respects, therefore, **functional performance has been replaced by appearance, price, service and other more intangibles** as opportunities for market share and profitability.

3.2 Supporting this view is the fact that the average person, in the UK, takes only 12 minutes in order to decide which refrigerator, washing machine or vacuum cleaner to buy. This implies that **much less detailed consideration is being given to performance variables**.

3.3 Moreover, many consumer item purchases are '**distress**' transactions: people buy a new freezer because their existing one has irrevocably broken down, rather than because they want to upgrade. When making a 'distress' purchase, customers are often anxious to reduce the pain of the exercise, for example by reducing the time taken.

3.4 Equivalent to a distress purchase is the **distress telephone call**, when customers find it necessary to contact, say, one of the utilities, or a servicing organisation, or a retailer, in order to make enquiries, place orders, report problems and so forth.

3.5 A 1998 survey by the Henley Centre found that only 10 per cent of customers start out feeling 'cheerful and optimistic' when embarking on a telephone call to an organisation; and most of these are **rapidly driven to 'anger and fury'** as a direct result of their efforts. Phrases calculated to irritate many customers to distraction include:

> Your call is being held in a queue
>
> If you have a touch-tone telephone press button number one if your query concerns ...

3.6 The key factor **pleasing customers**, not surprisingly, was the extent to which calls were received by 'live' operators. Relatively speaking, banks scored highly on this front, whilst the utility companies' handling of customers over the telephone resulted in one in four feeling 'irritated, furious or annoyed'. Although the use of interactive voice response (IVR) systems was occasionally welcomed - notably in booking cinema seats - **fewer than one in five customers felt happy** with the telephone service they received, according to Henley. As their study pointedly concludes: 'Thousands of times each day the perceived brand values of many companies are being shaped and distorted by the way they treat their customers on the telephone.'

Marketing at Work

Bernard Katz (*How to turn Customer Service into Customer Sales*, 1987) tells the following story.

He made telephone enquiries to ten companies: British Airways, British Rail, Alpine Double Glazing, Crittall Windows, Thermobreak, Bristol Street Motors, Oxford Motors, Kwik Fit Euro, Electricity Board and Anglia Water. All the calls were tape-recorded.

The tapes were **played** to course members. Before listening to the calls, the delegates were told the name of the company and the nature of the enquiry made. Participants were asked to rate, on a scale of 1 to 10, the expectation of service that would be provided. If an extremely bad response was expected, the rating was 0. If superlative service was expected, the rating was 10.

After listening to the calls, delegates are asked to rate the same company again. What quality of response did they now expect from the company, in the light of what they had just heard?

The results of this exercise are always the same:

- Where a company is **upgraded**, the level of expectation rises by an average of **one point**.
- Where a company is **downgraded**, the level of expectation falls by an average of **three points**.

This is reminiscent of the experience of the Ford Motor Company in the USA, who carried out a survey of customers buying their cars.

- Satisfied customer, on average, tell 8 people
- Dissatisfied customers, on average, tell 22.

Four factors contributing to a good telephone manner

Good communication

3.7 Good communication is achieved when messages sent by one party are received by the other party in the same format, without distortion. Good communication requires that:

- both parties have the **same frame of reference**
- both parties agree to use **common units and scales**
- both parties **check frequently** to confirm that **meanings are clear** and as intended
- **language is simple** rather than complicated; sentences are **short** rather than long

Speaking clearly

3.8 The following lists of Do's and Don'ts suggest what should be done and what should be avoided.

- **Do's** about speaking clearly

  Hold the **mouthpiece** in correct position   **Pause** occasionally
  Breathe normally   Speak **slowly**
  Use **short sentences**

- **Don'ts** about speaking clearly

  Don't **mumble**   Don't use **jargon**
  Don't **eat, drink or smoke** while talking   Don't **interrupt yourself** or others
  Don't **shout**

Empathy

3.9 Empathy is seeing the situation from the **other's point of view**: understanding (and predicting) how the person being spoken to is reacting to (or is likely to react to) what is being said.

Courtesy

3.10 Irrespective of the nature of the phone call, **courtesy** should be an integral part of the process. Lack of courtesy is often an emphatic indicator of the **emotional feelings of the speaker.**

Golden rules for answering a phone call

Smile as you pick up the receiver

3.11 Whether face-to-face or from the other end of a telephone, a friendly and courteous manner communicates itself. Smiling at the end of the day is harder than smiling first thing in the morning, but with practice, smiling becomes a habit.

Give the incoming call your undivided attention

3.12 **Don't try to combine answering the phone with something else,** like signalling your coffee order to a colleague, or reading the newspaper, or doodling. The fact that you are distracted (and therefore not paying attention) is likely to transmit itself to the caller, especially if he/she hears you speaking to someone else during the call.

Identify (yourself and) your department

3.13 It is important to **say who you are**: 'Hello' is friendly but is neither productive nor efficient. When the call is through a switchboard, giving the name of your department may be sufficient, and certainly the company or department name should be given before your own.

3.14 The **actual name** of the person answering the call is **not relevant all the time**. It's not applicable, for example, when someone is asking the price of theatre seats, seeking a telephone number from directory enquiries, or needing the day's weather forecast. On the other hand, the name is **important if the caller is likely to expect action** arising from the call, because a name then becomes the **point of contact**.

Establish the caller's needs

3.15 Find out by **questioning**. Sometimes the needs are volunteered by the caller, but not everyone is articulate and many people have difficulty in expressing themselves - they may not even be sure what they want, or whether they are talking to someone appropriate. Questions, if required, should pinpoint the **general area** of help needed in the first instance, and then gradually **home in on the more localised and specific issues**.

3.16 Callers' needs should be **written on a pad**. Many companies have special **forms**, or use appropriate **software/hardware** incorporating VDUs.

Provide the information

3.17 **Telling the customer what you're doing,** whilst you're doing it, breaks up the silence. If it is necessary for you to put the telephone down or leave the desk/counter for a moment, say so. If you are going to transfer the caller to another extension or number, say what you're doing and give a positive reason for doing it (rather than creating the impression that you're just passing the buck).

3.18 In the case of **calling back**, procedure must be very strict. Promises that are not kept create bad business and poor relationships. It is best to present the customer with **options** ('Will you hold on, or shall I call you back?') and also to undertake to ring back **within a designated period** or at a **specific time** ('I'll contact you between 3.30 and 4, if that's going to be convenient for you').

Close the call

3.19 Make sure that the customer concludes the enquiry with the feeling that the company/ department **cares**. Enquirers after information are thanked for their interest; callers seeking action must go away believing that the organisation is going to respond. It is especially relevant, for 'action' calls, to give and re-emphasise your name (as the person to contact if anything further goes wrong).

Dealing with complaints

3.20 The main requirement is to **listen** in order to elicit the full details of the complaint. Never argue.

Dealing with angry customers

3.21 Angry customers do not always slot easily into the standard response format. The anger is communicated strongly the moment contact with a company employee is achieved. The important rules to remember are: **listen,** be **sympathetic,** be **diplomatic,** and **never argue**.

3.22 The prime emphasis must be on **listening**. The customer who is not materially interrupted will eventually defuse his/her anger to the point where appropriate action can be set in motion in accordance with normal customer response procedures.

Keep callers informed

3.23 When action has been promised and delay is occurring, telephone the caller to advise the situation. **Good customer relations disintegrate rapidly when promised action fails to materialise**.

3.24 When it is apparent that a promised schedule or deadline is not going to be maintained, one phone call represents the difference between customer tolerance and customer anger.

Automated call handling

3.25 Robert Hollier, who helped compile a report for Cable and Wireless on British telephone-based services, has found that the way companies use telecommunications has a **direct impact on profits**. 'If you can get it right then you can reduce your payroll burden by 60 per cent with people working from their homes,' he says. 'But what has been omitted until now has been the consumer's reaction' (report in the *Sunday Telegraph*, 1998).

3.26 It is certainly true that **automated call handling (ACH),** where the robot voice asks callers to make choices by pressing phone buttons, enables user organisations to enjoy considerable cost savings. In some fields, too, the increased application of ACH has not caused customer-satisfaction backlash. Odeon Cinemas, for example, installed a £1 million automated call centre in Bromley in the face of rising cinema attendance and a related appetite for pre-booking; the system handles bookings for 52 cinema sites nationwide, and fortunately only a relatively small proportion find it daunting to talk to a machine. Odeon has not been indifferent to the reactions of this group, and they now provide an option enabling customers to **switch to a human operator** if that is what they prefer.

3.27 Stephen Farish, editor of *PR Week* (quoted in *Management Today*, April 1997) has a commonsense approach for all organisations deciding whether automated call handling is for their customers as well as themselves: 'The guiding principles with all these systems is **whether it makes the customer's life easier or not**.' He draws an unfavourable comparison with another major automated development from the 1980s, namely, hole-in-the-wall banking, which was readily accepted by customers (though, again, not by all of them). Getting customers to accept ACH or IVR is, relatively speaking, an uphill struggle.

Customer feedback

3.28 Customer feedback is an essential piece of management information and is a cheap source of market research. To quote Ted Johns (*Perfect Customer Care*) companies need to be able to find out answers to the following questions.

- Who are our customers?
- When are they likely to be our customers?
- Why are they our customers?
- What do our customers want?
- How do our customers feel?
- What do our customers think?
- How can we make our customers feel valued?
- What sort of initiatives would our customers appreciate?
- What can we do to keep our customers?
- How can we give ourselves a competitive advantage as far as our customers are concerned?

3.29 There are various ways of finding out what customers want. Relying on personal experiences, anecdotal evidence and customer complaints management can produce valuable lessons for any organisation. Formal customer research (surveys and questionnaires) and informal data collection (customer feedback phone lines) may also be used. Other methods are described below.

Focus groups

3.30 Group discussions are useful in providing the organisation with qualitative data about customer opinions of products and services. Qualitative data can often provide greater insight than quantitative data.

3.31 Group discussions usually consist of up to 20 respondents and an interviewer taking the role of group moderator. The group moderator introduces topics for discussion and intervenes as necessary to encourage respondents or to direct discussions if they threaten to wander too far off the point. The moderator will also need to control any powerful personalities and prevent them from dominating the group.

3.32 Group discussions are often used at the early stage of research to get a feel for the subject matter under discussion and to create possibilities for more structured research. Four to eight groups may be assembled and each group interviewed for one, two or three hours.

Complaints management

3.33 This was discussed in Chapter 2.

Suggestion schemes

3.34 Another variant is the **suggestion scheme**, where payments or prizes are offered to customers (or staff) to come up with workable ideas on improving efficiency or quality, new marketing initiatives or solutions to problems. There is motivational value in getting staff involved in problem-solving and planning, and staff are often in the best position to provide practical and creative solutions to their work problems or the customer's needs. Added incentives will help to overcome any reluctance on the part of staff to put forward ideas (because it is seen as risky, or doing management's job for them, or whatever).

Direct marketing

3.35 Theodore Levitt once stated that 'The sole purpose of a business is to create and keep a customer'. In brief, the aims of direct marketing are to **acquire and retain customers**. Here are two further definitions.

(a) The Institute of Direct Marketing in the UK define direct marketing as 'The planned recording, analysis and tracking of customer behaviour to develop relational marketing strategies'.

(b) The Direct Marketing Association in the US define direct marketing as 'An interactive system of marketing which uses one or more advertising media to effect a measurable response and/or transaction at any location'.

3.36 It is worth studying these definitions and noting some key words and phases.

(a) **Response**: direct marketing is about getting people to send in coupons, or make telephone calls in response to invitations and offers.

(b) **Interactive**: it is a two-way process, involving the supplier and the customer.

(c) **Relationship**: it is in many instances an on-going process of selling again and again to the same customer.

(d) **Recording and analysis**: response data are collected and analysed so that the most cost-effective procedures may be arrived at. Direct marketing has been called 'marketing with numbers'. It aims to take the waste out of marketing.

(e) **Strategy**: direct marketing should not be seen merely as a 'quick fix', a 'one-off mailing', a promotional device. It should be seen as a part of a comprehensive plan stemming from clearly formulated objectives.

3.37 Direct marketing creates and develops a direct relationship between the customer and the company on an individual basis. It is a form of direct supply, embracing both a variety of alternative media channels (like direct mail), and a choice of distribution channels (like mail order). Because direct marketing removes all channel intermediaries apart from the advertising medium and the delivery medium, there are no resellers, therefore avoiding loss of control and loss of revenue.

Components of direct marketing

3.38 Direct marketing encompasses a wide range of media and distribution opportunities which include the following;

- Television
- Radio
- Direct mail
- Direct response advertising
- Telemarketing
- Statement stuffers
- Inserts
- Take-ones
- Electronic media
- Door to door
- Mail order
- Computerised home shopping
- Home shopping networks

In developing a comprehensive direct marketing strategy, organisations will often utilise a range of different yet complementary techniques.

Marketing at Work

Land Rover won the gold award in the 1995 Direct Marketing Association/ Royal Mail awards for the second time.

'The reason is not hard to find. Having developed the first all-new Range Rover for 25 years – a major investment that is crucial to the future of the company – Land Rover took the gutsy decision to launch it solely through direct marketing.

The total cost of the direct marketing programme was £340,000 – small beer against the £6m which many car manufacturers would earmark for an important launch – but although it involved high-quality creative work, appropriate for customers prepared to spend £40,000 on a car, the major part of the budget went on logistics involved in managing a very complex operation.

The database included 7,000 Range Rover owners, past and present, and a further 5,000 prospects who were owners of other luxury cars. They were invited to a series of launch events which 127 Range Rover dealers were staging over two days.

As part of the launch, the Range Rover was to be sent on three epic expeditions – to Vermont, Patagonia and Japan.

Exploiting this, Craik Jones [the agency] developed three teaser postcards to fix the launch date in the prospects' minds – one consequence of which, incidentally had the agency trying to find 12,000 autumn leaves in the middle of summer. Personal invitations followed from the local dealers.

Showrooms were crowded on the launch days, with attendances averaging over 94%. And sales were high, with at least one dealer selling his first three months allocation on the spot.

Source: Marketing: The 1995 DMA/Royal Mail Direct Marketing Awards (1996)

Direct mail

3.39 Direct mail has been one of the largest and fastest growing advertising media of recent years. Between 1981 and 1991, the number of mailings received per head of household increased from 18 to 31.

3.40 Direct mail tends to be the main medium of **direct response advertising**. The reason for this is that other major media, newspapers and magazines, are familiar to people in advertising in other contexts. Newspaper ads can include coupons to fill out and return, and radio and TV can give a phone number to ring. Direct mail has a number of strengths as a direct response medium.

(a) The advertiser can target down to **individual** level.

(b) The communication can be **personalised**. Known data about the individual can be used, and parts of a letter can be altered to accommodate this.

(c) The medium is good for **reinforcing interest** stimulated by other media such as TV. It can supply the **response mechanism**, such as a coupon.

(d) The opportunity to use different **creative formats** is almost unlimited.

(e) **Testing potential** is sophisticated: a limited number of items can be sent out to a test segment and the results can then be evaluated. As success is achieved, so the mailing campaign can be rolled out.

(f) What you do is **less visible to your competitors** than other forms of media.

3.41 There are, however, a number of weaknesses with direct mail.

(a) There is obvious concern over the negative association with **junk mail** and the need for individuals to exercise their right to **privacy**.

(b) **Lead times** may be considerable when taking into consideration the creative organisation, finished artwork, printing, proofing, stuffing envelopes and finally the mailing.

(c) The most important barrier to direct mail is that it can be very **expensive** on a per capita basis. A delivered insert can be 24 to 32 times more expensive than a full page colour advert in a magazine. It therefore follows that the mailshot must be powerful and **well targeted** to overcome such a cost penalty.

Customer service & electronic commerce - customer perceptions

3.42 E-commerce is an avenue for generating a close relationship between customer and supplier. Every visitor to a company website is there because he wants to be there to see what the company has to offer. The first part of the connection has been made, but many companies engaging in e-commerce then fail to capitalise on it. The following is a review of some studies into customer perceptions of e-commerce.

Report by Shelley Taylor & Associates (1999)

3.43 The majority of online stores do not offer the degree of customer service that consumers receive at offline stores. Many merchants are failing to create a successful shopping experience.

3.44 A quarter of online stores do not provide a navigation guide for moving around the store; the same proportion fail to give any pre-sale assistance; 32 per cent offer no purchase instructions; only 12 per cent offer third-party reviews of products; 30 per cent of sites offer information on product availability; only 8 percent update consumers about the items currently included in their online shopping cart.

Forrester Research (1999)

3.45 So far, today's sites are not addressing the real potential of the Internet economy. Look-to-buy ratios are low - similar to typical direct-mail yields - with 2.7 buyers for every 100 visitors. Today's sites mostly take orders for low-consideration products; most orders completed over the Net are for easy-to-buy, strongly branded products.

Booz & Hamilton (1999)

3.46 The survey ("Competing in the Digital Age: Will the Internet Change Corporate Strategy?") was conducted in conjunction with the Economist Intelligence Unit; it involved 525 interviews in various European countries. The majority (89 per cent) had corporate Websites, but only 56 per cent offered customer service and 37 per cent were e-commerce enabled.

Marketing at Work

Safeway Palm Pilots

Source: *Daily Telegraph*, 29 April 1999

Safeway has given away PalmPilots to around 200 ABC card holders currently using the Collect-and-Go service at Basingstoke.

BPP PUBLISHING

Safeway is able to analyse four months of purchases for each shopper and come up with a definitive list of the items they buy. Most of us have a personal shopping list of no more than 150 items, so this makes a manageable subset of the store's 25,000 lines.

Shoppers can select their order from this list, or scan the barcodes of items in their cupboards, couple the PalmPilot to the telephone and download the order.

Safeway is also able to produce promotional items likely to appeal to individual customers - these are downloaded automatically whenever the PalmPilot is connected.

Safeway already works with Abbey National on financial services, so electronic banking is a further option for this approach.

---

4 CUSTOMER/SUPPLIER PARTNERSHIPS AND AGREEMENTS

Relationships with suppliers

4.1 While relationship marketing is concerned with customers, long-term business relationships can be built up with **favoured suppliers**. There are several factors behind this trend.

(a) Some firms have relationships with favoured suppliers rather than a free-for-all of suppliers competing for business on the basis of price.

(b) Just-in-time production methods, whereby supplies are delivered often and in small quantities, require a relationship of trust between supplier and customer.

(c) Relationships with favoured suppliers are encouraged by the total quality movement.

4.2 Supplier relationships can be built up in a number of ways. Here are some examples.

(a) Staff secondments.

(b) Joint research and development projects.

(c) Electronic Data Interchange (EDI), which link the sales order and stock control system of both companies.

4.3 The end result of the relationship approach from the company's point of view is a **reduction in vulnerability to changing customer and supplier demands**: the bargaining powers of customers and suppliers are effectively managed in a marketing network.

> **Exam tip**
> Check that you can give a clear definition of relationship marketing. This could be asked for in the exam.

Partnership sourcing and partnership marketing

4.4 **Partnership sourcing** and **partnership marketing** are other concepts which you may be asked to compare. The emphasis is on working together with all members of a value chain (suppliers, wholesalers, retailers and so on) to make sure that customer's needs are met profitably.

Key Concepts

From the perspective of a manufacturer, **partnership sourcing** implies a company seeking co-operation as it works back through the value chain. By contrast, **partnership marketing** implies co-operation as it works forwards through its value chain.

4.5 Essential features of partnership sourcing are as follows:

- joint involvement in new product development
- joint solution of distribution problems
- emphasis on long-term price stability
- quality standards which are consistent and to an agreed level

4.6 Partnership marketing implies the following:

- joint **promotional activity** shared by a manufacturer and its wholesalers and retailers

- joint **research** to assess customers needs

- joint **monitoring** of quality standards

- joint **new product development** which is focused on meeting customers' identified needs

4.7 Another type of arrangement is the **co-maker agreement**. The examples below illustrate them at work, and show the benefits to be gained.

Marketing at Work

From Mustang Industrial Corp web site

Co-maker relationships: The 'co-maker' relationships between our customers/suppliers and us are well established. Before our customers develop their new products, their designers will ask for our comments from the view points of a tool maker. With this kind of **communication**, the designers can avoid many mistakes and impractical designs.

Before we start to make products for our customers, we keep **feeding back** our professional suggestions, such as how to improve the design for increasing productivity and quality for the customer's benefit. Furthermore, we believe that 'our suppliers and us are on the same boat.'

Our quality control section staff are willing to help our suppliers to improve their quality and management in order that we can help each other.

From Magneti Marelli web site

Magneti Marelli is a leading international company in automotive systems and components with a high electronics content.

The basic product and process know-how within a company is no longer the key factor in achieving an effective and efficient product development process. Rather, the number and complexity of technologies in today's products require a **wide range of technological capabilities and competencies** and huge investments in human, technological and financial resources. These investments are both too large and too risky to be undertaken by a single company.

Rather, companies prefer to establish a **network of relationships** that allows them to **share costs, benefits an risks** when a new product must be designed and launched. Know-how and knowledge is provided by people who contribute to product development either as single individuals or as a team. The way these teams and individuals are organised to carryout product development is critical to business growth.

Given these various changes, all companies in the car industry are continuously seeking new ways to address competitive pressures. Recognising the need to shorten development cycles, improve quality and increase productivity has historically led these companies to **collaborative relationships** - relationships that can be facilitated and supported by the implementation of information and communication technologies.

BPP PUBLISHING

This increasing collaboration has in turn changed the industry's **competitive structure**, so that the competition is increasingly between groups of companies rather than between individual companies. These groups of companies, organised as networks, are composed of both competitors and suppliers.

The agreements linking network members may take various forms - partnerships, joint ventures, **co-maker relationships** and so on. Within a network, various inter-organisational projects are established to strengthen and leverage trust and openness relationships.

Against this background, at the end of the 80s Magneti Marelli changed it mission and organisation from product supplier to **strategic partner** capable of providing complete high-tech solutions. Recognising the importance of collaborative relationships, the company has formed and participated in several networks and network related projects.

Chapter roundup

- Long term relationships with customers are generally more profitable than one-off transactions.

- Loyalty can be defined as 'voluntary repurchasing and referral'.

- Marketers are increasingly classifying customers according to their level of commitment to brands, using terminology such as **'entrenched'**, **'average'**, **'shallow'** or **'convertible'**.

- The argument continues to rage about whether it is still legitimate to segment customers into large groups unified against only one dimension or whether segmentation is now dead and has been superseded by the ultimate **segment of one**: the individual customer.

- Relationship marketing changes the focus away from **getting customers** (which is still seen as vital) towards **keeping customers**. This **change in emphasis** is the most fundamental distinction.

- Customers can be regarded as assets because they can bring future benefits in the form of repeat business.

- Recently there has been a backlash against relationship marketing especially as applied to the consumer sector. Not all customers want a relationship and resent the potential intrusion.

- Customer care is fundamental to a marketing orientation.

- Customer feedback is an essential piece of management information and is a cheap source of market research.

- The Institute of Direct Marketing in the UK define direct marketing as 'The planned recording, analysis and tracking of customer behaviour to develop relational marketing strategies'. Direct marketing creates and develops a direct relationship between the customer and the company on an individual basis.

- E-commerce is an avenue for generating a close relationship between customer and supplier. But many companies engaging in e-commerce fail to capitalise on it.

- While relationship marketing is concerned with customers, long-term business relationships can be built up with **favoured suppliers**.

Quick quiz

1   What are satisfied customers likely to do? (see para 2.1)

2   What is mass customisation? (2.8)

3   What might organisations have to do in order for mass customisation to work? (2.18)

4   What are some distinguishing characteristics of relationship marketing? (2.32)

5   What is a 'distress' transaction? (3.3)

6   What does good communication require? (3.7)

7   What are some golden rules for answering a phone call? (3.11-3.24)

8   How can a company find out what customers want? (3.29)

9   How can suggestion schemes help with customer service? (3.36)

10   Give some examples of media and distribution opportunities that employ direct marketing. (3.40)

11   What are some of the strengths of direct mail? (3.42)

12   Why might a company want to cultivate a long term relationship with a favoured supplier? (4.3)

Action Programme Review

1   Here are some suggestions.

(a)   It means that regular customers will support the supplier when times are hard. It will be difficult for competitors to attract customers away from their favoured supplier.

(b)   Regular customers provide reliable income and turnover.

(c)   It is possible to build rapport with customers over time. This helps the supplier understand their needs more easily, thus making the marketing process more straightforward.

(d)   Customer loyalty is also a source of goodwill. It will enhance the supplier organisation's image and can be a source of very potent advertising in that customers may recommend the supplier to their friends or colleagues.

7 Innovation and the culture of continuous improvement

Chapter Topic List	Syllabus reference
1 Setting the scene	2.4
2 Avenues for customer-focused innovation	2.4
3 Sources of innovation	2.4
4 Organisational barriers to innovation	2.4
5 Marketing research and customer-focused innovation	2.4

Learning Outcomes

- After studying this chapter you will appreciate the role that innovation has to play in the arena of customer service.

- You will know about the sources of innovation and understand some of the barriers that can hamper it.

Key Concepts Introduced

- Innovation
- Invention
- The learning organisation

- Bureaucracy
- Procedure

Examples of Marketing at Work

- Philips
- Nestle

- Distribution
- British Airways

1 SETTING THE SCENE

1.1 **Innovation** is a term that is often associated with change.

> **Key Concept**
>
> **Innovation** is making something new or doing something in a different way. It may be a new product, but it also covers new ways of satisfying customers, new ways of carrying out routine activities, new linkages in the value chain, new approaches to work and organisation structure.
>
> **Invention** is more precise in meaning, as it refers to a new technique, 'gadget' or product.

1.2 For most firms, a strategy of growth or even survival must include plans for innovation.

(a) Innovation provides the organisation with a **distinctive competence** and with the ability to maintain such a competence.

(b) It helps maintain the organisation's **competitive advantage**. Innovation might underpin one of the generic strategies. Innovation in products is a source of differentiation, and enables the maintenance of this strategy.

(c) New products and/or markets might achieve **greater profitability** than mere expansion.

(d) A **leaner structure** - layers of management or administration may be done away with, and the need for specialist support may be reduced.

(e) Less formality in structure and style leads to **better communication**.

1.3 One of the necessary corollaries of innovation is **increased delegation**. Part of the creed is to give subordinates more authority so they can 'have their head' and act on creative ideas. In itself delegation has great value - morale and performance are improved, top management is freed for strategic planning and decisions are made by those 'on the ground' and therefore more 'in the know'. Most importantly the organisation benefits from the imagination and thinking of its high flyers.

1.4 The dilemma is between the need to be innovative and the need to retain control so as to prevent anarchy. This can be done simply by giving employees and managers parameters within which discretion can be exercised, and by ensuring that they know they are accountable for their actions.

2 AVENUES FOR CUSTOMER-FOCUSED INNOVATION

2.1 Some changes might result in going back to something that was done before: change doesn't necessarily mean doing something entirely new.

2.2 The rate of change might be fast or slow, depending on the organisation's circumstances, and the environment in which it operates. Organisations which operate in a rapidly-changing environment need to be innovative, and responsive to change, if they are to survive and grow. Very few organisations operate in a static environment.

The value of innovation

2.3 The chief object of being innovative is to ensure that organisation's survival and success in a changing world. It can also have the following advantages.

(a) Improvements in quality of **product and service**.

(b) A **leaner structure** - layers of management or administration may be done away with, and the need for specialist support may be reduced.

(c) Prompt and imaginative **solutions to problems** (through use of project teams).

(d) **Less formality** in structure and style - leading to better communication.

(e) **Greater confidence** inside and outside the organisation in its ability to cope with change.

Exam tip

Innovation can help a company stay ahead of its competitors. This fits in with the senior examiner's focus on customer power and the belief that 'the ability to relate proactively and **imaginatively** to their customers will be major opportunities for competitive advantage in the foreseeable future'.

Encouraging innovation

2.4 To encourage innovation the objective for management should be to create a more outward-looking organisation.

(a) People should be encouraged to look for new products, markets, processes and designs.

(b) People should seek ways to improve productivity.

2.5 Thomas Attwood suggests the following steps for creating an innovative culture from one which has previously existed in a cosy, unthreatening world.

(a) Ensure management and staff know what innovation is and how it happens.
(b) Ensure that senior managers welcome, and are seen to welcome, changes for the better.
(c) Stimulate and motivate management and staff to think and act innovatively.
(d) Understand people in the organisation and their needs.
(e) Recognise and encourage potential 'entrepreneurs'.

2.6 An innovation strategy calls for a management policy of **giving encouragement** to innovative ideas. This will require the following.

(a) Giving **financial backing** to innovation, by spending on R & D and market research and risking capital on new ideas.

(b) Giving employees the **opportunity** to work in an environment where the exchange of ideas for innovation can take place. Management style and organisation structure can help here.

 (i) Management can actively encourage employees and customers to put forward new ideas.

 (ii) **Development teams** can be set up and an organisation built up on project team-work.

 (iii) **Quality circles** and brainstorming groups can be used to encourage creative thinking about work issues.

(c) Where appropriate, **recruitment policy** should be directed towards appointing employees with the necessary skills for doing innovative work. Employees should be trained and kept up to date.

(d) Certain managers should be **made responsible for obtaining information** from outside the organisation about innovative ideas, and for **communicating** this information throughout the organisation.

(e) **Strategic planning** should result in targets being set for innovation, and successful achievements by employees should if possible be rewarded.

Creativity and innovation

2.7   Management can also create conditions in which risk-taking, creativity and enthusiasm for change is impossible.

Action Programme 1

Fishpaste Ltd is a business making adhesives. One of the employees, during the course of some research into adhesives, discovers a dryish glue that will not quite stick properly. It holds things in place, but two pieces of paper stuck together with this glue can be easily separated without damage to either. What do you do with the tub of glue and the employee?

The management of growth and stability

2.8   An organisation will usually seek to grow by increasing its range of products and markets, its sales turnover and its profits. At the least, it will seek stability with a secure and stable level of sales turnover and profits. Companies might seek to grow organically, by developing their own internal resources, or else to grow by merger and acquisition (in takeover). Many companies seek growth through a combination of the two strategies.

Innovation and growth

2.9   If a company operates in a market with a good prospect for growth, it can grow organically either by exploiting existing product-market opportunities or by diversifying. However, because existing products have a finite life, a strategy of organic growth must include plans for innovation - developing new products.

Innovation and stability

2.10   Stability calls for innovation too. An organisation cannot rely on its existing products and markets for ever, because products have a finite life, and customer demands change. An organisation which wants to maintain its sales and profits must therefore develop new or improved products, or new markets, to replace the old ones in decline. It is a case of having to keep on running just to stand still.

2.11   An innovation strategy should take a broad view of what sort of innovations should be sought. A product might be completely new, or just a different quality version of an existing product. A new product is not necessarily much different from existing products; rather, the essential characteristic is that it should be distinguishable from its predecessors in the eyes of its customers.

2.12   The car industry provides a very good example of the different types of product innovation. Some years ago, the hatchback was a fairly major innovation. Different quality versions of basically the same model are now a common feature of the car market. Modifications to existing models are made regularly, to keep consumers interested and wanting to buy.

New product strategies

2.13   Innovation can mean creating new markets as well as new products - creating extra demand from existing customers in a 'strengthened' market, or creating new demand from new customers. A matrix of new product strategies and new market strategies can be set out as follows. (The analysis was first presented by Johnson and Jones.)

New product and market strategies

Product

	No technological change	Improved technology	New technology
Market unchanged		Reformulation A new balance between price/quality has to be formulated	Replacement The new technology replaces the old
Market strengthened (new demand from same customers)	Remerchandising The product is sold in a new way — e.g. by repackaging	Improved product Sales growth to existing customers sought on the strength of product improvements	Product line extension The new product is added to the existing product line to increase total demand
New Market	New use By finding a new use for the existing product, new customers are found	Market extension New customers sought on the strength of product improvements	Diversification

Motives for growth

2.14 W H Starbuck suggested various motives for organisational growth.

(a) Organisations may pursue their mission by attempting to realise their ultimate objective. This may involve providing a more complete service to customers, say by expanding geographically or by vertical integration.

(b) Executives might like the **challenge and adventure** of a new gamble. Boredom with the existing situation might prompt changes.

(c) The **power** of individuals and their job security may be enhanced by growth.

(d) Executive **salaries** are likely to rise as a result of increasing turnover (rather than by increasing profits).

(e) Growth may lead to **profit maximisation**.

(f) Growth may lead to **economies of scale**.

(g) Large organisations tend to more **stable** than small ones. The desire for stability may lead to growth.

New products

2.15 The development of new products might be considered an important aspect of a firm's competitive and marketing strategies.

(a) New and innovating products can lower entry barriers to existing industries and markets, if new technology is involved.

(b) The market for any product changes over time and its life. The interests of the company are therefore best met with a balanced product portfolio. Managers therefore must plan when to introduce new products, how best to extend the life of mature ones and when to abandon those in decline.

2.16 A strategic issue managers must consider is their approach to new product development (NPD).

(a) **Leader strategy.** Do they intend to gain competitive advantage by operating at the leading edge of new developments - in which case there are significant implications for the R&D activity and the likely length of products life cycles within the portfolio.

(b) **Follower strategy.** Alternatively they can be more pro-active, adopt a follower strategy, which involves lower costs and less emphasis on the R & D activity. It sacrifices early rewards of innovation, but avoids its risks. A follower might have to license certain technologies from a leader (as in the case with many consumer electronics companies).

Marketing at Work

Philips, Europe's largest consumer electronics group, is to limit the extent to which it stakes its future on product breakthroughs - aiming for predictability in growth rather than seeking rewards in expensive and risky innovations.

The company - in earlier years inventor both of the compact disk and the failed V2000 video system - came close to bankruptcy in 1991 but recovered to achieve record net profits of Fl 2.52bn ($1.33bn)four years later before sliding back into a Fl 590m loss last year.

Mr Boonstra, new president for the company aids, 'Again and again we have proved vulnerable to market fluctuations, to the trade cycle, to success or lack of success with a particular product.

'We then put all our faith in a new invention, a new product, as if it is some magic wand that will solve all our problems with the market, the competition and price erosion. And if it fails to live up to its promise, we suffer setbacks.

'We are now seeking to break out of this cycle of all-or-nothing offensives.

Under Mr Boonstra's cuts a number of projects from the Timmer era have been abandoned.

(Financial Times, 25 March 1997)

2.17 What are new products? Booz, Allen and Hamilton identified the following categories in a survey of 700 firms

• New to the world	10%
• New product lines	20%
• Additions to product line	26%
• Repositionings	7%
• Improvements/revisions	26%
• Cost reductions	11/5

2.18 The term **new product development** encompasses a wide range of different types of activity ranging form the development of completely new products and technologies to repackaging of existing ones.

2.19 NPD is very risky, expensive and plagued with **failures**. Such results have created a NPD dilemma: it has strategic importance but there is high probability of failure. This dilemma has generated a considerable amount of research into the key factors for success in NPD.

The process of NPD

2.20 **Key factors for NPD success.** By recognising and adopting the characteristics of more successful NPD programmes managers should be able to reduce the levels of risk and likelihood of failure of their own NPD projects. A systematic NPD process can be structured along the following lines. This is outlined in the diagram below.

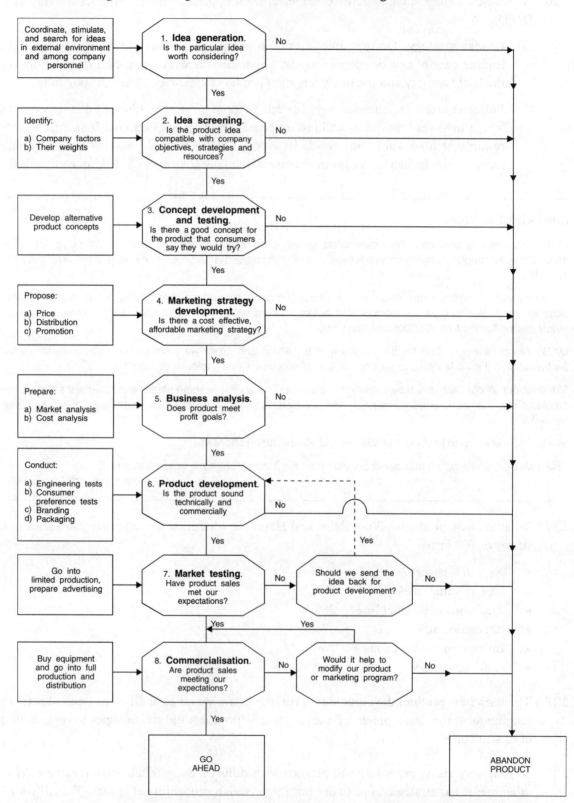

Step 1 **Idea generation** requires the maximum number of new ideas to be generated. This necessitates an active search of the environment and for no suggestion to be

rejected out of hand. Sources include employees, scientists, competitors, customers.

Step 2 **Screening** sorts the ideas for compatibility with organisational strategy, resources, distribution channels, competitive advantage etc.

Step 3 **Concept development and testing** is focused on customer needs. Can we find a concept that wraps the idea up into a package that will be adopted by enough consumers? Conceptual **positioning maps** are often used.

Step 4 **Marketing strategy**. The next stage is to draft a marketing plan including short and long term sales, profit and market share objectives and the structure of the marketing mix.

Step 5 **Business analysis** is focused on determining whether the product will meet the plan's objectives. Sales forecasting is used with estimates firstly on the level and speed of first-time sales and secondly the level of replacement sales. Costs and profits are also estimated.

Step 6 **Product development** involves the physical development of the product in the form of a prototype and a substantial increase in commitment and investment. Tests are then conducted (eg food, for taste and shelf life).

Step 7 **Market testing**. Test marketing is often used to arrive at a more reliable sales forecast and to pre-test marketing plans. Store tests are often used in consumer markets with product use tests and trade shows used more in industrial markets.

Step 8 **Commercialisation**. Often, market testing is omitted and full scale product launch occurs. The questions to ask at this stage are: when to launch? Where to launch? Which groups should be targeted? How should the product be launched?

R & D and marketing

2.21 A problem in NPD activity is the relation of the R & D department to marketing personnel who interact directly to the customer. This has three aspects.

(a) **Cultural**. The R & D department may have an 'academic' or university atmosphere, as opposed to a commercial one.

(b) **Organisational**. If R & D consumes substantial resources, it would seem quite logical to exploit economies of scale by having it centralised.

(c) **Work**. Marketing work and R & D work differ in many important respects. R & D work is likely to be more open ended than marketing work.

2.22 There are many good reasons why R & D should be more closely co-ordinated with marketing.

(a) If the firm operates the marketing concept, then the 'identification of customer needs' should be a vital input to new product development.

(b) The R & D department might identify possible changes to product specifications so that a variety of marketing mixes can be tried out and screened.

Marketing at Work

Nestlé once had a central R & D function, with regional development centres. The central R & D function was involved in basic research. 'Much of the lab's work was only tenuously connected with the company's business... When scientists joined the lab, they were told "Just work in this or that area. If you work hard enough, we're sure you'll find something"'. The results of this approach were:

(a) the research laboratory was largely cut off from development centres;

(b) much research never found commercial application.

Nestlé reorganised the business into strategic business units (SBU's). Formal links were established between R & D and the SBUs. This means that research procedures have been changed so that a commercial time horizon was established.

New forms of segmentation

2.23 Measures of advertising effectiveness are continuously being improved. One approach is to marry data which is currently gathered from two separate sources. Bar code scanners placed in selected homes track the food and grocery purchasing habits of over 8,000 individuals, whilst television meters (in distinctly separate homes) track the viewing habits of over 4,000 households in the UK. Merging this data can establish a possible link between commercials seen and products purchased.

Neural networks

2.24 Agencies and marketing departments are increasingly using 'neural networks' to evaluate advertising effectiveness. These are computer systems loosely modelled on the workings of the human brain. Given data of sufficient quantity and quality networks can 'learn' by being provided with examples. They are capable of recognising complex patterns within huge amounts of data and so detect subtle relationships between sales trends and other factors such as pricing strategy and advertising spending.

2.25 Some examples were given in the *Financial Times* in May 1995.

(a) 'McCann-Erickson, a London-based agency, has been using a neural network system for the last 18 months to evaluate the impact of advertising and improve the scheduling of advertisements. It has used its system to explore questions such as: what would happen to profitability if the price of the product was increased and extra money used on advertising? Is it better to concentrate the spending on advertising or to spread it throughout the year?'

(b) 'Kirsty MacEachen, brand manager of Club biscuits at Jacob's Bakeries in Reading, is also impressed with the neural network system which she has used since January. "So far, it appears to be very useful at pulling apart the various elements of the marketing mix," she says. "I believe it is the first time since I have been in marketing that we have had a clear indication of the contribution which advertising has made in the overall volume equation."'

E-commerce

2.26 E-commerce provides new mechanisms for delivering products and services to customers.

Supplier/customer continuity - just-in-time

Marketing at Work

Distribution is a key issue for the paper industry in Europe. Logistics here are viewed as a way of reducing costs and increasing efficiency, since there is a great problem from declining demand and the market penetration of low cost, low quality product from overseas competitors. Here, the buyer dominates the market and manufacturers are looking to their distribution specialists in order to implement supply systems which protect the product, and deliver in a form which involves minimum waste and keeps stockholding costs at ground level. Customers often require delivery of orders within 24 hours, and to accomplish this suppliers are establishing warehouses which are adjacent to the markets they are seeking to supply, in order to satisfy these time constraints. Margins are becoming squeezed and there are new techniques available to cope with these pressures, but also to provide creative means to accomplish new market opportunities.

2.27 Lancaster (1993) has argued that a 'new marketing' is emerging as a consequence of changing market conditions, but particularly the possibilities afforded by the new technologies for handling information. This is needed because, not only is technology affecting production processes, it is:

> '... transforming choice, and choice is transforming the marketplace. As a result, we are witnessing the emergence of a new marketing paradigm - not a "do more" marketing that simply turns up the volume on the sales trend of the past, but a knowledge and experience based marketing that represents the once-and-for-all death of the salesman.'   (McKenna)

2.28 Customers are, increasingly, faced with a plethora of companies striving to satisfy their needs. As a consequence, they have become more discriminating and competition has hotted up. Product differentiation and the identification and satisfaction of the precise needs of clearly targeted market segments means that companies must not only be aware of their customer needs but place them at the heart of their corporate thinking.

2.29 These needs can, and increasingly do, change very rapidly. Tom Peters has referred to this complex mix of factors as the 'chaos' of the modern marketplace, and the consequent acceleration of the pace of change as the 'nanosecond nineties'. To compete in this marketplace, a company must be aware not just of its customers but of competitors' strategies, the pace and scope of the market, and the technology available within it.

2.30 This cannot be accomplished by traditional marketing, which is bound by outmoded assumptions and formulated around a time-frame which makes it too slow to respond to change. Corporate structure, and the strategies which they evolve, are too rigid and hierarchical and find themselves unable to respond to market opportunities and changes in the tastes and behaviour of existing customers.

Just in Time: a creative competitive tool

2.31 Just In Time (JIT) is a system of inventory control invented by the Japanese. The benefit is that it allows 'pull' in the market, in contrast to the traditional system of 'just in case'. JIT is:

> 'an inventory control system which delivers input to its production or distribution site only at the rate and time it is needed. Thus it reduces inventories whether it is used within the firm or as a mechanism regulating the flow of products between adjacent firms in the distribution system channel. It is a pull system which replaces buffer inventories with channel member co-operation.'

JIT aims to:

> 'produce *instantaneously*, with perfect quality and minimum waste.'

Graham argues that JIT:

> 'completely tailors a manufacturing strategy to the needs of a market and produces mixes of products in exactly the order required.'

2.32 **Synchronisation** is an essential component of such systems. A successful channel will require precise synchronisation between suppliers, through the production units to retailers and finally suppliers. This depends crucially on **information** being freely passed back and forth between channel members; suppliers need to be informed about raw material deliveries, and also the components delivered to manufacturers. For their part, manufactures must be confident that their deliveries will arrive on time.

2.33 Customers need to be treated in a new way; loyalty is no longer to be taken for granted. Indeed, as consumers more and more realise the power they wield, and become more sophisticated in the criteria they apply when evaluating and choosing products, manufacturers find that they must become responsive to these needs and also be able to adjust themselves rapidly in order to satisfy them. The keyword of the modern marketplace is **flexibility,** and this is coupled with **profitability.**

2.34 This flexibility is now the key element in:

- the company meeting customer requirements
- the production process
- the company's organisation

2.35 Time lags are critical in these processes. Reducing times taken for the product to get from the design stage to the market place is critical for success. This is one of the crucial differences between the Japanese and European or American car manufacturers. Japanese manufacturers can get a concept into the marketplace in about 46 months - at least 13 months quicker than the Europeans and 14 months quicker than the Americans.

Action Programme 2

A system called ShopperTrak has been developed that tracks people entering and leaving stores, where they go when inside, and the average amount of time spent there. It can distinguish adults from children. The system uses infra-red sensors at strategic points linked to the retailer's tills or electronic point of sales systems.

What might be the uses of such a system?

2.36 If this synchronisation is effectively organised, a JIT system can meet consumer demand while at the same time profits may be maintained or enhanced, because stockpiles and inventory levels - and consequently, the costs of capital tied up unproductively in materials or products which are not being used - are cut dramatically.

3 SOURCES OF INNOVATION

The learning organisation

3.1 Innovation is essential. Why might this be so?

(a) One suggestion is given by a Japanese management theorist Ikujiro Nonaka.

'In an economy where the only certainty is uncertainty, the one sure source of lasting competitive advantage is knowledge. When markets shift, technologies proliferate, competitors multiply, and products become obsolete almost overnight, successful companies are those that consistently create new knowledge, disseminate it widely throughout the organisation, and quickly embody it in new technologies and products. These activities define the "knowledge-creating" company, whose sole business is continuous innovation.'

(b) Another way of expressing this is to state that 'where quality, technology and variety are all becoming widely available at relatively low cost, the only sustainable competitive advantage that a company can create may be the ability to learn faster than its rivals and to anticipate changes in the business environment'.

3.2 Constant innovation requires a **constant flow of ideas**. Where do these come from?

- From a caste of innovators?
- From management?
- From anyone?

As innovation can affect any aspect of an organisation's activities, so too can the ideas which drive it come from any part of the organisation, and in theory from any member of it.

3.3 Ikujiro Nonaka holds that the successful **creation of ideas,** as opposed to the mere processing of information, depends on a number of organisational factors.

(a) No one individual or group of individuals can be the source of all knowledge about a firm's activities;

(b) there must be a way whereby all individuals can communicate their insights to other members of the organisation, so that these insights flow into a pool of knowledge from which the whole company can draw.

(c) Furthermore, there is the idea that a company is 'a living organism'. This means that it can learn.

3.4 Once we combine the ideas that:

(a) an organisation is not only an arrangement of individuals but is also a social organism; and

(b) there is a need to create knowledge to ensure continuous innovation as a day to day activity;

we can say that organisations have to learn.

> **Key Concept**
>
> The **learning organisation** therefore:
> - encourages continuous learning and knowledge generation at all levels;
> - has the processes to move knowledge around the organisation;
> - can transform knowledge into actual behaviour.

3.5 Managers' plans for innovation will be influenced to a greater or lesser extent by stakeholders.

(a) **Customers'** demands will dictate decisions for investment in new products, development of existing ones and setting-up of new outlets. They will also affect the standards adopted for quality control, and the extent to which they can be enticed away by competitors' products will affect the planned advertising spend.

(b) **Suppliers' and distributors'** demands will affect the timing and amount of production, the amount of raw material and finished goods stock held and hence the financial planning which allows production to take place.

(c) **Employees'** attitudes and objectives will greatly affect the organisation and co-ordination required to put production plans into effect. Construction of departments and work groups, job design, workflow and the amount of training undertaken will all be matters in which management will have to take the employees' stake into account.

(d) **Specialised or professional employees** have two sets of priorities - their jobs, and the requirements of their professional bodies.

(e) **Trade unions** represent employees en masse and seek to ensure that pay, terms and conditions of employment, disciplinary and grievance procedures and employment protection policies are formulated with the employees in mind.

(f) **Legislation, regulations and the community at large**. At the planning level management discretion can be contained by a great number of restrictions which are put in place to protect the community as a whole. Examples are planning restrictions on a construction company, pollution controls on a chemical works and disclosure requirements for a financial services group.

Benchmarking

3.6 Some firms lead the way with technological innovation, and actively seek new products for their markets. Other firms react to what the leaders do - they 'follow my leader'. Either approach can be a successful strategy for innovation.

3.7 Imitation might even be a more successful approach than leadership in innovation, because the leader will make mistakes that the followers can learn from and avoid. A variety of 'follow-my-leader' is **benchmarking**, which compares business operations with what is known to be best practice in other companies or industries.

3.8 Benchmarking is at its simplest a measure of where we are now in order that at some future time we can take another measure to establish the degree of progress (if any). Benchmarks enable companies to set targets.

Creativity nurturing

3.9 Creative ideas can come from anywhere and at any time, but if management wish to foster innovation they should try to provide an organisation structure in which innovative ideas are encouraged to emerge.

(a) **Innovation requires creativity**. Creativity may be encouraged in an individual or group by establishing a climate in which free expression of abilities is allowed. Brainstorming could be used. The role of the R&D department and marketing will be significant in many organisations.

(b) Creative ideas must then be rationally analysed to decide whether they provide a viable proposition.

(c) A system of organisation must exist whereby a viable creative idea is converted into action through effective control procedures. In marketing terms constructive new product development frameworks would need to be established.

Corporate think-tanks

3.10 There is rarely one solution to a problem and much of a manager's skill will be exercised in framing, comparing and finally choosing between alternative solutions. Especially where creativity or innovation is required, it is advisable to generate as many options as possible.

3.11 **Brainstorming** sessions are problem solving conferences of 6-12 people who produce spontaneous 'free-wheeling' ideas to solve a particular problem. Ideas are produced but not evaluated at these meetings, so that originality is not stifled in fear of criticism. Brainstorming sessions rely on the ability of conference members to feed off each other's ideas. They have been used in many organisations and might typically occur, for example, in advertising agencies to produce ideas for a forthcoming campaign.

Creativity: different schools of thought

3.12 The teaching of creative thinking is quite big business in the US and inevitably different 'gurus' (including de Bono) shamelessly attempt to sell their methods and discredit others. Our advice would be to take from what follows anything that works for you.

Marketing at Work

The *Financial Times* reported on 11 November 1995 that British Airways had appointed Paul Birch as a 'Corporate Jester'.

'"A big company is a bit like a medieval court where the king can do no wrong." He adds. "No one questions the king or the senior courtiers. But if you are not careful this can lead you down into the abyss."

This is where the jester of old and his latter-day heir serve a serious role, as the mouthpiece for unorthodox criticism, couched as harmless jest. "Senior people in the company realise their very seniority gets in the way of people challenging them and asking questions," says Birch.

His task is to show things in a different light - negatively, unconventionally, humourously - as a foil to senior managers' conventional wisdom. "My job is about creativity and challenge," he says. His objective, drawn up by the head of BA's corporate strategy, is "to swan around, stick my nose into other people's business, and be a pain in the arse".

"I got into creative problem solving - ways of thinking around difficulties," he says. "I don't mean brainstorming sessions but methods to trigger Edward De Bono calls 'provocative operations'. I prefer Roger von Oech's phrase - 'a wack on the side of the head'."

"Any highly successful business, such as BA, is in danger of over-confidence," Birch says. "Success is probably the most dangerous time. You carry on doing things you know have made you successful while the world changes around you."

Birch says that channelling unorthodox thinking through a jester introduces creativity without jeopardising the stability of an organisation, the *realpolitic* that underpinned the jester of the medieval court. "The whole point is that it is very controlled anarchy. If it goes too far I get sacked."

Passive techniques

3.13 Many writers draw attention to the innate creativity of very young children. The argument is that, although this creative ability is ruthlessly and continually discouraged in early childhood through the process of learning what is conventionally 'right' and acceptable, it is never completely destroyed. It becomes submerged in the 'superconscious mind', a creative faculty that can occasionally be tapped. There is something rather mystical about this but it is appealing because we have all on some occasion had a good idea - a 'flash' of inspiration - apparently out of the blue.

3.14 The superconscious mind supposedly only works when one is concentrating totally on finding a solution to a problem or else when one is not thinking about it at all. Accordingly some of the techniques, like brainstorming, require an active approach, and others are entirely passive.

Mindstorming

3.15 This is like brainstorming for individuals. It entails choosing a time when it is possible to sit down without interruptions and writing down a problem at the top of a piece of paper **in the form of a question**. Then you force yourself to write 20 answers. The first three or four may come very quickly: the last few will be a struggle, but often the twentieth answer will be the ideal solution.

BPP PUBLISHING

Systematic 'solution-finding'

3.16 A step by step approach is favoured by some. The following is typical.

(a) Approach all problems as if they have a logical, workable solution: in other words do not be defeated before you start.

(b) Use positive language. Call a 'problem' a 'challenge' or an 'opportunity', or at worst a 'situation' that has to be dealt with.

(c) Clearly define the situation in writing.

(d) Work out what are all the possible causes of the situation and make a list.

(e) Now it should be possible to identify all the possible solutions. Again, make a list of all of them without prejudging them.

(f) From this point on think only in terms of *solutions*. There is nothing to be gained by going over and over the problem and all its problematic intricacies.

(g) Make a decision comprising one or a combination of the solutions that have been considered. If the decision cannot be made immediately, say, for want of information, set a deadline by which the decision must be made.

(h) Assign specific responsibilities for implementing the solution.

(i) Set a deadline. When must the solution be in place?

4 ORGANISATIONAL BARRIERS TO INNOVATION

4.1 Barriers to innovation include the following.

(a) **Resistance to change**

Any new method of management thinking can experience some resistance from established managers. This resistance may be due to concern to protect the status quo, or because managers are ignorant of the new thinking. Integrating marketing communications seems so obvious that it may be overlooked or seen as a superficial approach.

(b) **Old planning systems**

Old planning systems have sometimes downgraded promotional decisions to the tactical level. Advertising expenditure is decided on the basis of what the company can afford rather than what is strategically required. Promotion is seen as a series of short-term actions rather than as a long-term investment.

(c) **Old structures/functional specialists**

Complementing traditional planning systems are traditional organisation structures. These structures freeze out new thinking on integrated marketing communications strategy. Individuals have limited specific responsibilities - just for advertising, say, or just for public relations - and this inhibits new thinking on integration.

(d) **Centralised control**

If the chief executive keeps tight control of the organisation and of its planning and is unconvinced either of the benefits of marketing communication or of integrated marketing communications then the new integrated approach will not happen.

(e) **External agencies**

External agencies have formerly been organised in specialist areas such as advertising, public relations, sales promotion and marketing research and are not able to offer a complete and integrated service.

(f) **Cost consideration**

Replacing all old promotional materials with a new integrated set has cost implications.

4.2 Methods of overcoming these barriers include those described below.

(a) **Top management commitment**

The most effective way of overcoming these barriers to change is through the commitment of top management. The chief executive in particular needs to be convinced of the appropriateness of the new thinking and be enthusiastic about its implementation throughout the organisation.

(b) **Marketing reorganisation**

One way in which the chief executive can take advice is through a reorganisation of the marketing function in the organisation. In particular the company should seriously consider the appointment of an individual with overall responsibility for brining about the adoption of an integrated marketing communications program throughout the organisation.

(c) **Training and development**

It is one thing to change attitudes. It is another thing to be in a position to know exactly what to do. The integration of a marketing communications programme is not an easy or a short term task. It needs the services of individuals trained in strategic thinking. Such individuals also need to be aware of the appropriateness of a wide range of promotional tools. The individuals chosen to implement any new programme must be enthusiasts capable of overcoming resistance to change.

(d) **Communications as a competitive advantage**

Those with responsibility for implementing an integrated marketing communications programme must do so with the objective of developing communications as a sustainable, long term competitive advantage.

(e) **Producing the results**

Nothing succeeds like success. Producing the business results as a consequence of effective marketing communications will boost confidence and gain management converts to the new thinking on an integrated approach.

Obstacles to organisational learning

4.3 According to Peter Senge, there are seven sources of **learning disability** in organisations which prevent them from attaining their potential - which trap them into 'mediocrity', for example, when they could be achieving 'excellence'.

(a) **'I am my position'**. When asked what they do for a living, most people describe the **tasks** they perform, not the **purposes** they fulfil; thus they tend to see their responsibilities as limited to the boundaries of their position. As a result, individuals within departments can be performing efficiently, yet when you put the efforts of several departments together, the result is more poor quality and performance than would have been the case had the various departments pooled their efforts.

(b) **'The enemy is out there'**. A by-product of 'I am my position', a result of over-identification with the job is the fact that if things go wrong it is all too easy to imagine that somebody else 'out there' was at fault.

(c) **The illusion of taking charge**. True learning should lead to proactivity, but too often proactiveness can mean that the individual decides to be more active in fighting the enemy out there, trying to destroy rather than to build. Senge states that if we believe the enemy to be 'out there' and we are 'in here', then proactiveness is really reactiveness in overdrive: true proactiveness comes from seeing how our own actions contribute to our problems.

(d) **The fixation on events**. Conversations in organisations are dominated by concern about events (last month's sales, who's just been promoted, the new product from our competitor), and this focus inevitably distracts us from seeing the longer-term patterns of change. At one time, concentrating on events was essential to man's survival (you had to worry about whether you had a sabre-toothed tiger over your left shoulder) but today, according to Senge, 'the primary threats to our survival, both of our organisations and of our societies, come not from sudden events but from slow, gradual processes'.

(e) **The parable of the boiled frog**. Maladaptation to gradually building threats to survival is so pervasive in systems studies of corporate failure that it has given rise to the parable of the boiled frog. If you place a frog in a pot of boiling water, it will immediately try to scramble out; but if you place the frog in room temperature water, he will stay put. If you heat the water gradually, the frog will do nothing until he boils: this is because 'the frog's internal apparatus for sensing threats to survival is geared to sudden changes in his environment, not to slow, gradual changes'.

(f) **The delusion of learning from experience**. We learn best from experience, but we never experience the results of our most important and significant decisions. Indeed, we never know what the outcomes would have been had we done something else.

(g) **The myth of the management team**. All too often, the management 'team' is not a team at all, but is a collection of individuals competing for power and resources, forming short-term alliances when it suits them, looking for someone to blame when things go wrong. Chris Argyris believes that 'Most management teams break down under pressure. The team may function quite well with routine issues. But when they confront complex issues that may be embarrassing or threatening, the "teamness" seems to go to pot.'

Bureaucracy

4.4 Bureaucracy can pose barriers to innovation.

> **Key Concept**
> A **bureaucracy** is a type of 'authority structure' characterised by 'a continuous organisation of official functions bound by rules' (Max Weber).
> **Authority structure**. In a bureaucracy people obey commands because these commands have a rational, legal legitimacy (not because of devotion to a charismatic leader who commands by force of personality, or because of tradition).
> **Continuous organisation**. The organisation does not disappear if people leave: new people will fill their shoes.
> **Official functions**. The organisation is divided into areas (eg production, marketing) with specified duties. Authority to carry them out is given to the officials in charge.
> **Rules**. Rules and regulations specify precisely what must be done - they are designed to **reduce** individual initiative.

Characteristics of bureaucracy

4.5 Max Weber identified the characteristics of bureaucracy.

Characteristic	Description
Hierarchy	Each lower office is under the control and supervision of a higher one.
Specialisation and training	There is a high degree of specialisation of labour. Employment is based on ability, not personal loyalty.
Professional nature of employment	An organisation exists before it is filled with people. Officials are full-time employees, promotion is according to seniority and achievement; pay scales are prescribed according to the position or office held in the organisation structure.
Impersonal nature	Employees work full time within the impersonal rules and regulations and act according to formal, impersonal procedures.
Rationality	The 'jurisdictional areas' of the organisation are determined rationally. The hierarchy of authority and office structure is clearly defined. Duties are established and measures of performance set.
Uniformity in the performance of tasks	Regardless of who carried out the tasks, tasks should be executed in the same way.
Technical competence	All officials are technically competent. Their competence within the area of their expertise is rarely questioned.
Stability	The organisation changes rarely.

Policies, rules and procedures

4.6 The bureaucracy is run on rules and procedures to ensure that people are consistent in what they do.

4.7 **Policies** are general understandings which provide guidelines for management decision-making.

> **Key Concept**
> A **procedure** is a chronological sequence of required actions for performing a certain task.

4.8 **Procedures** exist at all levels of management (eg even a board of directors will have procedures for the conduct of board meetings) but procedures become more numerous, onerous and extensive lower down in an organisation's hierarchy.

4.9 **Benefits of bureaucracy**

(a) Bureaucracies are **ideal for standardised, routine tasks**. For example, processing driving license applications is fairly routine, requiring systematic work.

(b) Bureaucracies can be very **efficient**.

(c) **Rigid adherence to procedures is necessary** for **fairness**, adherence to the **law**, **safety** and **security** (eg procedures over computer use).

(d) **Some people like** the structured, predictable environment.

4.10 **Problems with bureaucracy**

(a) It results in **slow decision-making**, because of the complexity of the organisation.

(b) Uniformity creates **conformity**.

(c) Bureaucracies can **inhibit people's personal growth**.

(d) Bureaucracies are **bad at innovation**: they can repress creativity and initiative.

(e) Bureaucracies find it **hard to learn from their mistakes**.

(f) Bureaucracies are **slow to change**. Crozier stated that 'a system of organisation whose main characteristic is its rigidity will not adjust easily to change and will tend to resist change as much as possible'.

(g) **Communication is restricted** to the established structures, and important information may avoid detection.

(h) Bureaucracies find it **hard to deal with change in their environment**.

Resistance to innovation

4.11 New technology and ways of working have sometimes been resisted vigorously by the workforce affected by it. However, most people accept that new technology is inevitable, even desirable, even though it is disruptive.

Work organisation

4.12 Resistance to new technology may not be resistance to **machinery** as such, but instead may be resistance to new forms of **work organisation** imposed by management or employment conditions, or the threat of job losses.

4.13 The introduction of **scientific management** in some industries in the early years of this century generated outrage (strikes and so forth). Scientific management was unpopular because of:

(a) The increased **work discipline** that was regarded as necessary.

(b) The **fear** that enhanced productivity would result in **fewer employees** or that people would be working their way out of a job, despite the fact that it resulted in higher wages.

4.14 **Status.** Resistance to change can also result from a battle for status within the workforce itself. Introducing certain types of change may erode the differentials between different groups of workers.

4.15   Technological change may only be one in a whole gamut of factors in a situation of conflict between management and the workforce. Aspects of industrial relations include:

- Pay
- Hours
- Fringe benefits
- Overtime rates
- New work practices

4.16   **Interest groups**. Many existing groups have a strong interest in maintaining old technology and work practices.

4.17   **Skills**. Finally, people feel that their skills will no longer be useful.

Change and the individual

4.18   Change may present **opportunities** (for example, the development of new technology, a new trend in consumer fashions, or the 'dropout' of a competitor from the market) or **threats** (for example, competitors developing new technology or products rendering others obsolete, legislation imposing new controls on products, or costs of raw materials going up). The opportunities need to be seized upon, and the threats minimised.

4.19   Responding to changes - or staying 'adaptable' enough to be able to response to changes - is not easy for organisations, though. They may have formal organisation structures and ways of doing things that aren't flexible enough to allow for unexpected events or quick changes of direction. They may have to make long-term plans which don't take into account short-term influences, and can't quickly be 'shelved' or altered.

4.20   Perhaps the trickiest problem with managing organisational change is the fact that people dislike it. They frequently resist change to their jobs because:

(a)   any change makes people feel insecure and uncertain; they misunderstand the reasons for change;

(b)   they fear a threat to their competence or success in their jobs ('What if I can't pick up the technology?', 'What if the new manager doesn't like me?'); or

(c)   change disrupts the social structure and relationships they're used to - for example, if there is relocation, reshuffles, redundancies etc.

Conflict

4.21   Finally in this section we should consider the possibility of conflict when resisting innovations of any kind. Organisations are political systems within which there is **competition** for scarce resources and unequal influence. Competition can be healthy as it can:

(a)   Set standards, by establishing best performance through comparison.

(b)   Motivate individuals to better efforts.

4.22   In order to be fruitful, competition must be:

(a)   Perceived to be **open**, rather than closed. ('Closed' competition is a win-lose, or 'zero-sum' situation, where one party's gain will be another party's loss. 'Open' competition exists where all participants can increase their gains - for example productivity bargaining.)

BPP PUBLISHING

(b) Seen to be fair, and the determinants of success are within the competitors' control. If these preconditions are not met, competition may again degenerate into conflict.

Causes, symptoms and tactics of conflict

4.23 **Causes of conflict**

(a) **Differences in the objectives** of different groups or individuals.

(b) **Scarcity of resources**.

(c) **Interdependence of two departments** on a task. They have to work together but may do so ineffectively.

(d) **Disputes about the boundaries of authority.**

   (i) The technostructure may attempt to encroach on the roles or 'territory' of line managers and usurp some of their authority.

   (ii) One department might start **empire building** and try to take over the work previously done by another department.

(e) **Personal differences**, as regards goals, attitudes and feelings, are also bound to crop up. This is especially true in **differentiated organisations**, where people employed in the different sub-units are very different.

4.24 **Symptoms of conflict**

(a) Poor communications, in all 'directions'
(b) Interpersonal friction
(c) Inter-group rivalry and jealousy
(d) Low morale and frustration

4.25 **The tactics of conflict**

(a) **Withholding information** from another.

(b) **Distorting information.** This will enable the group or manager presenting the information to get their own way more easily.

(c) **Empire building.** A group (especially a specialist group such as accounting) which considers its influence to be neglected might seek to **impose rules, procedures**, restrictions or official requirements on other groups, in order to bolster up their own importance.

(d) **Informal organisation.** A manager might seek to by-pass formal channels of communication and decision-making by establishing informal contacts and friendships with people in a position of importance.

(e) **Fault-finding** in the work of other departments: department X might duplicate the work of department Y - hoping to prove department Y 'wrong' - and then report the fact to senior management.

5   MARKETING RESEARCH AND CUSTOMER-FOCUSED INNOVATION

5.1 The results of marketing research must always be seen as only one input in to the decision-making process.

> '(Marketing research) ... helps to reduce the risks in business decisions, but will not make the decision.'
> (Raymond Kent, *Marketing Research in Action*)

There are oft-quoted cases of marketing research which concluded that a product would be an utter failure, but which went ahead on the gut-feeling of the organisation and became a runaway success - the Sony Walkman being one. This illustrates the points that:

(a) while marketing research may help in decisions within the status quo, its results with respect to innovation can be misleading at best and disastrous at worst; and

(b) intuition, creativity and visionary flair may win the day when systematic and rational analysis of product innovation suggests otherwise.

5.2 To reduce risks, improve targeting and to get to know your customer's needs and competition better it is important to conduct marketing research yourself. Many small business people rely a great deal on intuition and may be reluctant to conduct research, but it will repay many times the effort devoted to it.

5.3 The design of the marketing mix will be decided on the basis of management intuition and judgement, together with information provided by marketing research. It is particularly important that management should be able to understand the image of the product in the eyes of the customer, and the reasons which make customers buy a particular product.

Chapter roundup

- **Innovation** is making something new or doing something in a different way. It may be a new product, but it also covers new ways of satisfying customers, new ways of carrying out routine activities, new linkages in the value chain, new approaches to work and organisation structure.

- Innovation provides the organisation with a distinctive competence and can help to maintain competitive advantage.

- The term **new product development** encompasses a wide range of different types of activity ranging form the development of completely new products and technologies to repackaging of existing ones.

- The ideas driving innovation can come from anywhere in the organisation. The learning organisation encourages such knowledge generation.

- Benchmarking compares business operations with what is known to be best practice in other companies or industries.

- Corporate think-tanks and brainstorming sessions can also generate new ideas.

- There are various organisational barriers to innovation, including old structures, resistance to change and centralised control. Bureaucracy can stand in the way of innovation.

- Perhaps the trickiest problem with managing organisational change is the fact that people dislike it.

- Marketing research can assist in developing innovative ideas, by testing customer reactions.

BPP PUBLISHING

Quick quiz

1 What is the distinction between innovation and invention? (see para 1.1)

2 What are possible steps for creating an innovative culture? (2.5)

3 What strategies can be adopted with regard to new product development? (2.16)

4 Outline a systematic approach to new product development. (2.20)

5 What are neural networks? (2.24)

6 What is a learning organisation? (3.4)

7 How can companies overcome organisational barriers to innovation? (4.2)

8 Why might the findings of marketing research not give the full story on success of a new product? (5.1)

Action Programme Review

1 You could have simply ignored the product, on the grounds that a glue which does not stick things together is not a glue that is worth making or selling. This is one response.

   Another response would be to discuss with the employee, and other employees, the possible use for such a glue. In this case, you might come up with a revolutionary idea - the 'Post-It' note. Then you reward the employee.

2 The main idea is to cut down long waits in check-out queues and weary searches by customers for staff. The system enables managers to adjust staffing to demand and so increase purchases per visit, encourage return visits and to lift 'conversion rates' – the percentage of people entering the stores who actually buy something. The system also provides information to improve the quality and style of service and enables stores to be designed and laid out more effectively.

Part C
Customer dynamics

8 The holistic perspective of customer behaviour

Chapter Topic List	Syllabus reference
1 Setting the scene	3.1
2 Modelling customer dynamics	3.1
3 Individuals, groups and organisations	3.1
4 Why new products succeed or fail	3.1
5 Dissatisfaction, satisfaction and delight	3.1

Learning Outcomes

After studying this chapter you will be in a position to:

- understand the (psychological, social, cultural and economic) factors influencing customer dynamics in particular marketing scenarios

- understand the impact of product/service improvement or innovation.

- analyse key issues in customer dynamics including segmentation, relationship marketing and the behaviour patterns found within the Decision Making Unit.

Key Concepts Introduced

- Diffusion and adoption
- Customer satisfaction and delight

Examples of Marketing at Work

- Microsoft/SDX Business Systems
- Daewoo
- Allders
- Woolworths
- Waitrose
- Mothercare

1 SETTING THE SCENE

1.1 This chapter introduces a number of themes that will be explored in more depth in the remainder of Part C.

1.2 Part C overall is about 'customer dynamics' - how and why customers make purchase decisions. It is vital that you understand how customers can be classified according to certain **types** and according to their **expectations** and **perceptions**.

BPP PUBLISHING

2 MODELLING CUSTOMER DYNAMICS

Rationale

2.1 The 'modelling approach' is based on the idea that any phenomenon or process can be **simplified,** by leaving out of the 'picture' any aspects or variables that are not of interest to the modeller, while still portraying something **meaningful** about the real phenomenon or process. This is particularly true of **consumer behaviour models**, since - in the words of Keith Williams - 'it has ... been found that it is possible to simplify consumer behaviour into its principal components and that, in practice, a relatively small number of variables account for the vast bulk of consumer behaviour'.

2.2 Because a model is a simplification of reality based on the modeller's interests, different models may be developed to describe the same phenomenon or process, showing different aspects of the same thing.

2.3 Chris Rice makes an analogy between modelling and mapping.

(a) Whilst all maps are representations of 'a real life phenomenon', maps of the same area are not all the same - contrast a road map of the UK with a meteorological map (rainfall etc) or geological map (clay, chalk etc). Each has been **adapted** by the cartographer to represent the information that is of use to the target audience.

(b) Not all maps are 'realistic' or to scale; instead, their significance is in the way they represent **connections**. Rice uses the famous example of the London Underground map, which usefully shows how the tube network fits together but contains no clue as to the relative distance between stations on the surface. For an underground traveller the map is invaluable; for an overground stranger to London it is famously misleading!

2.4 Thus maps and models give a simplified representation of how complex factors operate together in real life.

Applications

Micro versus macro

2.5 A micro-model deals with the **individual** or other small unit, while a macro-model deals with a **wider environment**.

Descriptive, diagnostic, predictive

2.6 Descriptive models **describe** historical or current phenomena, while diagnostic models set out to find **causes** - to explain - and predictive models try to show what **outcomes** will result from given inputs in given circumstances.

Low-level, medium-level, high-level

2.7 These terms denote the complexity of the model and the number of variables included.

Static or dynamic

2.8 A static model is a **'snapshot'** of a phenomenon at a **particular point in time**, while a dynamic model can take account of **variations over time**.

Qualitative and quantitative

2.9   Qualitative models do not make explicit variable **measurements**, while quantitative models do, weighting the variables according to importance and so offering a more accurate predictive model.

Data-based versus theory-based

2.10   A data-based model is based on logical analysis of **available data**, while a theory-based one is developed by means of logical **extension of existing theories**, often of marketing but sometimes of psychology or sociology.

Behavioural versus statistical

2.11   A behavioural model is based on **stimulus response theories**, that is on how people are expected to behave, while a statistical model uses numerical analysis without prior assumptions about motivation.

Generalised versus ad hoc

2.12   A generalised model is constructed to apply to a **wide range of markets**, while an *ad hoc* one applies just to one market or brand.

Objectives

2.13   The main objectives of a model, against which their effectiveness can be evaluated, are:

(a)   **to help researchers to develop theories**. Models provide a simplified framework within which research can be directed to confirm or refute/modify hypotheses about the relationships between variable and about the nature of the 'invisible' intervening variables;

(b)   **to describe and explain behaviour and aid prediction**. Models which have been substantially confirmed by research and practice offer a useful tool to the marketer who wishes to understand the consumer decision process, and to predict consumer reactions to a marketing strategy based on the manipulation of stimulus and intervening variables.

Limitations

2.14   Models may be defined as successful or unsuccessful according to their own functions, as defined by their developers: there is no universal prescription for a 'good' model. However, some general criteria (which you might like to use as a checklist for evaluating the models described below) laid down by Williams, *Behavioural Aspects of Marketing*, are as follows.

(a)   **Validity**. We should be able to verify the model, that is test its proposed relationships.

(i)   External validity - is the model generally applicable, or confined to a single research setting?

(ii)   Internal validity - can it be confidently claimed (and confirmed by testing) that the relationships between the variables are in fact as the model portrays?

(b)   **Factual accuracy**. Is the model consistent with known facts (even if it is an admittedly intuitive or theoretical model)?

BPP PUBLISHING

(c) **Rationality**. Is the model logical and internally consistent (not contradicting itself or requiring irrational 'leaps')?

(d) **Completeness**. The model may by definition leave out aspects of the phenomenon/process, but are all assumptions explicitly stated? Are the exogenous variables identified?

(e) **Simplicity**. Is the model accessible? Are the relationships portrayed as direct and easily-perceivable as possible?

(f) **Originality**. Does the model include new elements, or put elements together in a new way, which will further our insight or knowledge?

(g) **Effectiveness for its purpose**, whether that be:

    (i) **explanation**. Does the model show causal relationships which explain how and why the phenomenon occurs? or

    (ii) **prediction** - does the model enable the behavioural response/output to be predicted, given knowledge of the relevant input/stimulus and intervening variables? or

    (iii) **heurism** - does the model identify gaps in our knowledge, and so suggest new or further areas of research?

2.15 While we cannot expect all these criteria to be met, they do help us to evaluate each model.

Simple models of consumer behaviour

2.16 As examples we shall discuss some of the lower-level forms of modelling. These models:

(a) leave out the **internal** variables, the mental processes of decision making. These are black box models; or

(b) leave out the **external** variables, concentrating only on the mental processes of decision making. These are personal variable models.

Black box models

2.17 Black box models assume that observable behaviour is the only valid object of study, and that psychological constructs are part of an impenetrable box which should not be opened. Concentrating as they do on environmental factors, such models in the context of consumer behaviour are **market models** which may be used in market research to identify, for example:

(a) the **decision environment**. Factors external to the individual, which influence his buying behaviour, are shown - but the individual himself is a black box;

(b) the **marketing distribution process**. The 'flow' of products, or information, or influence, is plotted - from producer to salesforce to retail outlet to consumer to other consumers. Competitors can be similarly plotted on the model, along with government/regulatory bodies/consumer groups to build up a portrait of 'the market' as a whole;

(c) the **buying process** - taking into account only inputs and outputs.

Black box models

The decision environment

Reference groups

Retail outlets

Family —— Buyer —— Brands

Environmental factors

Marketing communications

The buying process

| Information inputs | Media channels | Buyer | | Purchasing responses |

2.18 Black box models can be useful because:

(a) they include **observable, quantifiable variables** which are easier to measure and to manipulate;

(b) they concentrate on a **manageable number of relevant input variables,** on which a strategy can be based - without 'analysis paralysis' from speculating about all the possible intervening factors.

2.19 Stimulus variables such as price, quality, availability, service, or advertising, can be identified by models, and the results of each - in terms of product/brand or supplier choice, quantity and frequency of purchase - set out in a simple, direct way. If a model indicates that decreased price results in increased purchase quantity, the marketer is able to respond accordingly: it does not matter, to an extent, why the phenomenon occurs.

2.20 Black boxes are, however, limited to **simple, unambitious functions**. They do not attempt to predict behaviour in a wide range of circumstances, nor to explain behaviour.

Action Programme 1

Analyse a simple regular purchase that you make - a pint of milk, say, or a chocolate bar - in terms of the black box model depicted above.

Personal variable models

2.21 Personal variable models are simple models of **internal processes** - beliefs, intentions, motives, perceptions etc - without any of the **external, environmental influences**. As we shall see later, such models are frequently used as the internal process components of high-level, comprehensive models, being insufficient on their own to explain or predict behaviour.

2.22 Personal variable models include:

(a) the **compensatory or trade-off model**. When faced with a choice between products composed of certain attributes or benefits in different proportions, a consumer will compromise on his image of the 'ideal' product, and accept less of one attribute in return for more of another. This is a judgement about which combination of attributes offers the highest overall utility, or value. It can be measured by asking the consumer to rank different attribute combinations in order of preference (for example: a car with standard features/standard price; all luxury features/high price; some luxury features/slightly higher price). The model really only works with specific variables, but can be useful in product planning and positioning;

(b) the **threshold model**. For each perceived attribute of a product, there is a perceived threshold of acceptability, below which the product will be rejected. Each attribute is assessed, until the product falls short on one (usually, price) and is discarded. This model has been used as a choice predictor within higher-level models;

(c) **linear additive models**. The individual's attitude towards an object is the sum of his evaluations of a number of attributes. Such models can, if well designed, give the marketer information about which attributes are considered important in a product, and about how consumers rate the product on the basis of each attribute: they can thus help with product design and positioning. However, the lack of other variables makes the model inadequate as a predictor of behaviour.

A simple decision process model

2.23   A simple descriptive model of the decision process consists of:

(a) **need/problem recognition**. Leads to motivation. (In a more complex model, would be shown to be triggered by psychological, physiological and social factors.) Marketers can identify needs/problems for the consumer, through product positioning;

(b) **pre-purchase/information search**. (In a more complex model, would be affected by sources, attitudes, perceptions.) Marketers can provide product information, tailored to need;

(c) **evaluation of alternatives**. Marketers can make products available for evaluation and provide comparative information about competing products: the important thing, though, is to get the product onto the short-list of options;

(d) **the purchase decision**. (In a more complex model, would be affected by situational factors: intention is not everything);

(e) **post-purchase evaluation**. Experience 'feeds back' to the beginning of the process, providing positive or negative reinforcement of the purchase decision. If the consumer is dissatisfied, he will be back at the problem recognition stage again. If the consumer is satisfied, the next decision process for the product may be cut short and skip straight to the decision, on the basis of loyalty (or, in a more complex model, expectations and learning constructs).

2.24   Such a model provides a useful descriptive framework for marketers, with indications of strategy requirements at each stage. It is still, however, too simple to be predictive, unless a large number of extra social, psychological and cultural variables are added or assumed.

3   INDIVIDUALS, GROUPS AND ORGANISATIONS

3.1   In the broadest sense customers fall into three 'types': individuals, groups and organisations. We shall devote most space in this text to individuals, since groups and organisations are ultimately composed of individuals.

3.2   Chapters 10 to 12 deal with this topic in depth, but here is an example to whet your appetite and get you thinking.

Action Programme 2

Read the following blurb and decide **who are the customers** that Delta Dental need to care for?

Delta Dental is a non-profit service corporation that was created in 1982 to provide high quality dental benefits programs for employee groups throughout the state. Delta Dental's programs are available to employee groups of 10 or more people. Groups can choose managed fee-for-service, preferred provider and HMO-type programs.

Delta Dental is a growing administrator of dental benefits programs in Indiana, covering more than 170,000 people in more than 200 groups.

The satisfaction of our customers is evidenced by our contract renewal rates, which exceed 97 percent each year.

Delta Dental annually pays approximately $20 million for dental treatment.

Some groups with Delta Dental coverage include the Indianapolis Public Schools, Indiana State University, and Kimball International Corporation, plus numerous other businesses, public schools, city and county governments, hospitals and universities throughout the state.

Additionally, Delta Dental Plan of Indiana offers dental benefits programs to people nationwide through our DeltaUSA program. Companies that are headquartered in Indiana and have employees located outside the state can provide quality consistent benefits to employees nationwide.

Delta Dental Plan of Indiana is a member of the Delta Dental Plans Association and is affiliated with Delta Dental Plan of Ohio and Delta Dental Plan of Michigan.

Delta Dental Plan of Michigan has a proud history of community service, which its employees enthusiastically support every year.

4 WHY NEW PRODUCTS SUCCEED OR FAIL

4.1 **New products** represent a significant opportunity to both **consumers** (who may find a better means of satisfying their needs) and **marketers** (who may find a new source of profit or competitive advantage). They also offer behavioural scientists the opportunity to study the way in which a new idea is **communicated, disseminated** and **accepted (or resisted)** by the consumer network. From the marketer's point of view, a new product or service represents a great deal of research and development and production expenditure which needs to bring a return. The **first buyers** of a product are the **most important**, since there is no established frame of reference within which the product will be considered: no experience, association or reference group adoption to build on.

4.2 A product may be considered an innovation because it is 'completely' new, or because it has not been manufactured by the particular organisation before, has new features, has only been purchased by a small percentage of the market before, has only been on the market for a short time, or is perceived to be new because it is being 'positioned' or promoted differently.

Diffusion of innovation

4.3   Diffusion is the process whereby acceptance of an innovation is disseminated, by communication and social influence, over a period of time. You may have noticed that some new ideas 'catch on' suddenly, while others take a long time to gain acceptance, and others never get beyond the fringes. The **rate and extent of diffusion** of an innovation depend on:

- the **characteristics** of the innovation/new product
- the **channels of communication** used
- the **social system** within which communication takes place
- the **stages of the adoption process** reached by members of the social system

Product characteristics that influence diffusion

4.4   Everett Rogers has identified five main characteristics which seem to influence the rate and extent to which consumers accept new products and ideas. (These do not offer a formula or prediction for marketers, but a set of guidelines as to a product's likely 'welcome'.)

(a)   **Relative advantage**

Relative advantage is the degree to which potential consumers perceive the product innovation to be **better than previous or competing products**.

Innovations which 'take off' immediately may do so because of relative advantage, if they have unique product features or improvements which are clearly communicated to the market. The fax' machine, for example, represented a **technological breakthrough** with clear advantages over telephone, post and courier services - and has been continuously improved ever since, with smaller size, better paper quality and so on: each 'generation' of machines is positioned as having relative advantage. Another form of relative advantage may be **promotional benefits**: money off next purchase coupons, a design award or British Standard qualification, money-back guarantee or whatever.

(b)   **Compatibility**

Compatibility is the degree to which potential consumers perceive the product innovation to be **comparable or consistent with their existing values**, attitudes, needs and practices. Schiffman and Kanuk use the example of the man's shaving razor. If a man uses a permanent razor, the innovation of disposable razors (or double-bladed, or swivel-headed razors) is easily adopted, because it is compatible with the wet-shaving ritual: it is less easy to imagine the shaver adopting an innovatory depilatory cream which removes facial hair more simply than the razor...

(c) **Complexity** is the degree to which potential consumers find the product innovation **difficult to understand or use**.

Innovations offering convenience - such as prepared and frozen meals, tea bags and instant coffee - are accepted faster than more complex propositions: the relatively fast adoption of video recorders and microwave ovens is a tribute to their relative advantages!

(d) **Trialability**

Trialability is the degree to which potential consumers can **test or sample** a product innovation **before committing themselves** to adopting it.

The greater the opportunity for sampling - through free trial offers, purchase on approval, in-store demonstrations, small-size sample packs and so on - the easier it is for consumers to evaluate the innovation with low risk. Expensive products with **low or no trialability** are high in perceived risk, and will be **adopted more slowly**, as consumers wait for general acceptance and others' experience to reduce the risk element.

(e) **Observability**

Observability, or 'communicability' is the degree to which a product innovation's benefits or attributes are **visible to the potential consumer** - by his own observation, or imagination, or the descriptions of others.

Fashion items, for example, have high 'social visibility' and are more easily disseminated than products for private use, which are 'shared' less with other people.

4.5 Note that each of these new product characteristics is **subjective** - dependent on the perception of the consumer, on the basis of his psychological and demographic characteristics.

4.6 **Resistance to innovation** is believed to increase with:

- low relative advantage
- low compatibility
- low trialability
- low observability and
- high complexity.

Action Programme 3

Whenever you see a product or service which claims to be 'new' in some way, apply the tests of relative advantage, compatibility, complexity, trialability and observability to it.

Marketing at Work

'It is an uncomfortable dilemma for a company. If you do not innovate, old products will be overtaken by new technology. If, on the other hand, you introduce a new range it can cannibalise the old product. Even more likely, sales of an existing model can dry up overnight once word gets out that a new product is imminent.

Yet companies must innovate. If you are Microsoft introducing Windows 95, this is less of a problem. Its marketing muscle and industry dominance are such that it could endure a fall in sales of Windows 3.1. When BMW announces a new 7-series, it has at least got sales of the 5-series and 3-series to tide it over should old 7-series sales slow down.

BPP PUBLISHING

This is not the case if you are a small one-product company, as SDX Business Systems was in 1991. When the management team, led by Frank Bretherton, bought the Welwyn Garden City-based company from Northern Telecom of the US it realised its digital telephone exchange had a limited life. But because the company had only one product Bretherton knew he would have to "bet the company" when introducing the new exchange called Index.'

Financial Times, 23 January 1996

Communication and social influence

4.7 Diffusion of innovation clearly depends on **communication** between marketers and consumers, and between consumers themselves. Marketers will need to consider such factors as:

(a) the **credibility of the communication medium**, the spokesperson, and/or retail outlet - in order to reduce the perceived risk of trying out something new;

(b) the **interactive nature of the communication medium** - so that doubts and questions can be addressed, to reduce perceived risk. Interpersonal communication through salespeople and opinion leaders is thought to be most effective - although mass media do achieve 'observability' more swiftly;

(c) the identification of **opinion leaders**, who tend to seek information about innovations, and be more knowledgeable about them (see Section 3 below); and

(d) the **orientation of the society**, with values and norms related to tradition and change.

(i) A **'modern'** society has a positive attitude to change and flexibility, with advanced technology, skilled labour, and a general respect for education and science: innovations are more readily accepted in such a climate.

(ii) A **'traditional'** society may, on the other hand, perceive innovation to be threatening of established customs and social order.

Rate of diffusion: 'adopter categories'

4.8 Diffusion research has indicated that diffusion of an innovation follows a normal distribution (a **bell-shaped curve**) over time, and that consumers can be classified according to the time they take to adopt an innovation, relative to other consumers.

4.9 **Five adopter categories** have been identified (by Rogers and others). (Note that although they are 'adopter' categories, we are still looking at 'diffusion', not 'adoption' as a process: we are still at the 'macro' level of society and the whole life of the product innovation.)

(a) **Innovators** (2.5% of the population that eventually adopts the product).

Innovators are the first people to adopt an innovation. Their main characteristic is said to be 'venturesomeness': they are not averse to risk, are eager to try new ideas, are varied and extensive in their social networking. Innovators also tend to be young, well-educated and with relatively high discretionary purchase power: they take a large number of publications in the search for innovative ideas. We discuss innovators in more detail in Section 2 below.

(b) **Early adopters** (13.5% of the population that eventually adopts the product).

Early adopters are next to adopt the innovation. Their main characteristic may be called 'respectability': they take fewer risks than innovators (watching to see how they get on before themselves adopting the innovation), and are integrated into their social system and culture. They have the highest number of opinion leaders and role models, and so are important in the communication process: they are perceived to be the people to 'check with' before adopting a new idea. They take fewer publications than innovators, but more than anyone else, and have greatest contact with sales people.

(c) **Early majority** (34% of the population that eventually adopts the product.)

The early majority are the first of the general mass of the population to adopt a new idea: just before the 'average' adoption time. Their main characteristic is said to be 'deliberation'. They are slightly above average in education, age and income, but tend to be followers, seldom holding leadership positions, and relying heavily on information from others. They deliberate for some time before adopting.

(d) **Late majority** (34% of the population that eventually adopts the product.)

The late majority are the last of the general mass of the population to adopt a new idea: just after the 'average' adoption time. Their main characteristic is said to be 'scepticism': they are cautious about new ideas and tend to adopt only as a result of economic necessity, or social pressure. They tend to be older, and less well educated, with less discretionary income: there are few opinion leaders among them, they take few publications and rely on information and influence from others.

(e) **Laggards** (16% of the population that eventually adopts the product).

Laggards are last to adopt. Their main characteristic is said to be 'traditionalism': they tend to be oriented to the past and custom, parochial in their social outlook and suspicious of anything new. They tend to be the oldest, least well-educated and poorest group, with almost no opinion leaders or information-search activities.

4.10 Remember that these are **not stages** people go through: they are '**types**' or categories of people. The stages refer to the diffusion process over time, and the points in it at which the different categories of people adopt the innovation. The normal distribution is illustrated as follows.

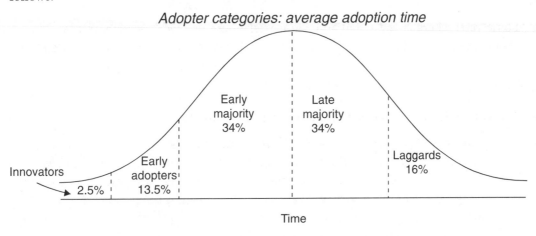

Adopter categories: average adoption time

4.11 The main problem with using this model is that the categories appear to add up to 100% of the social system - the target market. This is not a reflection of marketers' experience, since some potential consumers do not adopt/purchase at all. It has been suggested that an additional category should be added: **nonadopters,** or **nonconsumers**.

4.12 Some researchers prefer a two or three category scheme, comparing innovators/early triers with later triers and/or non-triers. This enables them to generalise the characteristics of the **important innovator/early trier segments**, which has practical significance for marketing. (We will discuss the characteristics of the consumer innovator below.)

Adoption

4.13 Adoption is the process by which a consumer arrives at a decision to try (or not to try) and - having tried - to continue using (or discontinue using) a new product.

4.14 Based on the premise (not universally accepted) that consumers tend to engage in fairly extensive information search and problem-solving in order to reach a purchase decision, a five-stage model of product adoption has been proposed.

(a) **Awareness.** Consumers have been exposed to the product innovation, and are aware that it exists, but their attitudes to it are neutral at this stage.

(b) **Interest.** Consumers become curious about the innovation or aware of its potential to fulfil a need or want of theirs: they become interested in it to the extent of seeking out more information.

(c) **Evaluation.** Consumers use the information they have gathered in order:

(i) to decide whether more information is necessary: delayed decision;

(ii) to establish a positive or negative attitude (favourable or unfavourable evaluation) of the innovation; and

(iii) to decide whether to purchase/try or reject the innovation.

The perceived product characteristics discussed earlier will influence this stage.

(d) **Trial.** Consumers try out the innovation, if possible on a limited, low-risk basis: their experience then provides them with the decisive information to adopt or reject.

(e) **Adoption** (or rejection). Based on evaluation ('mental trial') and physical trial of the innovation, consumers decide to continue to use it on a full committed basis - or to reject it.

4.15 Some researchers suggest that following trial, there are **two intermediate stages** (direct product experience and product evaluation: confirmation) before rejection or adoption.

Value of the adoption model

4.16 The adoption model offers a useful framework for marketers:

(a) to concentrate on **relevant aspects of the consumers' state of mind** at each stage. The most important goal, initially, will be to get attention, in competition with other stimuli. The next will be to arouse interest by suggesting motivations. The next will be giving information relevant to evaluation, then making the product available for trial etc;

(b) to study **which information media are most effective at each stage.** Awareness is best served by mass media, but in later stages, especially evaluation, mass media influence declines in favour of more personal sources: salespeople, opinion leaders and so on.

4.17 However, the traditional adoption model has been **criticised** for:

(a) **leaving out the problem/need recognition stage**, which may have to precede awareness if the message is going to be perceived;

(b) **suggesting that the stages are distinct and in sequence.** In practice, evaluation may take place throughout the decision-making process. Trial may occur before evaluation or interest - or not at all;

(c) **leaving out the possibility of post-adoption discontinuance**, because of further experience, post-purchase dissonance, forgetting and competing innovations.

Characteristics of innovators

4.18 It is of crucial importance to the marketer of an innovation to know who the innovators/early triers are, and how they can be reached and influenced. 'Consumer innovators' is a term for the relatively small group who are the earliest purchasers of a new product or service (whether this is defined as the first 2.5% of adopters of a particular new product, or the people who purchase a number of new products and are therefore inferred to be 'innovative'.)

4.19 Characteristics which distinguish innovators from later adopters and non-adopters include the following.

(a) **Interest in the relevant product category**. People who show an interest in fashion or technological inventions, say, are more likely to be the ones who will try out a new 'look' or device. Innovators can be identified and targeted by their tendency to seek information on the areas of their interest from special-interest mass-media sources - publications, conferences and exhibitions. Attitude surveys and lifestyle analysis may also pinpoint people with particular interests.

(b) **Opinion leadership**. We noted earlier that opinion-leaders tend to be innovators, and are therefore gatekeepers of new product information: if the opinion leaders get interested and have positive experience of the innovation, they will tell and influence others. By identifying opinion leaders, marketers can target motivational communication at innovative individuals. We will examine opinion leaders in more detail in Section 3 below.

(c) **Personality traits**, including:

(i) attitude flexibility, or open-mindedness;

(ii) independence of judgement;

(iii) variety-seeking, and the ability to deal with complex or ambiguous stimuli;

(iv) high tolerance for risk, low perception of risk, 'venturesomeness'. Innovators tend to be willing to risk a poor choice in order to increase their exposure to new ideas and experience.

Non-innovators seem to possess the opposite characteristics. Separate promotional approaches might therefore be required. Innovators respond to informative messages appealing to their interest, open-mindedness and willingness to make independent evaluations. Non-innovators respond to reference group influence, and the use of trusted/well known spokespersons, to reduce perceived risk and give their evaluation the support of others' opinions.

(d) **Consumption habits**. Innovators are less brand loyal, willing to switch to other brands for variety and respond more to promotional 'deals'. They also consume heavily (in volume) in the product areas in which they are the innovators.

(e) **Media selection**. Innovators expose themselves to more magazines and journals - especially those related to their particular interests. Targeting innovators can thus be efficiently achieved through advertising/editorials in special interest publications.

(f) **Social profile**. Innovators are more socially involved and accepted than non-innovators, meaning that they are more likely to belong to social groups and organisations. They therefore also function well as opinion leaders.

(g) **Demographic factors.** Innovators tend to be younger than non-innovators, although this depends to an extent on the nature of the product. They tend to have higher status in terms of education, occupation (three quarters have professional or technical jobs) and income. Innovators may thus be targeted through the use of geo-demographic techniques.

5   DISSATISFACTION, SATISFACTION AND DELIGHT

Key Concepts

Customer satisfaction signifies the fulfilment of basic product/ service criteria, ie the purchased commodity delivers what it says it will deliver, the packaging and other surrounding factors are acceptable, and the price paid is thought to be justified.

Delight, on the other hand, suggests a conscious feeling of elation, of pleasure, of fulfilment and gratification, arising from the enormous psychological benefit associated with the purchase or the awareness that some special, probably unique and remarkable degree of service has been rectified.

5.1   It used to be thought that the differences in behaviour between the customer who is 'very satisfied' and the customer who is merely 'satisfied' would be almost unnoticeable. In reality the differences are truly significant - and have dangerous implications for the organisation which becomes complacent because the vast majority of its customers claim that they are 'satisfied' with the company's current product/service offer. **The customer who is merely 'satisfied' is between 7 and 10 times more likely to move to another supplier than a customer who is 'very satisfied'.**

5.2   It is the 'very satisfied' customer who is genuinely loyal - who will, in other words, **repurchase.** Further, if the organisation makes a mistake or delivers unusually poor service to the 'very satisfied' customer, then a very strange thing happens: **the customer will forgive the organisation** arguing that the mistake or the poor service was an unfortunate aberration which will soon be corrected. What a wonderful situation!

5.3   Unfortunately only a few companies enjoy this kind of reputational asset - until very recently Marks & Spencer was one of them - and ultimately, if enough 'mistakes' are made, then the organisation will lose its reputational advantage and will have its work cut out trying to retrieve it.

5.4   The opposite situation occurs when the organisation has a reputation for customer service which **is so bad** that whenever they get something right, this is normally attributed to the random operation of Murphy's Law ('If anything can go wrong, it will' plus its corollary, 'If anything can go right, then occasionally it will do so, but at totally unpredictable times and for totally mysterious reasons'.) Why would we ever give our business to companies or organisations with this kind of image? Well, sometimes we **don't really have a choice,** because the organisation operates as a monopoly supplier of compulsorily-purchased services (local authorities, the Inland Revenue, the DSS); sometimes we do have a choice, but naively we believe that things may now be different, or we are activated by concern for price over all other conditions; now and again we like a challenge. By and large, however, most people would prefer to deal with organisations which enjoy a positive reputation for (a) their products and (b) the service package that goes with them, especially if benefiting from the reputation does not entail any, or any significant, price implication.

5.5   There are two action implications for organisations arising from what has been said here.

(a) If seeking long-run viability, it is **preferable to have a positive reputation**: you get more business, you stimulate repeat business, you attract more highly-motivated employees, and you can often secure higher margins because of the perceived added-value derived from your reputation.

(b) It you have a positive reputation, however, you **cannot afford to become complacent**. Competitors may be snapping at your heels; customer aspirations are always escalating upwards; occasional 'mistakes', if left alone, may become the norm. A reputation once destroyed is very difficult to rebuild; every error committed within the rebuilding phase is widely construed as further 'proof' that nothing has really changed.

Marketing at Work: Daewoo

'The motor industry case is probably an exemplar of the entire customer-care genre.......The growth of Daewoo in the UK owes much to its philosophy of scrubbing the discredited dealership system of car retailing and providing an after-sales service that delivers things rather than vague promises.

Since it started 30 years ago with seed capital of $10,000, Daewoo has grown to have a worldwide turnover of $88bn (£55bn), making it the fastest-growing international corporation and Korea's fourth-largest company. It took a year to achieve a one per cent market share in the UK after its 1995 launch (Mazda took 24 years to get to 1.2 per cent). So it must be getting something right.

My guess is that, by luck or judgement, Daewoo has hit the UK market with a customer-care philosophy that suits the moment and has pushed many more Anglo-Saxon operations in the some direction...

That philosophy is really one of back to basics – establish what customers want and give it to them.'

Marketing Week, 18 September 1997

Must be/alone is better/delighters

5.6 It is also important for all organisations to differentiate between what Dr Noraki Kano has called the **must be**, the **more is better**, and the **delighters** in the customer's perception profile of any given product or service.

5.7 The **must be** factors are those characteristics or features which we take for granted, like the fact that when turn the ignition key, the car's engine will wake up. The **must be** factors are only noticed when they are **missing**: we are annoyed when the engine does not fire, but take it for granted when it does.

5.8 If we are disappointed when a need is not met, but become progressively more satisfied and even elated as more of the need is fulfilled, then we are operating in the arena of the **more is better** factors. We can easily become annoyed if we have to wait for a spare part; when it is supplied immediately, without question and without the necessity for payment, then we can be delighted; something inbetween would probably evoke no reaction at all.

5.9 The **delighters** are the features or characteristics which surprise customers positively. They solve a need which the customer didn't know could be solved, or didn't think anyone would solve. Unfortunately, once a delighted has been experienced once or twice, the customer begins to entertain **expectations** that it will be provided permanently: it then becomes a **must be** ingredient, thereby losing its magic but retaining the necessity for its continued presence.

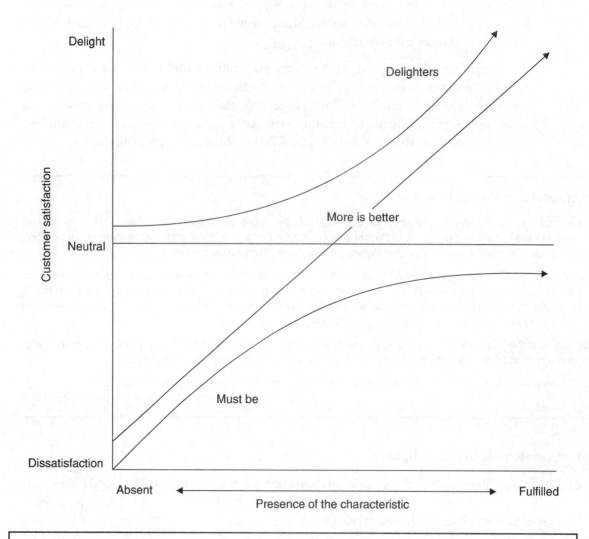

Kano's model of customer perceptions

Action Programme 4

A well-known theory of human motivation at work suggests that some aspects of a job, like working conditions, are 'hygiene' factors - only noticed if they are bad - and others, such as gaining recognition and promotion, are motivator factors.

Think of a product or service that you use and apply this idea to the 'satisfaction/delight' contrast.

5.10 Creating delighters represents a **critical success factor** for the organisation because this is how it can differentiate itself from the competition. The must be factors, on the other hand, are **critical failure factors**: organisations have to supply them, because not to do so would inevitably mean competitive disadvantage; however, relying on the must be factors alone does nothing more than ensure that the organisations remains in competitive contention, since must be factors cannot deliver genuine differentiation.

Marketing at Work

Here are some examples of companies providing their customers with delighted sensations; quite commonly, the sensation is produced through the behaviour of the front-line customer-service practitioner, rather than through the application of any codified corporate procedures.

In Nottingham, a grandmother bought two high chairs (for twins) at Allders. Both chairs split and were taken back. Allders immediately replaced them with two better quality and more expensive chairs, but at no cost to the purchaser.

In Swindon, a customer wanted to buy her daughter a dress from Woolworths, but the correct size was unavailable. The assistant phoned all the Woolworth stores in the country until the right dress was found - and then it was delivered to the customer free of charge.

In Fleet (Hampshire), the supermarket company Waitrose lends a fish kettle to its customers. One lady, having booked the fish kettle in advance for a particular Saturday, found that when she arrived to pick it up it was for some reason unavailable. The Waitrose employee promised that if she returned home, the company would make alternative arrangements and advise her within the hour: what they did, in fact, was to secure another fish kettle from their Oxford store and bring it to the customer's house by taxi.

Again in Swindon, a purchaser of a self-assembly children's cot, from Mothercare, found that a key component was missing. On phoning the store, with no great expectation that the component could be obtained quickly, the customer was told that a Mothercare staff member would bring the part round at once. Not only that: the visitor assembled the cot himself, and then produced a compensatory gift voucher.

5.11   If companies want to create meaningful customer 'loyalty' (ie the intent to repurchase), then in many respects all they have to do is to create circumstances in which employees across the board behave like these people from Mothercare, Waitrose, Woolworths and Allders.

Exam tip

Note particularly that the requirement is not principally to generate some elegant-sounding customer-focused strategies, but to stimulate, promote, reinforce and encourage **employees to build relationships** and to provide the kind of service which

- stimulates customers to **return**, and keep on returning, sometimes for life, and
- energises customers to **recommend** organisations to others.

These are the senior examiner's own words and reflect how it should be possible to generate customer loyalty, by employing the right people. Note here the emphasis that fancy strategies are not necessarily required!

Action Programme 5

Consider this. An article in *Svenska Dagbladet,* a Swedish newspaper, on 10 February 1989 began as follows.

'After 40 years as a customer in the [unnamed] bank, Ragnar Jones, who has an antiquarian bookshop on Norrtullsgatan in Stockholm, has been told that his routines do not suit the bank. He should therefore change banks.'

Customers at the Jones bookshop often paid by cheque. At the same time Ragnar needed cash to purchase books and give change. Therefor he would visit the bank several times a week to cash the cheques. But this was no popular with the bank because Jones was an unprofitable customer, according to the branch's deputy manager. The bank saw Jones as old-fashioned.

The bank's attitude was that Jones was a small customer, causing the bank a lot of trouble for little or no reward: he was uncooperative, refusing to open a cheque account and leave the day's takings in a bank box. Ragnar Jones, like many other of the bank's customers, is a peaceful businessman who does not show when he is annoyed. 'We have always used [the unnamed] bank and we cannot understand why we must change to suit the bank. It is the bank that introduced the cheques and not we businessmen. Why should they now refuse to cash them when we come into the bank?'

His anger led to the article in a national newspaper, and also to an opportunity for the bank to respond and gain publicity for its customer care. In fact the bank's reply, published in a subsequent issue of the paper, included the following statement:

'We have offered him alternatives but he will not accept them. In any case, we do not really want retailers as customers with their daily takings and need for change.' Could the bank not make an exception for customers like Ragnar and his wife, Siri? 'No, we reckon that the system we have proposed is goo for both the bank and the customer.'

Source: *Quality of Service: Making it really work,* Bo Edvardsson, Bertil Thomasson and John Ovretveit

Having read this Norseland saga, what is your reaction? Select any one of the following three:

(a)   The bank is quite correct, and Ragnar Jones should be arrested, prosecuted and conceivably executed for his failure to comply with the bank's preferred way of operating.

(b)   Jones is right, and the bank should at all times adapt its policies and systems to fit round the ways in which its customers choose to function.

(c)   The bank is entitled to be choosy about whom it wants as customers - so in concentrating its efforts on those customers from whom it currently makes a profit, it is acting wisely so far as the interests of its shareholders are concerned.

Chapter roundup

- Consumer behaviour models are popular because, in the words of Keith Williams, 'it has ... been found that it is possible to simplify consumer behaviour into its principal components and that, in practice, a relatively small number of variables account for the vast bulk of consumer behaviour'.

- Models help researchers to develop theories, describe and explain behaviour and aid prediction.

- Types of model include black box models and personal variable models.

- In the broadest sense customers fall into three 'types': individuals, groups and organisations.

- The **rate and extent of diffusion** of an innovation depend on:

  o   the **characteristics** of the innovation/new product
  o   the **channels of communication** used
  o   the **social system** within which communication takes place
  o   the **stages of the adoption process** reached by members of the social system

- Adopter categories have been identified as:

  o   innovators
  o   early adopters
  o   early majority
  o   late majority
  o   laggards

- It is of crucial importance to the marketer of an innovation to know who the innovators/early triers are, and how they can be reached and influenced.

- **The customer who is merely 'satisfied' is between 7 and 10 times more likely to move to another supplier than a customer who is 'very satisfied'.** It is the 'very satisfied' customer who is genuinely loyal and will repurchase.

- The **delighters** are the features or characteristics which surprise customers positively.

Quick quiz

1   What is the basis of the modelling approach? (2.1)

2   What are the limitations of models? (2.14)

3   What can black box models be used for? (2.17)

4   What does the decision process model consist of? (2.23)

5   What is diffusion? (4.3)

6   Why might a new product fail? (4.6)

7   What are the five adopter categories? (4.9)

8   What characteristics distinguish consumer innovation? (4.19)

9   Distinguish between satisfaction and delight. (5.1)

10 What is a 'must be' factor? (5.7)

11 When does a 'delighter' cease to be a 'delighter'? (5.9)

Action programme review

1   Just do it!

2   Does Delta Dental sell to employee groups, in which case what do those groups have in common? Or does it sell to companies? What are the consequences for Delta Dental if an individual member of an employee group has a grievance? There are no straightforward answers. Hopefully this generated some discussion. Other aspects of the passage are of interest too, for instance the reference to 'satisfaction'.

3, 4   Again, just do it!

5   If you choose (a), you probably work for or run an organisation which is constantly irritated by the untidiness of the ways in which customers operate. If only they would conform, you think, in your paternalistic (and not unkindly) way, then we would be happy, and they too would be contented.

If you chose (b), you have fallen for two of the most pervasive myths in the field of customer service: the first is that 'the customer is always right' and the second is that 'the customer is king' [or queen]. In reality, as we shall see, there are circumstances where it is more sensible to admit what we would often prefer to deny, namely, that the customer is wrong or, at least, misguided: we can then part company without endless recriminations.

If you chose (c), then you could be right, but you could also be dangerously mistaken. The trick lies in the fact that if you only concentrate on those customers from who you *currently* make a profit, then you could be ignoring the next generation. More and more organisations now realise that they have to address not just the profit to be made from each individual transaction with their customers, but also the lifetime profit from, say, 50 years of supermarket purchases, or 5 years of take-away pizzas. Moreover, you can't afford to neglect the damage it potentially does to your reputation if you appear to favour some customers over others. Even the ones you favour may feel uncomfortable about the 'privileges' they enjoy if they think that these are bought through the rejection of others. It is doubtful, in the scenario presented, whether the reported comments of the bank's spokesperson actually did anything to ensure that the bank's existing customers were impressed or that new customers were attracted - however sensible the logical arguments of the bank actually were.

9 *Classifying customers for competitive advantage*

Chapter Topic List	Syllabus reference
1 Setting the scene	3.2
2 The purpose of segmentation	3.2
3 Demographics	3.2
4 Social status and social class	3.2
5 Psychographics	3.2
6 Customer groups: family life cycle	3.2
7 Customer groups: cultures	3.2
8 Segmenting organisations	3.2
9 New approaches to classifying customers	3.2

Learning Outcomes

- After studying this chapter you will understand more about classifying customers and its key purpose.

- You should understand the following:

  - Market segmentation aims to group potential customers according to identifiable characteristics relevant to their purchase behaviour, thereby allowing marketers to more effectively target one or more particular segments of the market.

  - Demographic market segmentation is carried out in practice on the basis of age, gender, income, education and occupation. Geo-demographic segmentation groups together people who live close to one another.

  - A customer's buying decision will depend to a certain extent on his social status and social class.

  - The family life cycle is a method of classifying family units in a way that is significant for social/ consumer behaviour.

  - Psychographics or lifestyle segmentation attempts to classify people according to their values, opinions, personality characteristics and interests.

  - Culture can be used to segment a market.

  - Industrial market segmentation is worthwhile.

Key Concepts Introduced

- Segmentation
- Demographics
- Psychographics

Examples of Marketing at Work

* Men and marketers

* Compaq

* Nissan

1 SETTING THE SCENE

1.1 In this chapter we examine some of the main types of customer segmentation systems used by marketers.

> **Key Concept**
> **Segmentation** is the process by which consumers are grouped together according to identifiable characteristics which are relevant to their buying behaviour. It allows marketers to target people with research to discover their needs and preference, so that all the elements of the marketing mix can be directed towards the potential market.

1.2 This is obviously a vital area in marketing and allows the marketer to understand his or her customers by attempting to get as close as possible to them.

2 THE PURPOSE OF SEGMENTATION

2.1 **Every purchase is different**. Consumer and industrial buyers can be influenced by a wide range of factors and find themselves in a variety of buying situations. The motives, moods and personality of the buyer and seller all play a part in determining the outcome of a particular purchase opportunity. It is helpful if the total market of potential customers can be, at least in the first instance, dealt with on a larger scale.

2.2 Clearly there are many possible characteristics of buyers which could be used to segment markets. There is a **variety of criteria** which can be used to identify the most effective characteristics for use in market segmentation. Irrespective of the approach that is used, there are a number of **requirements for effective market segmentation**. The market must be measurable, accessible and substantial.

(a) **Measurable**

This refers to the degree to which information exists or is obtainable cost effectively on the particular buyer characteristics of interest. Whilst a car manufacturer may have access to information about location of the customers, personality traits of buyers are more difficult to obtain information about.

(b) **Accessible**

This refers to the degree to which the company can focus effectively on the chosen segments using marketing methods. Thus whilst a new car dealer may be able to access potential corporate customers in their area, by direct mail or tele-sales, identifying individual customers with family incomes in excess of £30,000 pa would not be easy.

(c) **Substantial**

This refers to the degree to which the segments are large enough to be worth considering for separate marketing cultivation. As devising different marketing approaches is expensive, a minimum size of a segment can be set and measured (perhaps by potential profitability). Thus, whilst a large number of people in social group DE aged over 65 could be identified, their potential profitability to a retailer is likely to be less in the long term than a smaller number of 17-18 year olds. This latter group might be worth cultivating using a specially devised marketing approach whereas the former might not be.

This list of requirements for effective market segmentation should be supplemented by Horam Wind's point that any given segment should be '**homogenous** in its response to marketing variables'. In other words, those in the segment should **react in a broadly similar fashion** when, for example, prices rise or fall or supply increases or decreases.

2.3 Besides the overall aim of improved profit contribution, a number of **other benefits** can emanate from successful market segmentation.

(a) The company should be in a better position to spot **new marketing opportunities**. This benefit should flow from a better understanding of consumer needs in each of the segments.

(b) **Specialists** can be used for each of the company's major segments.

(c) The total marketing **budget** can be allocated to take into account the needs of each segment and the likely return from each segment.

(d) The company can make **finer adjustments to the product and service offerings** and to the marketing appeals used for each segment.

(e) The company can try to **dominate particular segments** thus gaining competitive advantage.

(f) The product range can more closely reflect **customer need differences**.

(g) Improved segmentation allows **more highly targeted marketing activity** and allows the team to develop an in-depth knowledge of the needs of a particular group of consumers.

2.4 Segmentation as a strategy is widely recognised as one of the **most important marketing tools**. Recognising that within a particular market there will be any number of sub-groups with their particular needs and requirements is a first step in putting the marketing philosophy of consumer orientation into practice.

2.5 However, the process of segmentation has to bring with it **benefits** if it is to be a worthwhile and viable exercise.

(a) Segmentation should **increase benefits to consumers** by providing products and benefits more closely meeting their ideal specifications.

(b) Segmentation enables the firm to identify those groups of customers who are **most likely to buy**. This ensures that resources will not be wasted, and marketing and sales activity can be highly focused. The result should be lower costs, greater sales and higher profitability.

(c) Across the industry, segmentation will provide **greater customer choice**.

Exam tip

Imagine you are the marketing consultant for a construction firm, and you are asked in the exam to provide a memo for your client's marketing director to set out the benefits of customer/market segmentation and recommend the most suitable segmentation system for your client.

We suggest that the memo begins with a definition of segmentation and then sets out the benefits of marketing segmentation. The various approaches to segmentation should be briefly described. You will need to apply your knowledge to the question scenario and suggest an appropriate segmentation system. And, of course, a solution would not be complete without a conclusion.

3 DEMOGRAPHICS

Key Concept

Demography is the study of measurable statistics of a population, such as **age**, **gender**, **marital status**, **income**, **occupation** and **education**.

3.1 Demographics are often used as the basis of market segmentation because:

(a) the data are **more easily measurable and quantifiable** than psychological or sociocultural variables;

(b) the data are relatively **accessible** and **cost-effective** to gather;

(c) demographic information helps to **locate a target market** (whose motives and behaviour can then be explained and predicted using psychological or sociocultural investigation). It identifies potential for sales and consumption of a product, although it does not identify why, or by whom, a particular brand is used;

(d) demographic variables reveal **trends relevant to marketers**, such as shifts in age and income distributions.

3.2 Most secondary data, including census data about a population, are expressed in demographic terms, showing how many people (and what percentage) of a given population are of a given gender, age, income bracket, occupational bracket, household size, family size etc.

If you live in the UK, you may have had to fill out detailed forms for the 1991 Census of Population. A census is held every ten years, to take a kind of statistical 'snapshot' of the demography of the nation on a particular day. Derived from the census data, there are various digests and directories (such as *Social Trends* published by Her Majesty's Stationery Office) which make the statistics available. (Individual census forms themselves are considered sensitive personal information, and are not published for 100 years.)

3.3 Demographic market segmentation is carried out in practice on the basis of:

(a) **age**, particularly teenage, young adults and retired. Baby foods, teen fashion, 'yuppy' accessories etc are age-related niche products, although psychological variables such as self-image, health concerns (for the elderly) or status-consciousness (for young adults) are often added, since purely chronological segmentation can be misleadingly stereotyped: how do you appeal to the 'glamorous granny', for example?;

(b) **gender,** a major distinguishing variable in relation to gender-related family purchase roles. New market niches have been created by the blurring of traditional gender demarcations: male cosmetics, women's office accessories etc. Another consequence of changing roles is the relative inaccessibility of women, now that many of them work outside the home: magazines have replaced daytime television and radio as the premium media for reaching women. Meanwhile, men are more readily accessible through in-store promotions. Male homemakers are expected to be a major market for the future;

(c) **income, education and occupation**. Income alone is a commonly-used segmentation variable (and the 'affluent consumer' a much sought-after segment), but it is limited in only being able to indicate the ability to consume/purchase, rather than the criteria for product choice. Income is therefore matched with other demographic variables, to produce segments such as the 'affluent elderly', the 'yuppie' or the 'affluent woman'. Consumers' attitudes, values and tastes are more accurately reflected by occupation and education, which - together with income - are often combined in the index of social class, discussed below.

Geo-demographics: ACORN

3.4   **Geo-demographic market segmentation** is based on the notion that **people who live close** to one another, within the same physical geography, **share broad characteristics** of financial means, tastes, lifestyles and purchase habits. Consumers can be 'clustered' according to lifestyle, with is correlated with geographic areas as identified by post codes.

ACORN (A Classification of Residential Neighbourhoods) is a system which classifies every address in the UK into one of thirty-eight types, according to the demographics of its immediate 'neighbourhood'. The extract below divides the population into six main groups.

- Thriving (19.7%)
- Expanding (11.6%)
- Rising (7.8%)
- Settling (24.1%)
- Aspiring (13.7%)
- Striving (22.7%)

		% of population
C	**Rising (7.8% of population)**	
C6	*Affluent Urbanites, Town and City Areas (2.3%)*	
6.16	Well-Off Town and City Areas	1.1
6.17	Flats and Mortgages, Singles and Young Working Couples	0.7
6.18	Furnished Flats and Bedsits, Younger Single People	0.4
C7	*Prosperous Professionals, Metropolitan Areas (2.1%)*	
7.19	Apartments, Young Professional Singles and Couples	1.1
7.20	Gentrified Multi-Ethnic Areas	1.0
C8	*Better-Off Executives, Inner City Areas (3.4%)*	
8.21	Prosperous Enclaves, Highly Qualified Executives	0.7
8.22	Academic Centres, Students and Young Professionals	0.7
8.23	Affluent City Centre Areas, Tenements and Flats	0.4
8.24	Partially Gentrified Multi-Ethnic Areas	0.7
8.25	Converted Flats and Bedsits, Single People	0.9
D	**Settling (24.1% of population)**	
D9	*Comfortable Middle Agers, Mature Home Owning Areas (13.4%)*	
9.26	Mature Established Home Owning Areas	3.3
9.27	Rural Areas, Mixed Occupations	3.4
9.28	Established Home Owning Areas	4.0
9.29	Home Owning Areas, Council Tenants, Retired People	2.6

D10 Skilled Workers, Home Owning Areas (10.7%)		
10.30	Established Home Owning Areas, Skilled Workers	4.5
10.31	Home Owners in Older Properties, Younger Workers	3.1
10.32	Home Owning Areas with Skilled Workers	3.1

4 SOCIAL STATUS AND SOCIAL CLASS

4.1 In Britain, a complex social class system is usually encapsulated in the popular terms: 'working class', 'middle class' and 'upper class'. People have **stereotypes** about the attributes of a particular class, and the whole topic tends to be very emotive on the basis of these stereotyped perceptions.

4.2 **Subjective definitions** of class relate to the way in which people **consider themselves**. A white-collar job, an owned home or particular leisure pursuits may cause a person to identify himself as 'middle class'; others may consider anyone who 'works' to be 'working class'; others may preserve a sense of being 'working class' because of their family background, though their own social circumstances have changed.

4.3 **Objective measures** of social class consist of selected **demographic** - mainly **socio-economic** - variables: income, education and occupation are the most common. (These can then be combined with geo-demographic data about social class location and distribution, to offer useful information for market segmentation.) Other variables sometimes added - to supplement the limited value of a pure 'amount of income' measurement - include value/quality of residence or residential area, source of income (eg earned, inherited, assisted), and possessions in the home.

4.4 Social grade definitions vary.

(a) **Two-category schemes**

Producers of goods and services	Managers and organisers
'Blue-collar'	'White collar'
'Lower-class/working class'	'Middle class'

(b) **Five or six category schemes**

Jicnar's social grade definitions (A-E), correspond closely to what are called Social Classes I-V on the Registrar General's Scale. (The latter are to be revised in the 2001 census and the term 'class' will probably be dropped.)

Registrar General's Social Classes	Jicnar Social Grades	Social Status	Characteristics of occupation
I	A	Upper middle class	Higher managerial/professional eg lawyers, directors
II	B	Middle class	Intermediate managerial/administrative/ professional eg teachers, managers, computer operators, sales managers
III (i) non-manual	C_1	Lower middle class	Supervisory, clerical, junior managerial/ administrative/professional eg foremen, shop assistants
(ii) manual	C_2	Skilled working class	Skilled manual labour eg electricians, mechanics
IV	D	Working class	Semi-skilled manual labour eg machine operators

BPP PUBLISHING

Registrar General's Social Classes	Jicnar		Characteristics of occupation
	Social Grades	Social Status	
V			Unskilled manual labour eg cleaning, waiting tables, assembly
	E	Lowest level of subsistence	State pensioners, widows (no other earner), casual workers

(c) Some definitions also add a **seventh** stratum: upper class, consisting of the aristocracy (titled landowners) and the very wealthy (through ownership or investment). This stratum undoubtedly still exists in the UK, and this 1% of adult population is reckoned to own one quarter of the wealth of Britain!

Action Programme 1

How can you market your organisation's goods or services to the person who has everything?

The value of class as a segmentation variable

4.5 Consumer research has found some evidence that **each of the social classes shares a number of specific lifestyle factors** (attitudes, values, activities etc), and that these factors distinguish members of that class from members of all other classes. This theory has been used to determine the appropriate marketing mix for each social stratum, depending on researched buying preferences and habits. When banks, for example, have branded facilities for 'high net worths', they are targeting a class segment. 'Luxury' branded products and magazines catering for high-status readers (*Country Houses*, say, or *Boardroom* are similarly positioned).

4.6 In particular, social class has been found to correlate with:

(a) **tastes in clothing and fashion**. Higher-class individuals tend to seek a more subtle look, with fewer external points of identification such as badges, brand names and logos etc;

(b) **home decoration**. Some social status scales include furnishings and possessions, as well as home tidiness and cleanliness. (As an interesting related point, it seems that lower-class families have their television sets in the living room, while middle/upper class families are more likely to have them in a bedroom or other family room. If you were marketing a very expensive TV set, you would need to associate it with the latter setting);

(c) **leisure activities**. The choice of recreational activity correlates with class. Theatre, concerts, bridge parties etc are upper-class activities, while lower-class consumers tend to watch television, go to football matches or the pub, or do craft activities;

(d) **money management**. Upper-classes tend to invest, while lower-classes save less. Lower class consumers tend to use credit cards or instalment purchases to 'buy now, pay later' on desired and otherwise unaffordable items, while upper-class credit users simply use credit as a convenient substitute for cash, and pay in full each month.

4.7 Such analyses must, however, be **cautious** in their use of 'social class' as a variable.

(a) It is **not exactly or consistently defined**.

(b) **Social mobility,** to the extent that a class group is defined, may make it difficult to use the concept in a meaningful way. People commonly perceive themselves to be in a different class to that in which they are objectively classified, and/or may aspire to membership of a higher class: their consumption behaviour will be affected accordingly. In addition, more general affluence and educational attainment has blurred the edges between working and middle class, and increased the expectation of mobility still further.

(c) Conventional gradings take into consideration the occupation of the head of the household, but with **dual-income families,** fluctuating **family/household patterns,** the **mobility of labour** and **changes in employment** circumstances (eg redundancy or insolvency), this may give a rather **misleading** picture.

(d) 'It is certainly the case that people in the same social class have many things in common - the same monopoly or lack of access to scarce resources, for example; the same good or bad standards of housing; the same access to, or restrictions on, educational opportunity; the same shared experiences of comfort, travel, hardship or enjoyment. But all of these cultural characteristics are the consequences of social class rather than the causes of it. People's lifestyles are a reflection of their economic condition in society, not the reason for their position'.

(Jane Thompson: *Sociology Made Simple*.)

For this reason, consumer researchers are starting to concentrate more on the lifestyle variables and 'clusters' and less on the class-related terminology that has accompanied them.

5 PSYCHOGRAPHICS

> **Key Concept**
> **Psychographics** is a form of consumer research which builds up a **psychological profile of consumers in general**, or users (or potential users) of a particular product. It is the main basis of psychological segmentation of a market, and appropriate product positioning.

5.1 Psychographics is also commonly referred to as:

(a) **lifestyle** analysis; or

(b) **AIO analysis** - Activities (how consumers spend their time), Interests (or preferences) and Opinions (where they stand on product-related issues).

5.2 Psychographics is **different** from:

(a) **demographics** - which we have seen consists of quantitative data about population characteristics like age, income, gender and location. Psychographics tends to include qualitative data about motives, attitudes and values; and

(b) **motivation research.** Psychographics includes qualitative factors, like motivation research, but its findings are presented as quantified, statistical information in tabular format. They are also based on larger samples of the population reached through less intensive techniques like self-administered questionnaires and inventories. We shall discuss these distinctions in Part B of this text.

Psychographic segmentation

5.3 Psychographics or life style segmentation is a method which seeks to classify people according to their **values, opinions, personality characteristics, interests and so on,** and by its inherent nature should be very dynamic. The relevance of this concept is bound up in its ability to introduce various new dimensions to existing customer information, for example customers' disposition towards savings, investment and the use of credit, general attitude to money, leisure and other key influences.

5.4 In a competitive world where innovation is the key to improved organisational performance a system which is able to introduce new perspectives is worthy of investigation. Life style segmentation fits this criterion because it deals with the person as opposed to the product and attempts to discover the particular unique life style patterns of customers, which will give a **richer insight into their preferences** for various products and services. Strategists who use this segmentation tool will be better able to direct their marketing energies to meet the future needs of these identified groups.

5.5 **Lifestyle** refers to distinctive ways of living adopted by particular communities or sub-sections of society. Lifestyle is a **manifestation of a number of behavioural factors**, such as motivation, personality and culture, and depends on accurate description. When the numbers of people following it are quantified, marketers can assign and target products and promotion upon this particular target lifestyle group. The implications of lifestyle for marketing, and the problems of definition involved, can perhaps best be illustrated by some examples.

5.6 Lifestyle is a controversial issue, and a full analysis of the argument is beyond the scope of this text. One simple example generalises lifestyle in terms of four categories.

(a) **Upwardly mobile, ambitious**

People seek a better and more affluent lifestyle, principally through better paid and more interesting work, and a higher material standard of living. Persons with such a lifestyle will be prepared to try new products.

(b) **Traditional and sociable**

Compliance and conformity to group norms bring social approval and reassurance to the individual. Purchasing patterns will therefore be 'conformist'.

(c) **Security and status seeking**

'Safety' needs and 'ego-defensive' needs are stressed. This lifestyle links status, income and security. It encourages the purchase of strong and well known products and brands, and emphasises those products and services which confer status and make life as secure and predictable as possible. These would include insurance, membership of the AA or RAC etc. Products that are well established and familiar inspire more confidence than new products, which will be resisted.

(d) **Hedonistic preference**

The emphasis is on 'enjoying life now' and the immediate satisfaction of wants and needs. Little consideration is given to the future.

5.7 The **'green movement'** has become part of many lifestyle segments. Companies segment some market clients according to whether they are 'pale' or 'dark' green in their attitude to the environment and therefore how significant environmentally friendly product attributes will be to the purchasing decision.

5.8 In a typical **psychographic research study**, an inventory is compiled, in which consumers are asked to **react to a variety of statements** - as individuals or as a family or household. They may be asked to react by degree of agreement (Do you strongly agree, agree, disagree or strongly disagree?) or by the importance they attach to a concept (is it very important, important, fairly important, unimportant?), or by the amount of time they spend on an activity or interest. Psychographic statements may be about general lifestyle or specific product categories, products or even brands: ideally the inventory would contain both.

Action Programme 2

Psychographic statements: Traveller's cheques
adapted from Schiffman and Kanuk, Consumer Behaviour

Individual/personal

'Traveller's cheques are for people who are experienced travellers.'

'I think about my safety and security when planning a trip.'

'I almost always keep some traveller's cheques in my wallet.'

'I use a seat belt even when going to the local store for milk.'

Product specific ———————————————————————— *General*

'We wouldn't even go on an overnight trip without traveller's cheques.'

'When we go on holiday, our family is always shopping.'

'We really appreciate the peace of mind that traveller's cheques provide.'

'We use the hotel safe to store our valuables when away on a family trip.'

Family/ household

What are the implications for a marketer of traveller's cheques of a potential customer's strong agreement and strong disagreement with each of these statements?

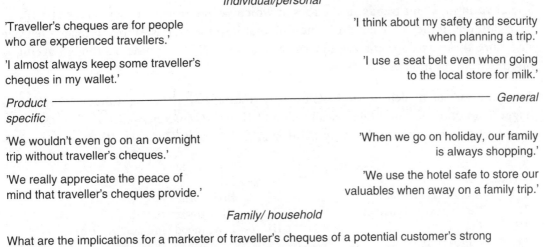

Action Programme 3

Suppose you were considering the responses to the following questionnaire.

'Time spent' inventory

Please tick the box that best indicates how often you have engaged in the activity during the past 12 months.

	0 times	1-4 times	5-9 times	10+ times
Went to a library	☐	☐	☐	☐
Went abroad on holiday	☐	☐	☐	☐
Went to a museum	☐	☐	☐	☐
Went to the cinema	☐	☐	☐	☐
Watched television	☐	☐	☐	☐

If 60% of your sample went to the cinema 1-4 times in one year, but 100% watched TV 10+ times, where would you advertise your product?

---

6 CUSTOMER GROUPS: FAMILY LIFE CYCLE

6.1 Family life cycle (FLC) is a method used by sociologists (and latterly consumer researchers) to classify **family units** in a way that is significant for social/consumer behaviour. It is frequently used as the basis of market segmentation, since it gives a composite picture of commonly-used demographic factors (marital status, family size, age, employment status) and their variation over time. You should be careful to distinguish in your mind - especially in the exam - between **life-cycle analysis,** discussed here, and **life style analysis** (or psychographics), discussed in the previous section - although both can be applied to the family in useful ways for marketing research and market segmentation.

6.2 The concept of family life cycle is based on the idea that the structure, membership and lifestyle of a family **change over time**, with the **age of the individual members**. The family progresses through a number of common stages of development. Researchers note that the family's economic character - income, expenditure and consumption priorities - will also change.

6.3 **Social variations and trends** in the ages at which people marry (if they marry at all) and have children (if they have children) indicate that it would be misleading to relate life-cycle stage directly to age: specific age ranges are not normally determined, although ageing is inferred from the progressive stages.

6.4 There are various models of the FLC used by researchers, including different numbers of stages. One synthesis, by Engel, Blackwell and Kollat (*Consumer Behaviour*) suggests nine stages, while a simpler synthesis by Schiffman and Kanuk (*Consumer Behaviour*) suggests only five.

9-stage FLC		*5-stage FLC*	
I	Bachelorhood	I	Bachelorhood
II	Newly-married couples	II	Honeymooners
III	Full Nest I	III	Parenthood ('full nest')
IV	Full Nest II		
V	Full Nest III		
VI	Empty Nest I	IV	Post-parenthood ('Empty nest')
VII	Empty Nest II		
VIII	Solitary survivor I	V	Dissolution
IX	Solitary survivor II		

The profiles of the nine stages appear on the next page.

6.5 There has been some **criticism** of the traditional FLC model as a basis for market segmentation in recent years. (See, for example, Rob Lawson, 'The Family Life Cycle: a demographic analysis', *Journal of Marketing Management* (Summer 1988).)

(a) It is modelled on the **demographic patterns of industrialised western nations** - and particularly America. This pattern may not be universally applicable.

(b) While the FLC model was once typical of the overwhelming majority of American families, there are now **important potential variations** from that pattern, including:

(i) childless couples - because of choice, career-oriented women and delayed marriage

(ii) later marriages - because of greater career-orientation and non-marital relationships: likely to have fewer children

(iii) later children - say in late 30s. Likely to have fewer children, but to stress 'quality of life'

(iv) single parents - (especially mothers) because of divorce

(v) fluctuating labour status - not just 'in labour' or 'retired', but redundancy, career change, dual-income etc

(vi) extended parenting - young, single adults returning home while they establish careers/financial independence; divorced children returning to parents; elderly parents requiring care; newly-weds living with in-laws

The family life cycle

	I	II	III	IV	V	VI	VII	VIII	IX
	Bachelor Stage	*Newly married couples*	*Full nest I*	*Full nest II*	*Full nest III*	*Empty nest I*	*Empty nest II*	*Solitary survivor in labour force*	*Solitary survivor(s) retired*
	Young single people not living at home	Young, no children	Youngest child under six	Youngest child six or over	Older married couples with dependent children	Older married couples, no children living with them, head of family still in labour force	Older married couples, no children living at home head of family retired		
	Few financial burdens.	Better off financially than they will be in the near future.	Home purchasing at peak.	Financial position better.	Financial position still better.	Home ownership at peak.	Significant cut in income.	Income still adequate but likely to sell family home and purchase smaller accommodation.	Significant cut in income.
	Fashion/ opinion leader led.	High levels of purchase of homes and consumer durable goods.	Liquid assets/ savings low.	Some wives return to work.	More wives work.	More satisfied with financial position and money saved.	Keep home.	Concern with level of savings and pension.	Additional medical requirements. Special need for attention, affection and security.
	Recreation orientated.	Buy cars, fridges, cookers, life assurance, durable furniture, holidays.	Dissatisfied with financial position and amount of money saved.	Child dominated household.	School and examination dominated household.	Interested in travel, recreation, self-education.	Buy medical appliances or medical care, products which aid health, sleep and digestion.	Some expenditure on hobbies and pastimes.	May seek sheltered accommodation.
	Buy basic kitchen equipment, basic furniture, cars, equipment for the mating game, holidays.	Establish patterns of personal financial management and control.	Reliance on credit finance, credit cards, overdrafts etc.	Buy necessities foods, cleaning material, clothes, bicycles, sports gear, music lessons, pianos, holidays etc.	Some children get first jobs; others in further / higher education.	Make financial gifts and contributions.	Assist children. Concern with level of savings and pension. Some expenditure on hobbies and pastimes.	Worries about security and dependence.	Possible dependence on others for personal financial management and control.
	Experiment with patterns of personal financial management and control.		Child dominated household.		Expenditure to support children's further / higher education.	Children gain qualifications; move to Stage I.			
			Buy necessities washers, dryers, baby food and clothes, vitamins, toys, books etc.		Buy new, more tasteful furniture, non-necessary appliances, boats etc holidays.	Buy luxuries, home improvements eg fitted kitchens etc.			

(vii) non-family households   -   unmarried (homosexual or heterosexual) couples

         -    divorced persons with no children

         -    single persons (mainly women, or older products of delay in first marriage)

         -    widowed persons (especially women, because of longer life-expectancy).

6.6   An alternative or modified FLC model is needed to take account of consumption variables such as:

(a) spontaneous **changes** in brand preference when a household undergoes a **change of status** (divorce, redundancy, death of a spouse, change in membership of a non-family household);

(b) **different economic circumstances** and extent of consumption planning in single-parent families, households where there is a redundancy, dual-income households;

(c) **different buying and consumption roles** to compensate/adjust in households where the **woman works**. Women can be segmented into at least four categories - each of which may represent a distinct market for goods and services:

- stay-at-home homemaker
- plan-to-work homemaker
- 'just-a-job' working woman
- career-oriented working woman

Action Programme 4

'The portrayal of non-traditional FLC stages in contemporary advertising of products and services is evidence that marketers are eager to expand their markets and make their products and services more relevant to varying family lifestyles.'   (Schiffman and Kanuk)

Identify examples of non-traditional FLC stages and circumstances in the advertising that you are exposed to.

Marketing at Work

(a) 'Those marketers who continue to deride their male audience may find themselves missing out on a host of new areas and markets in which male consumers are playing a more prominent part....

...According to Mintel/TGI, nearly 90 per cent of men shopped for groceries in 1992, compared with under 80 per cent in 1980. Nearly one in five men in 1992 said they did their grocery shopping single-handed, and this proportion rises to one in four among men in their early 20s. (Suddenly, that Sainsbury's ad, where the lone male shopper begins an imaginary affair with a lone female shopper, doesn't seem so contrived, after all.)

So what do today's marketers make of males in the 1990s? Men's fashion chain Hugo Boss launched a new male fragrance last summer which, it claimed, was designed to break the mould. Called HUGO, its design was like a hip flask and it was targeted at "disillusioned, highly critical uncompromising" young men of the so-called X-generation age group (16-28). These consumers are "true individuals, setting their own pace and defining reality in their own terms."

Maryann Barone, executive creative director of The Chelsea Partnership, which handled HUGO's advertising and promotion, says men are still an "untapped market". "When you consider how many single male households there are going to be by the year 2000 you start to realise just how many new opportunities for targeting there will be. We may not be too far from the day when household products like laundry and cleaning items will be targeted specifically at men."

For the moment, however, the tactics are not quite so overt. Enlightened marketers are taking care not to alienate male consumers by appearing to hurry them into strange new terrain.

Take L'Oreal, for example, which produced a brand extension of its famous Ambre Solaire suncare product in 1992. Called Ambre Solaire UV Sport, the range was aimed squarely at male consumers, who had traditionally given the sun protection market a wide berth. But this product was different: it played on the male-biased world of sports, it used a "male" pack design, and it carried the ultimate male descriptor: "Sweat resistant, non-greasy lotion, won't run in eyes". These attributes were highlighted, and the product has been a success, claims L'Oreal.

Pepsi showed the same marketing flair when it launched Pepsi Max. The TV ads show four "adrenalin-junky" dudes, living life "to the Max", but what they are in fact drinking is a diet product, Diet Pepsi in all but name - even thought Pepsi makes a song and dance about how different the two brand extensions are.

Pepsi pandered to a much-cherished male myth - the all-conquering action man - while recognising the reality that most men today are as concerned about their weight and health as are women....

....Now there is talk of Unisex, er, Thing. Calvin Klein has been advertising its new CK One fragrance, aimed at young trendies of either sex. Levi's produces two gender-bending TV ads - one featuring a tarty woman who turns out to be a transvestite man; the other produced in two versions, one where a boy goes into a drugstore to buy condoms, the second where a girl does the same thing. Elida Gibbs also does two executions of its Organics commercial - one featuring an endorsement from a women's magazine, the other endorsed by a men's magazine. What exactly is going on? "'All markets are beginning to merge", opines Nicola Fawssett, a director at marketing consultancy, New Solutions. "Traditional male markets like cars and financial services have opened their doors to women and vice versa. Consumers will increasingly be defined in terms of age and lifestyle rather than gender. It's about group identities." '
Marketing Business, February 1996

(b) 'The Cognac industry is to follow the lead of whisky distillers by targeting young drinkers. Allied Domecq's cognac brand Courvoisier is to be promoted for the first time to under 25s in pubs and clubs....

…The company will run a promotional campaign in the autumn in bars and clubs to encourage under 25s to mix Courvoisier with orange juice, cola or ginger ale or to use it as a base for cocktails.

It follows a route taken by whisky distillers especially United Distillers which ran a similar promotion last year in a bid to get drinkers to try its Bell's brand with mixers.' *Marketing Week*, August 2 1996

(c) 'In a first for a detergent company (Lever Brothers, the UK detergents arm of Unilever), young men who have graduated from taking their washing home to mum will be targeted, through magazines such as Loaded and GQ, and encouraged to phone the "careline". They will find out how to avoid what Lever terms "red socks syndrome", when shirts and underwear gain an unintended pink hue from red clothes in the wash.'

(d) 'Although men represent half the population, advertisers still find male consumers a difficult group to target both in the placement and the content of ads……In addition to finding the right arena in which to advertise products [magazines aimed at men represent less than a seventh of the female market in circulation terms], advertisers have also had difficulties in finding the kind of adverts that make men spend……However, the recent success of campaigns for American-made Dockers trousers demonstrates the huge potential for marketers who can effectively tap into the male psyche. Three out of four US men between 25 and 55 now own a pair of Dockers, and since their launch in Europe last year, sales are up 135 per cent.' *Times,* 3 September 1997

(e) In January 1998 the Express on Sunday newspaper spent £5m on launching a 48-page sports supplement as a further push into its target market of young males. *Financial Times*, 30 April 1996

7   CUSTOMER GROUPS: CULTURES

7.1   Knowledge of the **shared values, beliefs and artefacts of a society** are clearly of value to marketers, who can adapt their products and appeals accordingly, and be fairly sure of a sizeable market. Marketers can also plan to participate in the teaching process that creates culture, since mass media advertising, in particular, is an important agent by which cultural meanings are attached to products, people and situations.

7.2　Culture is deeply embedded in everyday behaviour, but is susceptible to measurement to some extent, using:

(a)　**attitude measurement techniques** (discussed later in this text);

(b)　**projective techniques, depth interviews** and **focus group** sessions (discussed later in this text);

(c)　**content analysis** - examining the content of the verbal, written and pictorial communications of a society: what kind of people are shown in advertisements, what criteria are used in design (is the society verbal or non-verbal? does it favour simplicity or complexity?), what 'themes' and images recur etc;

(d)　**observation** of a sample of the population by trained anthropological researchers, in the field (eg in store), followed by inference of the underlying reasons for the observed behaviour;

(e)　**surveys** or 'value inventories', measuring personal values.

7.3　Cultural market segmentation tends to stress **specific, widely-held cultural values** with which the majority of consumers are expected to identify. Some products may have an appeal specific to a particular culture; others may be 'cross-cultural' - but require a different promotional message or 'positioning' in each culture.

8　SEGMENTING ORGANISATIONS

8.1　Although industry sectors are usually **smaller and more easily identified** than consumer markets segmentation is generally very worthwhile, allowing a modified marketing strategy to be targeted at specified groups of organisations within the total market.

8.2　A number of methods for segmenting organisations exist and are again able to be used in combination. Improved data bases provide additional intelligence information allowing much tighter targeting of industrial customers.

(a)　**By location**

Already covered under consumer segmentation, but many business sectors are concentrated in particular locations for example steel in Sheffield, computer companies along the M4 corridor etc.

(b)　**Customer size**

The size of a company either by turnover or employees can give a broad indication of their needs for certain products such as management training services.

(c)　**Usage rates**

Customers can be segmented as heavy, medium or light users; this is most relevant in raw material and parts markets and the market for some business services, for example telecommunications and travel.

(d)　**Industry classification**

This classification indicates the nature of the business.

(e)　**Product use**

Different products may be used in different forms or ways, for example an organisation may buy a fleet of cars for use by its salesforce, or to hire out to the public as the basis for its service. Different uses are likely to be associated with different needs.

Marketing at Work

Many examples of the potential of segmentation of businesses are given in Ames and Hlavacek, *Market Driven Management* (1989), including the following.

'Compaq Computer Corporation identified what they believed to be a small market need for a high-end portable personal computer. Although IBM dominated the general personal computer business it did not have a portable personal computer at year end 1985. Compaq was quick to spot this void and rapidly got a product to the market. Only five years after its first product was introduced in 1982, the company posted revenues in excess of a billion dollars - a feat unmatched in all US industry.'

8.3   However, as Ames and Hlavacek observe, many companies in the past have failed to realise that time devoted to segmentation of organisations is worthwhile. This is why smaller firms are often able to capture significant niches: somebody with an entrepreneurial bent spots a **niche opportunity** and sets up a business specifically to serve the needs of that niche with a better product, better delivery, better price or better service.

8.4   Common **reasons why organisations fail to segment industrial markets** successfully are set out in Ames and Hlavacek.

(a)   Not giving enough thought to their markets or lacking the expertise and understanding to research and analyse the markets correctly.

(b)   Assuming that methods that work in the **consumer goods** world will work in the **business** market. 'However, segmentation for consumer and industrial markets is as different as potato chips and integrated circuit chips'. (Ames and Hlavacek)

(c)   Thinking of customers as **people rather than organisations**. Organisational market segmentation must be based on common economic, application or usage considerations: demographic and psychographic distinctions provide little basis for segmenting business markets.

(d)   **Thinking too broadly**: 'An industrial firm's division charter states: "The division is a supplier of hydraulic pumps and hoses to machinery markets." Again, a general industry is being defined, not market segments. Further analysis revealed that the division was primarily supplying certain types of farm equipment manufacturers, three kinds of construction machinery producers and heavy-duty truck makers'.

(e)   **Thinking too narrowly**: some firms do not think beyond their two or three major customers, or beyond their existing products and capabilities.

(f)   Identifying **too many or too few segments**.

8.5   Ames and Hlavacek suggest that the best way for an organisation to exploit small but attractive growth markets is to **break themselves down into many small business units** which can stay closer to changing market requirements and are quicker to identify and pursue new market opportunities. There must be a willingness to learn new skills and capabilities and selling staff need to be equipped with appropriate training and selling aids.

9   NEW APPROACHES TO CLASSIFYING CUSTOMERS

9.1   A word of caution is appropriate. Although segmentation supplies an opportunity for enhanced customer choice, it is arguable that nowadays **customers are not interested in choice if none of the choices available exactly matches their requirements**. Thus it is possible that a car manufacturer may offer 19 variants for a popular model, but still not supply a mixture of ingredients which entirely meets the expectations of some customers (who may want, for example, a two-door car with automatic transmission, but are faced with

BPP
PUBLISHING

a 'choice' between two-door versions with manual transmission or four-door cars with automatic transmission).

Segmentation versus customising

9.2   Such thinking is the basis for what is called **mass customisation,** that is, the creation of individually-designed products and services, tailored to the precise requirements of the individual customer, whilst minimising the cost implications so that, by and large, the economies of (mass-production) scale can be sustained. Joseph Pine's book *Mass Customisation* (Harvard Business School Press, 1993) indicates some of the possibilities.

(a)   **Component-sharing modularity** - where the same component is used across multiple products to provide economies of scale, yet enable a considerable variety of products to be made. Black & Decker completely redesigned its power tool product lines - twice - to take advantage of component-sharing modularity to greatly reduce costs whilst providing **more** variety and **speedier** product development.

(b)   **Component-swapping modularity** - where different components are paired with the same basic product, creating as many different products as there are components to swap. Examples include Swatch, Create-A-Book (where children's names can be inserted at appropriate points in a pre-printed text), and legal documents.

(c)   **Cut-to-fit modularity** - where variables in the product or service can be modified in an almost infinite number of ways in order precisely to match customer requirements. The National Bicycle Industrial Co, a subsidiary of Matsushita, provides individually customised bicycles. Its factory, as *Fortune* relates, 'is ready to produce any of 11,231,862 variations on 18 models of racing, road and mountain bikes in 199 colour patterns and about as many sizes as there are people.'

(d)   **Mix modularity** - where components are mixed together in ways which make the result totally unlike a straightforward combination of the components themselves. When particular colours of paint are mixed together, for example, the components are no longer visible in the end product.

(e)   **Bus modularity** occurs when different components are attached to a standard structure: examples include track lighting or bus services whose routes can be modified in accordance with passenger (customer) preferences.

(f)   **Sectional modularity** provides the greatest degree of customisation because it allows any number of differing components to be attached together in arbitrary ways - as long as each component is connected to another at standard interfaces. The classic example is the Lego building process with their locking-cylinder interfaces.

Marketing at Work

Full mass customisation of automobiles in the first year of the 21st century utilising all forms of modularity but also time-compression, point-of-sale manufacturing, customisability.

'The most important objective is to create a system to produce low-volume, special-niche vehicles at reasonable cost. The great numbers of such models make it obvious that very fast, inexpensive new model development is necessary ... Reducing the time and cost of new model development and start-up is the number one priority of the Japanese auto industry heading into the 1990s ...

Many assembly ideas have been considered. All of the most promising ones assume final assembly of cars from large modules with each module being sub-assembled on a short line ...

Cars would have to be designed with structural modules that can be sub-assembled in different locations, then brought together for final assembly of the structure, followed by attachment of the body panels. The external shape of the completed body is thereby partly independent of the form of the structural framework ... If the design could ingeniously allow for dimensional variations, final assembly might even be done at the dealership ...

The success of the concept depends on cultivating the *automotive prosumer.* The prosumer participates in the design of his vehicle at a work station in the dealership. Using the car company's CAD/CAM software, the prosumer can first select a combination of body structures, drive train components, and suspension components that have been tested for safety and performance. The car company's system will permit selection of only safe, durable combinations of these modules ...

Many features of the car can be custom-designed, depending on how much the customer wants to pay, of course. The seat contour can be fitted to the customer, the car's lighting system designed as the customer likes, the instrument panel layout modified to suit personal preferences - again with safety checks. Within limits, prosumers can create the shape of body panels, design their own trim, and 'imagineer' sound systems to their own tastes ...

In ten years, some of the features may be commonly modified on the run. For example, the stiffness of suspension can be adjusted while the car is in operation.

The prosumer design system will check whether final designs are feasible ... *The leadtime to delivery: three days.*

Source: 'Manufacturing 21 Report: The Future of Japanese Manufacturing', *AME Research Report* (Association for Manufacturing Excellence), 1990.

Chapter roundup

- Segmentation groups customers according to identifiable characteristics relevant to their purchase behaviour. For a market to be usefully segmentable, it must be measurable, accessible and substantial.

- Demographics is the process by which a population is analysed according to the relevant characteristics it demonstrates, such as gender, age, occupation etc. Geo-demographics, combining these factors with geographical location on the basis of post codes, is a very useful variation of demographics.

- Status (power and authority) and the awareness of it allow marketers to position a product as, say, aspirational to customers of low status or congratulatory to high status customers. Status and social class is the basis on which more traditional but open societies such as the UK are stratified. However, society is becoming increasingly open and mobile, so social class is no longer of such importance when it comes to segmentation.

- Psychographics builds up a psychological profile of consumers in general, or of consumers of a particular product. Also known as lifestyle analysis, psychographics help to segment markets at the same time as suggesting concrete ways to appeal to particular segments.

- Family life-cycle analysis classifies families so as to give a composite picture of the family in terms of commonly-used demographic factors. There are various models of the FLC; Schiffman and Kanuk's has five stages.

  o Bachelorhood
  o Honeymooners
  o Parenthood ('full next')
  o Post-parenthood ('empty nest')
  o Dissolution

- There have been criticisms of the FLC in recent years.

  o It is modelled on patterns in industrialised western nations.
  o There are now important potential variations from the model.

- Because of the increasingly global nature of marketing, cross-cultural psychographics is of increasing interest to marketers, by which the different mind-sets of people from different cultures are analysed.

- Organisational markets are also open to segmentation, often on a universal basis, ie *all* potential customers can be identified and analysed, since the population is by definition smaller than that of general consumers.

BPP PUBLISHING

Quick quiz

1   What is market segmentation? (see para 1.1) What are its benefits? (2.3)

2   Why is demographic segmentation often used? (3.1)

3   What are geo-demographics? (3.4)

4   With what does social class correlate? (4.6)

5   Why must care be taken when using 'social class' as a variable? (4.7)

6   What is AIO analysis? (5.1)

7   What is psychographic segmentation? (5.3)

8   What is meant by the Family Life Cycle? (6.1)

9   What are the five stages of Schiffman and Kanuk's FLC? (6.4)

10 How can cultural influence be measured? (7.2)

11 How can industrial customers be segmented? (8.2)

12 Describe the main reasons why organisations have failed to segment organisational markets. (8.4)

Action Programme Review

1   Given that the P of price is only an issue if it is too low, you concentrate on extraordinarily high quality products and services, promoted so as to lend them a high degree of exclusivity, and probably distributed by taking them directly to the customer.

Flick through *Vogue* and visit stores like Harrods or Harvey Nichols to get some more ideas. Leave your credit cards at home!

For interest, here is the text of a glossy advertisement that appeared alongside an article on malt whisky in *The London Magazine*. Compare it with a typical lager advert.

Whisky

The Spirited Investment

FOR FURTHER INFORMATION CONTACT ONE OF OUR CONSULTANTS WHO WILL BE PLEASED TO ADVISE YOU OF A PROFITABLE AND CONGENIAL METHOD OF EXPANDING YOUR INVESTMENT PORTFOLIO

The Napier Spirit Company

SALES OFFICE: 42 Southward Street, London, SE1 1ON
Telephone: 0171 378 7722 Facsimile: 0171 378 7744

10 The individual as customer: attitudes and behaviour

Chapter Topic List	Syllabus reference
1 Setting the scene	3.1, 3.3
2 Understanding buyer motives	3.1, 3.3
3 Attitudes and behaviour	3.1, 3.3
4 The relevance to the marketing customer interface	3.1, 3.3

Learning Outcomes

- After completing this chapter you will have an understanding of attitudes and behaviour in the buying decision, and its relevance to the marketing customer interface.

- The buying decision is not simply a result of a psychological process. It is also the outcome of an interaction between the buyer, the seller, the product and the situation.

Key Concepts Introduced

- Attitude

Examples of Marketing at Work

- Whiskas
- Daley Thomson and Lucozade
- Oxfam

1 SETTING THE SCENE

1.1 The **buyer** of a product has many individual characteristics and experiences which influence his or her buying decision. These influences are described later; for the moment, it is sufficient to note that they will be a varying mixture of personal, cultural, social and psychological factors. Although each person is different from the next, marketing managers may nevertheless be able to make generalisations about different types of consumer. Type A will make a particular buying decision, type B can be influenced into buying.

1.2 The characteristics of the **seller** will affect the consumer's decision to buy or not buy, because he or she will have some impression of the quality of the firm's after sales service, its experience in the field, its reliability and 'friendliness'. Marketing management can take action to control these seller characteristics.

1.3 In the same way, management can control the characteristics of the **goods** sold by their organisation. The quality, durability, price, design features etc of the product will influence the buying decision. However, it is useful to note here that consumer goods (goods made for the ultimate consumer) may be of three types.

(a) **Non-durable goods**, ie goods which are consumed in one or a few uses, such as food or soap. Since they will usually be purchased frequently, they should be made available in many locations, profit margins will be low and producers will try to encourage brand loyalty.

(b) **Durable goods**, ie goods which are used up very slowly and only after many uses (for example cookers, books). They may be purchased infrequently, and *may* need more direct selling effort.

(i) In the UK and elsewhere, customers now expect such consumer durables to function effectively, irrespective of whichever brand or manufacturer's products are being purchased. As a result, perceived quality is less significant as a brand discriminator than once was the case when (for example) the reports of the Consumers' Association were assiduously studied in order to isolate the 'best buy' in any given product field. In many respects, functional quality has been replaced by appearance and price as opportunities for market share.

(ii) Supporting this view is that fact that the average person, in the UK, only takes 12 minutes in order to decide which refrigerator, washing machine or vacuum cleaner to buy. This implies that much less detailed consideration is being given to performance variables.

(iii) Moreover, many consumer goods purchases are what are known as 'distress' transactions: in other words, people buy a new freezer because their existing one has irrevocably broken down, rather than because they seek an upgrade or a straightforward change. When making 'distress' purchases, customers are often anxious to reduce the pain of the exercise, eg by reducing the time.

(c) **Consumer services**, such as hairdressing, dry cleaning and laundry services. Quality, reliability and continuous availability are likely to be important aspects of the service to would-be purchasers.

1.4 The buying **situation** concerns the surroundings and circumstances under which the decision to buy or not to buy is taken. Some of the factors in the buying situation might be subject to management control, for example whether the products are available in supermarkets, dispensing machines, exclusive stores, or on the doorstep; whether sales assistants or sales literature such as home-purchase catalogues are helpful; and whether impulse goods are readily available on convenient promotion stands in stores. Other factors may be outside the control of management: for example the weather may influence decisions to buy umbrellas or electric fans.

2 UNDERSTANDING BUYER MOTIVES

2.1 Motives sit between **needs and action**. Motives are derived from needs in that a need motivates a person to take action. The difference between needs and motives are as follows.

(a) Motives **activate behaviour**. Being thirsty (need) causes (motivates) us to buy a drink (action). If the need is sufficiently intense, we are motivated to act.

(b) Motives are **directional**. Needs are general but motives specify behavioural action. A general need to belong may lead to a specific motivation to join a badminton club.

(c) Motives serve to **reduce tension**. If we are too cold, we are motivated to reduce the tension in our bodies that this causes by seeking a source of warmth. If we are not accepted by those we regard as important, we aim to reduce the tension this causes by seeking to change our behaviour so as to gain acceptance by those we value. This tension is also known as dissonance. When it exists, we aim to reduce it. We shall look at **dissonance** in more detail later in this text.

2.2 Although we know that motives arise from needs and can lead to purchase actions, motives do not tell us **how** consumers choose from the options available to satisfy needs. Other influences are clearly at work.

Psychological influences on buyer behaviour

2.3 **Attitudes**. Some writers have suggested that a buyer's attitude towards a product is an important element in the buying decision. However, there is no empirical evidence to link a favourable attitude directly with consumer purchases, therefore it is not certain that any great practical value can be derived from an attempt by management to analyse and influence consumer attitudes. Attitudes are discussed in more detail later.

2.4 **Learning**. J A Howard (1963) developed a model of buyer behaviour which included a learning curve of buyer behaviour. The curve was divided into three major phases.

(a) **Initial stage**. A buyer has limited experience of the product, and seeks information to discriminate between different models. Advice comes from sales assistants, magazines, friends, or hear-say. The consumer probably makes a rational purchase decision.

(b) **Intermediate stage**. The buyer relies more on his or her own experience and less on outside information to make his selection.

(c) **Final stage**. The buyer knows what he or she wants, and will probably buy the same again unless put off by a very bad experience (frequent breakdowns, poor service) with the current model. Buying may even become perfectly routine and 'automatic response behaviour' might occur.

2.5 **Loyalty**. A consumer may demonstrate a loyalty towards a particular company's goods or to a brand, or even to a particular shop or retail chain. It is not clear, however, that marketing efforts can be successful in trying to increase customer loyalty. Although it is an important phenomenon, it may well be outside the sphere of management influence or control.

2.6 **Personality**. Inevitably, a consumer's buying behaviour will be influenced by his or her personality. Kotler noted seven broad personality variables. For example, the latest computer might be purchased by a customer whose personality traits include self confidence, dominance and autonomy. Coffee producers, on the other hand, have discovered that heavy coffee drinkers tend to have sociability as a principal personality trait.

The effect of culture

2.7 Cultural differences raise many purchasing issues influencing every facet of life. Cultural differences can affect purchasing in terms of:

- **what** is bought   (style, colours, types of goods/service);
- **when** things are bought (Sunday shopping, for instance);

229

- **how** things are bought   (bartering, haggling about price);
- **where** things are bought (type of retail outlet);
- **why** things are bought   (influence of culture on needs, wants and hence motives).

Action Programme 1

Why is it that it is accepted practice to haggle about the price of some purchases (a house, or a second-hand car, say, in the UK) but not others?

The consumer's motivation mix

2.8 Customer behaviour is therefore determined by **economic, psychological and sociological** considerations. The reasons for buying a product may vary from person to person, or product to product, or the reasons may be the same, but the weighting given to each reason in the mind of the customer may vary. These reasons make up the motivation mix of the customer.

2.9 **Research in order to understand the customer** therefore forms the basis for efficient marketing. A company can make decisions on price, pack, brand name, advertising contents, choice of retail outlets, etc which will appeal to the conscious or sub-conscious motivations of consumers.

2.10 The **motivation mix** leads a customer to choose:

(a) the type of goods or services he wants to buy (food or a new hairstyle, say);

(b) the brand;

(c) the quality;

(d) the quantity;

(e) in what place;

(f) from whom;

(g) at what price;

(h) by what method of payment (cash, cheque, credit card);

(i) the timing of his purchase: will the customer purchase on credit card, or will the customer save up the money, and so delay the purchase?

2.11 The motivation mix of a customer for **consumer goods** will be different from that of a buyer of **industrial goods**.

(a) The **domestic buyer** might buy on impulse, attracted by the branding, packaging or display of an article, as well as to meet the family's needs within the shopping budget. The homemaker has a variety of demands to satisfy, within the limits of the family budget.

(b) An **industrial buyer** might be expected to give more emphasis to rational motives for purchasing - a clear need for the article, its price and quality, delivery dates and after-sales service.

2.12 Although customers are not motivated to buy for the same reasons, the market for a specific item may have a special feature or character. Its appeal may be restricted to a certain industry, social class or income group, geographical area, or customers of a certain age, gender, level of education, occupation, race, religion or even life style. As we have seen this allows for **segmentation** and tight **targeting** of the marketing and sales effort.

3 ATTITUDES AND BEHAVIOUR

3.1 An **attitude** is a **relatively consistent, learned predisposition** to behave in a certain way in response to a given object.

(a) **Relative consistency**. Attitudes are not permanent: they can be changed, as we will see later. However, they tend to be reasonably well established, and to lead to behaviour with a reasonable degree of predictability. (If someone prefers coffee to tea, he is likely to choose coffee over tea fairly consistently.)

(b) **Learned**. Attitudes are 'learned' or conditioned, formulated with experience as a result of learning factors such as motivation, association and reinforcement. They are therefore also dependent on individual perception. If a product is associated with positive concepts in its promotional message, reinforced by experience, you may develop a positive attitude.)

(c) **Predisposition**. Attitudes are a predisposition to behaviour: they do not imply that a given behaviour will *necessarily* follow.

(d) **An object**. Attitudes relate to some aspect of the individual's environment: it may be a thing, person, event, concept or whatever.

> ### Key Concept
> A technical definition of **attitude** is: 'a mental and neural state of readiness, organised through experience, exerting a directive or dynamic influence upon the individual's response to all objects and situations with which it is related.' (Allport)

Attitude and behaviour: intervening factors

3.2 There is no automatic, direct relationship between attitude and behaviour. Insofar as attitudes and behaviour are inter-related, the process may be portrayed as a **tendency** for an individual to behave in a given way: not a **prediction** of how he will behave.

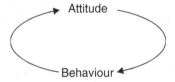

3.3 Situational factors affect our behaviour: attitudes are not the sole variable involved.

(a) An individual's **behaviour** may be influenced by the **situation**, to contradict his attitudes. For example, you may have a strong liking for organically-grown produce (you believe it is 'right' to buy such produce, and you intend to buy it) - but it is more expensive in the supermarket, so for economic reasons you do not buy it every week. From your behaviour, it could be inferred that you had a negative or neutral attitude to organic products: not so.

(b) An individual's **attitudes** may also be influenced by the **situation**. People who generally avoid chocolate for health and figure reasons may feel differently in situations where they are physically exhausted and need a boost in blood sugar, or where they are in a festive mood and sharing a bar/packet/cake with friends -especially if told that 'A Mars a day helps you work, rest and play!'

3.4 Situational or environmental factors include the following.

(a) **Physical environment**, the surroundings you find yourself in. If you are freezing cold in the office, would your behaviour be dictated by your attitude that 'it's silly to wear a coat indoors'?

(b) **Social environment**, including other people. If you are eating in the home of a vegetarian, would you insist on acting on your attitude towards 'good red meat'? Would you go to work in jeans, because you 'hate' suits, if everyone else dressed formally?

(c) **Time of day, season, or 'temporal perspective'.** You may be prevented from acting on your attitudes by having insufficient time, by office/shop opening hours, or by seasonal availability of product. Your attitudes may also change according to the time of day, or your time of life;

(d) **Task definition**: how the individual perceives the task to be accomplished, which may be inconsistent with particular attitudes. You may 'hate' going to the dentist, but it fulfils your objective of keeping healthy teeth and gums;

(e) **Temporary conditions** obtaining at the time of behaviour, such as mood, illness, availability of cash.

You may note that situational factors may affect our **attitudes**, or our **ability to act on our attitudes**.

3.5 Other factors in whether or not we act on, or consistently with, an attitude include:

(a) the **strength** of the attitude; and

(b) the **other attitudes** we have which may:

(i) **conflict** with it, and so inhibit our acting on it; or

(ii) be **stronger** or **more relevant** to the particular situation, and so distract us from acting on it at that time.

3.6 Because of these problems of predicting a particular behaviour, on the basis of a particular attitude, psychologists have formulated complex models of the attitude-behaviour relationship as a dynamic process. What happens when we hold an attitude? Why do we modify our behaviour in some situations - and our attitudes in others? We will now go on to look at some of the major theories.

3.7 As a general introduction we can chart the relationship between attitudes and behaviour in the following ways.

(a) Attitudes can **cause behaviour**. For example, a person who is fanatically keen on football and, for whatever reason, supports Arsenal is likely to *purchase* Arsenal football club memorabilia.

(b) Some attitudes are **not linked to behaviour at all**. For example a person's attitude towards Arsenal football club is unlikely to influence that person's purchasing behaviour in a supermarket: an attitude has an **object**. Moreover, the individual may have no choice or may be unwilling to exercise it: many people are distressed by images of factory farming or maltreatment of animals, but continue purchasing food products made in these 'cruel' processes.

(c) **Some attitudes produce dissonant behaviour.** People may believe in healthy eating, but over-indulge in cream cakes. ('Naughty but nice' was an advertising slogan encapsulating this element of guilt.)

(d) **Behaviour causes attitude change.** Doing something may change one's attitude towards it. This is prevalent in attitudes to food, because people are perhaps afraid to experiment. The same might be true of other cultural products: watching adaptations of Jane Austen novels on TV (eg *Pride and Prejudice*) might lead people to a more favourable attitude towards the books themselves which might have an unjustified image of being 'difficult' or an elite 'high culture' product.

Attitudes and behaviour

Attitude formation

3.8 Attitudes are **learned** predispositions; people are motivated to form attitudes about things in four ways.

- We tend to seek rewarding objects and avoid negative ones.
- We need to protect our self-concept.
- We need to express and reflect our innermost beliefs and values.
- We need to make sense of our environment by gathering knowledge and beliefs.

Attribution theory describes attitude formation as a product of people's interpretations of their own behaviour and experiences. People make inferences about the causes of their own and other people's behaviour and in so doing form an attitude. If a salesman offers you a more expensive model because it is 'vastly superior to the cheaper one', you may attribute to him the motive of trying to get a bigger commission and judge him insincere about the model's quality: your attitude will be negative.

3.9 Three major attitude theories emerged in the 1940s and 1950s, based on the premise that individuals seek **cognitive consistency**.

- Consistency between the attitudes they hold
- Consistency between their attitudes/perceptions and their experience of reality
- Consistency between their behaviour and their self-image

3.10 When **discrepancies or inconsistencies** occur (and are perceived) the individual experiences **tension**. In order to alleviate that tension, the individual has to change one or more of the factors creating the inconsistency: to **change one of his conflicting attitudes** to 'fit' the other, to change his attitude to 'fit' his behaviour, or to change his behaviour to 'fit' his attitude. Let us see how this idea works in the three main consistency theories.

- Balance theory (F Heider)
- Congruity theory (C E Osgood & P H Tannenbaum)
- Cognitive dissonance theory (L Festinger)

Balance theory: Heider

3.11 **Balance theory** is mainly concerned with what happens when one person receives information (to which he may have a positive or negative attitude) from another **person** (to whom he may have a positive or negative attitude).

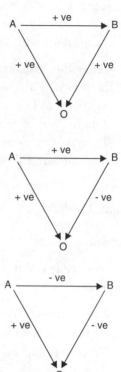

(a)   If person A has a positive attitude to an object O (whatever it may be), and a positive attitude to person B, there will be no inconsistency when person B expresses a positive attitude to O: their agreement conforms to A's expectations. This system is said to be balanced for A.

(b)   If person A has a positive attitude to object O, and a positive attitude to person B, he will however feel some tension when person B expresses a negative attitude to object O: maybe person A is wrong to like O, if B dislikes it? or maybe he is sure about O, in which case he has to doubt B?

This system is said to be unbalanced for A, and requires adjustment of one of his attitudes.

(c)   If person A has a positive attitude to object O, while person B has a negative attitude to it, the situation would however be balanced if A had a negative attitude to B. There would be no conflict for A between his attitudes to O and B: in fact he would expect to disagree with B.

3.12   Balance theory is simple, which is useful when it comes to application. However, it has been **criticised** as too simple adequately to portray the complexity of attitude systems and conflicts, particularly since it **uses only the dimensions 'positive' and 'negative'** without taking into account the **strength** of positive or negative feeling, which would allow us to predict which way people would choose to resolve an unbalanced situation.

An application of balance theory

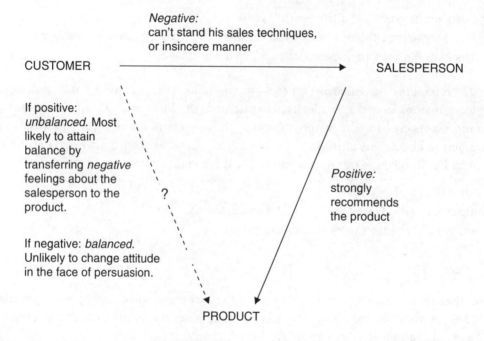

Congruity theory: Osgood and Tannenbaum

3.13   *Congruity theory* adds to the 'balance' model a measurement of the **strength or intensity** of positive and negative attitudes, on a scale of -3 to +3.

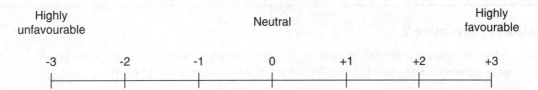

The theory is mainly concerned with what happens when there is a **discrepancy** or **'incongruity'** between:

(a) an individual's evaluation of an object; and

(b) his evaluation of a person who endorses or is associated with that object.

(If he likes or dislikes the object *and* the person who recommends/praises it, there is no discrepancy, and no need for attitude change.)

3.14 Congruity theory states that for congruity (consistency of attitudes) to be achieved, there **has to be an adjustment of both evaluations towards each other**, until their ratings are the same. The adjustment therefore must in total equal the amount of the initial discrepancy between them, but because stronger attitudes are harder to change than weaker ones, the evaluation whose rating is further from 0/neutral (in either direction) will be adjusted less.

(a) If a product say, is rated at +2 (favourable), but the salesperson recommending it is rated -2 (unfavourable), there would be a discrepancy of 4. Because the valuations are equally strongly held in either direction, congruity would be achieved by each attitude changing by 2 points: the product would lose popularity (-2) and the salesperson gain (+2). They would reach the same rating at 0 (neutral).

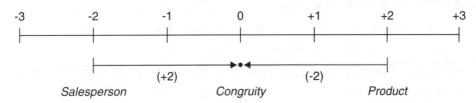

(b) If the product were rated at +3 (highly favourable) and the salesperson only slightly unfavourably, at -1, the discrepancy would also be 4. However, the stronger attitude might only change by 1 point, and the weaker by 3, so that congruity was reached with both rated +2 (favourable). The product would still have 'lost' by being recommended by someone the individual did not like, but not by much, since the initial attitude to the product was so positive.

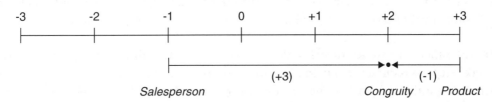

> ### Action Programme 2
>
> Linda McCartney was not a popular figure when she first met and married Beatle Paul in the late sixties/early seventies. She was a figure of fun during Paul McCartney's Wings days.
>
> In the early 1990s, however, 'perhaps the most successful mass-market celebrity brand [was] Linda McCartney's vegetarian range, produced by Ross Young's, which has a 25 per cent share of the £100m frozen meat-free products sector.'   *Financial Times*, June 1995
>
> Why do you think this was?

Cognitive dissonance theory: Festinger

3.15 **Cognitive dissonance** is the discomfort experienced by an individual when he receives **new information which appears to contradict a belief or attitude he holds**. The theory is particularly concerned with **decision-making**.

(a) In making a decision - for example, to buy a product - individuals frequently have to **weigh up positive and negative factors** and compromise on that basis. Post-purchase dissonance occurs when somebody regrets or feels anxious about a choice they have made.

(b) He may also find himself acting in a way that appears to contradict a belief or attitude he holds: he has chosen a foreign-made car because of a special financing deal or promotional campaign, when he has previously always believed in 'buying British'.

3.16 The extent to which the individual will experience psychological discomfort as a result of this conflict depends on the following.

(a) The **significance of the decision**. Post-purchase dissonance is more severe following the selection of expensive items such as cars, houses etc.

(b) The **positive attributes of the rejected options**, and the **negative attributes of the selected option**, of which the individual becomes aware. If the decision was very close in terms of relative value, the uncertainty will be more acute. On the other hand, if all the alternatives are perceived as being alike, with similar characteristics ('cognitive overlap'), the decision will be supported ('it makes no difference anyway'), and the dissonance less.

(c) The **number of rejected alternatives**, since the more are rejected the more 'wrong' choices may have been made, and the greater the uncertainty.

(d) The **duration and intensity of the attitude or belief** that has been contradicted by the individual's decision or behaviour.

3.17 As with other consistency theories, this theory suggests that dissonance propels individuals to take steps to **reduce the tension and discomfort** felt as a result of conflicting knowledge/beliefs (cognitions), by achieving consonance, or consistency. This can be done in a number of ways.

(a) By **making the decision more attractive**, to reduce the impact of conflicting information.

(i) The individual can seek out information (eg from ads, or satisfied customers) that supports his choice, while avoiding information that is positive about dissonance-creating alternatives.

(ii) The individual can rationalise his choice by finding new information and beliefs which harmonise it with his attitudes. ('This is a foreign design - but it is *made in Britain*.').

(b) By **devaluing the source of information** which creates dissonance ('well, they would say that, wouldn't they?').

(c) By **devaluing the attitude or belief** with which the new information/behaviour conflicts. ('What does it matter whether it's British or not? I don't really care.').

(d) By **changing the attitude or belief** with which the new information/behaviour conflicts. ('Actually, this is much better than any British car. They aren't what they used to be.').

(e) By **revoking the decision**, in order to act in consonance with his original attitudes. ('No, it's no good. I'll trade it in and go back to my British model.') This can be an expensive option, even if possible.

Action Programme 3

Have you suffered from 'cognitive dissonance' as a result of the mad cow disease scare? Did you try to achieve consonance and if so, how?

3.18 Marketers can use dissonance theory in several ways.

(a) To persuade people to **try or buy first** and develop a **positive attitude afterwards**. If you induce someone to try a product (even if they don't 'normally' like it) - with coupon offers, competitions or persuasive advertising - they will experience post-purchase dissonance, and try to convince themselves they like the product! The greater the post-purchase dissonance, the greater the subsequent brand loyalty, according to one study.

(b) **To reinforce purchase decisions**. The consumers will only be able to convince themselves they like the product if you *tell* them in your advertising they've done the right thing! You can make the rationalisation process easier if your advertisements stress the good points of the product and provide plenty of information, if you have guarantees or warranties and post-purchase service and customer care, and if you can get word-of-mouth recommendation working.

(c) **Be careful to avoid disappointing your customers**. Faced with dissonance, the customer will be haunted by the bad points of the product he has chosen: if it is one of yours, you do not want to provide him with 'ammunition' in the form of poor quality or failure to live up to advertised claims.

3.19 Dissonance theory is also useful in changing attitudes in an **employee management** context. If an individual thinks, for example, that toeing the company line on a new customer care initiative will bring him fulfilment - but his closest, most admired friends despise management and regard compliance as betrayal of class values - he will experience dissonance. This will only be alleviated if he:

(a) changes his own attitude to customer care (although this creates another dissonance - the discrepancy between his past and current attitudes);

(b) changes his attitude to his friends - down-grading them so that their dissonant input need no longer concern him;

(c) does not expose himself to dissonant information, or seeks only information which confirms his attitude.

3.20 The implications of this for an organisation wishing to change attitudes, say towards customer care, are these.

(a) If the **source** of dissonant information is **not highly regarded**, the individual will experience **less discomfort**, and will not be moved to change his attitudes.

(b) If you **pay people to change**, they may change their behaviour - contrary to their attitudes - but they will be able to explain away the resulting dissonance by justifying their actions with the reward. They will suffer **less discomfort**, and will not need to change their views.

(c) **Public commitment** to, or admission of 'ownership' of, an attitude or course of action makes it very **difficult to renounce** without painful dissonance.

Note that a change in behaviour (ie compliance) does not imply a change in attitude. The latter is harder to achieve, but lasts much longer.

Marketing at Work

The following extracts look at the way in which a petfood company coped with the BSE scare.

'Mars-owned Pedigree Petfoods is axing all varieties of Whiskas containing offal in an effort to reassure shoppers worried about 'mad-cow' disease.

The company's flagship catfood brand has lost market share after an onslaught from Spiller's Felix, and is in the process of being relaunched. The relaunch is being supported by a three-month £6m campaign, breaking in the first week of October.

Kidney, heart and liver flavours are being dropped as part of the overhaul of 400g cans, which will be rebranded 'New Whiskas'. The sub-brands Select Cuts and Fine Cuts will be dropped in favour of prominent labelling saying In Jelly and In Gravy. The Supermeat sub-brand will stay the same.

Whiskas' 200g cans and aluminium trays (sub-branded Select Menu) have not been changed as they do not contain offal. The liver variety of Whiskas Supermeat is being axed and the Beef & Kidney, Duck & Heart and Lamb & Kidney Select Cut varieties are being reformulated, with other meats replacing offal.

Sources say the move is in response to consumers' fears over BSE, and follows the trend to 'humanise' petfood, making it sound more appetising to pet-owners.' *Marketing Week*, 2 August 1996

4 THE RELEVANCE TO THE MARKETING CUSTOMER INTERFACE

4.1 If we accept that attitudes and behaviour are linked then as **marketers** we will be much concerned to change attitudes if we want people to change their behaviour - that is, to buy our products.

Factors affecting attitude change

4.2 Rice (*Consumer Behaviour: Behavioural Aspects of Marketing*) identifies **six major factors which affect attitude change** (as shown below).

Factors affecting attitude change

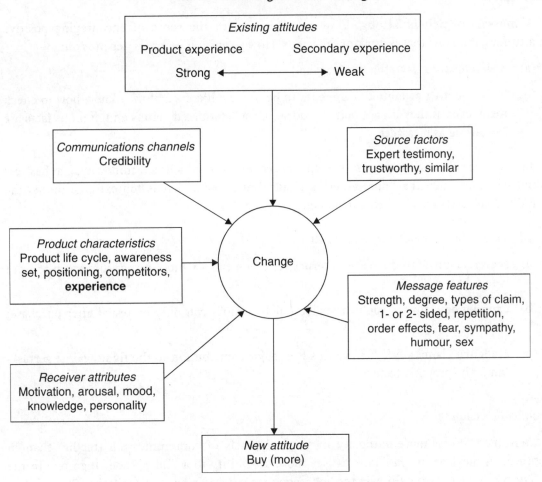

4.3 When we looked at **congruity theory** we saw that in a conflict situation between two attitudes, the final attitude that results tends to be closer to the original attitude that was **more strongly felt**. This means that changing an attitude depends very much on **how committed** the individual is to the existing attitude. In addition, an existing attitude which was formed on the basis of **direct product experience** will be more difficult to change than one formed on the basis of secondary experience, that is tales of product experience passed on by third parties.

Source factors

4.4 The influence of a marketing message designed to change an attitude can be greatly affected by its source. A 'man in a white coat' has the authority of an **expert**; a **TV star** who **endorses** a cereal may have the authority of trustworthiness. Ideally, the source should have both 'expertness' and **trustworthiness**.

Marketing at Work

Daley Thomson is perceived to have both 'expertness' and trustworthiness and hence was an ideal celebrity to endorse Lucozade. Of the two factors, trustworthiness is the most important factor - if a celebrity is felt to be untrustworthy then no amount of expertise will compensate. Imagine Ben Johnson endorsing Lucozade, and remember the action of Pepsi when faced with the Michael Jackson child abuse scandal.

4.5 A source who is a celebrity, physically attractive and similar to the target audience is ideal.

Message features

4.6 **A message which is 'strong'** is more persuasive, in the sense of encouraging positive attitudes, than one that is weak or fallacious. How strong a message is depends on:

 (a) how **relevant** it is to the receiver; and

 (b) how **objective or factual it appears to be**. People like facts if they know how to check them, even if they do not actually do so. Unsubstantiated claims and dubious facts are less strong as messages.

4.7 The **degree** of the message also has an impact. A claim which is a minor change has less impact on attitude than one which is major, but a claim that is too extreme means the individual's self-concept feels threatened.

4.8 Advertised claims are categorised by Rice as:

 (a) **search** claims - 'find a better alternative, if you can' - which the consumer can test out before he buys;

 (b) **experience** claims - 'you'll never be lonely again' - can only be tested after purchase; and

 (c) **credence** claims - 'We believe this is a major contribution to the fight against germs' - cannot be properly tested.

Communication channel

4.9 Consumers invest more authority in some channels of communication (media) than in others. A message in *The Times* carries more credibility to a *Times* reader than one in the *Sun* could have. Generally **written messages** are seen as **more authoritative** than spoken ones.

Receiver attributes

4.10 A number of features of the individual consumer will affect how or whether his attitudes can be changed.

 (a) **Motivation.** This is discussed in detail in the next chapter.

 (b) **State of arousal.** A message needs to be recognised for what it is before the individual's attention and awareness can be roused. The consumer needs to be conscious of the message but not so excited that he cannot concentrate on it.

 (c) **Knowledge.** Where the consumer has a fair amount of knowledge already about the product then he is more open to technical messages.

 (d) **Mood.** The consumer's mood has some bearing on how influenced he will be by a message. Some messages seek to create a mood (such as Cadbury's Caramel) which will make the consumer open to attitude change. Marketers will be very careful to place the message in a medium and at a time when the consumer's mood is likely to be favourable, for instance in the middle of a favourite TV comedy.

 (e) **Personality.** Some individuals need to have messages 'spelled out' to them, while others can elaborate a subtle or peripheral message. Elaboration is the process whereby we use comparisons with previous experience, values, attitudes and beliefs to evaluate information.

Product characteristics

4.11 Changing a customer's attitude towards a product is very much tied up with features of the product itself.

(a) **Situation in the customer's awareness set**. The consumer may be unaware of either the organisation or the product; if the product is in the inept set then it is time for an attitude change!

(b) **Stage in the product life cycle**. Whilst the product life cycle is outside the scope of this text, it is very important when considering how to change a customer's attitude towards it. Products go through a number of stages from their introduction on the market - growth (rising sales), maturity (steady, high sales), decline (falling sales) and senility (removal from the market). Whilst a far from perfect model, it shows us that attitude change will be important particularly in the innovation/growth phases, while maintenance of 'good attitudes' will be vital in the maturity phase via brand image

(c) **Relative performance** to competitor's products. A product that objectively performs better than any other can be reinforced by facts; a rather obscure message is required where this is not the case.

(d) **Product positioning**. If a product is positioned as a cut price good then the message needs to be different to that of a luxury good.

(e) Last but not least, **product experience**, good or bad, will always exert more influence than a message.

How to change attitudes

4.12 In changing attitudes, we can change:

- **cognition**, what people know or believe about a product
- **affectivity**, what people feel abut a product
- **conation**, what people actually do, their behaviour

Changing the way people think

4.13 **Cognition** involves **knowledge, perception and beliefs** about the product. Our aim would be to change beliefs, to change the relative importance of existing beliefs, to develop new beliefs, and/or to change beliefs as to what is ideal. Messages which change cognition should then have a 'knock on' effect on the other two components, leading to an overall change in attitude.

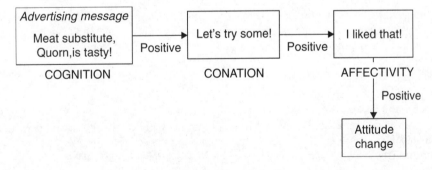

Marketing at Work

'A group of models sashay along a brightly lit catwalk in leopard prints, glitter and Seventies "retro". Supermodel Karen Elson struts across the screen and declares: "I love it when people come up to me and say 'darling, where did you get that dress' and I say 'Oxfam. Forty quid'."

Oxfam's latest television and cinema ad has broken the mould of charity advertising. Gone are images of suffering and helplessness. The UK's largest charity is taking a retail approach to encouraging donations.

The idea behind the new ad, says Sheckleton [Oxfam shops marketing manager], was to present people with images of clothes they would love to own and then surprise them with the word "Oxfam" at the end. '

Marketing Week, 6 November 1997

Changing the way people feel

4.14 Marketers can attempt to influence customers' feelings (**affectivity**) directly before touching either beliefs or behaviour. The idea is to make the experience of using the product seem an enjoyable one (or a worthy, or exciting one).

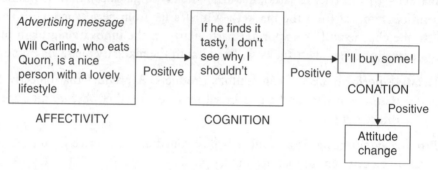

4.15 There are three main ways in which a message can change affectivity.

(a) **Repetition** of positive messages when the product is one in which the consumer is not much involved (eg washing up liquid).

(b) **Likeable advertising** means that the consumer is more inclined to like the product, although an ad which is too good may distract the customer from the product!

(c) **Classical conditioning** by linking the product name with a stimulus that is liked by the consumer, such as music.

Changing the way people behave

4.16 Often a consumer will try or **experiment** with a product before either his beliefs or his feelings are changed, most usually because a product with fairly **low involvement** is **reduced in price**.

> **Exam tip**
>
> Would you be able to describe the connections between attitudes and behaviour so far as customers are concerned, amplifying your arguments with relevant examples?
>
> An answer could open with an introduction providing a general description of behaviour and attitudes. Attitudes and attitude components could then be considered in more detail. The links between attitudes and behaviour could subsequently be examined using the following four scenarios.
>
> * Attitudes lead to behaviour.
> * Attitudes are influence by behaviour.
> * There is no link between attitudes and behaviour.
> * Attitudes lead to behaviour but other factors play a role.
>
> Finally you must draw a conclusion. It is at this point that it might be useful to introduce the impact of environmental issues. There is, of course, no right or wrong conclusion. Provided you justify yourself you may conclude that any of the four scenarios is an accurate reflection of reality.

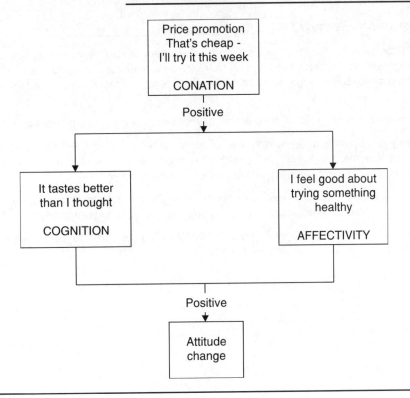

Chapter roundup

- Individuals are important in all buying decisions, either for themselves or on behalf of an organisation. Marketers need to understand their motives, psychology and influences, and how these combine to form a motivation mix.

- A consumer's self-image may lead him to choose brands which support him and help him towards his expected self-concept.

- An attitude is a relatively consistent, learned predisposition to behave in a certain way in response to a given object.

- Attribution theory states that attitudes are formed by people's interpretations of their own behaviour and experiences.

- Consistency theories state that individuals seek cognitive consistency, experiencing tension if this is not achieved.

- Marketers often seek to change attitudes. Factors affecting attitude change are existing attitudes, source factors (who is telling us), message features, the communication channel, receiver attributes and product characteristics.

Quick quiz

1 What are the three types of consumer good? (see para 1.3)

2 What is the difference between needs and motives? (2.1)

3 How can cultural differences affect purchasing? (2.7)

4 Why will the motivation mix of a customer for consumer goods be different from that for industrial goods? (2.11)

5 What is attribution theory? (3.8)

6 How can marketers use dissonance theory? (3.18)

7 What are the six major factors affecting attitude change? (4.2)

8 What is conation? (4.12)

9 What is another term for customers' feelings, that marketers may attempt to influence? (4.14)

BPP PUBLISHING

Action Programme Review

1   In general the extent of haggling depends upon the number of customers or suppliers and their relative economic power. When you go to the supermarket you are just one of many customers. However, if a business supplies regular large quantities to relatively few customers compromises will be made about price.

Your answer will also depend on the customs in your own country, if you do not live in the UK.

2   In the early days, Linda was probably the victim of envy. Later, however, the endorsement worked because there was a real branding proposition there. She was not after some publicity. She genuinely espoused vegetarianism and that gave her credence with consumers.

3   Perhaps you said to yourself, 'Well, I've always thought about becoming a vegetarian'. Maybe you decided to go on a diet: 'Well, I ought to stop eating junk food like hamburgers, anyway'.

Or possibly you decided that there is little point in not eating beef, as you ate it when it was dangerous and so you could well have the disease already.

11 *Individual customers: external influences and personality profiling*

Chapter Topic List	Syllabus reference
1 **Setting the scene**	3.3
2 **Socialisation**	3.3
3 **Reference groups**	3.3
4 **Roles**	3.3
5 **Psychological theory**	3.3
6 **Motivation: needs, wants and goals**	3.3
7 **Motivation theories relevant to marketers**	3.3

Learning Outcomes

- After studying this chapter you will understand more about the influences on individual customers.

- This chapter continues and concludes our discussion of the **individual** as a customer.

Key Concepts Introduced

- Socialisation
- Reference group
- Role

- Learning
- Trait
- Self concept

Examples of Marketing at Work

- Trainers
- 'Best' advice

- Ratners
- The Post Office and BT

BPP PUBLISHING

1 SETTING THE SCENE

1.1 The first few sections of this chapter look at how the individual is **influenced** by his or her **personal environment** - the family, the many groups with which an individual interacts, and his or her position in relation to all of these.

1.2 We then go on to look briefly at some of the issues in an individual's **personality profile**, in particular the psychological factors that motivate different individuals in different circumstances.

2 SOCIALISATION

> ### Key Concept
> According to Keith Williams (*Behavioural Aspects of Marketing*), **socialisation** is 'the process by which the individual learns the social expectations, goals, beliefs, values and attitudes that enable him to exist in society'. In other words, socialisation is the process by which he acquires sufficient knowledge of a society and its ways to be able to function and participate in it.

2.1 The **learning** of gender-related, consumer and occupational roles is part of the socialisation process: what it means to 'be' or 'behave like' a girl or boy, what money is for, what 'buying' is, what 'work' is and what sorts of work different 'sorts' of people do.

2.2 The **family** is the earliest contact through which socialisation is achieved, although other socialising influences on children include formal education, **reference groups** (particularly **peer groups**, at a young age), and the **mass media**. Socialisation is an on-going process, however, and reference groups, the mass media and all social interactions continue to influence the behaviour of adults towards conformity to newly-encountered roles, norms and values.

2.3 As a learning process, **socialisation** may function through the following ways.

2.4 **Classical conditioning.** Children (and indeed adults) try out various **social behaviours**, which are **reinforced** either positively (with satisfaction, approval or rewards) or negatively (with failure, disapproval or punishment). A treat or praise, a rebuke or punishment, may be used by parents to shape a child's behaviour to desirable norms and to eradicate 'deviant' behaviour. An adult adjusts his own behaviour to **social norms** in the same way, when confronted with approval, acceptance, rejection or embarrassment.

2.5 **Cognitive learning.** The child develops a cognitive 'map' of various situations in which behaviour succeeds or fails, gathering information for use in later situations when there is a particular goal to be achieved or problem to be solved.

   (a) A **range of options or principles is learned**, rather than particular responses to particular stimuli. (Taking **gender-related** roles as an example, a girl may learn through experience a number of behaviours 'suitable' to 'being a girl' in a number of situations. This information is processed through perception and stored, so that given an appropriate stimulation or motivation, a relevant behaviour can be selected.)

   (b) This depends on the **stage of cognitive development** the individual has reached: although young children are active information gatherers, reasoning powers are relatively undeveloped, and older children have more complex learning abilities.

2.6 **Imitation of observed behaviour.** Imitation is a common behaviour in animals as well as humans, usually based on curiosity or observed reinforcement of the behaviour (for example, in 'it worked for him - it can work for me' types of advertising);

2.7 **Identification.** Deeper than imitation, identification involves the adoption of the perceived values and attitudes of the role models, usually in an attempt or aspiration to become like him. Behaviour then emerges from the values and attitudes, in certain situations;

Role experimentation, exploration, or role play

2.8 Children (and adults) explore not only their own roles, but those of others: they not only **observe others in roles** related to them, but **'try out' some of those roles** to experience for themselves the patterns of behaviour expected in those roles in relation to other people.

  (a) Children play at being nurses or doctors, policemen, parents or whatever: dolls and other toys and accessories can be very important in establishing the images and expectations associated with those roles.

  (b) Adults also 'play' at occupying unaccustomed roles, in social situations, and are often encouraged to do so in training for managerial or other interpersonal jobs, and in situations where they would find it difficult to express their feelings 'as themselves', for example in therapy.

2.9 **'Consumer socialisation'** is the process by which children acquire the skills, knowledge and attitudes that enable them to **function in society as consumers**.

  (a) **Children** observe the consumption behaviour of their parents or older siblings (while pre-adolescents), or their peers (once adolescents and teenagers), and model their own behaviour accordingly. This applies to specific brand attitudes/choices and pricing/budgeting skills, as well as to shopping behaviour: 'co-shopping' (parent and child shopping together) can encourage both sorts of learning.

  (b) **Parents** use consumption-related events to socialise children generally: promises of gifts or shopping expeditions are used as incentives to behave in a desired way; withholding of money for self-directed purchases is threatened as a deterrent to undesirable behaviour.

  (c) **Children** are socialised into attitudes, values and motivations which are indirectly related to consumption: products or particular brands are means of satisfying socialised needs and wants. Socialisation creates consumer motivations.

2.10 We can therefore identify a number of agencies who are instrumental in the socialisation of individuals.

  (a) The **family** is probably the most enduring and extensive source of influence, because it is here that the dependent child learns from his or her parents and siblings. The family is a particularly strong influence on the child's perception of appropriate roles and on his or her self-esteem, which in turn affects aspirations.

  (b) **School** is an important source of values, particularly as they relate to other people.

  (c) **Peer groups** exert influence on social groups which can control a person's social and emotional satisfactions, say by appointing a person unelected leader or by 'sending him to Coventry'. As a person grows, peer groups become more of an influence, eventually superseding the family.

  (d) The **mass media** is extremely pervasive and has a profound effect on all of us.

3   REFERENCE GROUPS

Key Concept

Reference group theory was formulated in the 1940s by Herbert Hyman, to describe the way in which **an individual uses groups as a point of comparison** or 'reference' for his own judgements, beliefs and behaviour.

3.1   Groups can serve as a benchmark for:

(a)   general behavioural norms; and/or

(b)   specific attitudes or behaviour - such as 'fashionable' product purchases.

3.2   An individual may be influenced by a non-contactual or secondary group, as well as a primary one with which he is intimately in contact. Note, too, that the individual **does not need to be a member of a group** in order to measure his behaviour by it.

(a)   An **aspirational group** can impel an individual to act as it does, or to wear the same 'badges', in order to feel closer to attaining actual membership.

(b)   A **dissociative group** can impel an individual to disown any behaviour or object associated with it.

3.3   There are various inter-related factors on which reference group influence depends.

(a)   Individuals **must be aware of the reference group**, and of its norms and values - otherwise they will have nothing concrete to model their behaviour on.

(b)   Individuals must **identify themselves** to a lesser or greater extent with the particular group - otherwise there will be no impulse towards conformity with that group's norms. The degree of identification is known as 'affectivity'. This in turn will depend on the reference group's:

- attractiveness;
- credibility; and
- power.

(c)   The **power** of the group depends on its ability to **impose sanctions** - whether positive or negative - to encourage conformity. In fact, few individuals wish to be complete conformists, and there is usually a range of acceptable alternatives within given norms: in consumer terms, for example, the group might dictate the product (a personal organiser, say) or even the brand (Filofax), but the sense of independence will be maintained by the choice of size, colour and so on.

(d)   Individuals must have little or **no information or experience** that:

(i)   **undermines** the reference group's credibility, by contradicting its message; or

(ii)   makes **reference outside** the individual's own rational choice irrelevant or unnecessary.

3.4   Reference groups influence a buying decision by making the individual **aware** of a product or brand, allowing the individual to **compare** his attitude with that of the group, encouraging the individual to **adopt an attitude consistent** with the group, and then **reinforcing and legitimising** the individual's decision to conform.

Marketing at Work

An example of how reference groups affect behaviour derives from the vogue for Nike trainers. Nike itself maintains that trainers are sports shoes, no more no less. Parents who have to fork out £50-£100 know differently!

3.5   It has been suggested that we adopt **different reference groups** for **different areas** of our lives and consumer choices. Miles carried out a study of adolescent girls, and found that the peer group was most influential in, for example, the choice of clothes and books, while in matters such as the choice of boyfriends, their **parents'** opinions were more valued. Reference groups may even conflict: the member of a shop-floor work team who also aspires to managerial status and lifestyle may face a dilemma over the kind of behaviour that will gain acceptance in either circle or both.

3.6   **Youth,** however, is the stage at which we are most **personally insecure,** and at which the reference group has the most power: consider the market for training shoes or music, for example.

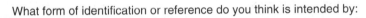

Action Programme 1

'Reference group appeals are used very effectively by some advertisers to segment their markets. Group situations, or people with whom a segment of the audience can identify, are used to promote goods and services by subtly inducing the prospective consumer to identify with the pictured user of the product. This identification may be based on admiration (eg of an athlete), on aspiration (of a celebrity or a way of life), on empathy (with a person or situation), or on recognition (of a person - real or stereotypical - or a situation). In some cases, the prospective consumer thinks, "If she uses it, it must be good. If I use it, I'll be like her." In other cases, the prospective consumer says to himself: "He's got problems I've got. What worked for him will work for me."'   (Schiffman & Kanuk)

What form of identification or reference do you think is intended by:

(a)   'slice-of-life' family situation advertisements, (like Oxo)?

(b)   advertisements in which celebrities - or their characters - endorse products (like Bob Hoskins telling us 'it's good to talk' in BT commercials)?

(c)   advertisements in which celebrities use or are associated with products (Linford Christie *et al* drink milk, Jackie Charlton eats Shredded Wheat)?

(d)   an 'expert' extols the virtue of a product (a man in a white coat praises a toothpaste or washing powder)?

(e)   special interest or 'image' magazines, such as *Vogue, The Face, Viz* or whatever?

(f)   product ratings (for example in *Which?* magazine) which endorse a product, or give popularity ratings?

4   ROLES

Key Concept

A **'role'** is the sum or 'system' of expectations which other people have of an individual in a particular situation or relationship. Role theory is concerned with the roles that individuals act out in their lives, and how the assumption of various roles affects their attitudes to other people.

4.1   An example may help to explain what is meant by 'roles'. An individual may consider himself to be a **father** and **husband,** a good **neighbour** and an active member of the **local**

community, a **supporter** of his sports club, an amateur **golfer**, a conscientious **church-goer**, a man of certain **political** views, a **professional** and a **marketer**. Each organisation to which he belongs provides him with one role or several such roles to perform. His perceptions of other people and interactions with other people will be influenced by his varied roles, although in any particular situation one role is likely to have a stronger immediate bearing than others on what he thinks and does.

4.2 The other individuals who relate to him when he is in a particular role are called his **role set**. At work, he will have one role set made up of colleagues, superiors and subordinates, and any other contacts in the course of business: at home, he will have another role set consisting of family members.

4.3 Roles are **shaped** by:

(a) the **expectations** of other people as to how a person in a given role should or usually does behave; and

(b) **norms** - the customs and informal 'rules' of behaviour which society has formulated.

4.4 We learn, growing up in society and experiencing different role sets, **what is expected of us**, and what the 'rules' are in given situations.

(a) We learn, for example, the **'appropriate' behaviour for our gender**, and the roles it puts us in the family and in society: these gender roles are by no means universal and innate, but are shaped by our particular culture through learning or 'socialisation' (as discussed later in this text).

(b) When we start a **new job** - or first become a student - we are confronted with a whole new set of expectations and norms, and have to 'learn the ropes': if our behaviour does not 'fit' we are soon made aware of social disapproval designed to make us adjust our behaviour to the role expectations and norms.

(c) For many companies in the service sector, **uniform** is an important part of the branding, and is as much part of corporate identity as **logos** or other aspects of physical evidence.

(i) Uniform identifies **who is** the employee of the company and **who is not**. The uniform conveys authority on the part of individual (eg to give instructions abut safety procedures).

(ii) Uniform conveys an **image** of the company, for example in the uniform of airline cabin crew.

4.5 Individuals give expression to the role they are playing at any particular time by giving **role signs**. One example of role signs is **clothing or uniform**.

(a) A businessman will **wear a suit** at work, in his role as executive, but when he returns home in the evening, he may change into casual wear.

(b) A **white coat** indicates that an individual is performing his role as a hospital doctor, a certain shirt indicates that an individual is acting in the role of a **football team** supporter, and a **college scarf** is a sign that a person is in the role of student.

4.6 Note that **role signs** can be embodied as **particular products**. Many products are purchased because they reflect or reinforce social roles. Clothing and accessories are bought as symbols of role, for example; people buy gifts for each other which reinforce the nature of their role relationship (intimate and familial or formal and professional).

4.7   The nature of roles is not dependent on the particular people who fill them: people fit into roles. Roles are therefore valid units of analysis, in themselves. Knowledge of roles can:

    (a) **enable marketers to predict the kind** of role signs people will want to buy, for a wide range of roles;

    (b) **suggest role models** - ideal figures who embody the highest expectations of particular roles - who can be associated with a product (through licensing, advertising or promotions) in order to appeal to the aspirations of people in those roles;

    (c) offer the basis of **market segmentation** and product positioning: categories such as executives, or young mothers, carry with them a range of role expectations, norms and signs which can be appealed to or catered for.

4.8   Since roles depend on learning and perception, and since an individual occupies multiple roles, there are situations in which **problems** occur.

    (a) **Role ambiguity** is a term which describes a situation when the individual is not sure what his role is, or when some members of his role set are not clear what his role is.

Marketing at Work

Role ambiguity is perhaps inherent in the way certain complex financial services, such as pension plans, have been sold. Is the person that sells the pension a 'financial advisor' or 'an insurance salesperson'?

The difference is important - a financial advisor is required to offer 'best advice' to the customer but, at the same time, may be required to meet sales targets.

Role ambiguity might sometimes emerge as 'conflict of interest'.

    (b) **Role conflict** occurs when an individual, acting in several roles at the same time, finds that the roles are incompatible. A businessman who receives a telephone call from his wife, who wants him to leave work and go home, will experience conflict in his roles as businessman and family man. Similar conflict might be experienced by a working woman, who must reconcile her roles as a businesswoman and a mother. A trade union member may be reluctant to obey a strike call, because he disapproves of its reasons.

4.9   Consider how a **product's image** may be enhanced by being positioned as (or associated with) the **solution to such problems**.

    (a) A man resolves the conflict between his roles as a manager in a recession (having to make staff cuts) and as a friend and drinking partner to 'the lads', by selling the executives' company cars to maintain the wages bill. This man drinks a certain brand of beer with 'the lads' afterwards, as a symbol of the 'winning' role.

    (b) A woman finds she cannot fulfil satisfactorily the (stereotyped) roles of worker and wife, because at the end of the day she cannot cook a 'proper' dinner, or get the laundry sweet-smelling enough. Fortunately, there are convenience products to help her. (There are lots of advertisements of this kind, and while they alienate most women, they appeal to a sense of **role-related 'guilt'** or inadequacy in some.)

Marketing at Work

Ratners was a jewellery chain famous for its 'cheap and cheerful' products. Its managing director told an audience of investors that the products were 'crap', to explain its market position. This suggests role conflict between:

(a)   The MD's role as being responsible to investors, explaining the business strategy.

(b)   The MD's role as spokesman for the company as a whole to its other publics, including its customers.

5   PSYCHOLOGICAL THEORY

5.1   We looked at a fair amount of psychology in the previous chapter. Also relevant are psychologists' ideas about **learning**.

> **Key Concept**
>
> **Learning** can be defined as the process of acquiring, through experience, knowledge which leads to changed behaviour. The common factors of any learning situation are motivation, association and reinforcement.

5.2   There are two main approaches to **learning theory**.

(a)   **Conditioning theories** are based on the formation of associations between stimuli and responses. The connectionist/associationist/stimulus-response/behaviourist approach:

- classical/respondent conditioning (Pavlov);
- instrumental/operant conditioning (Skinner).

(b)   The cognitive/information processing/stimulus-organisation-response approach. **Cognitive theories** stress the purposive nature of people's behaviour and their capacity to rationalise and choose from a number of possible means to achieve ends, which may be 'present' in his mind as a 'cognitive map'. These might be known as **mean-end chains**.

5.3   **Stimuli and responses** can become connected in the mind through **repeated experience** of the connection in practice. This is the basis of an approach to learning theory variously called the 'connectionist', 'associationist', 'stimulus-response' or 'behaviourist' approach.

5.4   **Reinforcement** is a process of gathering feedback about the results of actions/ responses, and having those actions/responses confirmed (positive reinforcement) or rejected (negative reinforcement).

(a)   Where an association is established between a given behaviour and **positive reinforcement**, the individual is more likely to respond in that way in future. If every time you choose Brand X you get good results, you will tend to choose Brand X in future. If every time you wear a certain outfit you get the praise and approval of your friends, you will feel confident about wearing it again. If every time you reach your sales targets, you get a financial reward, you will work equally hard to do the same again.

(b)   **Negative reinforcement** works in the same way. If a product lets you down, you say: 'I'll know better than to use that next time.' If you take a lengthy lunch-hour and get a severe reprimand from your boss, you will think twice before going out again the next day.

Pavlovian ('classical' or 'respondent') conditioning

5.5   According to stimulus-response psychology, there can be **no response (behaviour) without a specific stimulus** to invoke it. The Russian physiologist Ivan Pavlov formulated the theory that behaviour which is associated with one stimulus can be 'attached' to another stimulus by conditioning: the behaviour is the same, but has been redirected. In Pavlov's experiment, whenever **dogs** were shown the meat, a bell was rung. After a while, the sound of the bell became associated with the sight and smell of the meat, and the normal response to the meat (salivation) became 'attached' to the new conditioned stimulus (bell).

Skinnerian ('instrumental' or 'operant') conditioning

5.6 The American psychologist B F Skinner argued that in the more complex human mind **behaviour does in fact occur in the absence of a specific stimulus**: random or spontaneous behaviours of this kind are called operants (as opposed to 'respondents'), and are also susceptible to conditioning. Skinner demonstrated how new behaviours and behaviour patterns become established, through being associated with a stimulus which **offers a reward or 'reinforcement'** of some kind. Unlike respondent conditioning, operant conditioning can be used to shape behaviour in **specific** ways.

5.7 **Any behaviour which is positively reinforced** - even if it is completely random - will **tend to be repeated** in that same situation or context. The phenomenon is called 'instrumental' conditioning because behaviours conditioned in this way must be instrumental in gaining a reward which is:

- of **value** to the subject and
- **associated** with the behaviour concerned.

5.8 In a **marketing** context, consider how this works.

(a) You may try several makes of shoe, before you find one that fits comfortably and looks good. The comfort and sense of pride act as a positive reinforcement to your 'behaviour' in choosing that make of shoe. Next time, you may try on another make - but the discomfort or unfavourable comparison with your previous pair act as a negative reinforcement to trying other makes. You try on your previous make - and get positive reinforcement from its comfort and style once again. 'I've learned my lesson', you say. 'I'll buy these from now on.'

(b) Marketers can offer reinforcements in the form of product features, and also discounted prices, promotional gifts, after-sales service etc.

5.9 It is worth looking a little more closely at some of the **terms** associated with reinforcement and its role in operant conditioning.

(a) **Positive reinforcement** is 'reward': it offers the satisfaction of a need or want, and is therefore 'goal-directed' or motivated.

(b) **Negative reinforcement** is also related to a need or want - to avoid unpleasantness, pain or a threat to safety: negative reinforcement is the 'stick', where positive reinforcement is the 'carrot'. Having experienced a negative or 'aversive' stimulus, an individual will modify his behaviour to avoid it in future, either by:

(i) **passive avoidance** - not putting himself into any situation where the stimulus is likely to occur ('if you don't like the heat, stay out of the kitchen'); or

(ii) **active avoidance** - making a specific response to prevent the stimulus occurring ('if you don't like the heat, wear an oven glove, or prepare cold food instead!').

Cognitive approaches

5.10 The cognitive or 'information processing' approach to learning is based on the following.

(a) Human behaviour is **not dependent on stimuli** from the senses, but relies on **reasoning** as the basis for understanding. Sensory information is merely raw material

BPP PUBLISHING

on which the mind imposes organisation and meaning, not merely by sorting and abstracting, but by active and discriminating interpretation. Our image of the world is more elaborate than a mere sensory mosaic.

(b) The realisation that **experience** influences behaviour through **reinforcement** - but in **more complex** ways than 'conditioning' implies. Feedback information on the results of past behaviour must be processed - received, interpreted and used in decision-making.

5.11 In a sense, cognitive learning theory makes life more difficult for the marketer, rather than easier. After all, it admits that consumers are active organisers rather than passive receivers of stimuli presented to them. It admits that there are very many intervening variables between stimulus and response, and that the combination of these variables will be unique to each individual.

6 MOTIVATION: NEEDS, WANTS AND GOALS

6.1 Human behaviour is **purposive**: we have goals, aims, wants, desires and needs. Moreover, we exercise **choice** in the purpose of our behaviour, and in the way we behave to further our ends - whether we actually stop and think about it or not. It is important to us to **ascribe meaning** to our own behaviour and that of others. We want to know why we behave as we do: 'motiveless' crimes frighten us; 'aimless' or 'senseless' actions baffle us.

6.2 Obviously, it is **in an organisation's interests** to know the reasons or motives behind people's behaviour. The reasons why people choose to seek a product or product category, and how they go about obtaining it, will be of vital importance to the marketer.

6.3 Let us look more closely at some of the concepts involved.

Needs

6.4 Needs are the basis of motivation. An unfulfilled need creates a tension which impels individuals to action to reduce this tension, or stress. There are different types of need.

(a) **Biogenic/physiological needs**. These are innate (as opposed to learned or acquired) needs, and include the need for food, water, oxygen, shelter, self preservation: they are also called primary needs or motives, because they relate to the sustaining of life. The sex drive and maternal drive are also primary needs, although related to the survival of the species rather than the individual.

(b) **Psychogenic needs**. This category of innate needs or motives does not relate to physiological stimuli at all, although it ensures the individual's competence to survive in a changing environment: these needs include explanation, learning and experimentation, and self-expression.

(c) **Learned or secondary needs**. Learning attaches meaning to naturally neutral stimuli, which are than capable of arousing motivation. Depending on the other people you have interacted with as your personality develops, and on the culture of your society, you may acquire secondary goals such as power, status, achievement, the approval and esteem of others, family or friendship or a structured and orderly life. These goals are not innate or universal: they are shaped by experience and cultural values (socialisation).

6.5 Primary and secondary - unlearned and learned - needs are related in complex ways.

(a) We may decide to **satisfy intellectual and emotional needs before - or even instead of - primary needs**. Religious orders, for example, may require disciplines such as celibacy or fasting. People give up much-needed sleep for all sorts of reasons (even studying!). The self-preservation drive may be overcome by concern for other people (altruism) or by other goals, in dangerous situations.

(b) We retain **freedom of choice** about how we **satisfy** our needs.

6.6 A consumer may **need to purchase food to fulfil one of the primary needs** - hunger - of his family. However, he does not buy just any food: his choices will be directed by secondary needs to gain his family's **esteem and recognition**, to eat foods that are culturally acceptable (and not, for example, breaking any religious taboos), to recall food he was brought up on, to impress dinner guests - or whatever. He may not be aware of the operation of any of these needs in the choices he makes, although he is more likely to be aware of the physiological hunger for food.

Wants

6.7 **The means of satisfying needs are wants**. For instance, a customer's need for food may be crystallised into wanting a cheese sandwich. Depending how strongly he wants one he will take action to satisfy the want, and go and buy a cheese sandwich.

6.8 The wants of an individual specify the outcomes which will act as motivators to act in a certain way. Motivation is thus the driving force within individuals that impels them to action to achieve wants.

Goals

6.9 **Goals** are then the outcomes that have become sought-after (buying the cheese sandwich), the 'ends' of motivated behaviour. Goals may be:

(a) **generic:** general categories of outcomes that people expect to fulfil their needs; or

(b) **specific:** specific 'wants' which are expected to fulfil needs. From a marketer's point of view, product- or brand-specific goals are desirable. From the generic goal of, say, needing a thirst-quenching drink we may develop a specific goal of drinking a Coke.

6.10 Many 'goals' may be appropriate to satisfy a given need. Which specific goal or goals will be selected depends on:

(a) **past experience**, and the reinforcement that may have accompanied it, to make goals seem desirable and attainable;

(b) personal **physical capacity or ability** to attain a given goal;

(c) **learned cultural norms and values**, acquired through, say, family and education, social interaction or religious instruction. As Buchanan and Huczynski note, 'those behaviours that are typical and conventional tend to become socially necessary, as those who do not conform may be shunned, or even imprisoned. Polygamy is a crime to us, but a social norm and a sign of male achievement, wealth and status in parts of the Arab world';

(d) the **accessibility of the goal** in the individual's physical and social environment;

(e) the **individual's self image**, and whether the goal reflects or enhances it;

(f) the **stage of life** the individual is at. There is usually a process of gradual 'goal shift' with age, career pattern, family development etc - as well as radical re-evaluation as a result of physical events (illness or menopause, say), career events (change of career, redundancy, retirement) and family events (divorce, birth of child).

6.11 Schiffman and Kanuk (*Consumer Behaviour*) give the amusing example of an individual with a strong hunger need.

> 'If he is a young American athlete, he may envision a rare sirloin steak as his goal object; if he is also an orthodox Jew, he may require that the steak be kosher to conform to dietary laws. If he has a sore gum, he may not be able to chew a steak; he may have to select hamburger instead. If he has never tasted steak... he will probably not even think of steak, but will select a food that has previously satisfied his hunger... If he were having dinner with his mother, she might frown on his consuming red meat, and insist he have fish or chicken instead. If he were shipwrecked on an island with no food provisions or living animals, he could not realistically select steak as his goal object, though he might fantasise about it.'

6.12 We might add that if he perceived himself to be a health-conscious, ideologically- sound vegetarian, the sirloin would also be incompatible with his self image - and if he had just been made redundant, he might reappraise his priorities as far as paying for expensive cuts of meat went.

Positive and negative motivation

6.13 **Motives may be positive or negative**: we have needs for positive satisfactions, but also needs to avoid dissatisfactions and threats. Negative drives are sometimes called 'fears' or 'aversions', but essentially they impel behaviour in the same way as 'needs', 'wants' and 'goals' (positive drives). A safety need, for example, may impel us to seek shelter in a storm: this is both a desire for warmth and dryness, and to avoid cold, wet and lightning.

6.14 **Goals can also be positive ('approach objects') or negative ('avoidance objects')**. You may have the positive goal of **finishing this Study Text** as soon as possible, and the negative goal of collapsing from stress and exhaustion: your behaviour will be directed accordingly and you will work on the text for a sensible number of hours each week!

Arousal of motives

6.15 Most of our needs are latent or 'dormant' most of the time: we are not constantly aware of them, until they are stimulated or 'aroused'. The **arousal of a given need** or set of needs at a given moment may be one of the following.

(a) **Physiological**. Internal physical stimuli (a drop in blood sugars, or surge of adrenaline, say) trigger biogenic needs such as hunger, thirst or flight from danger. Hormone release triggers the sex drive.

(b) **Emotional**. Imagination and fantasy can arouse latent needs, creating frustration until action is taken to satisfy them. Social aspirations, sexual fantasies and daydreams are of this kind. A man whose fantasy was to play football for Liverpool might respond to products endorsed by the team's star players. Ads for perfumes (and chocolates) often arouse desires related to sexual fantasy.

(c) **Cognitive**. Thoughts or achievements can trigger recognition - cognitive awareness - of a need.

Marketing at Work

The Post Office and British Telecom both advertise their services to consumers in a way that reminds people of the need to write/speak to a friend or family member. 'That reminds me, I must...' is a typical response to cognitive arousal.

(d) **Environmental**. Environmental or situational 'cues' or stimuli can be associated with need arousal by conditioning: you feel hungry when you hear the 1 o'clock or 6 o'clock news theme, when you smell certain foods or hear them spoken of. A desire is frequently aroused by the sight of a goal object: if you see a car, or item of clothing, that is 'better' than your own, you become dissatisfied with what you have and experience a need for something new. Television advertising is not kind in this respect: it actively arouses desires that many viewers will have little hope of fulfilling.

Action Programme 2

Why were you motivated to study for the CIM qualification? Which needs were aroused? What are your goals? Have you been motivated to behave in a certain way by other people's expectations of you?

7 MOTIVATION THEORIES RELEVANT TO MARKETERS

7.1 There are various theories (and indeed categories of theories) of motivation. Here, we will examine **theories about the need systems individuals have**. Some of these consist of rather lengthy lists of needs and motives that humans experience, but these are cumbersome for marketers to use. More useful are the theories which suggest categories of need, into which the variety of human experience can be fitted.

(a) Maslow's 'hierarchy of needs';

(b) Alderfer's existence, relatedness and growth;

(c) McClelland's three motivating needs (including the important concept of achievement need); and

(d) Vroom's expectancy theory.

Maslow's hierarchy of needs

7.2 The American psychologist Abraham Maslow formulated a widely popular theory of universal human needs ranked in a **'hierarchy of relative pre-potency'** (overriding force) from **biogenic** needs upwards to **psychogenic** needs. According to the hierarchy theory, the **lowest 'level'** or need which is unsatisfied is **dominant**. Once it is satisfied, the next level 'up' becomes the dominant motivating impulse, until it in turn is satisfied - or until a lower-level need becomes dominant again, through renewed deprivation.

7.3 Since no need is ever completely satisfied, the levels **overlap** in practice, and more than one level of need may operate at the same time, but the prime motivator - the dominant impulse within the individual at a given time - is said to be the lowest level of need that is substantially unsatisfied.

7.4 Maslow's need categories are as follows.

Physiological needs	food, water, air, shelter, sex
Safety and security needs	freedom from threat, health, but also security, order, predictability, 'knowing where you are with people'
Social or companionship needs	for friendships, affection, sense of belonging
Esteem or ego needs	for self-respect and self-confidence, competence, achievement, independence, prestige and their reflection in the perception of others
Self-actualisation needs	for the fulfilment of personal potential: 'the desire to become more and more what one is, to become everything that one is capable of becoming'

Maslow's hierarchy of needs

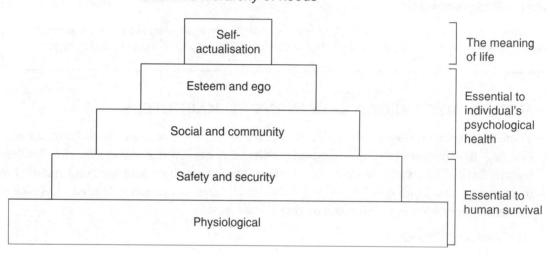

Evaluating the hierarchy of needs

7.5   There is a certain **intuitive appeal** to Maslow's theory. After all, you are unlikely to be concerned with status or recognition while you are hungry or thirsty - primary survival needs will take precedence. (As Maslow said: 'For the man who is extremely and dangerously hungry, no other interest exists but food - he dreams food, he remembers food, he thinks about food, he emotes only about food, he perceives only food and he wants only food.') Likewise, once your hunger is assuaged, the need for food is unlikely to be a motivating factor. Unfortunately, **research does not bear out the proposition that needs become less powerful as they are satisfied**, except at the very primitive level of 'primary' needs like hunger and thirst.

7.6   There are various **problems** associated with Maslow's theory.

(a)   **Empirical verification for the hierarchy is hard to come by**. Physiological and safety needs, as we mentioned before, are not always uppermost in the determination of human behaviour. It is still not clear, either, whether the higher order needs are innate or learned: it would be pleasant to believe, with Maslow, that they are innate, but, as Buchanan and Huczynski suggest: 'Maslow may simply have reflected American middle class values and the pursuit of the good life, and may not have hit on fundamental universal truths about human psychology.'

(b)   **It is difficult to predict behaviour using the hierarchy**: the theory is too vague. It is impossible to define how much satisfaction has to be achieved before the individual progresses to the next level in the hierarchy. Different people emphasise different needs. Also, the same need may cause different behaviour in different individuals: one person may seek to satisfy his need for esteem by winning promotion, whereas another individual might seek esteem by ram-raiding.

(c) **Self-actualisation**, in particular, is **difficult to offer in practice**: it depends on what we perceive to be our personal potential, which in turn depends largely on social values, beliefs, ideals and customs. People's perception of their own worth and potential is bound up with the expectations and roles imposed on them by their culture; men are supposed to find fulfilment in paid work, and women in child-rearing, in traditional Western societies. In addition, the need for self actualisation may be expressed in an infinite variety of ways, according to individuals' orientations towards creative or sporting pursuits, physical or mental achievement, business or service of others and so on.

(d) The '**ethnocentricity**' of Maslow's hierarchy has also been noted. It does seem broadly applicable to Western English-speaking cultures, but is less relevant elsewhere.

7.7 However, the hierarchy offers a **simple and readily understood model** of motivation for marketers in the broadly Western cultures to which it is most applicable. It is particularly useful to marketing strategists, because the marketing concept is based on the satisfaction of consumer needs, and consumer goods and services are available to satisfy each of the need categories put forward by Maslow. Physiological needs are met by food and drink, houses and clothes; safety needs by insurance, job training, double glazing and seatbelts; social needs by cosmetics, personal hygiene products and pets; esteem or ego needs by luxury items, bigger cars and designer clothes; self-actualisation needs by education and training services, health-club membership and career consultancy.

The hierarchy of needs as an operational tool

7.8 The hierarchy of needs can be adapted to:

(a) facilitate **market segmentation**, by enabling advertisers to focus their messages on a need category that is likely to be shared by a sizeable segment of the target population; and

(b) facilitate **product/brand positioning**, by enabling advertisers to establish the product/brand in people's perception as the means to satisfy a particular need category.

Examples of segmentation and positioning by need category

	Segment
Physiological needs	Ads for 'Stop smoking' products: targeting people worried about cancer
	Position
	Gas Central Heating ads: creating the perception of central heating as a 'survival' tool (blizzards in the unheated hallway etc)
Safety needs	*Segment*
	Pensions and insurance ads: target people with families and houses, career peak age-groups etc
	Position
	Volvo ads: creating the perception of Volvo as the safe car

	Segment
Social needs	*Segment*
	Soft drink ads: target young people (associated with 'good times together' situations)
	Position
	Mail/telephone service ads: creating the perception of putting you in touch with people you love and miss.
Esteem needs	*Segment*
	Luxury car ads: target high-income, high-status groups
	Position
	Alliance and Leicester Building Society ads: creating the perception that you can be proud of yourself for making a smart choice.
Self-actualisation needs	*Segment*
	Health product ads: target at body-conscious young people
	Position
	Courvoisier brandy ads: creating the perception that you deserve the best, after your efforts/ achievements

7.9   Schiffman and Kanuk point out the **versatility** of the model. They use the example of potential promotional appeals for a home exercise machine.

Physiological:	Improves body tone and health.
Safety:	Safe to use at home. Sturdy and dependable.
Social:	Fun to use with a friend. Makes you more attractive.
Esteem:	Be proud of your physique. Impress your friends.
Self-actualisation:	Give yourself a perfect physique. You deserve the convenience and luxury of home exercise after a hard day at work.

Action Programme 3

How would you segment the following products and services in terms of Maslow's categorisation of needs?

(a)   Private health insurance
(b)   Designer sunglasses
(c)   Mobile phones
(d)   Word processing course
(e)   Underwear

Alderfer's existence, relatedness and growth

7.10   Clayton Alderfer has suggested a **three factor hierarchy of needs** known as ERG - existence, relatedness and growth.

Alderfer's ERG model

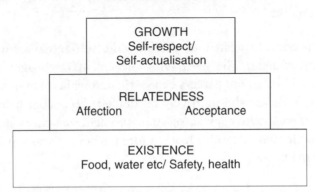

7.11 In many ways the theory is similar to Maslow's, but Alderfer adds an interesting amendment to the **force** of each need:

(a) a need becomes **more important the less it is satisfied**;

(b) satisfaction of a **lower need** means the **next need** becomes more important;

(c) the **less** a higher need is satisfied, the **more** important the lower need becomes.

In other words, **individuals who cannot get what they want demand more of what they can get**.

7.12 From a marketing point of view this theory highlights the role of **frustration** and the possibility that a person who cannot afford the Georgio Armani suit she wants may buy three Emporio Armani suits she can afford instead.

McClelland's three motivating needs

7.13 Another **three-motivating-needs** model, which has particularly been applied to motivation at work, is David McClelland's model of the needs for **power, affiliation, and achievement**.

7.14 **Power needs** are to do with the individual's need to **control his environment** - including the resources needed for survival, and also other people. (It therefore includes elements of physiological, safety and ego or esteem needs.) People with strong power needs will tend:

(a) to be **motivated at work by promotion** to positions of control over others, autonomy for themselves and control over resources. This is an important attribute for a successful manager;

(b) to select **products which are positioned to offer power or superiority** - such as very fast cars, dominant clothing styles - or any product associated with a streetwise, dominant role model.

7.15 **Affiliation needs** relate to social needs for **friendship, acceptance and belonging**. People with high affiliation needs will tend to depend on the approval and judgement of others, and so will:

(a) be motivated at work by **opportunities to form and develop social relationships** within the 'team' and organisation. Not usually an attribute of the successful manager;

(b) conform to **'team' norms** of output and behaviour, even against managerial pressure to do otherwise;

(c) select goods that will be **approved of by their friends, peers and role models**, adapting their purchase behaviour to that of reference groups (discussed in Chapter 1);

(d) respond positively to **co-operative and friendly sales personnel**; and

(e) select **distribution channels that offer social opportunities**: fairs and shows, shopping malls and the like.

7.16 **Achievement needs** are related to **esteem and self-actualisation needs**, focusing on personal accomplishment. The need for achievement is thought to be related to **early socialisation**. Children whose parents expect them to gain early independence, and impose few restrictions on them, who positively reinforce independent behaviour, and who foster an atmosphere of competitiveness, aspiration and achievement at home, are more likely to develop high achievement needs than children whose parents dominated, restricted or 'molly-coddled' them.

7.17 There has been less work done on achievement needs in the consumer context, although the need for feedback on their performance, the enjoyment of calculated risk, and the enjoyment of personal responsibility for making decisions may indicate that **high achievement needers**:

(a) respond to **information appeals** which give them the responsibility for making choices and finding solutions;

(b) respond to **innovative products** and 'do it yourself' products - houses that 'need some work', cars that 'take some driving', knitting kits instead of ready-made knitwear;

(c) respond to **'symbols' of success and status,** which allow them to feel they are doing well;

(d) respond to **'self-evaluation' opportunities** - quiz books and games, 'beat the computer' chess, competitive sports and so on.

Action Programme 4

Attempt to classify a member of your family, a close friend and somebody you work with in terms of McClelland's three motivating needs. By which need are they most motivated?

Vroom's expectancy theory

7.18 The expectancy theory of motivation is based on the **assumptions that human beings are purposive and rational,** that is, aware of their goals and behaviour.

7.19 Essentially, the theory states that the **strength of an individual's motivation** to do something will depend on the extent to which he **expects the results of his efforts,** if successfully achieved, to **contribute towards his personal needs or goals.**

7.20 In 1964 Victor Vroom, another American psychologist, worked out a **formula** by which human motivation could actually be assessed and measured, based on an expectancy theory of work motivation. Vroom suggested that the strength of an individual's motivation is the product of two factors:

(a) the strength of his **preference for a certain outcome.** Vroom called this **valence.** It may be represented as a positive or negative number, or zero - since outcomes may be desired, avoided or considered with indifference; and

(b) his **expectation that the outcome will result from a certain behaviour.** Vroom called this **subjective probability**: it is only the individual's expectation, and depends on his perception of the probable relationship between behaviour and outcome. As a probability, it may be represented by any number between 0 (no chance) and 1 (certainty).

7.21 In its simplest form, the 'expectancy equation' therefore looks like this.

Vroom's expectancy equation

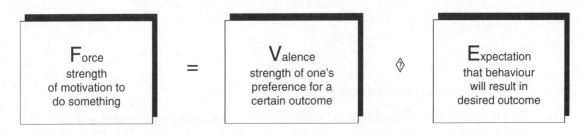

7.22 Expectancy theory attempts to measure the **strength** of an individual's motivation to act in a particular way. It is then possible to compare 'F' values for a range of different behaviours, to discover which behaviour the individual is most likely to adopt. It is also possible to compare 'F' values for different individuals, to see who is most highly motivated to behave in the desired (or undesirable) way.

7.23 This is what you would expect: if either valence or expectation have a value of zero, there will be no motivation. In marketing terms:

(a) a consumer has a **high expectation that a purchase will result in a certain outcome**, such as getting drunk, but he is **indifferent** to that outcome (he doesn't want the hangover), V = 0, and he will **not be motivated** to purchase beer.

(b) the consumer has a great desire for a good time - but **doesn't believe that the purchase of beer** will secure it for him, E = 0, and he will still **not be highly motivated**.

Trait-factor theories

> ### Key Concept
> A **trait** is a stable characteristic of a person. Traits are not directly observable but they are important because they allow us to understand and predict other people's behaviour.

7.24 Trait theories assume that the basic motivation of human behaviour is to fit in with our environment. One of the best-known trait factor theories is **Holland's theory**.

7.25 Holland's theory contains four assumptions.

(a) Most people can be characterised as one of **six types** (these are shown in the diagram below).

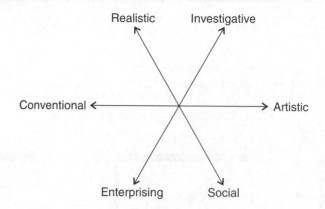

(b) There are also six types of **environment**

(c) People search for environments that will let them **exercise their skills** and express their attitudes

(d) Behaviour is an **interaction** between someone's personality and their environment

7.26 Trait factor theories find their most common use in career counselling, and deal mainly with achieving satisfaction at work, but marketers may also be able to use them in understanding customer behaviour.

Self-concept theories

Key Concept
Self-concept can be defined as the perceptions that people hold regarding their own personal existence – who they are and how they fit into the world. They can be a primary motivating force in human behaviour. The 'self' is seen as a social product, developing out of interpersonal relationships.

7.27 As with trait theories, self-concept theories are most often employed in counselling, but again they can be of use to marketers. As self-concept is **learned through experience**, it can be **developed and manipulated**, and therefore could be used to the marketer's advantage when targeting customers. Customers are **dynamic** and constantly assimilating new ideas (your new product?) and getting rid of old ones (a competitor's product?). Marketers can design programmes that are specifically designed to stimulate this learning process.

Exam tip
Psychological theory, motivation theory, trait-factor theory and self concept theories are specifically mentioned in the tutor's guidance notes. Use your knowledge as a route to devising product/service improvements and innovations and thereby make it applicable to the exam. Put the theory into practice!

Chapter roundup

- The individual is influenced by his or her personal environment.

- Socialisation is the process by which knowledge of society and its rules is acquired, to enable participation in that society. The family is the earliest contact through which socialisation is achieved.

- Groups can serve as a benchmark for behavioural norms and specific attitudes.

- Reference groups influence buying decisions.

- Knowledge of roles can enable marketers to predict the kind of items (role signs) that people will want to buy.

- Motivation can be understood by reference to needs, wants and goals.

- This chapter also looked at relevant motivation theories:

  o Maslow's hierarchy of needs
  o Alderfer's existence, relatedness and growth
  o McClelland's three motivating needs
  o Vroom's expectancy theory

  It is important to examine these in a marketing context.

- Trait factor theories and self concept theories can also assist the marketer.

Quick quiz

1   What is 'consumer socialisation'? (2.9)

2   How can reference groups influence a buying decision? (3.4)

3   What is a role set (4.2) and a role sign? (4.5)

4   How can knowledge of roles help with market segmentation and product positioning? (4.7)

5   What is reinforcement? (5.4)

6   What are the different types of need? (6.4)

7   How can Maslow's hierarchy of needs be used as an operational tool in marketing? (7.8)

8   What are the six types of people identified by Holland's theory? (7.25)

Action Programme Review

3   (a)   Safety
    (b)   Esteem
    (c)   Social
    (d)   Self-actualisation
    (e)   Physiological

12

Groups and organisations as customers

Chapter Topic List	Syllabus reference
1 Setting the scene	3.1, 3.4
2 The primary group DMU	3.1, 3.4
3 Secondary groups: the social environment	3.1, 3.4
4 Secondary groups: cultural issues	3.1, 3.4
5 Implications for national, international and global marketing	3.1, 3.4
6 The DMU within organisations	3.1, 3.5

Learning Outcomes

- After studying this chapter you will be able to move beyond individual customers and explain the influences on groups and organisational customers.

- The organisational DMU is explored further - its characteristics and implications for marketing.

Key Concepts Introduced

- Group
- Status

- Micro-culture
- Cross-cultural marketing

Examples of Marketing at Work

- The home PC market
- Left-hand and right-hand drive, watches, jeans, ice-cream
- Nestle, Monopoly, Häagen-Dazs
- Global products

- Benetton, American Express

- Hoover
- Coke and Lever Bros

1 SETTING THE SCENE

> **Key Concept**
> Edgar Schein (*Organisational Psychology*) defines a group as 'any number of people who (i) interact with one another, (ii) are psychologically aware of one another, and (iii) perceive themselves to be a group.' The point of this definition is the distinction it implies between a random collection of individuals and a 'group' of individuals who share a common sense of identity and belonging.

Groups as decision making units

1.1 Groups offer certain **advantages and disadvantages** for decision making.

(a) Groups have been shown to produce **fewer, although better evaluated, new ideas** than the individuals of the group working separately.

(b) A group will often produce a **better solution** to a problem than even its best individual, since 'missing pieces' can be added to the individual's thinking by the rest of the group.

(c) Group decision making allows the **voicing of various different viewpoints**. The disadvantage of this is that the decision-making process may be rather cumbersome, especially if consensus is sought. The advantage is that the decision will be representative, and decisions reached by consensus tend to have ready acceptance - not merely compliance.

(d) Groups provide a **sense of belonging, 'solidarity' and strength to individuals**. This can help them where unpleasant and risky decisions need to be taken (although it may be a problem where risk is undesirable, say in business). It will also tend to strengthen group attitudes - whether positive or negative.

1.2 In order for a group to be an **effective** decision making unit it needs:

(a) clear **terms of reference** or objectives;

(b) sufficient **information** to make the decision;

(c) **leadership and guidance** of the debate; and

(d) the **appropriate mix of** 'roles' for the task - which are the roles we saw in our analysis of the DMU.

Consumer-relevant groups

1.3 Some reference groups or groupings are **particularly relevant to marketers** in their influence on consumer behaviour.

(a) The **family** is the main **primary group** for most individuals, involving the most frequent contact and the greatest significance or perceived importance to the individual. Family norms and influences on all behaviour are particularly strong. (We will discuss the family separately below.)

(b) **Work groups are also primary**, if only because of the sheer amount of time people spend at work. The opinion of colleagues can be an important factor, especially if they are also part of informal friendship groups in the workplace. 'Politics' at work also influences the choice of products which enhance status and image.

(c) **Friendship groups** are an important influence on buyer behaviour, since the desire to form and maintain friendly relationships is one of Man's basic motivations, and since

267

people trust their friends to advise them in their best interests - particularly those friends whom they perceive to share their values and goals. Marketers frequently depict product choice, in advertising, in the context of friendly sharing, advice and encouragement.

(d) A particular off-shoot of this is the **shopping group** - people who regularly or occasionally shop together and form a buying Decision-Making Unit. The shopping group offers social diversion and company, but also enables the purchaser to confirm that a purchased item will be socially acceptable, or to get the security of a 'second opinion'.

(e) **Interest or action groups**. Membership of a particular interest or 'pressure' group may have an influence on purchase behaviour. A 'consumer action' or 'consumerist' group, for example, may address directly consumer-relevant issues by boycotting a product that is thought to be dangerous or deceptive. Other groups - animal rights, anti-fur, anti-apartheid or whatever - may include in their programmes purchase-oriented behaviour.

1.4 Any group (including an aspirational or symbolic group) that serves as a 'frame of reference' for an individual's behaviour, and may therefore influence that behaviour, is called a **reference group**.

Exam tip

Organisational customer care is, in some ways, much more straightforward because it is much easier to identify the customer, but in other ways more complex because of the 'organisational' factors that come into play.

2 THE PRIMARY GROUP DMU

2.1 The **family** is perhaps the **most important primary group** for any individual, although its structure, behaviour and influence will vary greatly from society to society, and even according to individual circumstance. Such questions as who looks after children, how and for how long, are vital to understanding the family unit.

2.2 A family has traditionally been defined as a number of people who are related by blood, marriage or adoption - and who usually reside together. Such a family unit may be:

(a) a **married couple** who have not yet 'started a family' (had children - a reflection of the child-oriented nature of the family unit) or who have already raised children and seen them leave home;

(b) a **nuclear family**, consisting of a couple or single parent plus one or more children, living together; or

(c) an **extended family**, consisting of the parents, children and other relatives (grandparents, aunts and uncles, in-laws etc). Since increased mobility in industrialised nations has tended to separate parents from their adult offspring, and siblings from each other, the extended family is less common than it was in such cultures, and the nuclear family has become the main decision-making unit for consumption activity.

In addition there is the **pseudo-family unit, the household**. A household - or number of people sharing a residence and its consumption decisions - may be a family, but may also be a number of unrelated people living together: boarders/lodgers, house/flat sharers, unmarried couples and so on.

2.3 The family can be regarded as any of the following.

(a) A **network of relationships**, the dynamics of which can be very complex. This network can fulfil the crucial love and security needs of its members, although not every family unit is experienced as secure, happy, socially constructive and mutually supportive.

(b) A **social unit**, both earning and consuming, and therefore a model of economic behaviour. It has been suggested that the ideal of 'normal' family life is defined to suit the prevailing economic system (developing properly submissive labour forces - both wage-earning and domestic - for the future) and the preservation of the social structure.

(c) A **reference group**. The family exerts an important influence on the following.

(i) The **socialisation** of children: informal training encouraging the kind of values, attitudes and behaviour that their society will later expect of them. Families, as institutions, are norm-setting units: members are taught to conform to shared norms of attitude and behaviour.

(ii) **Role definition**. The family is the first context in which individuals take on a role - as son, daughter, brother, sister etc - and learn what to expect, and what is expected of them, in relation to others (in appropriate roles as mother, father, adult). The family also provides role patterns for sexual, social and 'economic' behaviour. To take a stereotypical example:

Woman = wife and mother = household maintenance and child-rearing;
Man = husband and father = breadwinner.

(iii) **Self-awareness and perception**. The way an individual perceives himself and other people, events and the world around him will be highly subjective and selective, and will partly be influenced by his expectations. These in turn arise out of past experience. The experience of the earliest 'formative' years of childhood and adolescence is therefore likely to colour the whole perceptual world of the emerging adult.

(iv) **Goal-formation and articulation**. The satisfaction or denial of childhood needs can determine needs in later life. Family members also act as role-models or patterns, whose goals and achievements may be emulated (or indeed avoided, if the pattern is a negative one: the family may also act as a dissociative group).

(v) **Consumer behaviour**. As a reference group over a broad span of the individual's life, the family can influence his understanding of the use and value of money, his perception of what products are 'normal' and valuable, his perception of his own role as a selector and decision-maker; and the criteria on which products are chosen (eg for family use).

Family decision-making roles

2.4 Multi-individual decision making involves several **decision-making roles**. It is obviously of relevance to marketers whether the woman or man in the household is the buyer or decision-maker, or whether it is the parents or children; who usually finds out first about products and brands; who in the family has the power to persuade the buyer to make a particular brand choice and purchase. This kind of information determines the product's **positioning** (masculine/feminine, youthful/mature image?) distribution and **promotion pattern**, and **target audience** for information. Marketers must also be aware how the shifting pattern of family roles (with financial independence for working women, the acceptance of household tasks by men, and the earlier age at which children expect their own independence) is changing the composition of traditional target markets.

Family consumption roles

Initiator	suggests the idea of buying a particular product
Influencer	provides information about a product/service to other members
Gatekeeper	controls the flow of information about a product/service into the family (for example by 'giving the gist' of a consumer article, or selecting the advertising message that is relayed to the family).
Decider	has the power to determine whether to purchase a specific product/service
Buyer	makes the purchase of the product/service
Preparer	makes the product into a form suitable for family consumption (by preparing food, say, or assembling DIY furniture)
User	consumes or utilises a particular product/service
Maintainer	services or repairs a product so that it continues to satisfy
Disposer	initiates or performs the disposal or termination of the product/service

The family DMU

2.5 Within a family group as a decision-making unit various members may occupy these roles. Morden gives the examples of the purchase of a child's toy and a family car.

Toy		*Car*	
Initiator:	Child	Initiator:	Father, salesperson
Influencer:	Parents	Influencer:	Mother
	Relatives		Family
	Friends		Friends/colleagues
	Salesperson		Salesperson
Decider:	Parents	Decider:	Father, mother
Buyer:	Mother	Buyer:	Father
User:	Child	User:	Father, mother

2.6 **Marketers will be interested in reaching each of these roles**: to make the product attractive to the initiator (if it is not a product automatically bought), influencer and decider in particular. They would need to make the product readily available for the purchaser, and satisfying enough for the user to initiate future repurchase.

2.7 These roles - and the number and nature of the individuals who adopt them - will **vary from product to product, and from family to family**. One person (say, whichever family member buys routine grocery supplies) may occupy several of these roles, by browsing in the shop alone, unilaterally selecting and buying items without any influence. That individual may or may not also be the preparer of a meal, and will probably not be the sole user of all items (the family share the meal, but the individual uses his/her own purchased toothbrush, lipstick or whatever).

2.8 If the **buyer** of a product is a **different** person from the **decision-maker**, the marketer would need to **redirect promotional effort** from packaging and point of sale (attracting the buyer in-store) to advertising and promotional activity outside the store (where the decision-maker would be reached). If powerful influencers can be identified, they can be targeted as a way of getting to decision-makers.

2.9 **Media** which are designed for **sharing by the whole family** unit like television, Sunday newspapers, or cinema (when 'family' films are showing) offer marketers the opportunity of reaching influencers, decision-makers, buyers and users at the same time, facilitating discussion and influence within the decision-making unit.

The influence of gender

2.10 The pattern of decision-making roles has also **varied in society generally**, over time, particularly in relation to **gender roles**. The relative influence of male and female partners is of particular interest to consumer researchers, who commonly classify decisions as being male-dominated, female-dominated, joint, equal or 'syncratic', or unilateral or 'autonomic' (independent).

2.11 The relative influence of male and female partners, and the extent to which decisions are shared, may vary according to:

(a) the **family's attitudes to gender roles**. These may have changed significantly in the last three decades. A family which is 'modern' in its outlook on gender-based stereotypes will tend to distribute decisions (traditionally either male - eg cars - or female - eg household items) between partners, and share decision-making more, through discussion and consensus. It will in particular distribute financial decisions more evenly: women who undertake paid work tend to make more independent decisions about aspects of family finances;

(b) the **surrounding culture's attitudes to gender roles**. According to cross-cultural studies, some societies - notably Latin cultures and less developed societies - retain much stronger traditional gender role patterns, and the male partner makes significantly more unilateral decisions than in other cultures. Micro-cultural factors such as religious orientation may also affect decision-making roles through the maintenance of traditional gender-role patterns;

(c) the **product or service**. Car purchase is a particularly interesting example: several decades ago, it was strongly male-dominated, while now, although still mainly male-dominated for the purchase of the main family car, the female car-buyer forms a rapidly expanding market segment (for second cars, cars for single and/or working women etc). The reverse trend is true for products like food and household items. There are still strong perceptions, however, that there are male-chosen products (like insurance and legal services) and female-chosen products (like clothes and cookware), while some decisions are widely shared - choice of holidays or the family doctor, say.

Action Programme 1

(a) Look out for car advertisements featuring women buyers and drivers, stressing independence and equality.

(b) Look out for advertisements in which the male partner (or even child) is 'sent out' shopping for food, washing powder and other such items: note how some choices they make change the female partner's mind and the family purchase pattern ('Well done. We'll be getting your brand from now on. Won't *you*?')

(c) Look out for advertisements which, on the other hand, reinforce traditional gender-related buying patterns: 'You're not a 'real'/'proper' mum if you don't buy/give them X.' 'Real men buy x.'

The influence of children

2.12 Children also have (or attempt to have) an influence on purchase decisions, not only those which are **relevant** to their particular wants ('I want toy X', 'I want chocolate bar Y') but also those which - **however irrelevant to them personally** - they relate to attractive messages they have seen and heard on television, or at friends' houses (a brand of dishwashing liquid marketed as having lots of soft bubbles, a car that a friend's dad has etc).

2.13 Particular **aspects of child influence** on consumption include the following.

(a) **Latchkey children**, who are at home alone for part of the day while both parents work. Consumer studies have shown that these children are able to operate household appliances more than other children, and also participate more in housework and household shopping. This makes them a market for a wide range of products, at a young age (so that brand loyalty can be established early and for a potentially longer time).

(b) The **increased spending power of teenagers and students**. A significant number of teenagers and post-teens work - at least part-time or in casual jobs - and may also, or otherwise, receive money 'gifts' or allowances from the family. Teenagers with working parents may participate in household purchasing, with some discretion as to the products selected (particularly for their own sole consumption - snacks etc). The **market for personal discretionary spending by teenagers**, however, is **highly developed**: a market for clothes, accessories, music, entertainments etc, usually segmented by lifestyle. **Students** are also an important target market for necessities such as books, clothing and transport, as well as discretionary purchases such as entertainment and travel.

In addition to independent purchases and influence on family purchases, teenagers and students are important to marketers, because it is believed that the young adult years are a **formative period** in terms of the establishment of shopping habits and brand preferences.

(i) Note how keen **banks and building societies** are to attract student customers.

(ii) Note how prominent **brands and 'labels'** are in advertising to teenagers when it comes to training shoes, jeans and other such items.

(c) **Television**. There is still controversy over whether pre-school children are able to distinguish between television programmes and advertising: the impact of television in general, however, is undeniable, because of its **power of creating associations** which become part of child learning. Older children are able to recall slogans and recognise symbolism in TV advertising. Advertising directed at adults can influence children's perceptions (by associating products with 'being grown-up') as much as those directed at children.

2.14 Parent groups frequently show concern that advertising to children:

(a) leads to **family conflict**, as the child attempts to exert influence in purchases; and

(b) **influences children to want things** which they are **not capable of evaluating objectively** (independently of the advertisers' message) and which may not be in their best interests, such as 'junk' food, expensive designer clothes and so on.

Action Programme 2

'Today's seven to eight year olds are more cynical about advertising and promotions than previous members of that age group, according to a report from Handel Communications, *The New Generation*.

"They are hard to please and tend to view campaigns aimed at them as childish. They want to be treated as adults and have an 'instant gratification' philosophy with regard to promotions," says Handel chairman Kleshna Handel.

Its findings are based on its own research, as well as continuous Child Track research by Carrick James Market Research.

Handel also reveals that most seven to 12-year olds in Britain are growing up wary, fearful and anxious to be like their parents. They see school as the passport to a good job and are keen to achieve financial security.

Of seven to eight year olds, 38 per cent regularly collect special offers or gifts attached to products. That figure falls sharply as they get older. Their attitude to promotions parallels this trend.

The financial muscle wielded by today's seven to 12 year olds cannot be ignored. The Carrick James Child Track study reveals that seven to eight year old girls receive £2.24 a week in pocket money and nine to 12 year old girls £4.14. Boys aged seven and eight get about £2,80 a week, rising to £4.62 when they are aged between nine and 12. This, combined with their 'pester power' - more than 60 per cent of parents confirmed that their shopping bill was more expensive if a child was with them - make them a force to be reckoned with.'   *Marketing Business*, July/August 1995

What evidence of these trends do you see in marketing aimed at children? You may have to watch a bit of children's TV, glance through a few magazines aimed at children or pay a visit to Toys R Us to get a good understanding of these customers.

3   SECONDARY GROUPS: THE SOCIAL ENVIRONMENT

3.1   If we are to understand our customers we need to have some idea of how far the individual's cognitive processes and behaviour, including his/her decision whether to become our customer, depend on his/her perception of and interaction with **other people**. In this section we will cover two particular ways in which we see ourselves, and behave, **in relation to others**.

Status

3.2   Some roles are perceived as **superior or inferior** in relation to others. The roles of employer and employee, or parent and child, have this connotation in traditional Western societies. One role may be superior to another because it is perceived that a person in that role has power or authority.

(a)   **Power**. Power is the capacity or ability to control or influence the actions of others. It may have as its source:

(i)   **physical** power, or superior force;

(ii)   **personal** power, or charisma;

(iii)   **resource** power - control over resources which are valued by the individual or group being controlled. An employer has this sort of power over an employee; or

(iv)   **expert** power - if the individual is acknowledged by others to have knowledge or expertise that they need or value.

(b)   **Authority**. Authority is the 'legal' or socially acknowledged right to control or influence the actions of others. In formal organisations, it is conferred on an individual by his position or job title. (Because it depends on social recognition, it may also be conferred by expertise or other factors - if they are acknowledged as giving the right to exercise power.)

3.3 A combination of such factors - power, wealth, expertise, position - determines 'where' a person is in relation to other people, or in the framework of society as a whole. This relative position of superiority or inferiority is called status.

> ### Key Concept
> **Status** has been called 'a kind of social identification tag': as such, it is the basis of the determination of social class, or social stratification. It also forms part of the individual's self-image.

3.4 **Status** may be:

(a) **ascribed,** or attributed to someone by society, on the basis of perceived factors such as their sex or age, intelligence or race. Improved status comes automatically with seniority in some cultures - such as the Japanese - while the male has traditionally had higher status than the female in Western cultures; or

(b) achieved by **deliberate effort** on the part of the individual. Professional and occupational status are *achieved*.

3.5 Status may be ascribed to an individual on the basis of their role or roles: in a **matriarchal society,** for example, the female role in the family carries with it high status. Once ascribed, status may also define a person's role or roles: low-status individuals are expected to take on subordinate roles and behaviour, in society and at work.

Status may be achieved by **acquiring appropriate roles and behaviours** (becoming a student and joining the CIM to achieve **professional status,** say). Once status is achieved, it will also determine the roles a person will be able to fill, consistent with his status.

3.6 **Some cultures are 'status-conscious', while others are not.**

(a) In the past, Western organisations tended to **perpetuate the divide** between management and workers, through symbols such as executive restaurants and other facilities, executive cars and car-parking places, suits for the managers, formal modes of address, offices for managers only and so on. Attitudes have changed in the 1990s, however. Big institutions in the City of London have 'dress down days' when all staff wear casual clothes.

(b) Japanese organisations tend to have no executive-only facilities; all staff eat in the same staff restaurant, wear overalls and are on first-name terms. This culture has been transferred to Japanese organisations operating in the UK.

3.7 **Marketing,** as well as management, will need to take into account the extent of status-awareness. **Low-status** individuals, in a status-conscious society, may **aspire to achieve higher status**: products can be positioned accordingly. **High status** individuals may wish to be 'congratulated', or to emphasise the exclusivity and power of their position in society: premium quality (and price) products frequently appeal to this sense.

Social class: stratification of UK society

3.8 However, in practice, class strata or divisions are commonly derived from the specific **demographic factors** of:

- **wealth/income** - economic resources;
- **educational** attainment; and
- **occupational** status.

3.9 Social class, based on status, could be thought of as a range of social positions in rank order. However, it has been thought more helpful to divide this continuum up into categories or strata (hence the term 'stratification'), called 'classes'. Each class is then presumed to share a common level of status, relatively higher or lower than other classes in the 'hierarchy' of society. From a marketer's point of view, it is also possible to infer **shared values, attitudes and behaviour within a social class,** as distinct from those of a higher or lower class: some research has been able to relate consumption behaviour to class standing. This makes social class an attractive proposition for market segmentation.

Exam tip
Various categorisations have been prepared offering different ways of stratifying society, but you should note that 'class' is also a highly **personal and subjective** phenomenon, to the extent that people are 'class-conscious' or class-aware, and have a sense of belonging to a particular social group. Be flexible in your approach.

Class distinction and mobility

3.10 Social class tends to perpetuate itself, **where people are highly class-conscious: they do not tend to move between classes,** or indeed to interact socially with members of other classes. Sociologists note that some societies have a very rigid class system, while others do not.

(a) **Closed societies** have a rigid structure, with very little social or class mobility (movement into another class): you are a member of the class or 'caste' you are born in, and have 'ascribed status' accordingly. The most obvious example is the Indian caste system, in which membership of a caste is ascribed at birth, and interactions (especially marriage) between castes is restricted by caste rules: no contact at all is permitted with those 'untouchables' who have no caste. To rectify this situation the Indian government reserves a proportion of government jobs for 'scheduled castes'

(b) **Open societies** have a less rigid system where it is possible to achieve status through the acquisition of knowledge, wealth and power, and thereby to move into a higher class 'bracket' - or to lose status, by an opposite process. Industrialised countries are now by and large open - although the older ones, such as Britain, contained elements of a closed society in the feudal system of the Middle Ages, until the rise of the merchant class gained momentum with the increase in trade.

3.11 Social mobility has several **implications for marketers.**

(a) **People aspire to upward mobility,** given a reasonable expectation of success, and will exhibit purchase and consumption patterns suitable to the class to which they aspire. (Consider the boom in products for 'yuppies' - by definition 'young upwardly mobile' people in the late 80s - and in demand for owned homes, foreign holidays, private education and health clubs, all of which used to be considered 'exclusive' to the upper middle class.)

(b) The **'lower' classes will become a less significant proportion of the population** (and therefore target market), as people move up out of them - assuming that the country's economy can support a widespread increase in per capita income.

(c) People are **afraid**, in a society of increasing inequality, of **downward mobility**.

3.12 A society in which there is **social mobility** will give plenty of examples of people changing their social class. Upward social mobility does occur (eg the trapeze artist's son who became Prime Minister (John Major)), as does downward mobility. However, the fact that some individuals, or even a significant number of them, are able to climb up to another rung on the ladder does not mean that socio-economic status is unimportant as a factor affecting the average person's life chances. These are now described in the context of the UK.

Education and achievement

3.13 *Social Trends* (1998) reports that 16% of the UK's male working age population and 21% of the UK's female working age population have **no qualifications**. However, it is likely that more and more people will become qualified.

(a) *Social Trends* reports that the workforce is becoming **increasingly well qualified**, with an increase (1975 - 1997) in the proportion of adults with GCSE grades A - C or equivalent rising from 27% to 62%.

(b) The number of people leaving school without qualifications is lower than the past. Women are doing increasingly well. In fact, fewer girls leave school without educational qualifications than boys. Overall in the UK, **girls outperform boys**.

3.14 There is also a **definite correlation between an individual's academic attainments and their socio-economic group**. The following comparisons may be made for 1996-97.

	Socio-economic group	
Qualification obtained	*Professional*	*Unskilled Manual*
Degree	66	-
Higher Education	16	1
A Level	7	5
GCSE grades A - C	5	16
CSE grades D - G	1	11
Foreign	4	2
None	2	65
	100 (1% rounding)	100

The differences are marked, but the sample on which these data were collected is based on all persons **between the ages of 25 and 69**. A breakdown by **age** would reveal fewer differences because of:

(a) the expansion of higher education after World War II;
(b) increases in the school leaving age;
(c) government policy, which has been to extend the scope of education.

Socio-economic position, income and wealth

Action Programme 3

'Comparing people's income is a simple matter. All you need to do is compare income after direct tax and social security contributions to see how well off people are.'

Do you agree with this statement?

3.15 The exercise above indicates some of the **problems collecting and presenting data** relating to wealth and living standards. This is because some households are taxed more than they benefit, and others benefit more than they are taxed. Let us look at some figures, comparing the poorest 20% to the wealthiest 20% (1995-96).

	Bottom 20% £	*Top 20%* £	*All* £
Total original income (wages, pensions)	2,430	41,260	17,200
Gross income (original income + cash benefits)	7,340	42,450	20,450
Disposable income (after tax, NIC, etc)	6,210	31,980	16,170
Post-tax income (after interest taxes)	4,280	26,890	12,820
Final income (after education, NHS, school meals etc)	8,230	29,200	15,920

3.16 **Wealth, too, is related to social structure.** In the UK, a large proportion of wealth is held as **property**, and so any increase or falls in property prices affects wealth. In 1971 26% of personal sector wealth was in dwellings. In 1991 this had risen to 36%. Since the recession, and the fall in house prices, this proportion fell to 25% in 1996. Of national wealth, in 1994 the richest 10% owned 51% of marketable wealth (including dwellings). The proportion of wealth excluding dwellings held by the richest 50% has increased from 88% in 1976 to 94% in 1994.

Buying patterns

3.17 Demography and the class structure are relevant in that they can be both **behavioural determinants** and **inhibitors** of household buying behaviour.

(a) **Behavioural determinants** encourage people to buy a product or service. The individual's personality, culture, social class, and the importance of the purchase decision (eg a necessity such as food or water, or a luxury) can predispose a person to purchase something.

(b) **Inhibitors** are factors, such as the individual's income, which will make the person less likely to purchase something.

3.18 **Socio-economic status can be related to buying patterns** in a number of ways, both in the amount people have to spend and what they spend it on. It affects both the quantity of goods and services supplied, and the proportion of their income that households spend on goods and services. Let us compare, for 1995-6, household expenditure of the poorest 20% to that of the wealthiest 20% (*Social Trends* 1998).

Item	*Bottom 20%* *% of total* *purchases*	*Top 20%* *% of total* *purchases*
Housing	15	18
Fuel, light, power	7	3
Food	24	15
Alcohol and tobacco	7	5
Clothing and footwear	5	6
Household goods and services	13	14
Motoring and fares	11	16
Leisure goods and services	13	18
Other	5	5
(After rounding)	100 (£158 per week)	100 (£477pw)

3.19   As you can see the wealthiest households spend less of a **proportion** of their total income on food and more on leisure, than do the poorest. This does not imply they spend any less in absolute terms of course: they just have more available to spend on other things.

3.20   The effect on social class on leisure is an example of how **discretionary spending sometimes varies from class to class**.

  (a)   In 1996 41% of members of social class AB took a **short break holiday**, compared to 28% of class C2 (according to *Social Trends*, 1998).

  (b)   For 1996, 47% of members of social class AB had been to the **cinema**, in the three months prior to the interview, compared with 35% of members of Class C2. **Bingo** enjoyed the patronage of 14% of members of social class E, compared with 2% of social class AB, in the three months prior to the interview.

  (c)   **Other activities are enjoyed equally**. 26% of ABs and 27% of C2s went to a disco/night club and 14% of each class visited a theme park.

4   SECONDARY GROUPS: CULTURAL ISSUES

4.1   **Culture** embraces the following aspects of social life.

  (a)   **Beliefs** are perceived states of knowing, or cognition: we feel that we know about 'things', on the basis of objective and subjective information. *Values* are the comparatively few key beliefs which are:

    (i)   relatively enduring;

    (ii)   relatively general - not tied to specific objects;

    (iii)   fairly widely accepted as a guide to culturally appropriate behaviour - and therefore as a 'standard' of desirable and undesirable beliefs, attitudes and behaviour.

  (b)   **Customs** are modes of behaviour which represent culturally approved ways of responding to given situations: usual and acceptable ways of behaving.

  (c)   A **ritual** is a type of activity which takes on symbolic meaning, consisting of a fixed sequence of behaviour repeated over time. Ritualised behaviour tends to be public, elaborate, formal and ceremonial - like marriage ceremonies. Ritualistic behaviour, however, is any behaviour a person makes a ritual out of (performing certain superstitious acts on the morning of an exam, for example). Rituals commonly require ritual artefacts (representing, for the marketer, products): think of the 'accessories' that attend a wedding.

  (d)   The different **languages** of different cultures is an obvious means of distinguishing large groups of people. Language can present a problem to cross-cultural marketers as we shall see.

  (e)   **Symbols** are an important aspect of language and culture: the symbolic nature of human language sets it apart from animal communication. Each symbol may carry a number of different meanings and associations for different people, and some of these meanings are learned as part of a society's culture. The advertiser using slang words or pictorial images must take care that they are valid for the people he wants to reach - and up-to-date.

  (f)   Culture embraces all the physical **'tools' or artefacts** used by people for their physical and psychological well-being. In our modern society, the **technology** we use has a very great impact on the way we live our lives, and new technologies accelerate the rate of social change.

(i) **Appearance and dress**. Cultures vary widely on what is accepted and desirable in the way of apparel and general appearance. In Muslim countries, for example, females cover themselves up while in Western societies, depending to some extent on the ebb and flow of fashion, female semi-nudity is accepted. Obviously this has a great impact on marketing; for instance, the market in the UK for ties is much larger than in Australia where 'dressing down' even in a business context is the norm.

(ii) **Food and eating habits**. Different cultures have different attitudes to food and eating together, with some cultures embracing the idea of convenience food (the US, UK) while others devote a great deal of time and effort to food preparation (France, Japan).

(iii) **Gender roles**. In different cultures the expectations and rules governing male and female behaviour vary widely. Increasingly the extent to which women have broken away from the traditional role of nurturer in Western society has been reflected in advertising campaigns, while in other societies the male/breadwinner-female/homemaker imagery persists.

(iv) **Mental processing and learning styles**. In Western societies, a great deal of store is set by rationality and logic when it comes to business and other commercial decisions. This is often in stark contrast to the more intuitive and political decision making that goes on in Eastern countries.

(v) **Time and time consciousness**. Time horizons vary considerably across cultures. In British business, a week can be a long time; in British retail, particularly with Just in Time distribution systems, a day is a long time. This contrasts sharply with other cultures; how many times have you heard colleagues say 'Well, time seems to have no meaning there'?

The transfer of cultural meaning

4.2 Some consumer researchers talk about the 'transfer of cultural meaning' at different stages of the marketing process. The 'culturally constituted world' produces products which are invested with cultural meaning or significance by advertising and 'fashion'. Those consumer goods, symbolic of cultural values, are then sold to individual consumers, who thus absorb the cultural values. Meanwhile, by using the products in rituals of possession, exchange, grooming or whatever, the consumer adds further cultural meaning to the goods.

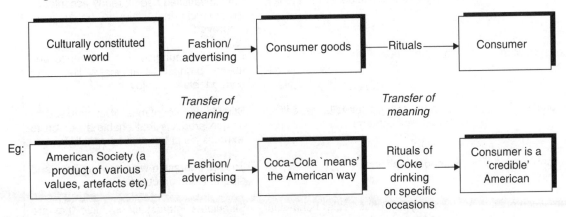

Characteristics of culture

4.3 Having examined the areas included in the definition of culture, we can draw together some of the underlying characteristics of culture itself.

(a) **Social**. Culture exists to satisfy the needs of people in a society. 'It offers order, direction and guidance in all phases of human problem solving, by providing "tried and true" methods of satisfying physiological, personal and social needs';

(Schiffman & Kanuk)

(b) **Learned**. Cultural norms and values are taught or 'transferred' to each new member of society, formally or informally, by socialisation. This occurs in institutions (the family, school and church) and through on-going social interaction and mass media exposure in adulthood;

(c) **Shared**. A belief or practice must be common to a significant proportion of a society or group before it can be defined as a cultural characteristic;

(d) **Cumulative**. Culture is 'handed down' to each new generation, and while new situations teach new responses, there is a strong traditional/historical element to many aspects of culture;

(e) **Adaptive**. Culture must be adaptive, or evolutionary, in order to fulfil its need-satisfying function. Many factors may produce cultural change - slow or fast - in society: eg technological breakthrough, population shifts, exposure to other cultures, gradual changes in values. (Think about male-female roles in the West, or European influences on British lifestyles.)

Action Programme 4

Schiffman & Kanuk (*Consumer Behaviour*) give the following summary of American core values and their relevance to consumer behaviour. Consider how far they are applicable to your social culture.

Value	General features	Relevance to consumer behaviour
Achievement and success	Hard work is good; success flows from hard work	Acts as a justification for acquisition of goods ('You deserve it')
Activity	Keeping busy is healthy and natural	Stimulates interest in products that are timesavers and enhance leisure time
Efficiency and practicality	Admiration of things that solve problems (eg save time and effort)	Stimulates purchase of products that function well and save time
Progress	People can improve themselves; tomorrow should be better than today	Stimulates desire for new products that fulfil unsatisfied needs; ready acceptance of products that claim to be 'new' or 'improved'
Material comfort	'The good life'	Fosters acceptance of convenience and luxury products that make life more comfortable and enjoyable
Individualism	Being oneself (eg self-reliance, self-interest, self-esteem)	Stimulates acceptance of customised or unique products that enable a person to 'express his or her own personality'.
Freedom	Freedom of choice	Fosters interest in wide product lines and differentiated products
External conformity	Uniformity of observable beha-viour; desire for acceptance	Stimulates interest in products that are used or owned by others in the same social group

Humanitarianism	Caring for others, particularly the underdog	Stimulates patronage of firms that compete with market leaders
Youthfulness	A state of mind that stresses being young at heart and a youthful appearance	Stimulates acceptance of products that provide the illusion of maintaining or fostering youthfulness
Fitness and Health	Caring about one's body, including the desire to be physically fit and healthy	Stimulates acceptance of food products, activities, and equipment perceived to maintain or increase physical fitness

Micro-culture

4.4 Culture is a rather broad concept, embracing whole societies. It is possible to subdivide (and for marketers, further segment) a macro-culture into **micro-cultures** (or **sub-cultures**) which also **share certain norms of attitude and behaviour**.

> **Key Concept**
> A **micro-culture** is a distinct and identifiable cultural group within society as a whole: it will have certain beliefs, values, customs and rituals that set it apart - while still sharing the dominant beliefs, values, customs and rituals of the whole society or 'mainstream' culture.

4.5 The main **micro-cultures relevant to the UK** are defined by the following factors.

(a) **Class** (discussed in detail earlier).

(b) **Nationality**. Nationality refers to the birthplace of one's ancestors. In the UK there are different national groups within the indigenous ('native') population - English, Scots, Welsh and Irish - as well as immigrants from Africa, the West Indies, Asia and Europe. Immigrant populations tend to be assimilated into the host culture - especially after the first generation - but commonly preserve elements and awareness of their national identity (language, food, customs): there is therefore a market for ethnic food, music, art, reading matter and so on.

(c) **Ethnicity**. Ethnicity refers to broader divisions into white, black and Asian groups. There are identifiable differences in lifestyles and consumer spending patterns among these groups, but it is only relatively recently that attention has been given to reaching and serving racial minority market segments, as distinct from mass marketing which would 'also reach' the racial minorities. Personal grooming products have most notably been targeted specifically at the Afro-Caribbean market in the UK.

(d) **Geography or region**. Even in such a small country as England, there are distinct regional differences, brought about by the past effects of physical geography (poor communication between communities separated by rivers or mountains, say) and indeed its present effects (socio-economic differences created by suitability of the area for coal-mining, say, or leisure, or urbanisation). Speech accents most noticeably differ, but there are also perceived (often stereotyped) variations in personality, life style, eating and drinking habits (perhaps due to socio-economic factors) between the North and South, or the South-West and South-east - and even between West and East London! Some regions, such as Yorkshire, have a particularly strong self-image and loyalty to 'home' products.

BPP PUBLISHING

Marketing at Work

'In fact, regional differences in consumer purchasing are often directly related to classic marketing product lifecycle models..... [A recent report] shows certain products and services enter the market and mature at different times within different regions, and product penetrations vary most dramatically at the earlier and later stages of the cycle.

The home PC market is a good example of a developing sector. At present, ownership penetrations vary dramatically from 24 per cent in Scotland, to 39 per cent in the South-east. These regional contrasts are linked to differences in income, skill sets and the nature of local employment. Variations are also closely linked to reasons for purchase. In the South-east, the rationale for purchase is work-oriented, whereas in Scotland the rationale is predominantly children's education. All this evidence suggests that companies should tailor their marketing activity to accommodate these regional disparities.'   *Marketing Week*, January 29 1998

(e) **Religion.** Adherents to religious groups tend to be strongly oriented to the norms, beliefs, values, traditions and rituals of their faith. Food customs are strict in religions such as Judaism, Hinduism and Islam. Values and lifestyle are also likely to vary according to the teachings and customs of the religion. Even secularised or non-religious sections of society are affected as consumers by religious festivals: consider the consumer booms associated with Christmas and, to a lesser extent, Easter.

(f) **Age.** Age micro-cultures vary according to the period in which individuals were socialised, to an extent, because of the great shifts in social values and customs in this century. (You may have seen specially branded products for 'Baby-boomers': those born between 1946 and 1964 in the post-war birthrate explosion. 'Yuppies' are an important sub-group of 'Baby Boomers'.)

Age micro-cultures also vary through each individual's life, according to the life cycle concept. Each individual progresses through the **'teen' or 'youth'** (14-24 year old) micro-cultures, which are the most strongly bonded and identifiable groups, with shared - often exaggerated - values and 'badges' of belonging. The **elderly** are another distinct micro-culture and an increasingly attractive market segment, as mortality ages (and age distributions) get higher, and discretionary income for the elderly also gets higher (with dual-income retirers). Unlike traditional stereotypes, it has been suggested that the 'new age' elderly perceive themselves to be younger than their chronological age, are self-confident about consumer decisions, are market-aware and innovative, and feel financially more secure.

(g) **Gender.** We have already discussed gender roles in family buying behaviour, and their gradual erosion - despite which, marketers make frequent appeals to gender-linked stereotypes. The Working Woman and the New Man are perhaps the most important current micro-cultural markets segmented on this basis.

4.6 Marketers need to be aware of micro-cultural variations. Not all may be significant enough to be a basis for segmentation of the market for a particular product. Some may be particularly **sensitive** (eg marketing 'prohibited' foods to a religious group).

4.7 Marketers also need to **avoid exaggerating the exclusivity of micro-cultures**. Promotional strategies need not target a single micro-cultural membership, since each consumer is **simultaneously a member of many micro-cultural segments**. (You do not need to sell cornflakes specifically to a ethnic minority, when its members are also Protestants, women, young people, living in the West Midlands - and part of the mainstream UK culture, as far as cornflake consumption is concerned.)

Action Programme 5

(a) Find at least one example of marketing targeted at a segment of each of the above micro-cultures. You do not have to confine yourself to commercial enterprises or to TV advertising. The Metropolitan Police, for example, recently ran a recruitment drive using a poster that featured a white man chasing a black man - or so one concluded until one read the copy. Actually both men were policemen chasing an unseen villain.

(b) Visit shops or look through magazines that are not targeted at the micro-cultures into which you happen to fit. Make a note of the differences that you perceive.

---

5   IMPLICATIONS FOR NATIONAL, INTERNATIONAL AND GLOBAL MARKETING

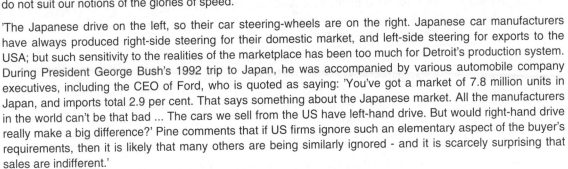

Key Concept

Cross-cultural marketing broadly means trying to market a car made for, say, the US market in, say, the UK. Such an enterprise presents difficulties which the marketer cannot afford to ignore.

Marketing at Work

Using our car example, the primary difficulty is that in the UK we drive on the left, so we want right-hand drive, while in the US they drive on the right, so they produce left-hand drive cars. Historically, they have also produced large cars, which do not fit in some of Britain's more width-challenged roads, and slower cars, which do not suit our notions of the glories of speed.

'The Japanese drive on the left, so their car steering-wheels are on the right. Japanese car manufacturers have always produced right-side steering for their domestic market, and left-side steering for exports to the USA; but such sensitivity to the realities of the marketplace has been too much for Detroit's production system. During President George Bush's 1992 trip to Japan, he was accompanied by various automobile company executives, including the CEO of Ford, who is quoted as saying: 'You've got a market of 7.8 million units in Japan, and imports total 2.9 per cent. That says something about the Japanese market. All the manufacturers in the world can't be that bad ... The cars we sell from the US have left-hand drive. But would right-hand drive really make a big difference?' Pine comments that if US firms ignore such an elementary aspect of the buyer's requirements, then it is likely that many others are being similarly ignored - and it is scarcely surprising that sales are indifferent.'

(B Joseph Pine II, *Mass Customisation - The New Frontier in Business Competition*, 1993, slightly adapted.)

Generally speaking, the answer to this marketing problem is to adapt to what the customer wants, which in the UK appears rarely to be left-hand drive cars. There are exceptions to this, however.

(a) Some products can be marketed cross-culturally because technologically and culturally there is no reason why not (eg watches).

(b) Some products can be marketed so as to appeal to certain common groups in each culture - such as jeans for the world's teenagers, Chicken McNuggets for the world's children (although it is interesting that recently McDonalds have realised that the imposed, American greeting does not appeal to the world's parents).

(c) Häagen-Dazs ice-cream is available in green tea flavour in Japan.

5.1   Most cultures are identified with a nation, although some regions have strongly independent cultural identities. Cultural segmentation must be considered particularly carefully, therefore, in an **international** context: the marketer would need to understand the beliefs, values, customs and rituals of the countries in which a product is being marketed in order to alter or reformulate the product to appeal to local needs and tastes, and reformulate the promotional message to be intelligible and attractive to other cultures.

BPP PUBLISHING

(a) **Legal and regulatory provisions** with regard to advertising vary from country to country: the showing of cigarettes in ads, for example, the use of comparative advertising, or the use of children in advertising.

(b) Products are positioned as **exotic imports** with the specific appeal of their country of origin (Australian lager, Italian pizza, French mineral water) - while in the domestic market they are sold on **familiarity and cultural loyalty.**

Marketing at Work

(a) Nestlé, the Swiss coffee maker, sells different strengths and styles of coffee in Europe than in America.

(b) Board games such as Monopoly are sold worldwide - with nationally-relevant street/area names, money and tokens.

(c) Häagen-Dazs ice cream is available in green tea flavour in Japan.

Exam tip

There are two ways of looking at cross-cultural marketing.
Localised marketing strategy stresses the diversity of consumers in different national cultures.
Global marketing strategy stresses the similarities of consumers worldwide.
Related to this is the standardisation v adaptation debate.

Localised marketing strategy

5.2 The marketer will be interested in the extent of the differences between two countries.

	Potential problems
Language	A promotional theme may not be intelligible - or properly translatable - whether in words or symbols.
Needs and wants	The benefits sought from a product in one country may be different in another.
Consumption patterns	One country may not use a product as much as another (affecting product viability), or may use it in very different ways (affecting product positioning).
Market segments	One country may have different demographic, geographical, socio-cultural and psychological groupings to another.
Socio economic factors	Consumers in one country may have different disposable incomes and/or decision-making roles from those in another.
Marketing conditions	Differences in retail, distribution and communication systems, promotional regulation/legislation, trade restrictions etc may affect the potential for research, promotion and distribution in other countries.

5.3 **A failure to understand cultural differences** may thus cause problems with each of the four Ps.

(a) **Product.** Nestlé coffee, Camay soap and a host of similar products are marketed internationally - with different names, flavours, aromas, and other characteristics. Coffee is preferred very strong, dark and in ground form in Continental Europe - but weaker, milder and instant in the USA. Colour is another interesting element in product and packaging: it means different things to different cultures. Blue is said to represent warmth in Holland, coldness in Sweden, purity in India and death in Iran! Product benefits also vary in appeal: Pepsodent apparently tried to sell their toothpaste using the slogan 'You'll wonder where the yellow went!' in South-East Asia where chewing betel nuts is considered an elite habit (giving status-enhancing brown teeth!).

(b) **Promotion.** Customs, symbols and language do not always travel well. Apparently the Chevrolet Nova failed to sell in Latin America because in Spanish 'no va' means 'doesn't run'! 'Come alive with Pepsi' was translated as 'Pepsi brings your dead ancestors back to life' in one Far Eastern country! Advertising practices such as the extent and frequency of nudity used may vary widely from culture to culture, as do government regulations and voluntary guidelines on a number of issues.

(c) **Price.** Large package sizes may not be marketable in countries where average income is low, because of the cash outlay required.

(d) **Place.** Distribution tastes may vary. Supermarkets are very popular in some countries, while others prefer intimate personal stores for groceries and other foodstuffs. Newly-opening markets such as Eastern Europe exhibit poor distribution systems and very low salesperson effort and productivity - compared to Japan, say, which rates very highly.

Global marketing strategy

5.4   However, it should be remembered that **culture is dynamic and adaptive**: it changes as new values and behaviours are learned. Now that satellite television and other forms of communication, and the speed of air travel, make the world more accessible to more people, **cross-cultural exposure is increasing**. So, too, is the **global perspective** encouraged by concerns for peace and the environment, which are global issues.

5.5   Consumers are **more able to try out goods and customs from other national cultures** - beyond those which already form subcultures within their own nation. They may experience different customs/products abroad, and adopt them into their lifestyle when they return home - a process made easier by the fact that immigrants from the other countries bring those customs/products with them, so they can also be tried out (and/or subsequently adopted) at home.

Marketing at Work

Apart from ethnic foodstores, which have become increasingly fashionable, there are hitherto unfamiliar products in UK supermarkets: Vegemite (yeast extract) from Australia, fromage frais from France, star fruit, papaya, plantain and other exotic fruits/vegetables from all over the world. There are sushi bars and Karaoke clubs from Japan. Meanwhile McDonalds hamburgers have invaded Red Square in Moscow and Coca Cola is everywhere.

5.6   Consumers are also **encouraged to become positively cosmopolitan and cross-cultural in their outlooks**. International festivals of culture, foreign holidays, global environmental problems, the European Market and the opening up of Eastern Europe all contribute to widen people's horizons, and make parochial, narrowly nationalistic viewpoints unfashionable. This is **not an easy process**: witness the UK's struggle with aspects of the European movement - giving up cultural emblems such as the pint, the mile, or the pound sterling.

5.7 Nevertheless, consumers in the UK are starting to learn languages, to drink wine as well as beer, to cook with garlic and herbs, to try other cuisines/music/arts.

5.8 Some marketers have argued that **standardised marketing strategies** are, therefore, becoming **more and more feasible,** as cultural assimilation makes markets more and more similar. There are world or global brands, which are manufactured, packaged and positioned in the same way in all the countries in which they are sold.

Marketing at Work

Two instances of a global marketing strategy in action are Benetton and American Express. The rationale for their thinking is summarised below.

(a) *Benetton*

    (i) The European domestic markets are relatively small and a successful concept can reach saturation coverage fairly quickly.

    (ii) The development of 'lifestyle retailing' based on clear segmentation of the target market is the perfect platform for global marketing.

    (iii) There is in some real sense a proprietary technology - not in a technical sense, but in the inter-relationships with other elements of Benetton's strategy which gives a sustainable competitive edge, as it is not easily imitated.

    (iv) International systems provide the channel for fast response to shifts in consumer demand and risk-free low inventory (stockholding) costs.

(b) *American Express*

    (i) Deregulation has opened up international markets to international competition.

    (ii) Interactive IT systems networks provide 24-hour global trading (with the collapse of geographical time-zone, regulatory and market boundaries).

    (iii) The company's international presence is critical to future growth.

    (iv) Global coverage is required in order to remain competitive and retain both clients and staff.

5.9 Given the case histories mentioned earlier, however, it is as well to be **cautious about the feasibility of global marketing in general**. Global manufacturing and promotion brings efficiencies and economies - where it works.

Marketing at Work

Hoover (UK) wanted to sell washing machines in Europe, but found that the number of different features wanted by consumers in different countries would have made the expansion plan simply not viable.

Exam tip

As a marketing student you should distinguish between:

- **global promotion**
- **globally standardised** products.

You must also understand the distinction between:

- **global strategy** and
- **global execution**.

See the example below.

Marketing at Work

(a) Even Coca Cola, with a mainly global strategy, adds an element of local variation in execution. The 'I'd like to buy the world a Coke' song advertisement is international in the people shown, and is featured in 21 languages in 16 countries. Other campaigns, however, show different people, settings and celebrities, according to local culture.

(b) 'Another important lesson learnt [by Lever Brothers, the UK detergents arm of Unilever] from Persil Power days is the necessity for each European market to construct its own marketing campaign. While the balance of ingredients that make up the Stain Release System will be broadly consistent in all markets, timing and presentation will be decided locally. Clothes washing habits vary widely across cultures.'

Financial Times, 30 April 1996

Action Programme 6

Make a brief list of products and services that have a global appeal and another of those that do not. Now try to identify what it is about each product or service that determines the internationality or otherwise of its market. (There will be many factors involved.)

---

6 THE DMU WITHIN ORGANISATIONS

6.1 The market for an **industrial or business good** is more clearly demarcated than for a **customer good**, and it is not unusual to find markets where **every potential customer is known**. As the customer will **not buy beyond his economic need** (again, unlike consumers) the **extent of his demand** can also be estimated with accuracy. The ability to see the potential market clearly can be an advantage in organising sales promotion to suit the market.

6.2 In many industrial goods industries, **individual buyers** are very important, because there are only a **few customers** buying **infrequently** and placing orders of **high value**. It may also be necessary for the supplier to secure an even flow of orders to keep design staff and employees in all aspects of production fully occupied at all times. Occasionally, one customer dominates the market (eg British Telecom in the UK market for telephone exchange equipment) and can negotiate with suppliers from a position of strength. In markets where individual buyers are important, customer-orientation involves a marketing policy by the manufacturer which is specifically designed to cater for their idiosyncrasies.

6.3 The industrial market is marked by a curious, seemingly irrational, **inertia,** whereby there is a **great loyalty amongst industrial buyers to 'traditional' suppliers** (more so than in the consumer market). The reasons for this inertia in favour of existing suppliers is that they are **already known** - the quality and reliability of their goods and services have been tested and proven and personal links have been established - whereas a new supplier is an unknown and untried quantity, and not even a more favourable price might win an order for him in the face of competition from a 'traditional' supplier. Once inertia has been established in favour of a supplier, the supplier's marketing task should be to **maintain the advantage**.

Features of industrial buying decisions

6.4 In spite of the restrictive influence of inertia industrial buyers are **much more rationally motivated** than consumers in deciding which goods to buy. Sales policy decisions by a supplier are therefore more important than sales promotion activities in an industrial market. **Special attention** should be given in selling to **quality, price, credit, delivery**

dates, after-sales service etc, and it is the importance of these rational motivations which makes it difficult for an untried newcomer to break into an industrial goods market.

6.5 A study by Schary (1982) of head office buyers for a major UK food product group produced the following **hierarchy of customer service elements**.

1	Product availability	7	Pricing
2	Prompt quotation	8	Merchandising
3	Representatives	9	Product positioning
4	Order status	10	Invoice accuracy
5	Distribution system	11	New product introduction
6	Delivery time	12	Advertising

6.6 All **organisational buying decisions** are **made by individuals or groups of individuals**, each of whom is subjected to the same types of influences as they are in making their own buying decisions. However, there are some real **differences** between personal and organisational buying decision processes.

(a) Organisations buy because the products/services are **needed to meet wider objectives**: for instance, also to help them to meet their customers' needs more closely. (However, as individuals also do not buy products and services for themselves but for the benefits they convey, it could be argued that both are forms of derived demand.)

(b) A **number of individuals are involved** in the typical organisational buying decision. Again, a personal buying decision may involve several family members, for example, and so may not be very different in some cases.

(c) The **decision process may take longer** for corporate decisions: the use of feasibility studies, for example, may prolong the decision process. Tendering processes in government buying also have this effect.

(d) Organisations are **more likely to buy a complex total offering** which can involve a high level of technical support, staff training, delivery scheduling, finance arrangements and so on.

(e) Organisations are **more likely to employ experts** in the process.

6.7 There are many examples of **different types of organisational buying behaviour** ranging from simple **reordering** (for example, of stationery supplies) to **complex purchasing decisions** (such as that of a consortium to build a motorway with bridges and tunnels, for example).

Exam tip

Although it is difficult to identify a useful overall categorisation scheme, there are **common features** which can be discussed.

Who buys? Is it an individual or a committee? What is the job title of the buyer? Who influences the process?

How does the organisation buy? Are there discernible stages in the buying process?

Why does the organisation buy? What are the factors which influence the decision process and what is the relative importance of these factors?

6.8 One system of categorisation for corporate buying decisions, devised by Howard and O'Shaughnessy, is based on the **complexity of organisational behaviour**. They identify three types.

(a) **Routinised buyer behaviour.** This category is the habitual type, where the buyer knows what is offered and is buying items which are frequently purchased. It is likely that the buyer has well-developed supplier preferences and any deviation in habitual behaviour is likely to be influenced by price and availability considerations.

(b) **Limited problem solving.** This category is relevant to a new or unfamiliar product/service purchase where the suppliers are nevertheless known and the product is in a familiar class of products, for instance a new model of car in a company fleet.

(c) **Extensive problem solving.** This category relates to the purchase of unfamiliar products from unfamiliar suppliers. The process can take much time and effort and involve the need to develop criteria with which to judge the purchase. For example, the construction and refurbishment of new offices where previously buildings were looked after by managing agents.

The DMU in organisations

6.9 The **DMU is a particularly useful concept** in marketing industrial or government goods and services where the customer is a **business or other organisation**. The marketing manager then needs to know **who** in each organisation makes the effective buying decisions - this might be one person, or a group of people - and the DMU might act with formal authority or as an informal group reaching a joint decision. Many large organisations employ **buyers** - but the autonomy of the buyers will vary from situation to situation.

6.10 **Purchasing decisions may be influenced by several people** in the consuming organisation.

(a) **Employees or managers** in operational departments might make recommendations about what type of supplies should be purchased.

(b) A **junior buying manager** might decide what he would like to buy, but **submit his recommendation** to a superior for approval.

(c) In large organisations, there will be **several buying managers**, who might work independently, but might also work closely together, either formally or informally.

(d) Technical specifications for component purchases might be provided by **engineers or other technical staff**.

(e) **Accountants** might set a limit on the price the organisation will pay.

(f) Large items of purchase might require approval from the **board of directors.**

6.11 The marketing department of a supplier aiming at corporate clients therefore needs to be aware of:

- **how buying decisions are made** by the DMU;
- how the **DMU is constructed**; and
- the **identities** of the most influential figures in the DMU.

6.12 The relationships between **members of the buying centre** are also important.

(a) The **user** may have influence on the technical characteristics of the equipment (and hence the cost) and on reliability and performance criteria.

(b) The **influencer** is particularly useful where the purchase relies on technical knowledge. Unlike personal purchasing behaviour where opinions may be sought from colleagues, friends and family, competitive pressures and trade secret constraints may limit the sharing of information between companies. In this environment the salesperson can be a respected technical link with the buyer and so be able to influence the purchasing process. Trade journals and trade associations or professional bodies can often be a good source of influential information in addition to sales staff of the supplying company. Also, there is a tendency not to copy competitors, but to seek one's own solution and thus demonstrate independence.

(c) The **buyer or decider**. As already noted, decisions are, in the final analysis, made by individuals or groups of individuals. These individuals have personal idiosyncrasies, social pressures and organisational and environmental pressures. Thus each has a set of rational factors (task variables) and non-economic factors (non-task variables).

(d) The **gatekeeper** who controls the flow of information about the purchase may be senior or junior but is important because he/she influences the communication flow within the organisation.

Action Programme 7

Whenever you have the chance - when visiting clients, when browsing in the newsagents, at the dentist's or hairdresser's - browse through the trade magazines that you find (*Campaign, Farmer's Weekly, Banking World, Engineering Today* or whatever).

What do you notice about the way products and services are marketed in such publications? Is more technical language used? Are the ads less 'glossy'? What do you learn about price and place?

The American Marketing Association model

6.13 The AMA model suggests that influences come from **within the buying department**, from **other departments** within the organisation, and from buying and other departments in **other organisations**. Placing the departmental and organisational influences on the axes of a cruciform chart, we can express the model as follows:

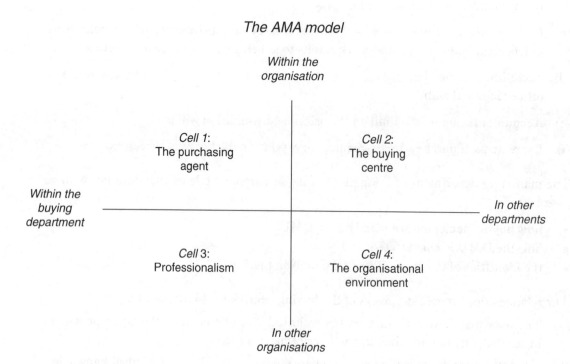

The AMA model

The purchasing agent

6.14 The purchasing agent is the **buyer within the buying department** within the organisation. The intra-departmental, intra-organisational **influences** on his decisions are:

(a) **social factors,** mainly the personal relationship of the purchase agent with the supplier or supplier's representative, which is believed to have considerable importance - despite inconsistency with the supposed rationality of organisational decisions. The influence of other members of the DMU is also relevant;

(b) **price/cost factors**. Price may be more or less important, depending on:

- the product, and the value/benefits it offers;
- pressure on profit margins in the buying organisation;
- budgetary control on the purchasing function;
- competition on price in the market for the product;
- the background and price-consciousness of the purchasing agent;

(c) **supply continuity**. The desire to keep a consistent source of supply will be greater if the number of potential suppliers is small;

(d) **risk-aversion**. The purchase agent may perceive the risks of a decision to be high or low, depending on the price of the product, reputation of the supplier or manufacturer, reputation of the brand, and past experience. He may try to reduce or avoid risk by further information search, premium brand choice, product sampling etc - just like individual customers.

The buying centre

6.15 The 'buying centre' is, like the DMU, the group of people within an organisation but in **different departments,** who participate in the buying decision. The inter-departmental, intra-organisational **influences** on the decision are as follows.

(a) **The organisational structure**. This will determine the composition of the DMU, and the authority delegated to the purchasing function. Some decisions will be centralised (kept at a senior level or within a specialised function) while others will be decentralised (delegated downwards or outwards from the centre of authority): the purchasing department may make decisions, or implement the decisions of a planning department - or purchasing may be done by the user departments themselves. Inter-departmental decisions depend on the effectiveness of communication and co-ordination mechanisms.

(b) **Organisational politics**. 'Politics' in organisations is the way in which individuals and groups compete for power and resources. The extent of perceived conflict of interest between departments, and the mechanisms for conflict resolution, will determine how effectively departments can work together in co-operative buying decisions, and who has the greatest influence or power to enforce their preferences.

To retain and even increase his organisational status, the buyer might use a variety of techniques designed to stress the buyer's role over that of financial or operational specialists.

(i) **Role-oriented tactics** involve keeping to the formal rules of the organisation where these rules work in favour of the buyer's intentions.

(ii) **Role-evading tactics** involve passive resistance to the rules where these rules do not work in favour of the buyer's intentions.

    (iii)   **Personal-political tactics** involve manipulating the relationship between informal and formal relationships in the process.

    (iv)   **Educational tactics** include using persuasive techniques.

(c)   **The gatekeeper.** An important role in the DMU belongs to the person who gathers, 'edits' and disseminates information about new brands, suppliers and terms of business to other members of the buying centre.

Professionalism

6.16   Professionalism links members of the same department, or function, in **different organisations**: all marketers, say - or in this case, all purchasing professionals. Intra-departmental, inter-organisational influences are:

(a)   **word of mouth communication** between fellow professionals in the purchasing field. This allows the exchange of information about products and suppliers, which can be used as one of the inputs to the buying decision. A professional body - or perceived professionalism - acts as a reference group;

(b)   **specialist journals and conferences,** trade shows etc. Specialist publications and meetings also allow the exchange of targeted, technical information, and reference group effects. (They also offer opportunities for suppliers to advertise or be represented to the defined market segment);

(c)   **supply-purchase reciprocity**. Two organisations may supply each other as part of the trading relationship.

The organisational environment

6.17   The environment of the organisation includes those **outside the purchasing function** and **outside the organisation**. Inter-departmental, inter-organisational influences on the purchaser include:

(a)   **technology** and technological change;

(b)   the **legal, political and social** environment: influencing trading practices, contracts, and purchaser 'values' - such as buying environmentally-friendly products, supporting trade sanctions etc;

(c)   **economic, commercial and competitive** factors - influencing price/cost sensitivity, purchasing power etc;

(d)   the **nature of the supplier**: large companies may offer less risk, but be less flexible and accommodating, and less willing to enter into price competition with other suppliers;

(e)   **co-operative buying**: organisations may get together as purchasing consortia, in which case compromises on all the other factors may need to be reached.

Chapter roundup

- Individuals are important in all buying decisions, either for themselves or on behalf of an organisation. Marketers need to understand their motives, psychology and influences, and how these combine to form a motivation mix.

- The family is of critical importance to individuals, as a network of relationships, reference group and social unit. The decision making unit operates most often is a family context, with different family members adopting different consumption and hence DMU roles.

- Organisational decision-making is based on the same DMU model but is generally more rational yet inert. The interaction of DMU members is influenced by a great many variables. The AMA model can be used to describe this.

- The term 'culture' encompasses the sum total of learned beliefs, values, customs, rituals, languages, symbols, artefacts and technology of a society or group.

- Different societies vary greatly in most aspects of culture, but all culture is social, learned, shared, cumulative and adaptive.

- Products can be invested with cultural meaning by marketing efforts; that meaning is transferred to a buyer who uses the product in a cultural context and hence imbues it with further cultural meaning. This is called transfer of cultural meaning.

- Micro-cultures within a culture are usually structured on the lines of class, nationality, ethnicity, geography, religion, age and gender.

- Marketing cross-culturally has many advantages for marketers but brings with it a number of new challenges. Two approaches can be used: localised markets (marketing a product so that it fits into the existing culture) or global marketing (capitalising on the fact that culture changes and develops, so a 'foreign' product can gain acceptance into different cultures in the same form worldwide).

- The DMU is a particularly useful concept in marketing industrial or government goods and services where the customer is a business or other organisation.

- The marketing department of a supplier aiming at corporate clients therefore needs to be aware of:

  - M how buying decisions are made by the DMU;
  - M how the DMU is constructed; and
  - M the identities of the most influential figures in the DMU.

Quick quiz

1 What is a group? (see para 1.1)

2 What are the advantages and disadvantages of groups for decision making? (1.1)

3 How does a family operate as a reference group? (1.3)

4 List the nine family consumption roles. (2.4)

5 What affects the relative influence of male and female partners, and the extent to which decisions are shared? (2.10)

6 Describe the influence of children on family consumption. (2.12)

7 How can the marketer use status awareness? (3.7)

8 What is 'the transfer of cultural meaning'? (4.2)

9 How can a failure to understand cultural differences cause problems for the marketing mix? (5.3)

10 How does organisational buying differ from that of an individual? (6.6)

11 Describe the effect of the different DMU roles in an organisational buying decision. (6.10)

12 Describe the AMA model of organisational buying behaviour. (6.13)

13 What are the inter-department, intra-organisational influences on a purchasing decision? (6.14)

BPP
PUBLISHING

Action Programme Review

3   Unfortunately the issue is not that simple. Firstly, there is indirect taxation (VAT). Households on different incomes are more or less exposed to this. Secondly, there is the issue of mortgage interest relief, which is not available to people renting their accommodation. Thirdly, there are additional social benefits such as education. It is hard to combine all these factors together.

Part D
Investigating customer dynamics

13 *The basic principles*

Chapter Topic List	Syllabus reference
1 Setting the scene	4.1
2 Techniques for studying customer dynamics	4.1
3 Problems with investigating customer dynamics	4.1
4 The creation of meaningful populations	4.1
5 The reliability of customer responses	4.1
6 Factor importance and factor satisfaction	4.1

Learning Outcomes

After studying this chapter you will be able to:

- design and carry out operational investigations into customer dynamics, customer perceptions of product/service performance, and customer satisfaction/delight.

Key Concepts Introduced

- Sampling

Examples of Marketing at Work

- BMW
- BA
- Organic vegetables
- Air Miles

- Ford
- 3M
- Cullens

1 SETTING THE SCENE

1.1 Information about customer dynamics is **acquired in a variety of ways** and the data is systematically collected and analysed to provide useful information. A **field sales force** or a **telephone sales force** are usually the first line of customer contact points. These are the people who acquire information which may pieced together with **other systematically collected** and **ad hoc information**. Environmental scanning, trade exhibitions and trade press may also provide the organisation with information about customer dynamics that may help in formulating strategies that serve the customer needs.

1.2 For years the rhetoric of marketing has been that of **warfare**: targets, campaigns, offensives. The macho approach has been one of trying to beat the 'enemy' into submission and 'win' new customers. Now, at last, many organisations have begun to realise that there is more to be gained from alternative strategies.

(a) Investing in activities which seek to **retain** existing customers, based on the argument that it may cost between 5 and 15 times more to attract new customers (depending on whether the product is a consumer durable or a consumer option).

(b) **Encouraging existing customers** to spend more.

1.3 **Retaining customers** is the basis of such **relationship marketing** techniques as the Tesco ClubCard and loyalty discounts like the Barclaycard Profiles Scheme. These organisations see customers not only in terms of what they are buying today, but also in terms of their **potential for future purchases**.

Marketing at Work

The 'lifetime value' of a customer prompts car manufacturers like BMW to offer 'entry' products in the expectation of several sales to follow.

1.4 Most authorities and marketing practitioners say that **added services** and **quality of service** are the key to retaining customers.

Markeing at Work

BA's 'Putting People First' programme of improved service was aimed at retention; so are all frequent flier and Air Miles schemes.

1.5 The **implications for marketing research** are clear. To be effective at retention marketing, the organisation has to have a **really good database about present and past customers**, with details of the nature of the relationship; it has to know about their attitudes, their perceptions of the organisation's products and service, and their expectations. Just as importantly, the organisation must know, from systematically-acquired customer feedback, precisely what it is doing wrong.

2 TECHNIQUES FOR STUDYING CUSTOMER DYNAMICS

Exam tip

Whilst the CIM does not expect you to be a statistician, competent marketing managers should be able to assess the value and the validity of data upon which they are basing important decisions. Some approaches to this assessment are outlined below.

2.1 (a) **Common sense.** Clearly data which is dated, which emanates from dubious sources or which is based on unrepresentative samples should be treated with extreme caution, if not totally disregarded.

(b) **Statistical approaches.** There are a variety of sampling methods for survey data as already described, which are appropriate to different situations. All of them involve some degree of risk (some probability of error). The degree of risk of statistical error can, however, be computed as we have seen.

(c)   **Expert judgement.** 'There are lies, damned lies and statistics.' The same data can be interpreted differently by different people - you have only to look at differences between economists or between politicians of different parties on the latest figures to see ample evidence of this. The following array - 98.7, 98.6,. 98.6, 98.4, 98.1, 98.1- might be regarded by a statistician as a declining trend but to a marketing manager the figures may represent a very steady state, especially if they were percentages of actual sales against budgeted sales for the last six years. In using this approach, therefore, the marketing manager might be wise to consult more than one expert before making a decision.

(d)   **The intuitive approach.** Some people have a better feel for figures than others and seem able to judge the value and validity of data intuitively. For example, it is said that Rank Xerox ignored survey findings that there was no market for a dry copier and in doing so went on to become a world leader in this field. This approach, whilst perhaps successful for a chosen few, is not, however, recommended.

(e)   **The questioning approach.** Always question the origin and the basis of the data. Ask for further information. An actual spend of 180% of budget is not important if the amount concerned is only £10. A much smaller variance on a much large amount could, however, be quite serious. Recognise that human errors occur when manipulating data, that bias can occur in questionnaire design: ask to see the questionnaire, check the figures. The negative response to Rank Xerox's survey on the potential market for dry copiers could have been due to some of the following factors.

    (i)   The wrong people were asked.

    (ii)   People did not understand the dry copying concept (technologically).

    (iii)   The benefits of dry copying were not made clear.

    (iv)   The survey was conducted at an unfavourable time (when respondents had spent all their budget and were therefore not willing to countenance any potential extra expenditure.

    (v)   The question design was faulty.

    (vi)   Human errors were made in computing results.

    (vii) Statistical errors were made in computing results.

    (viii) Competitors sabotaged the research.

    (ix)   The questionnaire might have been too long, thus causing irritation.

    (x)   Interviewers could have been biased.

3   PROBLEMS WITH INVESTIGATING CUSTOMER DYNAMICS

3.1   You should be aware that **research cannot supply** marketers with perfect, irrefutable and comprehensive answers to all the questions that marketers may wish to ask. This may be because the research itself is badly designed (the sample populations inappropriate, the questions misleading and so on) but it can also happen because systematic research, by definition, can **only ask the questions which exist in marketers' mind** and elicit responses within the framework of respondents' imaginations.

3.2   As Nishikawa claims in his 1989 article for the *Journal of Long Range Planning*, the most important point in building marketing strategy is not logical analysis or investigative excellence, but creative action. Only proactive creativity, generating products and services **in anticipation of** customer needs and expectations, can create marketing advantage; organisations which are customer driven (as opposed to being customer focused) are invariably **reactive**. Responding to declared customer needs is acting too late for successful marketing: in order to forecast the future, organisations require creativity rather than responsiveness, challenge rather than passivity.

3.3 In particular, Nishikawa claims that marketing research linked to new products and services is especially defective, because of certain features in customer psychology.

(a) **Indifference**. Customers often provide negative responses to ideas for new products/services simply because they are indifferent to something they have not thought about or tried before.

(b) **Absence of responsibility**. People will say more or less anything when responding to research surveys, often out of a desire to please the researcher.

(c) **Conservative attitudes**. Most customers choose conventional and familiar products/services. To put it another way, only about three per cent of customers are Early Adopters.

(d) **Vanity**. Customers will try to put on a good appearance about their motives and will seldom want to admit that cheapness (for example) was the major reason for a purchase decision.

(e) **Insufficient information**. Researchers often approach customers with information and ideas seen from the seller's rather than from the customer's point of view.

3.4 One of Nishikawa's key points is that customers are most sincere when spending rather than talking.

Marketing at Work

Many growers and retailers, had been misled by surveys suggesting that 70 per cent of consumers would purchase organic vegetables and fruit. In the event only 11 per cent are doing so, the remainder have demonstrated by their actions that *behaviour* and *attitudes* are not necessarily synonymous. Perhaps they had not seriously considered the possibility that organic produce would cost more or that it would look less attractive; quite possibly they gave 'ethically correct' responses when completing a questionnaire, but had no real intention of acting differently.

What do customers want?

3.5 Curiously enough, most customers are easy to please. They simply want companies to do what they say they are going to do when they say they are going to do it. However, this kind of glib remark is not helpful. Much more constructive are the '**four fundamentals of customer satisfaction**' reported by Milind M Lele and Jagdish N Sheth.

(a) **Product-related variables**. The product - its functionality and design quality - is a key determinant of customer satisfaction. Product design, in particular, can enhance or restrict the company's ability to keep the customer happy during and after the sale: a strong, successful design increases the confidence of salespeople whilst a poor design makes them defensive. Bad design places constraints on promotional messages and also on channel choices; it can also add considerably to the cost and difficulty of providing customers with adequate after-sales support.

(b) **Sales and promotion-related variables**. Three key variables affect customer satisfaction in this area.

    (i) **Messages** which help to shape customers' ideas about the product's benefits before they have experienced it in use.

    (ii) **Attitudes** of everyone in the organisation who comes into contact with customers: salespeople, service staff, telephone operators, and so forth.

    (iii) The use of **intermediaries** to sell on behalf of the organisation: similar selection, training and performance criteria should be applied to intermediaries as are applied to an organisation's own staff.

(c) **After-sales variables**. There are two aspects of after-sales which are especially significant for organisations.

    (i) **Support services**. Covering traditional after-sales activities like warranties, parts and service, and user training.

    (ii) **Feedback and restitution**. The way the organisation handles complaints and the level of priority attached by management to such activities.

(d) **Culture-related variables**. The crucial question here is whether the corporate culture is built around maximising customer satisfaction, or whether management merely pays lip service to it. Would it be acceptable for an employee to postpone a meeting with the managing director in order to meet a customer, for example?

Marketing at Work

'Rude and unhelpful staff are the biggest single hurdle to developing customer loyalty, according to an Air Miles UK survey exclusive to *Marketing Week*.

The survey found that 54 per cent of the 1,000 people interviewed were most likely to become disloyal because of rude and unhelpful staff.

Young people in the 18-to-24 age bracket are the group most affected by rude staff – 60 per cent cited it as a reason for "disloyalty" to a retailer or service provider.

Judith Thorne, Air Miles UK marketing director, says: "This shows that customer service and the way companies interact with customers is an integral part of building customer loyalty."

According to Thorne, advertising which over-hypes the offer can seriously damage loyalty.

She says: "Advertising is fantastic for putting a thought into the consumer's mind, but people will be very disappointed if the promise isn't delivered."

One in five of the survey's respondents said poor value for money would challenge their loyalty and one in ten would turn their backs on suppliers who "do not seem to listen".

Complaints are most likely to come from extremely loyal customers while those claiming to "feel no loyalty" will simply switch retailer without explaining why.

Combining fair prices with good service is the surest way to win loyalty, say 54 per cent of respondents.'
Marketing Week, 5 March 1998

Problems with measuring customer satisfaction

3.6   Measuring whether customers have got what they wanted can be extremely problematic for a number of reasons.

(a) **Weak anecdotal evidence**, often based on single incidents, is given too much weight, especially if such evidence reinforces what people in an organisation want to hear (wishful thinking).

(b) Alternatively, **single-incident disasters** may be used by one part of the organisation to attack another, rather than as an opportunity for improving performance.

(c) The views of those **customers who complain, which may be atypical**, are not counter-balanced by the views of those who do not.

(d) **Many badly-served customers will not complain**, but will simply take their business elsewhere if they can. MORI figures for 1993 suggested that around only 17% of customers will voice their dissatisfaction to the organisation from which they bought the product or service, though they will complain to others (their friends, relatives, or anyone who will listen).

Marketing at Work

In 1986, the Ford Motor Company found that customers satisfied with their cars told (on average) eight other people, dissatisfied customers told 22 (who in turn told 22 more, with the story becoming more elaborate and embellished with each repetition).

(e) The opinions of **small numbers of highly articulate customers**, especially if of high status and personally known to top management, or expressed through the public media, will be **given excessive emphasis**.

(f) **Preconceptions within the organisation** about its customer-service standing and performance may be out-of-date or mistaken, especially if insufficient attention is paid to what the competition is doing.

The complexities of measuring customer 'loyalty'

3.7 Now there is hard evidence that **companies supplying poor customer service are likely to suffer financially**, through reduced profitability, reduced sales per customer, reduced numbers of customers and, ultimately, disaffected employees (people who deliver poor service rarely derive pleasure and satisfaction from doing so). A recent report from the Henley Centre for Forecasting concludes that an individual who would usually spend £100 a year with a given supplier is likely to spend only £266, half the usual amount, over the entirety of a five-year period, if customer service is believed to be inadequate. Worse: that customer is likely to pass on the bad news to friends and colleagues, thereby reducing the likelihood that they might spent money with the offending organisation.

3.8 Frederick Reichheld, author of *The Loyalty Effect*, argues that 'Good long-standing customers are worth so much that in some industries, reducing customer defections by as little as five points - from, say, 15% to 10% per year - can double profits.'

3.9 **Many organisations know little about their customers**, whether they are satisfied or not, whether they are delighted or not, whether they are about to defect or not, or even whether they are profitable or not. Increasing realisation of the need to know more has prompted an increasing number to take action, and to do so by concentrating on the aspects of customer behaviour which genuinely matter.

3.10 For several of these organisations, the focus has shifted away from trying to measure customer satisfaction and towards methods for identifying the ingredients of customer loyalty.

Marketing at Work

3M has set itself the Top Box Measure criteria, seeking out those customers who are 'completely satisfied', would 'definitely recommend' 3M, and would 'definitely repurchase'. The company's target is that at least 50% of its customers should be Top Box loyalists.

3.11 Organisations are also becoming **more sophisticated in their selection, use and interpretation of research methodologies**. Aware of the problems associated with focus groups, questionnaires, interviews, surveys, complaints analysis and the like, companies are more inclined to use a combination of both qualitative and quantitative techniques; moreover, they want to find out not only what customers think about each factor in the product/service offer, but also how important each of these factors is perceived to be. **There is no point in achieving perfection with activities which don't mean much to customers** - for example, in promoting friendly human contact by your front-line staff, when all your customers want is immediate response facilitated through a machine.

3.12 If you are a bank, for example, your surveys may show that customers don't like your cash dispensers. Armed with this information, you spend many hundreds of thousands of pounds in improving, upgrading, redecorating and revamping your cash dispenser - only to find that your customers are just as dissatisfied as they were before. Why is this? Plausibly, it occurs for a variety of reasons with which all of us can **identify**.

(a) First, respondents to questionnaires may express strong dissatisfaction with one aspects of the product/service offer because, **on one occasion when they used it two years ago, it did not work satisfactorily**, and that dismal experience has stuck with them ever since. If you tried to extricate money from a cash dispenser in 1996 and failed to do so and, worse, the dispenser ate up your bank card, then the memory lives on; not unreasonably, you **extrapolate that unique transaction** into a general hatred of cash machines, which then achieves catharsis when someone gives you a customer-service attitude survey to complete: and lo! there is a question about cash dispensers.

(b) Second, you may have **picked up rumours** about the way banks treat customers who complain about (supposedly) malfunctioning cash dispensers. You are not impressed, even though such treatment has never been meted out to you - and you think it was about time your bank (after all, it's much the same as the others) was taught a lesson. If banks believe their cash dispensers to be technologically infallible, your reasoning process runs, then I will suggest otherwise.

(c) Third, you may be one of those people who really does prefer to interact with human beings, and your feelings about cash dispensers are **just part of your general anti-automation view of the world**. In other words, your dislike of cash dispensers is entirely genuine: it isn't therapeutic, nor cathartic, nor embedded prejudice. Of necessity you may frequently use cash dispensers, but that frequency of use doesn't mean that you have to like them.

3.13 Whatever the psychological fine-tuning, it turns out that completion of the 'strongly dislike' or 'strongly disagree' box in the customer survey questionnaire **does not really tell us very much**. What we must know as well is **how important** the particular service ingredient is perceived to be, in the customer's system. If it is viewed as important, and your organisation's performance is thought to be poor, then you have to do something about it.

3.14 In practice you have a limited number of choices:

(a) Persuade your customers that the service ingredient in question is **not so important as they currently imagine it to be**.

(b) Persuade your customers that your organisation's performance is **better than they think it is**.

(c) Concentrate your efforts on **improving your organisation's performance** so far as the specific service ingredient is concerned.

3.15 In fact, although it may look as if you have three choices, you actually have only one, because you don't have any hope whatever of succeeding with either (a) or (b). Even if you could, the time, money and overall energy expended in trying to accomplish (a) or (b), or possibly both, will be huge; it will cost much less, and generate much more benefit, if you work on (c).

4 THE CREATION OF MEANINGFUL POPULATIONS

Key Concept

Sampling is one of the most important subjects in marketing research. In most practical situations a **population** will be too large to carry out a complete survey and only a sample will be examined. A good example of this is a poll taken to try to predict the results of an election. It is not possible to ask everyone of voting age how they are going to vote: it would take too long and cost too much. So a sample of voters is taken, and the results from the sample are used to estimate the voting intentions of the whole population.

4.1 Occasionally a population is small enough that **all of it can be examined**: for example, the examination results of one class of students. When all of the population is examined, the kcvey is called a **census**. This type of survey is quite rare, however, and usually the researcher has to choose some sort of sample.

4.2 You may think that using a sample is very much a **compromise**, but you should consider the following points.

(a) In practice, a 100% survey (a census) **never achieves the completeness** required.

(b) A census may require the use of **semi-skilled investigators**, resulting in a loss of accuracy in the data collected.

(c) It can be shown mathematically that once a certain sample size has been reached, **very little extra accuracy** is gained by examining more items.

(d) It is possible to **ask more questions** with a sample.

(e) The **higher cost** of a census may **exceed the value** of results.

(f) **Things are always changing**. Even if you took a census it could well be out of date by the time you completed it.

Action Programme 1

A recent advertising campaign by IKEA, the Swedish furniture retailer, is based on some very frivolous market research. This research has established that people with flowery sofas are thought to be snooty and people with green sofas might be more adventurous in bed.

The sample size for this particular piece of real-life research was 202 people, and the characteristics and products had to match up in 90 per cent of respondents to be included. What do you think about the sample size? Is it too small, about what you would expect or unnecessarily large? Do you believe the results?

The choice of a sample

4.3 One of the most important requirements of sample data is that they should be **complete**. That is, the data should **cover all areas of the population** to be examined. If this requirement is not met, then the sample will be biased.

4.4 For example, suppose you wanted to survey the productivity of workers in a factory, and you went along every Monday and Tuesday for a few months to measure their output. Would these data be complete? The answer is no. You might have gathered very thorough data on what happens on Mondays and Tuesdays, but you would have missed out the rest of the week. It could be that the workers, keen and fresh after the weekend, work better at the start of the week than at the end. If this is the case, then your data will give you a **misleadingly high productivity figure**. Careful attention must therefore be given to the sampling method employed to produce a sample.

Random sampling

4.5 To ensure that the sample selected is **free from bias**, random sampling must be used. Inferences about the population being sampled can then be made validly.

4.6 A simple random sample is a sample selected in such a way that **every item in the population has an equal chance of being included**.

4.7 For example, if you wanted to take a random sample of library books, it would **not be good enough to pick them off the shelves, even if you picked them at random**. This is because the **books which were out on loan** would stand no chance of being chosen. You would either have to make sure that all the books were on the shelves before taking your sample, or find some other way of sampling (for example, using the library index cards).

4.8 A random sample is **not necessarily a perfect sample**. For example, you might pick what you believe to be a completely random selection of library books, and find that every one of them is a detective thriller. It is a remote possibility, but it could happen. The only way to eliminate the possibility altogether is to take 100% survey (a census) of the books, which, unless it is a tiny library, is impractical.

Sampling frames

4.9 If random sampling is used then it is necessary to construct a sampling frame. A sampling frame is simply a **numbered list of all the items in the population**. Once such a list has been made, it is easy to select a random sample, simply by generating a list of random numbers using random number tables or the computer equivalent.

4.10 A sampling frame should have the following characteristics.

- **Completeness**. Are all members of the population included on the list?
- **Accuracy**. Is the information correct?
- **Adequacy**. Does it cover the entire population?
- **Up to dateness**. Is the list up to date?
- **Convenience**. Is the sampling frame readily accessible?
- **Non-duplication**. Does each member of the population appear on the list only once?

Action Programme 2

Why is a telephone directory an unsuitable sampling frame of the human population?

BPP
PUBLISHING

Action Programme 3

You want to take a random sample of people who live in a particular area. Why would the electoral register not be a satisfactory sampling frame?

4.11 In many situations it might be **too expensive** to obtain a random sample, in which case quasi-random sampling is necessary, or else it may not be possible to draw up a sampling frame. In such cases, non-random sampling has to be used.

Quasi-random sampling

4.12 Quasi-random sampling, which provides a **good approximation to random sampling**, necessitates the existence of a sampling frame. There are **three main methods** of quasi-random sampling.

Systematic sampling

4.13 **Systematic sampling** may provide a good approximation to random sampling. It works by selecting **every nth item** after a random start. For example, if it was decided to select a sample of 20 from a population of 800, then every 40th (800 ÷ 20) item after a random start in the first 40 should be selected. The starting point could be found using the lottery method or random number tables. If (say) 23 was chosen, then the sample would include the 23rd, 63rd, 103rd, 143rd ... 783rd items.

The gap of 40 is known as the **sampling interval**.

The investigator must ensure that there is no regular pattern to the population which, if it coincided with the sampling interval, might lead to a biased sample. In practice, this problem is often overcome by choosing multiple starting points and using varying sampling intervals whose size is selected at random.

Stratified sampling

4.14 In many situations **stratified sampling** is the best method of choosing a sample. The **population must be divided into strata or categories**.

4.15 If we took a random sample of all marketers in the country, it is conceivable that the entire sample might consist of members of the CIM working in commercial companies. Stratified sampling removes this possibility as random samples could be taken from each type of employment, the number in each sample being proportional to the total number of marketers in each type (for example those who are lecturers, those in commerce, those in the public sector and those in market research and agencies).

4.16 Note, however, that stratification requires prior knowledge of each item in the population. Sampling frames do not always contain this information. Stratification from the electoral register as to age structure would not be possible because the electoral register does not contain information about age.

Multistage sampling

4.17 The population is first **divided into quite large groups**, usually on a geographic basis, and a small sample of these groups is selected at random. Each of the groups selected is **subdivided into smaller groups** and again, a smaller number of these is selected at random.

This process is **repeated as many times as necessary** and finally, a random sample of individuals in each of the smallest groups is taken. A fair approximation to a random sample can be obtained.

Non-random sampling

4.18   Non-random sampling is used **when a sampling frame cannot be established**.

Quota sampling

4.19   In quota sampling randomness is forfeited in the interests of **cheapness and administrative simplicity**. Investigators are told to interview all the people they meet up to a certain quota. A large degree of bias could be introduced accidentally. For example, an interviewer in a shopping centre may fill his quota by only meeting people who can go shopping during the week. In practice, this problem can be **partly overcome by subdividing the quota** into different types of people, for example on the basis of age, gender and income, to ensure that the sample mirrors the structure or stratification of the population. The interviewer is then told to interview, for example, 30 males between the ages of 30 and 40 from social class B. The actual choice of the individuals to be interviewed, within the limits of the **quota controls**, is left to the field worker.

Action Programme 4

The number of marketers and their sex in each type of work in a particular country are as follows.

	Female	Male	Total
Lecturers	100	100	200
Commercial companies	400	300	700
Public sector	100	200	300
Marketing research and agencies	500	300	800
			2,000

What would an investigator's quota be, assuming that a sample of 200 is required?

Cluster sampling

4.20   Cluster sampling involves **selecting one definable subsection of the population** as the sample, that subsection taken to be representative of the population in question. The pupils of one school might be taken as a cluster sample of all children at school in London.

Action Programme 5

A publishing company carries out a national survey of adults' reading habits. To reduce travelling costs, the country is first divided into constituencies. A sample of 50 constituencies is then selected at random. Within each of these constituencies, 5 polling districts are selected, again using random techniques. Interviewers will visit a random selection of 30 people on the electoral register in each of the districts selected. What sampling method is the company using?

---

5   THE RELIABILITY OF CUSTOMER RESPONSES

5.1   There are several faults or weaknesses which might occur in the design or collection of sample data. These are as follows.

(a) **Bias**. In choosing a sample, unless the method used to select the sample is the random sampling method, or a quasi-random sampling method, there will be a likelihood that some 'units' (individuals or households etc) will have a poor, or even zero chance of being selected for the sample. Where this occurs, samples are said to be biased. A biased sample may occur in the following situations.

  (i) The sampling frame is out of date, and excludes a number of individuals or 'units' new to the population.

  (ii) Some individuals selected for the sample decline to respond. If a questionnaire is sent to 1,000 households, but only 600 reply, the failure of the other 400 to reply will make the sample of 600 replies inevitably biased.

  (iii) A questionnaire contains leading questions, or a personal interviewer tries to get respondents to answer questions in a particular way.

(b) **Insufficient data**. The sample may be too small to be reliable as a source of information about an entire population.

(c) **Unrepresentative data**. Data collected might unrepresentative of normal conditions. For example, if an employee is asked to teach a trainee how to do a particular job, data concerning the employee's output and productivity during the time he is acting as trainer will not be representative of his normal output and productivity.

(d) **Omission of an important factor**. Data might be incomplete because an important item has been omitted in the design of the 'questions'.

(e) **Carelessness**. Data might be provided without any due care and attention. An investigator might also be careless in the way he gathers data.

(f) **Confusion of cause and effect (or association)**. It may be tempting to assume that if two variables appear to be related, one variable is the cause of the other. Variables may be associated but it is not necessarily true that one causes the other.

(g) Where questions call for something **more than simple 'one-word' replies**, there may be difficulty in interpreting the results correctly. This is especially true of 'depth interviews' which try to determine the reasons for human behaviour.

5.2 One method of checking the accuracy of replies is to insert control questions in the questionnaire, so that the reply to one question should be compatible with the reply to another. If they are not, the value of the interviewee's responses are dubious, and may be ignored. On the other hand, the information that the interviewee is genuinely confused about something, and so offers contradictory answers, may be valuable information itself, or it may reflect the way the questions are structured.

Non-response

5.3 Non-response (of a sample member) cannot be avoided. It can, however, (apart from in mail surveys) be kept at a reasonable level. Experience has shown that the non-response part of a survey often differs considerably from the rest. The types of non-response are as follows.

(a) **Units outside the population**. Where the field investigation shows that units no longer exist (eg demolished houses), these units should be considered as outside the population and should be subtracted from the sample size before calculating the non-response rate.

(b) **Unsuitable for interview**. This is where people who should be interviewed are too infirm or too unfamiliar with the language to be interviewed.

(c) **Movers**. People who have changed address since the list was drawn up cannot be interviewed.

(d) **Refusals**. Some people refuse to co-operate.

(e) **Away from home**. People might be away from home for longer than the field work period and call-back might not be possible.

(f) **Out at time of call**.

5.4 These sort of problems occur chiefly in **random** sample surveys. Some of the above do not apply when interviewing is done in factories, colleges, offices, and so on. In quota sampling (c), (e) and (f) do not appear. Although the interviewer may miss some people for these reasons, he or she simply continues until he or she fills the quota.

5.5 An article in the *Financial Times* (29 June 1995) highlighted the **effect of social change on the level of non-response**. Rising crime means that householders may be afraid to answer the door to strangers and, with women increasingly looking for regular employment, it is becoming more and more difficult to find the standard type of person who used to be the backbone of fieldwork - the reasonably well-educated housewife looking for part-time work! Response rates are therefore slipping as more people either refuse to be or cannot be interviewed.

> The 'director general of the Market Research Society, the industry's professional body, says falling response levels are not just a UK phenomenon. He is concerned that the quality of research will begin to be affected, for the lower response rates are, the greater the departure from ideal cross-sections of opinion, and the less accurate findings are likely to be.'

5.6 Another problem pointed out in the article is that of '**data fatigue**', as the public becomes tired of filling in questionnaires and more cynical about the real motives of 'market researchers' because of 'sugging' (selling under the guise of research) and 'frugging' (fundraising under the guise of research).

How to deal with non-response

5.7 Taking **substitutes** (such as the next house along) is no answer because the substitutes may differ from the non-respondents. Instead the interviewer can try to increase response rate.

(a) Little can be done about **people not suitable** for interview.

(b) **People who have moved** are a special category. It is usually not practical to track them down. It is acceptable to select an individual from the new household against some rigorously defined procedure.

(c) To minimise '**refusals**', keep questionnaires as brief as possible, use financial incentives, and highly skilled interviewers. Refusal rates tend to be low (3-5 per cent).

(d) People '**away from home**' may be contacted later, if this is possible.

(e) People '**out at time of call**' is a common problem. The researcher should plan calling time sensibly (for example, as most breadwinnners are out at work in the day-time so call in the evening). Try to establish a good time to call back - or arrange an appointment.

6 FACTOR IMPORTANCE AND FACTOR SATISFACTION

6.1 A key element of customer care is finding out what customers think and what they want. These areas are essentially what the whole of this text is about, but it is worth bearing in mind that marketing research often concentrates on new products, while existing customers are in fact the bread and butter of the organisation. Customer feedback must be systematically gathered to ensure that they stay the organisation's customers. This can be done to find out:

- who the customers are and when they buy;
- what the customers think, feel and want;
- why they are not the customers of the organisation's competitors; and
- how the organisation can gain a competitive advantage with its customers.

Marketing at Work

Franchise food retailer Cullens launched a careline in 1997, enabling customers to call a freephone hotline displayed throughout the store and on the back of till receipts to give their opinion on the service received. Every call is followed up to find out what action was taken and the caller receives a written report. The caller information is analysed to provide information on branch and staff performance and to highlight where service levels need to be improved at each of the franchises.

6.2 It is emphatically not true that organisations should concentrate on improving their performance in the areas about which customers are evidently dissatisfied. What has to be evaluated, as well customer perceptions along a satisfied-dissatisfied scale, is the degree of importance which customers attach to the specific performance, product or service dimension being measured. Let us develop this important argument further.

6.3 Many customer surveys only measure what the customers think about the organisation, product or service as a whole, and about particular aspects of the organisation, product or service. Thus a customer survey designed by a bank may ask, 'What do you think of our cash dispensers (ATMs)?' Respondents are invited to select one from a range of alternative answers along what is known as a Likert scale, like the one illustrated below.

Very satisfied	Satisfied	No opinion	Dissatisfied	Very dissatisfied

6.4 If it were to turn out that a significant proportion of customers were 'dissatisfied' or 'very dissatisfied' with the bank's cash dispensers, then the bank may think that what it must do is to improve the functioning of its cash dispensers. There are two possible difficulties with drawing this conclusion.

(a) Customer reactions to cash dispensers are a matter of **perception** and, as such, are not necessarily founded on an analytical evaluation of the evidence. When Midland Bank asks its customers about cash dispensers, barely 40% say they are 'satisfied' or 'very satisfied' with them; when First Direct asks its customers the same question, the 'satisfied' and 'very satisfied' proportion rises to 80%. Both groups (because First Direct is a subsidiary of Midland Bank) are talking about the same cash dispensers: clearly, either Midland's customers are hyper-critical, or First Direct's customers are particularly tolerant: either way, opinions about cash dispensers have little to do with facts about the performance and responsiveness of cash dispensers, and a lot to do with the expectations of customers.

(b) The opinions being expressed may simply be a reflection of one or two disappointing and frustrating experiences, and take no account of the importance attached by customers to cash dispensers (and, indeed, to all other ingredients in the service delivery process). After all, it is not at all uncommon for customers to express vitriolic (or adulatory) opinions about an organisation, product or service, despite the fact that they have only experienced it once - or sometimes not at all.

6.5 If customer surveys are to generate authentic data, then questions need to be asked not only about how **satisfied** customers are with any given element in the service, but also how **important** that element is to them. If these dimensions of 'satisfaction' and 'importance' are combined, the organisation may then map customer perceptions.

Chapter roundup

- Information about customer dynamics is acquired in a variety of ways and the data is systematically collected and analysed to provide useful information. To be effective at retention marketing, the organisation has to have a really good database about present and past customers, with details of the nature of the relationship; it has to know about their attitudes, their perceptions of the organisation's products and service, and their expectations.

- Nishikawa emphasised creativity and understanding customer psychology. His key point was that customers are most sincere when they are spending, rather than when they are taking part in surveys.

- Lele and Sheth proposed four fundamentals of customer satisfaction.

    o product-related variables
    o sales and promotion related variables
    o after-sales variables
    o culture-related variables

- Companies are likely to use a combination of qualitative and quantitative techniques when undertaking research.

- Sampling is a key topic in marketing research. Various sampling methods were examined in this chapter.

- Customer responses may be affected by bias, or they may not respond at all.

- A key element of customer care is finding out what customers think and what they want.

Quick quiz

1 What approaches can be used when assessing the validity of data for decision making? (see para 2.1)

2 What features of customer psychology did Nishikawa highlight? (3.3)

3 How many people might be told about bad service by a disgruntled car buyer? How does this compare with the number likely to be told about good service? (3.6)

4 What factors make sampling worthwhile rather than a compromise? (4.2)

5 What is quasi-random sampling? (4.12)

6 Give some faults or weaknesses that may occur in the collection of sample data. (5.1)

7 What is 'data fatigue'? (5.6)

8 What features on a Likert scale? (6.3)

Action Programme Review

2 Not everyone has a telephone and not all of those who do have a telephone are listed.

3 (a) Those under 18 are not included on the register since they are not entitled to vote.

   (b) Mobile individuals such as students are frequently not registered where they live.

(c)   The register is not up to date and so those who have recently moved to the area are omitted and those who have recently left the area are still included.

4   The investigator needs to interview 200/2,000 × 100% = 10% of the population.

Using quota sampling, the investigator would interview the first 10 (100 × 10%) male marketing lecturers that he met, and the first 40 (400 × 10%) female marketers in commercial companies.

	Female	Male	Total
Lecturers	10	10	20
Commercial companies	40	30	70
Other commercial	10	20	30
Marketing research and agencies	50	30	80
			200

5   Multistage sampling

14 *Quantitative methodologies*

Chapter Topic List	Syllabus reference
1 Setting the scene	4.2
2 Questionnaire design	4.2
3 Interviews	4.2
4 Telephone surveys	4.2
5 Postal surveys	4.2
6 Experimental research	4.2
7 Continuous research	4.2
8 Recording data	4.2
9 In-home scanning	4.2
10 Observation	4.2
11 In-store testing	4.2
12 Retail shop audit	4.2

Learning Outcomes

- After completing this chapter you will have more understanding of the specifics behind designing and carrying out operational investigations into customer dynamics, customer perceptions of product/service performance, and customer satisfaction/delight using quantitative methodologies.

Examples of Marketing at Work

- Credit Card Sentinel
- The Appleyard Group, ICD Marketing Services
- Technology and marketing research

1 SETTING THE SCENE

1.1 This chapter looks at applying basic principles of research into customer attitudes and customer satisfaction.

1.2 A range of methods is explored.

2 QUESTIONNAIRE DESIGN

Designing the questionnaire

2.1 The sampling process can be an important contributor to the quality and value of the survey process. Nevertheless, where the survey is based on a substantial proportion of the population, the technical issues arising from sampling are likely to be relatively straightforward. In the majority of surveys, the most critical technical issue is likely to be not the quality of the sample, but the **quality of the survey instruments that have been used**. Where survey findings are technically suspect, this is most commonly because there are fundamental **flaws in the design of the questionnaire**. In this section, therefore, we will spend some time looking at some of the key issues involved in designing an effective questionnaire.

2.2 As with sampling theory, there is an **extensive range of literature** dealing with the complexities of questionnaire design. A large part of this literature deals with the design of questionnaires for **psychometric** and similar **experimental** purposes, where a particularly high level of rigour and precision is required. Although many of the core principles are undoubtedly relevant to the effective design of surveys, **the rigour required for managerial or organisational purposes is generally rather less**. In an organisational context, you will usually be interested in exploring, at a relatively straightforward level, **opinions or attitudes** relating to specific issues. You will not, for example, often be interested in exploring in detail the causal or other links between, say, behaviour and attitudes or in investigating the correlations between a range of different attitudes, values or beliefs. Even where there is a desire to explore these areas with some precision - for the purposes of individual development, for instance - you will most probably use professionally designed and well-validated instruments.

2.3 Nevertheless, even though most surveys are exploring comparatively straightforward issues, **the precision of the survey instrument should always be a primary concern**.

2.4 Expressed in these terms, our principles sound so obvious as to be **hardly worth stating** and, yet, in many questionnaires these apparently self-evident principles are **routinely disregarded**. All too often, there is little clarity about the information that is required, there is woolliness and imprecision in the framing of questions and there are confusions both about the meaning of the question and about the interpretation of the response.

2.5 The potential causes of this imprecision are numerous, but there are a number of common pitfalls that are worth highlighting (all the examples quoted are adapted from actual questionnaires encountered in organisations).

(a) **Ambiguity and uncertainty about language or terminology**. In framing a question, managers will often assume a common understanding or words or phrases where no such commonality actually exists. For example, a questionnaire might ask, 'Is the quality of work in your workgroup excellent/good/fair/poor?' This may be a useful question if it is followed by others that explore the respondents' understanding of the term 'quality' and its application in their workgroup. Frequently, though, this kind of question is allowed to stand alone, with neither explanation nor follow-up. In such cases, what is meant by quality? Do we mean quality in a technical sense of, say, 'fitness for purpose' or do we mean quality in the more colloquial sense? What measures of quality are we applying, and who is doing the measuring? Without answers to these (and many other) questions, the responses we receive are likely to be largely meaningless.

(b) **Lack of clarity about the information required**. Questionnaires are frequently weakened by a lack of clarity about the nature and detail of the information they are intended to collect. You should always stop and ask yourself some fundamental questions. Why am I asking this question? What is it intended to find out? What exactly do I want to know? **Will this question give me the information I need?** These questions are often not explicitly addressed, with the result that the wrong question (or only part of the right question) is asked. In one employee survey, for example, the questionnaire asked:

> Which of the following do you feel are barriers to your undertaking further training or development in your own time?
>
> Lack of spare time
> Lack of motivation
> Personal/domestic commitments
> Cost

Not surprisingly, many respondents ticked most if not all of these options. A moment's thought would have indicated to the survey designer that most of us will have seen these factors as barriers to personal development, even if we have managed to overcome them. The survey designer really wanted to ask not **whether** these factors were seen as barriers, but **which** were the most significant barriers and **how** significant they were. A more useful question might, for example, have asked respondents to indicate whether or not a given barrier had, in practice, prevented them from undertaking training.

(c) **Conflation of multiple questions into one**. One of the most common causes of confusion in questionnaire design is the entangling of several issues within one question, so that it is unclear what information is being provided by the respondent. In one survey, for example, respondents were asked, 'How often does your workgroup meet to discuss performance, quality and safety issues?' The assumption behind this question - which was part of the evaluation of a team development programme - was that managers called workgroups together to discuss all three of these issues, as they were required to do. In fact, practice varied considerably across the organisation. Some workgroups did not meet at all, some met infrequently and many met relatively often but only discussed performance issues. However, this fact, which was crucial to evaluating the effectiveness of the programme, only emerged during subsequent focus group.

(d) **Making unjustified assumptions**. Similar problems can arise when the phrasing of the question implies an assumption of a preconception that is not justified by the evidence available to you. It is not uncommon, for instance, to encounter questions such as, 'In reviewing your performance, which of the following methods does your manager use?' The assumption here, of course, is that the manager reviews the respondent's performance at all. If respondents feel that their performance is never reviewed, their only options are to add an extra narrative response or to leave the question uncompleted. In the latter case, it will be difficult to know how to interpret the response without additional evidence.

Leading questions

2.6 Even when the question has been very carefully and precisely planned, it may still provide misleading or inaccurate data if it appears to be **leading the respondent towards a particular answer**. It is important to remember that, even when you have carried out extensive preparation, a survey can still be a considerable source of anxiety. People may still feel **uncertain** about its outcomes and they may still feel **suspicious of your motives** for conducting it. In such cases, some may feel very keen to give the 'right' answer - the answer that they believe the organisation wants to hear. Regardless of your care in drafting the questionnaire, you may not be able to avoid this problem entirely. Some will always instinctively seek what they believe to be the 'socially acceptable' response (just as a few may react in the opposite direction). Nevertheless, you should avoid giving any kind of explicit steer to the respondent about the acceptability (or otherwise) of a given response.

2.7 This problem occurs most commonly when respondents are asked to **indicate their level of agreement or disagreement** with a particular statement. Although this can be a useful approach, there is a danger that the preferences or prejudices of the questionnaire designer can appear too obvious to the respondent. A series of positive statements about a particular aspect of the organisation may suggest to the respondent that a positive attitude to this issue is preferred. It is prudent, therefore, to include a **mixture of positive and negative statements**, which do not suggest any intrinsic preference.

2.8 In some cases, the choice of statement can **significantly undermine the value of the information obtained**. In one questionnaire, for instance, respondents were asked to indicate their agreement or disagreement with the statement, 'The quality of work in my department is generally excellent'. If the respondent agreed with this statement the meaning was clear - that he or she thought the quality of work in the department was generally excellent. However, if the respondent **disagreed** with the statement, the meaning was less clear. Did they think the quality was moderate or even poor? From the information provided by the question, there was no way of telling.

Question formats

2.9 Apart from the **'agree/disagree'** format, there are various **other ways** of structuring survey questions. In general, the questions in a written questionnaire should be of the **multiple choice** type, so providing the basis for quantitative analysis. The primary purpose of a written questionnaire is to facilitate **precise statistical analysis**. If the questionnaire includes too many narrative or open questions, analysis becomes very difficult.

2.10 **Survey questions** can be divided into two broad categories; those **exploring attitudes** or opinions and those **seeking some form of factual information**. In the former category would generally fall, for example, the 'agree/disagree' format, such as 'Safety is always a paramount concern for the organisation. Do you agree strongly/agree slightly/disagree slightly/disagree strongly'. In the latter category might fall questions about, say, the frequency of workgroup meetings or about recent experience of training.

2.11 Within these two broad categories, a number of formats can be applied. Questions on attitude or opinion generally ask the respondent to indicate both the direction and the strength of feeling - say, 'strongly agree' to 'strongly disagree'. Alternatively, you might ask for the range of opinion relating to a given topic with a question like 'Do you think the quality of work in your department is generally excellent/good/fair/poor?' In such cases, where you are effectively asking respondents to commit themselves to a specific opinion, you need to be aware of what is sometimes called, in an experimental content, the 'error of the central tendency'.

2.12 In other words, **respondents are commonly reluctant to give extreme responses** and prefer to hover around the middle ground. If you have an odd number of items in your scale, you may find that respondents disproportionately opt for the neutral option. Although in an experimental context there are some dangers in excluding the neutral option, for the cruder purposes of an employee survey there are benefits in forcing respondents off the fence by **offering only an even number of options**, so that the respondent has to choose between, say, 'agree slightly' and 'disagree slightly'. In this way, you gain a clearer perspective on the **true direction of opinion**.

2.13 Where you are asking to identify preferences from among a number of options, you may ask respondents to **rank the options against a given criterion**, such as 'Which of the following do you think are the most important contributors to high workgroup performance? (Please rank in order of importance.)' If you use this format, you should remember to indicate **how the ranking should be applied**. Is number 1 the **most** or the **least** important factor? Ranking questions can seem **confusing** to respondents and are best used sparingly. In any cases, it is rarely worth asking respondents to rank more than the first three or four items. Beyond that, rankings usually become fairly arbitrary. A more straightforward approach is to ask respondents simply to **select one item** - 'Which of the following do you think is the single more important contributor to high workgroup performance? (Please tick one only.)' Although slightly less detailed, this question is easier both to complete and to analyse.

2.14 In collecting factual information, you may again wish to **use scales** where the required information lies on a continuum. For example, 'How many days have you spent training in the past 12 months? Fewer than 3 days/4 - 6 days/6 - 10 days/more than 10 days.'

2.15 On the other hand, where you are exploring more discrete items of information, you may simply ask respondents to **select the most relevant items**. For example, you might ask, 'Which of the following types of training have you undertaken in the last year? (Please tick any that apply.)' In this case, you are not asking respondents to evaluate the options against one another, but simply to make a choice between those that are and those that are not significant. This format can also be applied in cases of **opinions and attitudes**, where you require respondents simply to indicate, rather than to evaluate, specific options - for example, 'Which of the following do you think are significant contributors to workgroup performance? (Please tick any that apply.)' It is worth noting that, by contrast with the ranking or single-choice format, this format will enable you to evaluate the options only on a collective basis (in other words, 87 per cent felt item A was significant, whereas only 42 per cent felt that item B was significant) and will provide no indication of individual preferences.

Building the questionnaire

2.16 The overall structure of the questionnaire can take a number of forms, depending on the purpose and nature of the survey. As a general rule, when you are exploring a given topic, you should aim to be as systematic as possible in **progressing from the general to the specific**. Typically, your initial aim should be to gain an understanding of the **broad context** within which opinions are held. You can then progress to gaining an understanding of the **nature and strength of opinion** in a given area. Finally, you can move, step by step, towards identifying the **detail that underpins these**.

2.17 To illustrate this, let us take a specific example - a questionnaire designed to explore issues to reward and recognition. The questionnaire might begin, for example, by asking a question about perceptions of reward and recognition in the organisation generally.

> How satisfied are you with the level of recognition and reward you receive for your achievements at work?
>
> Very satisfied
> Fairly satisfied
> Fairly unsatisfied
> Very dissatisfied?

2.18 The **responses** to this question will help provide you with a **context** within which you can interpret the more detailed information you will obtain from subsequent questions. For example, in interpreting employees' opinions about specific reward mechanisms, it is important to know whether or not these opinions are expressed in a general climate of satisfaction or dissatisfaction. Without such contextual information, it is difficult to gauge the significance of a given response. Does respondents' dissatisfaction with, say, the level of bonuses indicate a major concern or simply an awareness that, in an ideal world, bonuses might be higher? The context questions will help you understand just what kind and level of problems you have on your hands.

2.19 Having defined the broad organisational context, you can begin to focus more precisely on the detail of the specific topic. The next question might be:

> If you feel that your work achievements are recognised, what form does this recognition generally take? (Please tick any that apply.)
>
> Increased basic pay
> Bonus payment
> Other financial reward
> Promotion
> Verbal congratulations
> Non-financial reward
> Other (please specify)

2.20 This will provide you with an understanding of the **current perceptions of the topic** - what respondents' perceptions of the rewards they typically receive for work achievements are.

2.21 You may feel **tempted to omit** this kind of 'state of play' question on the basis that **you already know** enough about what happens currently in the organisation. It is easy to assume that **your** perceptions and perspective reflect those of the wider workforce. You may, for example, know that the company pays out very large sums every year as bonus payments and you may, therefore, assume that bonus payments are perceived by employees as the most significant form of reward. In practice, though, particularly if the bonuses are received only by a comparatively small number of employees, they may be perceived by the wider workforce as much less significant than other forms of reward. The broad rule, as in most aspects of employee surveying, is **do not make assumptions**. If you have any doubts at all about people's views or perceptions, test them out.

2.22 Having identified people's perceptions of the current state of play in the specific area, you can then move to the next level of detail and begin to explore, for example, internal customers' **preferences** for reward and recognition. You might ask:

> Which of the following forms of recognition for work achievements do you find most motivating? (Please tick one only.)
>
> Increased basic pay
> Bonus payment
> Other financial reward
> Promotion
> Verbal congratulations
> Non-financial reward
> Other (please specify)

2.23 Mapping these expressed preferences against the current perceived position should indicate very clearly **if or where there is gap between current and the desired**. This, in turn, will enable the organisation to focus its future activities very precisely on these areas, where they are likely to bring maximum pay-back. Having identified the most important issues in this way, you can then, of course, move on to look in detail at specific aspects of the topic.

Ensuring accurate responses

2.24 This general process of moving from the general to the specific is sometimes known as '**funnelling**'. Clearly, it is an important device for **ensuring precision in interpretation**. In addition, it may also help you to provide a meaningful interpretation of responses that may be influenced by extraneous factors, such as **self-interest**. The use of broad, contextual questions, however, will help you to interpret such responses against a range of other issues and concerns. You might, for instance, ask respondents, initially, to rank areas of potential dissatisfaction in order of significance. This will then provide you with a basis on which to evaluate any specific expression of dissatisfaction with the really important issue.

2.25 **Other questionnaire structures** can also be used to **minimise the influence of external factors**. If you are exploring a range of issues, for example, it can be helpful to distribute questions about each respective issue throughout the questionnaire, rather than bunching them in discrete sections. This can help reduce what is sometimes known as the 'halo effect', which is when overall positive or negative feelings about a given issue influence responses to individual questions. For example, if customers generally feel unhappy about delivery times, they may feel inclined to give negative responses to **all** questions relating to delivery, even though they may actually be highly satisfied with, say, quality of packaging. Distributing questions about delivery throughout the questionnaire may help to prevent such respondents establishing a **pattern of negative responses**.

Questionnaire length and layout

2.26 One of the most common questions asked by those conducting or commissioning surveys is, 'What length of questionnaire is acceptable?' As with sampling, there is **no straightforward answer**. It depends on the nature and complexity of the **questions** being asked. It depends on the **population** being surveyed, and their familiarity and confidence with questionnaires. It depends on the **methods being used** to administer the survey. It is also true that the appliance and format of the questionnaire may be just as important as its length. Everything else being equal, a well-designed and clearly laid out questionnaire can afford to be longer than a poorly constructed equivalent.

2.27 Above all, of course, there is generally a trade-off between questionnaire length and the level of response. The **longer and more detailed** the questionnaire, the **more likely** you are to encounter **resistance** from potential respondents. Ultimately, you will need to balance these two factors. In some cases, for instance, you may feel that a smaller response is justified by the need to obtain a higher level of detail from the questionnaire.

2.28 Despite these caveats, the following crude guidelines for different forms of questionnaire administration may be helpful.

(a) **Cold surveys**. Where the questionnaire is being sent out with no preparation and where respondents have no particular incentive to respond, you should aim for an absolute maximum of 4 sides of paper and no more than 15 to 20 questions (including sub-questions), but in many cases, it will be preferable to aim for just 1 or 2 sides of paper and even fewer questions. The key issue here is likely to be one of presentation. You will want to suggest that the survey is easy to complete and will involve comparatively little of the respondent's time. Therefore, simple, 'user-friendly' layout is likely to be an even more significant issue than the overall length.

(b) **Postal questionnaires**. Where respondents have been briefed and prepared, but are nevertheless expected to complete the questionnaire entirely in their own time, you should generally aim for a questionnaire of some 6 to 8 sides of paper, ideally with no more than 30 to 40 questions. You will still need to ensure that the form is not unduly intimidating or off-putting and, ideally, respondents should feel encouraged to complete it immediately rather than delaying. If potential respondents put the questionnaire to one side, the chances are that a substantial proportion will not get around to completing it at all.

(c) **Questionnaires completed in work time**. Where the organisation allocates some work time to completing the questionnaire, you can generally risk a rather longer questionnaire - probably up to 10 to 12 pages and 50 to 60 questions. Respondents will feel actively encouraged to complete the form, and it may be possible to include complicated questions or topics, that might not be appropriate for a questionnaire that is to be completed in the respondent's own time. In this kind of survey, as we have seen, it is not uncommon to obtain response levels of 80 per cent or above, even when the questionnaire is both long and highly detailed.

2.29 Some other general points about questionnaire design are also worth stressing. First, make sure that you provide **clear instructions** throughout, indicating precisely how the questionnaire should be completed. These should be simply phrased and as concise as possible. It is also a good idea to **provide some examples** of specific question types and how they should be completed. As always, one good example is worth several dozen words of explanation.

2.30 Try to **avoid over-complicated instructions**. In some cases, a degree of complexity may be inevitable - particularly where, for example, some respondents are required to skip a number of the questions. Nevertheless, the most effective questionnaires, in terms of ease of response, are those where all respondents are able to proceed straightforwardly through the questionnaire from the first question to the last.

Name	Description	Example

CLOSED-END QUESTIONS

Dichotomous — A question with two possible answers.

'In arranging this trip, did you personally phone British Airways?'

Yes ☐   No ☐

Multiple choice — A question with three or more answers.

'With whom are you travelling on this flight?'

No one ☐   Children only ☐
Spouse ☐   Business associates/
Spouse and   friends/relatives ☐
children ☐   An organised tour
                    group ☐

Likert scale — A statement with which the respondent shows the amount of agreement/

'Small airlines generally give better service

Strongly disagree 1	Disagree 2	Neither agree nor disagree 3	Agree 4	Strongly agree 5
☐	☐	☐	☐	☐

Semantic differential — A scale connecting two bipolar words, where the respondent selects the point

British Airways

Large ─ ─ ─ ─ ─ ─ ─ ─ ─ ─ Small
Experienced ─ ─ ─ ─ ─ ─ ─ Inexperienced
─ ─ ─ ─ ─ ─ ─ ─ ─ ─

Importance scale — A scale that rates the importance of some attribute.

Extremely important 1	Very important 2	Somewhat important 3	Not very important 4	Not at all important 5
☐	☐	☐	☐	☐

Rating scale — A scale that rates some attribute from 'poor' to 'excellent'.

Excellent   Very good   Good   Fair   Poor

Intention-to-buy scale — A scale that describes the respondent's intention to buy.

'If an inflight telephone was available on a long flight, I would'

Definitely buy 1	Probably buy 2	Not sure 3	Probably not buy 4	Definitely not buy 5
☐	☐	☐	☐	☐

OPEN-END QUESTIONS

Completely unstructured — A question that respondents can answer in an almost unlimited number of ways.

'What is your opinion of British Airways?'

Word association — Words are presented, one at a time, and respondents mention the first word that

'What is the first word that comes to mind when you hear the following'
Airline _____
British _____
Travel _____

Sentence completion — An incomplete sentence is presented and respondents complete the

'When I choose an airline, the most important consideration in my decision is _____ ,'

Story completion — An incomplete story is presented, and respondents are asked to complete it.

'I flew B.A. a few days ago. I noticed that the exterior and interior of the plane had bright colours. This aroused in me the following

Picture completion — A picture of two characters is presented, with one making a statement. Respondents are asked to identify with the other and fill in the empty balloon.

The inflight entertainment's good

Thematic Apperception Test (TAT) — A picture is presented and respondents are asked to make up a story about what they think is happening or may happen in the picture.

Laying out the questionnaire

2.31 (a) If respondents have to complete the questionnaire themselves, it must be approachable and as short as possible. Consider the use of **lines, boxes, different type faces and print sizes and small pictures.** Use plenty of space.

(b) Consider the use of **tick boxes**. Is it clear where ticks go or how to respond in each case? For analysis, will it be easy to transfer responses from the forms to a summary sheet or a computer? Consider pre-coding the answers.

(c) Explain the **purpose of the survey** at the beginning of the questionnaire and where possible guarantee confidentiality. Emphasise the date by which it must be returned.

(d) At the end of the questionnaire, **thank the respondent** and make it clear what they should do with the completed questionnaire.

Pilot tests

2.32 It is vital to pilot test questionnaires since mistakes, ambiguities and embarrassments in a questionnaire can be extremely expensive once the main data collection phase has been entered.

The Likert scale

2.33 (a) A list of statements is prepared about the topic being researched, and a test group of respondents is asked to rate each statement on a scale from strong agreement to strong disagreement.

(b) A numerical value is given to each response:

Strongly agree: 5 Agree: 4 Don't know: 3 Disagree: 2 Strongly disagree: 1

(c) Each respondent's scores for all the statements are added up to give a total score for the topic, which may reflect overall positive or negative attitudes: responses to individual statements can also be analysed to get more meaningful information about the pattern of responses.

2.34 Likert scales are simple to prepare and administer. You may have been asked to complete such an inventory test over the telephone, or seen one in a magazine. However, again you should be aware that scale values have no absolute meaning, and are limited in their statistical uses, on an 'interval' scale.

The Semantic Differential scale

2.35 (a) Scales are constructed on a number of **'dimensions'** - pairs of opposite attributes or qualities, expressed as adjectives - valued on a continuum from +3 to -3.

Profile of Car Model X

	+3	+2	+1	0	-1	-2	-3	
Modern								Old-fashioned
Fast								Slow
Attractive								Unattractive
Powerful								Weak
Responsive								Unresponsive
Glamorous								Ordinary

(b) Respondents are asked to **select the position of the object** being researched (in this case the car) on each continuum, according to the degree to which they think the adjective describes the object. (If the car is very powerful but not terribly responsive, say, it might rate +3 on the powerful-weak dimension, and +1 on the responsive-unresponsive scale.)

(c) A **'profile'** is thus built up by each respondent.

Profile of Car Model X

	+3	+2	+1	0	-1	-2	-3	
Modern								Old-fashioned
Fast								Slow
Attractive								Unattractive
Powerful								Weak
Responsive								Unresponsive
Glamorous								Ordinary

2.36   The main problem with Semantic Differential scales is the **subjectivity attached to language**. Words are mean different things to different people. (The word 'old-fashioned' in our car profile above may mean 'old-hat' to some and 'classic' to others.)

2.37   The other problem of measuring responses to, and perceptions of, different attributes of the same thing is that **one attribute can influence our perception of other attributes** and some attributes bring clusters of other assumed attributes with them (stereotypes). Think, for example, about our model X car: if it looks sleek and attractive, we may perceive it as a fast car - whether it is or not - and if we think of old-fashioned cars as glamorous (because of stereotypes of 'classic' cars and the people who drive them) we might distort our glamour rating.

3   INTERVIEWS

3.1   Most surveys in UK market research take place as **face-to-face** interviews. The interviewers are often freelancers but can be employees of a market research organisation. An interview is a social encounter, where the personal interface between interviewee(s) and interviewer is crucial.

3.2   There are five main styles of interview, classified according to where they occur.

(a)   **Street surveys** take place typically in busy town centres, with the interviewer approaching individuals as they pass by. They need to be brief (5 minutes is too long for most people in their lunch break or going to or from work) and should not require too much concentration from the interviewees, so getting them to consider show material should be avoided. A survey taking place in a shopping centre requires the centre's manager's permission, and a fee may be payable.

(b)   **Shop surveys** take place inside or just outside a particular shop, obviously with the shop's permission.

(c)   **Hall surveys** take place in a pre-booked location such as a hotel, where people are invited to attend to answer a few questions, usually being recruited from the street and being enticed by a give-away or refreshments. More complex tasks can be performed by the interviewee, for instance a display can be permanently set up and considered.

(d)   **Home interviews** are held in the interviewee's home (or doorstep), with the interviewer recruiting simply by knocking on doors. They can be pre-arranged by phone or by dropping a note through the door. Larger, in depth interviews often result but they are time-consuming, expensive and prone to interruption. Many people are reluctant even to answer their doors let alone let an interviewer in so recruiting for home interviews is often frustrating for the interviewer.

(e)   **Business surveys** take place on the interviewee's business premises and are always pre-arranged. Again they are prone to interruption and/or last minute cancellation.

3.3 It must always be remembered that people taking part in interview surveys are **doing the researcher a favour,** so the least one can do is ensure that the interviewer is well-prepared and does not make the interviewee feel that his or her time is being wasted. Good preparation will also save time in the long run and reduce the costs of hiring freelance interviewers. Finally, it will result in getting the data that is actually needed. It is vital, therefore, that the questionnaire or interview schedule is clear, unambiguous, and accurate.

3.4 The interviewer's other tasks are:

(a) to **locate respondents** (stopping in street, calling house-to-house as instructed by the researcher);

(b) to **obtain respondents' agreement** to the interview (no mean feat);

(c) to **ask questions** (usually sticking strictly to the interview schedule/questionnaire's wording) and take down answers; and

(d) to **complete records.**

3.5 Since the desired outcome of the survey is useful data, it is important to consider whether **interviewer bias** may affect the outcome. This comes about in selection of respondents (stopping people who look 'nice' rather than a reasonable cross-section), handling the interview (not annoying the respondent so his or her answers are affected) and so on.

3.6 The **advantages of interviews** as a survey method over telephone and postal surveys are as follows.

(a) Respondent **suitability can be checked** at the outset by asking quota questions but more effectively by assessment of the respondent (young man, woman shopping with children etc), so that the target number of interviews is achieved.

(b) Respondents can be **encouraged to answer as fully as possible** and the interview is usually completed.

(c) Questions are **asked in the right order,** and all relevant questions are asked.

(d) The **use of show material** is properly administered.

(e) **Response rates are higher** than for other forms of survey.

4 TELEPHONE SURVEYS

4.1 Surveys conducted over the phone rather than face-to-face have the following advantages.

(a) The response is **rapid.**

(b) There is a **standard sampling frame** - the **telephone directory,** which can be systematically or randomly sampled.

(c) A **wide geographical area** can be covered fairly cheaply.

(d) It may be **easier to ask sensitive or embarrassing questions.**

4.2 But there are considerable **disadvantages** as well.

(a) A **biased sample** may result from the fact that a large proportion (about 10%) of people do not have telephones (representing certain portions of the population such as old people or students) and many of those who do are ex-directory.

(b) It is **not possible to use 'showcards'** or pictures.

(c) Due to telesales the **refusal rate is much higher** than with face-to-face interviews, and the interview often cut short.

(d) It is **not possible to see the interviewee's expressions** or to develop the rapport that is possible with personal interviews.

(e) The interview **must be short**.

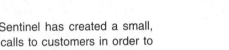

Marketing at Work

Credit Card Sentinel offers credit card holders a high degree of protection against loss, or theft, of their cards. If a credit card goes missing, then a single call to Sentinel, via a 24-hour helpline, will ensure that all relevant card-issuing organisations are alerted with minimum delay.

As part of its programme for keeping up-to-date with customers, Credit Card Sentinel has created a small, self-managed group called the Customer Attitude Team, which makes random calls to customers in order to collect feedback. In the view of the company such an approach is much more useful than questionnaires, which tend to attract responses only from those who are either greatly impressed or greatly unimpressed. CAT is a very interactive system because it is possible to discover what a broad range of customers really think; moreover, the CAT staff are empowered to bring any dissatisfied customers back on track, using whatever means they feel necessary.

5 POSTAL SURVEYS

5.1 **Approximately 25% of market research questionnaires are completed by postal survey.** We are using the term 'postal' survey to cover all methods in which the questionnaire is given to the respondent and returned to the investigator without personal contact. Such questionnaires could be posted but might also be left in pigeonholes or on desks.

5.2 Postal questionnaires have the following **advantages** over personal interviews.

(a) The **cost per person** is likely **to be less,** so more people can be sampled, and central control is facilitated.

(b) It is usually possible to **ask more questions** because the people completing the forms (the respondents) can do so in their own time.

(c) **All respondents are presented with questions in the same way.** There is no opportunity for an interviewer to influence responses (interviewer bias) or to misrecord them.

(d) It may be **easier to ask personal or embarrassing questions** in a postal questionnaire than in a personal interview.

(e) Respondents **may need to look up information for the questionnaire**. This will be easier if the questionnaire is sent to their homes or places of work.

Action Programme 1

What are the advantages of personal interviews over postal questionnaires?

Enumerators

5.3 A cheaper alternative to interviews is the use of an **enumerator** who will **deliver the questionnaire** and **encourage the respondent to complete it**. He will later visit the respondent again to collect the completed questionnaire and perhaps to help with the interpretation of difficult questions. This method results in a better response rate than for postal questionnaires.

5.4 It may be advisable to **encourage better response rates** from questionnaires, surveys and telephone studies. Methods of achieving this include putting all respondents' names into a **prize draw** or offering a product or service **discount** to all respondents.

Marketing at Work

(a) *The Appleyard Group, Peugeot Dealers from Chesterfield*

This company awards a cut-glass goblet to its 'Technician of the Month' - not the one with the best scores from the customer-feedback cards, but the technician who gets the most cards.

Designing the award in this way helps to stimulate all the technicians actively to encourage their customers to complete the feedback cards, so that customer feedback consists of comprehensive data and not merely a few selective instances.

Moreover, the system avoids the trap highlighted by Edwards Deming (one of the original US quality-improvement gurus) of rewarding the best at the expense of (relatively) punishing the rest. As Deming points out, all employees have a responsibility to improve: the rewards should go to those who generate the most data to help everyone to improve, rather than to the people who perform best at any given moment.

(b) *ICD Marketing Services*

'The balance between the advertising, market research and direct marketing industries could be altered for good this autumn after the launch of what is claimed to be the largest ever survey of UK consumer behaviour.

ICD Marketing Services plans to mail every household in the country, more than 20 million in all, with questionnaires grilling them on every aspect of their lifestyle, from reading habits to political beliefs and health.

With more than 1,500 questions and 2,500 possible responses, it aims to provide the first definitive national picture of consumer habits. ICD predicts a response from two million named households, giving information on the preferences of 3.6 million individuals. The survey will cost £7 million to set up.

ICD is even considering spending a further £1 million on an advertising campaign to stimulate response, and is allowing companies to sponsor individual questions for 25 pence per response. When you consider that some questions will receive three million replies, revenue could add up to £750,000 per question.'   The Times, 5 June 1996

6   EXPERIMENTAL RESEARCH

Laboratory experiments

6.1 An **artificial environment** is set up by the researcher in which most of the crucial factors which may affect the outcome of the research are controlled.

6.2 Laboratory experiments are most often used for measuring response to **advertisements**, to **product design** and to **package design**. They can take place before the item being tested is generally released (pre-testing), or after (post-testing). In pre-tests in particular it can be difficult to design an experiment which isolates the impact of one factor in a product or package from all the other factors which make up the proposed item, and which are likely to be the subjects of other experiments.

Field experiments

6.3 In a field experiment **a product is tested in realistic surroundings**, that is in the environment in which it will be bought and/or consumed once launched. Whilst the researcher has less control over extraneous variables, field experiments do give a more realistic idea of future behaviour.

6.4 Field experiments are usually carried out for products in what the marketer hopes is their final form. They are therefore **expensive** as the product has to be made and marketed in small quantities, and they are **risky** in that competitors will inevitably get a good look. Laboratory experiments are often preferred but there are some elements of the marketing mix, such as distribution, which do not lend themselves to laboratory tests.

6.5 There are **three main types** of field experiment.

(a) A sample of consumers **try the product out at home** and report findings, usually by completing a questionnaire. The consumers are often members of a carefully selected consumer panel. Such **in-home placement tests** are often used for toiletry and other personal products.

(b) **Retail outlets** are used as the site for testing merchandising, packaging and point-of-sale material (**store tests**). There should be a reasonable cross-section of stores, both by size and by region, and ideally a control group. Results are measured primarily by changes in sales by store, but sometimes also by interview surveys of consumers.

(c) **Test marketing** is an expensive but often vital experiment in which one or more marketing actions are **tried out in limited areas of the market** in order to predict sales volume, profitability, market share, consumer, retailer and distributor behaviour and regional variances. It is vital that the experiment be properly controlled since the prediction of a new product's success, or a successful change in the marketing mix of an existing product, very often depends on it. Mistakes can be expensive.

7 CONTINUOUS RESEARCH

7.1 The object of continuous research is to **take measurements regularly** so as to monitor **changes in the market,** either consumer, business or internally. Often syndicated because of the set-up costs, continuous research is usually undertaken by a large market research organisation. It can focus on the same consumers over time (panel research) or on a changing body of consumers.

7.2 Some research is continuous in the sense that measurement takes place every day, while in other cases measurements are taken at regular intervals.

Regular interval surveys

7.3 Where separate, independent samples of respondents are surveyed at regular intervals we have regular interval surveys. For marketing measurement these usually take the form of either omnibus surveys or market tracking surveys.

(a) An **omnibus survey** is a master questionnaire run by market research companies who 'sell' space on the questionnaire to marketing organisations who need data. Because the market research companies undertake the sampling, administration, processing and analysis, and spread the cost over the organisations needing data, it is a cost-effective method of research for all concerned.

The master questionnaire usually contains some of the same questions (age, gender, occupation) every time, while the remainder of the questions are either continuous (the same questions in the same place on the questionnaire as were asked of a different group, say, one week earlier) or *ad hoc* (inserted on a first-come-first-served basis but in a sensible order).

(b) Where the market research company designs the whole questionnaire seeking data on a particular market from regular different samples of respondents, rather than a panel, there is a **market tracking survey**. The results are sold by the company to as many marketing organisations as possible. Sometimes information on product usage is combined with data on media exposure.

8 RECORDING DATA

8.1 Most of the research methods discussed above make use of the questionnaire (when self-completed) or the interview schedule (when interviewer completed) as the means of capturing or recording market research data. These questionnaires may be conventional 'bits of paper' or, in the case of telephone surveys and some interview surveys, they may be in the form of on-line computer terminals when the questions are flashed on the screen and the interviewer inputs the answer directly into the analytical programme.

Diaries

8.2 A consumer diary allows the consumer to record behaviour on or between different dates or even times of the day. The diary is completed every time a certain behaviour occurs, rather than behaviour being recalled at times specified by the researcher. It is thus an **accurate means of recording repetitive information** for, say, a consumer panel.

8.3 Diary-filling **can be very detailed and onerous** and it is rare that a household, even a member of a consumer panel, is asked to complete one for longer than two weeks. The problem is that the data recorded needs to be both accurate and up-to-date, whilst the room for error, with new brands on the market for instance, is vast.

Recording devices

8.4 While questionnaires and diaries essentially record answers to direct questions, other devices are used to record **observations**, for instance of the order in which a consumer proceeds around a supermarket.

Manual recording systems

8.5 For a market researcher, some material is a recording device of marketing data but to other people it has a quite different use. For instance, to a marketer an **invoice** records a successful sale, a **credit note** a dissatisfied customer, while to an accountant they record financial information only.

Electronic recording systems

8.6 An explosion in market research data has been made possible by the development of **electronic recording devices**.

(a) **EPOS** (electronic point of sale systems) with scanners of bar-codes provide fast and accurate records of sales, times and prices.

(b) **Electronic questionnaires** and diaries, discussed above, allow information to be input directly into a computer system, so results can be reviewed at any time in the survey and range and topical checks applied.

(c) **Audio and video recording devices** may be used to record interviews, especially depth ones, and camcorders can be used to record consumer behaviour.

8.7 The key point about electronic recording devices is that **information recorded is complete,** so sampling and estimating are not required.

Marketing at Work

The impact of technology on marketing research is likely to be profound. The *Financial Times* carried an article on the subject in June 1995 from which the following is taken.

'First, the paper questionnaire-carrying clipboard is being rapidly replaced for many applications by the laptop computer. Computer assisted personal interviewing (CAPI) will probably be used in more than 60 per cent of face-to-face interviews by the end of this year, according to BMRB International, one of the UK's biggest market research agencies.

Computer-assisted telephone interviewing (CATI) is already firmly established as an alternative to the more laborious written questionnaires that telephone interviewers used to complete.

For both CAPI and CATI, interviews tap survey answers straight into a computer, cutting down on data processing time and improving accuracy. Surveys can be more complex and closely targeted because the computer automatically selects the interviewer's 'routing' - which question should follow on from a particular answer.'

---

9 IN-HOME SCANNING

9.1 Consumer panel research has traditionally relied on diaries or home audits to collect data. However, both Neilsen and AGB have recently launched new panels based on in-home scanning, where each household is equipped with a **hand-held laser scanner** or light pen for reading the bar-codes on the products they buy. This has revolutionised the consumer panel process because it obviates the need for diary completion and, plausibly, generates much higher levels of accuracy and comprehensiveness.

9.2 All panellists need to do is run the scanner or light-pen over the **bar-code** as they unpack their shopping. The bar-code instantly records the country of origin, the manufacturer, the product, and the product variant if applicable. Other **information can be keyed in** at the same time using the number keys attached to the scanner, including price, source of purchase, date of purchase, promotions, and who made the purchase.

10 OBSERVATION

10.1 Interviews and questionnaires depend on respondents answering questions on behaviour and attitudes truthfully. Sometimes it is necessary to **observe behaviour,** not only because respondents are unwilling to answer questions but because such questions do not record behaviour and are therefore unable to provide the researcher with answers.

10.2 The major categories of observations are as follows.

(a) **Home audit**. Also termed indirect observation, this involves the investigation of the respondent's home, office or premises so as to determine the extent of ownership of certain products/brands. (Note that the home audit and diary panels are termed *consumer panel* research.)

(b) **Direct observation**. This involves, not surprisingly, the direct observation of the behaviour of the respondent by the researcher. Tull and Hawkins (1990) claimed that an event must meet three criteria to be a fit subject for direct observation.

  (i)   The event being observed must only occupy a **short period** of time.

  (ii) It must be **frequently** performed.

  (iii) The event must be **visible** (and so feelings, beliefs and attitudes are not suitable topics for this technique).

(c) **High-tech recording devices**. Such devices record micro behaviour in laboratory settings and macro behaviour in natural settings.

  (i)   **Laboratory settings**

     (1) **Psychogalvanometers** measure a subject's response to, say, an advertisement by measuring the perspiration rate (which tends to increase when the subject is excited).

     (2) **Eye cameras** are used to assess those parts of, for example, an advertisement which attract most attention and those parts which are neglected.

     (3) **Pupilometric cameras** are used in assessing the visual stimulation derived from an image.

  (ii) In **natural settings** video and movie cameras are used to record behaviour. In such settings there is an increased chance of observing real behaviour but the researcher might have to wait a long time until the behaviour occurs.

10.3 During group discussion, **non-verbal communication** can be observed so as to assess the validity of a respondent's replies.

10.4 Observation can be **open** (the observer can be seen by the respondent) or **disguised** (the observer uses a physical disguise, a one-way mirror or a closed-circuit TV system, as is often the case in a natural setting), **structured** (the researcher must know what is to be observed) or **unstructured** (the situation does not allow for the data requirements to be predetermined).

Action Programme 2

Is the observation of the effectiveness of point-of-purchase promotional advertising material likely to be open or disguised?

10.5 Observation has the **advantage** over asking people questions of placing no reliance on respondents' memories, guesses or honesty but it does have a number of **drawbacks**.

(a) It may not be possible or feasible.
(b) It is labour intensive (one observer can only observe a limited number of things).
(c) Attitudes and feelings cannot be observed.

10.6 The use of observation as a data collection method has been stimulated by advances in electronics. EPOS systems allow firms to observe stock on hand, inflows, outflows and the speed at which stock items are moving through the store.

11 IN-STORE TESTING

11.1 Product testing in store may be a **relatively quick and inexpensive method** of gathering information about customer attitudes towards a particular product. In-store testing can be a useful, convenient way to gain insights into expected consumer behaviour before a full product launch is implemented. Selected stores can be chosen to test a product and gather information about likely buyer behaviour when the product is launched. In-store testing is also a way of promoting the product before, during and after a launch.

12 RETAIL SHOP AUDIT

12.1 Retail shop audits are used by organisations to assess consumer demand for their products.

12.2 At set intervals **researchers visit a sample of shops,** audit (count) the stock in question and record the details of any deliveries since the last audit. Using the fact that

$$\text{sales} = \text{original stock} + \text{deliveries} - \text{final stock}$$

they are able to calculate the sales of the product since the last audit.

12.3 **Shops are segmented** according to their type (multiples, independent, department) and by the volume of business. Those shops which sell the largest range of products in which the organisation is interested are usually the ones upon which the auditors concentrate.

12.4 Retail shop audits **investigate product types** and hence the client of the research company can be provided with information on their competitors' product as well as their own.

Chapter roundup

- This chapter looked at several quantitative methodologies for measuring customer responses and perceptions.

Quick quiz

1   What are the core principles of questionnaire design? (see para 2.3)

2   What are the five main styles of interview? (3.2)

3   What are the advantages of telephone surveys? (4.1)

4   Give some examples of electronic recording systems. (8.6)

5   What is a retail shop audit? (12.2)

Action Programme Review

1   (a)   Large numbers of postal questionnaires may not be returned, may be returned only partly completed or may be returned very late. This may lead to biased results if those replying are not representative of all people in the survey. Response rates are likely to be higher with personal interviews, and the interviewer can encourage people to answer all questions. Low response rates are a major problem with postal questionnaires, but low response rates can be avoided by:

    (i)   providing a stamped and addressed envelope or a prominently sited box for the return of the questionnaire;

    (ii)   giving a date by which you require the completed questionnaire;

(iii) providing an incentive such as a lottery number for those who return questionnaires on time; and

(iv) using a good covering letter.

(b) Misunderstanding is less likely with personal interviews because the interviewer can explain questions which the interviewee does not understand.

(c) Personal interviews are more suitable when deep or detailed questions are to be asked, since the interviewer can take the time required with each interviewee to explain the implications of the question. Also, the interviewer can *probe* for further information and encourage the respondent to think more deeply.

2   Disguised

15 *Qualitative methodologies*

Chapter Topic List	Syllabus reference
1 Setting the scene	4.3
2 Qualitative research	4.3
3 Projective techniques	4.3
4 Focus groups	4.3

Learning Outcomes

- After studying this chapter you will be able to design and carry out operational investigations into customer dynamics, customer perceptions of product/service performance, and customer satisfaction/delight, using qualitative methodologies.

Key Concepts Introduced

- Qualitative research

- Focus groups

Examples of Marketing at Work

- Focus groups

1   SETTING THE SCENE

1.1   This chapter looks at qualitative methodologies of examining customer attitudes and perceptions.

Exam tip

Projective techniques and focus groups are concentrated on as these are specifically mentioned by the senior examiner.

BPP
PUBLISHING

2   QUALITATIVE RESEARCH

Key Concept
Qualitative research is the process which aims to collect qualitative primary data, although qualitative data are also collected in the process of quantitative research, primarily questionnaires.
Its main methods are the open-ended interview, whether this be a depth interview (one-to-one) or a group discussion (focus group), and projective techniques.
The form of the data collected is narrative rather than isolated statements reduceable to numbers.
Its main purpose is to understand consumer behaviour and perceptions rather than to measure them.

2.1   The key to qualitative research is to allow the respondents to say what they feel and think in response to flexible, 'prompting' questioning, rather than to give their responses to set questions and often set answers in a questionnaire.

Unstructured interviews

2.2   Neither interviewer or respondent is bound by the structure of a questionnaire in an unstructured interview. Interviewers may have a checklist of topics to cover in questioning, but they are free to word such questions as they wish. The order in which questions are covered may also be varied. This will allow the respondent to control the data flow and for the interviewer to explore more thoroughly particular views of the respondent and why they are held. Unstructured interviews are a very useful way of capturing data which is qualitative in nature. Such interviews may also provide the researcher with relevant questions which could be put to a wider audience of respondents using structured or semi-structured interview techniques, especially if quantitative data is required.

Depth interviews

2.3   Motivational research often uses the psychoanalytic method of depth interviews. The pattern of questioning should assist the respondent to explore deeper levels of thought. Motives and explanations of behaviour often lie well below the surface which is only scraped by structured and semi-structured techniques of interviewing. It is a time-consuming and expensive method of data collection. Taped interviews and analysis of transcripts is often the way in which the depth interview and subsequent data analysis are conducted. A single individual or a small team may conduct depth interviewing. Depth interviews may have fewer than ten respondents.

2.4   The strengths of depth interviews include the following.

(a)   Longitudinal information (such as information on decision-making processes) can be gathered from one respondent at a time, thereby aiding clarity of interpretation and analysis.

(b)   Intimate and personal material can be more easily accessed and discussed.

(c)   Respondents are less likely to confine themselves simply to reiterating socially acceptable attitudes.

2.5   There are, however, disadvantages of depth interviews.

(a)   They are time consuming to conduct and to analyse. If each interview lasts between one and two hours, a maximum of three or four per day is often all that is possible.

(b)   They are more costly than group discussions.

(c) There is a temptation to begin treating depth interviews as if they were simply another form of questionnaire survey, thinking in terms of quantitative questions like 'how many' rather than qualitative issues like 'how', 'why' or 'what'.

(d) There is less opportunity for creativity.

2.6 In a depth interview the key line of communication is between the interviewer and the respondent. They have an open-ended conversation, not constrained by a formal questionnaire, and the qualitative data are captured as narrative by means of an audio or video tape.

2.7 The factors to consider when planning a depth interview are as follows.

(a) **Who should the respondent be?**

   (i) The kind of person depends on the subject being discussed. It may be a consumer interview for discussion of consumer goods or an executive interview for discussing industrial buying.

   (ii) The number of people undergoing depth interviews in the course of the research should be considered in the light of the time they take. 10-15 is usually more than enough.

   (iii) Respondents for consumer interviews are pre-recruited and asked to agree to the interview.

(b) **What type of interview?** Although depth interviews are usually one-to-one, there may be more than one respondent and there may also be an informant, there to give information about tangible things (eg how big the organisation's purchase budget is) but not about his own attitudes.

(c) **How long should it be?** Genuine depth interviews interpret the meanings and implications of what is said and can therefore take some time. By contrast, a mini-depth interview may take only 15 minutes, because it can focus on one, predefined topic like a pack design.

(d) **How structured should it be?** It can be totally open-ended, ranging over whatever topics come up, or it can be semi-structured with an interview guide and perhaps the use of show material.

(e) **Should show material be used?** The type of material that is commonly used includes mock-ups or prototypes, storyboards or concept boards, narrative tapes and animatics, a form of cartoon.

(f) **Where should the interview take place?** Usually at home or in the workplace.

3 PROJECTIVE TECHNIQUES

3.1 Many interview techniques rely on the assumption that you need only to ask people and they will tell you what you want to know. This is not always the case. People may respond differently to how they would act. People may tell you what they think you want to hear or give a different answer because their true answer may reflect badly on them or because they consider it too personal.

3.2 Alternatively, people may find difficulty in articulating their motives which lie buried deep within the sub-conscious mind. So as to overcome problems associated with articulating complex or sub-conscious motives, researchers have borrowed techniques developed by psychologists in their studies of mentally disturbed people who have difficulty explaining why they do things.

3.3 These techniques are referred to as **projective techniques**. Attitudes, opinions and motives are drawn out from the individual in response to given stimuli.

3.4 A number of techniques might be employed.

(a) In **inkblot tests**, subjects are shown inkblots and asked to describe what they see, in order to expose dominant imagery and preoccupations.

(b) **Third person**, or 'friendly martian' as it is sometimes called, is designed to get the respondent talking about issues which do not interest them. The researcher asks the respondent to describe what someone else might do (a friendly martian). For example, if someone wanted to buy a house, what do they need to do? Can you describe the steps they would need to take?

(c) **Word association** is based on an assumption that if a question is answered quickly, it is spontaneous and sub-conscious thoughts are therefore revealed. The person's conscious mind does not have time to think up an alternative response.

(d) **Sentence completion** is a useful way to get people to respond quickly so that underlying attitudes and opinions are revealed.

   Men who watch football are ....?
   Women wear red to ....?
   People who Morris dance are ....?

(e) In **thematic apperception tests** (TAT tests), people are shown a picture and asked to describe what is happening in the picture. They may be asked what happened just before or just after the picture. It is hoped that the descriptions reveal information about deeply held attitudes, beliefs, motives and opinions stored in the sub-conscious mind.

(f) **Story completion** allows the respondent to say what they think happens next and why.

(g) **Cartoon completion** is often used in competitions. There are usually speech balloons which need to be completed. A comment may be present in one and another left blank for the respondent to fill in.

(h) **Psychodrama** consists of fantasy situations. Respondents are often asked to imagine themselves as a product and describe their feelings about being used. Sometimes respondents are asked to imagine themselves as a brand and to describe particular attributes. For example, if a Chanel dress was a woman how would she differ from Dior, what would she be like?

Problems and value of projective research methods

3.5 There are a few problems associated with projective techniques.

(a) Hard evidence of their validity is lacking. Highly exotic motives can be imputed to quite ordinary buying decisions. (One study found that women preferred spray to pellets when it came to killing cockroaches because being able to spray the cockroaches directly and watch them die was an expression of hostility towards, and control over, men!)

(b) As with other forms of intensive qualitative research, the samples of the population can only be very small, and it may not be possible to generalise findings to the market as a whole.

(c) Analysis of projective test findings - as with depth interviews - is highly subjective and prone to bias. Different analysts can produce different explanations for a single set of test results.

(d) Many of the tests were not developed for the study of marketing or consumer behaviour, and may not therefore be considered scientifically valid as methods of enquiry in those areas.

(e) There are ethical problems with 'invasion' of an individual's subconscious mind in conditions where he is often not made aware that he is exposing himself to such probing. (On the other hand, one of the flaws in projective testing is that subjects may be all too well aware of the nature of the test. The identification of sexual images in inkblots has become a standard joke.)

3.6 The major drawback with projective techniques is that answers given by respondents require considerable and skilled analysis and interpretation. The techniques are most valuable in providing **insights** rather than **answers** to specific research questions.

3.7 However, motivational research is still in use. Emotion and subconscious motivation is still believed to be vitally important in consumer choice, and qualitative techniques can give marketers a deeper insight into those areas than conventional, quantitative marketing research.

Since motivational research often reveals hidden motives for product/brand purchase and usage, its main value lies in the following.

(a) Developing new promotional messages which will appeal to deep, often unrecognised, needs and associations

(b) Allowing the testing of brand names, symbols and advertising copy, to check for positive, negative and/or irrelevant associations and interpretations

(c) Providing hypotheses which can be tested on larger, more representative samples of the population, using more structured quantitative techniques (questionnaires, surveys and so on)

4 FOCUS GROUPS

4.1 Focus groups are useful in providing the researcher with qualitative data. Qualitative data can often provide greater insight than quantitative data and does not lend itself to the simple application of standard statistical methods.

> **Key Concept**
> **Focus groups** usually consist of 8 to 10 respondents and an interviewer taking the role of group moderator. The group moderator introduces topics for discussion and intervenes as necessary to encourage respondents or to direct discussions if they threaten to wander too far off the point. The moderator will also need to control any powerful personalities and prevent them from dominating the group.

4.2 Group discussions may be **audio or video tape recorded** for later analysis and interpretation. The researcher must be careful not to generalise too much from such small scale qualitative research. Group discussion is very dependent on the skill of the group moderator. It is inexpensive to conduct, it can be done quickly and it can provide useful, timely, qualitative data.

4.3 Focus groups are often used at the early stage of research to get a feel for the subject matter under discussion and to create possibilities for more structured research. Four to eight groups may be assembled and each group interviewed for one, two or three hours.

4.4 According to Raymond Kent (*Marketing Research in Action*), the **key advantages** of focus groups include the following.

(a) The group environment with 'everybody in the same boat' can be **less intimidating** than other techniques of research which rely on one-to-one contact (such as depth interviews).

(b) What respondents say in a group often **sparks off experiences** or ideas on the part of others.

(c) **Differences between consumers** are highlighted, making it possible to understand a range of attitudes in a short space of time.

(d) It is **easier to observe groups** and there is more to observe simply because of the intricate behaviour patterns within a collection of people.

(e) **Social and cultural influences** are highlighted.

(f) Groups provide a **social context** that is a 'hot-house' reflection of the real world.

(g) Groups are **cheaper and faster** than depth interviews.

4.5 The principal **disadvantages** of groups are as follows.

(a) Group processes may **inhibit some people from making a full contribution** and may encourage others to become exhibitionistic.

(b) Group processes **may stall** to the point where they cannot be retrieved by the moderator.

(c) Some groups may **take a life of their own,** so that what is said has validity only in the short-lived context of the group.

(d) It is not usually possible to identify **which group members said what,** unless the proceedings have been video recorded.

Focus groups

4.6 When planning qualitative research using focus groups, a number of factors need to be considered.

(a) **Type of group.** A standard group is of 7-9 respondents, but other types may also be used.

(b) **Membership.** Who takes part in the discussion depends on who the researcher wants to talk to (users or non-users, for instance) and whether they all need to be similar (homogenous).

(c) **Number of groups.** Having more than 12 groups in a research project would be very unusual, mainly because nothing new would come out of a thirteenth one!

(d) **Recruitment.** Usually on the basis of a quota sample: respondents are screened by a short questionnaire to see whether they are suitable. In order to persuade them to join in, the members are usually given an incentive plus expenses.

(e) **Discussion topics.** There will be decided by the researcher with regard to the purpose of the group discussion, that is the data that are required. There should be a number of topics since the interviewer needs to be able to restart discussion once a topic has been fully discussed.

Action Programme 1

What are the advantages and disadvantages of group discussions and depth interviews?

Marekting at Work

Focus Groups ['Focus groups fail to reach pin-sharp results'] Daily Telegraph, October 1998

Focus groups constitute a very popular mechanism through which customer attitudes and motivation can be teased out, analysed, measured and explored. Typically, a focus group will consist of between six and ten individuals, perhaps chosen because they have something in common (they might all be customers of a particular bank, for example, or alternatively could be linked by their readership of a specific local newspaper in which the focus group initiative has been advertised); the group is led by a moderator whose task is to encourage, clarify, facilitate, probe, and generally to ensure that everyone has the opportunity to contribute.

There are crucial doubts about the methodological purity of the focus group. On what basis are participants selected or recruited? Might there not be some distinctive features among those people who actively avoid focus group sessions? Of course, we do not know. What about the possibility of selective perception on the part of the moderator, or even the possibility that the focus group has been set up in the first place in order to supply some 'evidence' to justify a course of action which the marketing or customer service function has already decided upon? After all, the focus group session itself is usually conducted in circumstances of some secrecy; the result is that nobody can authoritatively challenge the moderator's report of the process and the outputs achieved. If the moderator has manipulated the event, so that certain contributions are highlighted (as 'typical') whilst others are ignored or downplayed, then who is to blow the gaff - especially if the people reading the moderator's report are ready to be persuaded anyway?

If the focus group cannot be justified by reference to methodological elegance and the robustness of its empirical achievements, then its popularity must be explained in other ways. Some have argued that the focus group is simply a child of the times: it exemplifies a move away from more quantitative, statistically-focused study incorporating testable hypotheses, carefully-structured samples, control/experimental groups, emergent conclusions and refined action programmes, towards an affinity towards 'touchy-feely' thinking. In addition, it has to be conceded that 'traditional' approaches to scientific investigation, at least in the field of marketing, have not yielded particularly impressive results so far as the prediction of customer behaviour is concerned.

Yet the limitations of the focus group should be clearly understood. First, if surveys have been properly pilot-tested, and if the samples are systematically chosen, then their results should permit the development of statistical inferences about people's behaviour. Predicting customer behaviour from the achievements of a focus group would be very foolish indeed: the groups are very small and (for that reason alone) unrepresentative; no two focus groups will generate the same material (if it is claimed that they have done, then somebody is manipulating the evidence); if different moderators are used for the same focus-group population, then the outputs will be different. In other words, focus group results are not replicable. Because the unreliable is seldom valid, then it is also likely that focus groups commentaries do not measure what they say they are measuring.

Furthermore, focus groups rejoice in individual differences. This is acceptable when large-scale systematic research is undertaken, since the effects of such differences can be ironed out, but within the confines of a focus group the expression of such differences simply means that the result is confused. Confusion is of no help to the decision-maker seeking clarity: if decision-makers wanted a confused picture, they could generate that themselves - why would they incur the expense of a focus group?

Finally, the focus group has to cope with the characteristic problems created when a collection of people works together. Some people have what is called 'evaluation apprehension', that is, they are frightened of appearing foolish and so will not say what they really think; others will join the focus group merely to take advantage of its immediate rewards and will contribute little; others contribute far too much, given the (often false) impression that their views reflect those of the majority or even of the group as a whole. Quiet, reflective types find it difficult to think constructively and to contribute intelligently because the group's 'discussion' is dominated by a few; sometimes they will tacitly admit defeat and present to support an opinion which in private they abhor.

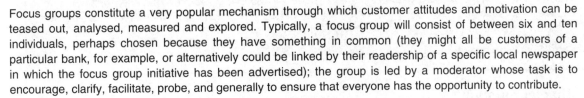*BPP*
PUBLISHING

As Furnham points out, research about brainstorming has consistently shown that compared with the pooled ideas of people working alone, brainstorming groups nearly always produce fewer and lower quality innovative ideas. Focus groups suffer from the same limitations. The process of being in one is often hugely enjoyable, and this leads to the delusion that the quality of the group's output is similarly worthwhile. We should face the truth: focus groups are often popular because they enable advocates of a particular customer-service or marketing innovation to secure some evidence that the recipients of the innovation will welcome it (there will always be at least one focus group contributor who will say the right things). To that extent, therefore, focus groups supply some - admittedly small-scale, admittedly qualitative, and admittedly spurious - support for an established position. This is a substantial advantage, especially for those innovators who suspect that 'proper' research, involving appropriately large-scale samples, might not yield the 'truth'.

Exam tip

The guidance notes for this syllabus refer to a need to appreciate features, benefits, hazards and applications associated with focus groups. The above article was supplied by the senior examiner for inclusion in this text.

Chapter roundup

- The main method of qualitative research is the interview.

- Projective techniques attempt to draw out attitudes, opinions and motives by a variety of methods.

- Focus groups concentrate on discussion of chosen topics in an attempt to find out attitudes. They do have limitations despite advantages such as the ability to observe a whole range of responses at the same time.

Quick quiz

1   What is an unstructured interview? (see para 2.2)

2   What are some strengths of depth interviews? (2.4)

3   Give some examples of projective techniques. (3.4)

4   What is the major drawback associated with projective techniques? (3.6)

5   What are the principal disadvantages of focus groups? (4.5)

Action Programme Review

1

Group discussions	Depth interview
Advantages	
(a) Less intimidating	(a) Decision making *processes* can be analysed
(b) Easily observed	(b) Majority *and* minority opinion can be captured
(c) Range of attitudes can be measured	(c) Sensitive topics more easily discussed
(d) Social aspect reflects real world	(d) 'Unusual' behaviour can be discussed
(e) Dynamic and creative	
(f) Cheaper	
Disadvantages	
(a) Participants may not express what they really think - they may be inhibited or they may be showing off	(a) Time consuming
	(b) Less creative
	(c) More expensive
(b) Views may be unrealistic - meaningful in a group context but not for the individual	

16 *Secondary information sources*

Chapter Topic List	Syllabus reference
1 Setting the scene	4.4
2 Secondary data	4.4
3 Internal secondary data	4.4
4 Published statistics	4.4
5 Market research agencies	4.4
6 Benefits, risks and dangers of reliance on secondary data	4.4

Learning Outcomes

- After completing this chapter you will be able to design and carry out operational investigations into customer dynamics, customer perceptions of product/service performance, and customer satisfaction/delight, using secondary information sources.

Key Concepts Introduced

- Secondary data
- Desk research

Examples of Marketing at Work

- Teenagers Europe

1   SETTING THE SCENE

1.1   The collection of **secondary data** involves the seeking out of **data which already exists in some form.**

> **Key Concept**
> **Secondary data** is not created specifically for the purpose at hand but is used and analysed to provide information where primary data is either not sufficient or is not being collected for whatever reason.
> **Desk research** is the term used to describe the proactive search for existing data, usually as an initial, exploratory research purpose.

1.2   Typical desk research activities include:

(a)   making use of **library sources**, such as journals, periodicals, recent academic books etc;

(b)   accessing the **organisation's information systems** and records, which is information gathered by another department for a different purpose to the research in hand. Internal data would include:

    (i)   production data about quantities produced, materials and labour used etc;

    (ii)   data about inventory;

    (iii)   data about sales volumes, analysed by sales area, salesman, quantity, profitability, distribution outlet, customer etc;

    (iv)   data about marketing itself - ie promotion and brand data etc;

    (v)   all cost and management accounting data;

    (vi)   financial management data relating to the capital structure of capital tied up in stocks and debtors etc;

(c)   tapping into **industry internal on-line databases**;

(d)   **buying in data and reports** prepared externally, either as primary data for another organisation which is then syndicated, or as secondary data material for all users.

Action Programme 1

Can you think of any limitations to desk research?

1.3   Common sense suggests that it would usually be unwise to embark on substantial amounts of primary research **without doing some desk research first**; checking what is currently known can give insights into how and what to investigate further. In addition, database material can go back several years, and so **trends** may be extrapolated. Finally, a lot of research is done on the **business-to-business market** - the industrial market - and so market research in non-consumer areas is more likely to have a desk research phase.

2   SECONDARY DATA

2.1   As consumers ourselves (as well as marketers) we are continually using secondary data for our own purchasing decisions. Secondary data is data neither collected by, nor specifically for, the user, and is often collected under conditions not known by the user. If you plan a trip to the theatre you will read the reviews or talk to friends who have seen the production. **We make use of such secondary data sources on a daily basis.** However, these sources **cannot replace the experience itself**, nor the more energetic enquiries we might decide to make ourselves. You might see a dress or suit you like in a fashion magazine, but you would still go out and look at the garment 'in the flesh', feel it, try it on and so forth, before you decided to buy it.

The use of secondary data

2.2   With the developments over the last few years in communications technology, **information is now available in every form and on a huge scale**. The problem is how to decide what information is required.

2.3   The use of secondary data will generally come early in the process of marketing research. In some cases, secondary data may be sufficient in itself, but not always. Newson-Smith (1988) states that secondary data:

- can provide a **backdrop to primary research**;
- can act as a **substitute for field research**;
- can be used as a **technique in itself**;
- can be used in **acquisition studies**.

Backdrop to primary research

2.4   In **unfamiliar territory**, it is natural that the marketer will carry out some **basic research** in the area, using journals, existing market reports, the press and any contacts with relevant knowledge. Such investigations will aid the marketer by providing guidance on a number of areas.

- Possible data sources
- Data collection
- Methods of collection (relevant populations, sampling methods and so on)
- The general state of the market (demand, competition and the like)

Substitute for field research

2.5   The (often substantial) **cost** of primary research **might be avoided** should existing secondary data be sufficient. This data would not be perfect for the needs of the business; and to judge whether it *is* enough, or whether primary research ought to be undertaken, a cost-benefit analysis should be implemented.

2.6   There are some situations however, in which secondary data is bound to be **insufficient**. Where, say, the constitution of the marketing mix is being investigated, each situation is so unique that primary research will be a necessity.

A technique in itself

2.7   Some types of information can **only be acquired through secondary data**, in particular **trends** over time. The historical data published on, say, trends in the behaviour of a market over time, cannot realistically be replaced by a one-off study. It has also been pointed out (by Baker 1991) that such data is usually gathered by census, a superior method to sampling.

2.8   Secondary data may also be used to set the parameters for primary research.

Acquisition studies

2.9   In the secretive and competitive world of takeovers (particularly contested takeovers), **primary research is not always possible**. Field research would show the aggressor's hand too soon and so secondary data sources would be exploited, mainly in two areas.

    (a) **Company description**: history, structure, financial situation, production methods, employee resources and so on

    (b) **Products and markets**: products and product policy, promotional activity, competitors and markets

2.10 In spite of all these uses of secondary data, it has been shown that many businesses do not use secondary data to full advantage. Many sources are left untapped.

3 INTERNAL SECONDARY DATA

3.1 Internal secondary data are **records inside the organisation**, gathered by another department or section for the research task in hand. They therefore include the following.

(a) **Production data** about quantities produced, materials and labour resources used and so on

(b) Data about **stock**

(c) Data about **sales volumes**, analysed by sales area, sales person, quantity, price, profitability, distribution outlet, customer and the like

(d) Data about **marketing** itself, such as promotion and brand data

(e) All **cost and management accounting data**

(f) **Financial management data** relating to the capital structure of the firm, capital tied up in stocks and debtors and so on

3.2 Webb (1992) gives an alternative summary of internal sources of data.

(a) **Accounts.** Contain information on:

- customer's name and location
- type and quantity of product purchased
- costs of sales, advertising and so on

(b) **Sales records.** Contain information on

- markets
- products
- distribution systems

(c) **Other reports.** Contain information on

- trade associations and trade fairs
- exhibitions
- customers' complaint letters
- previous marketing research reports
- conferences

3.3 You can see that some of the **information collected** by particular departments in an organisation would be **useful to other departments** within the business. It is often the case, however, that there is little inter-departmental communication of such information. In an organisation with good information channels between departments, such data would be reported to other interested departments. For example, bad debt and credit control analysis should be passed from accounts to the sales department. Similarly, the breakdown of customer by geographic location indicated by the return of guarantee cards could be sent to the sales department from the customer service department (Webb, 1992).

3.4 A problem may be that information passed from one department to another is in a **format which is unsuitable** for that second department to use. The increasing use of management information systems has made data manipulation straightforward. This allows inter-departmental data to be adjusted as required.

3.5 Webb also points out the **failure** of most information systems to incorporate a **reporting system** which can **use the expertise and knowledge of customers held by the sales force**. These people are, after all, the only ones in the company to meet the customers face to face.

3.6 Despite the problems associated with internal secondary data, it can be extremely useful for sales and marketing, as the following examples show.

(a) **Order/sales statistics (by customer)**. An understanding of who the customers are allows marketing activity to be directed appropriately (promotions, invitation to sponsored events and so on). Having a correct view of the types of existing customers and where they live allows consumer product companies to use geodemographic databases to target other like-minded people susceptible to buying the product.

Sales representatives need to understand **who their most important customers are** to be able to manager their time effectively. Very important customers may be categorised as needing contact once a month, medium-sized customers as needing to be seen every quarter and so on.

Trends need to be monitored as the 'league table' of customers will change and new important customers should be given the most appropriate treatment.

(b) **Sales statistics (by product)**. These allow product managers to monitor the popularity of products to help decide where to direct the marketing activity and which products to withdraw so that the most appropriate ones are available. Having an appropriate mix of products is required to maintain good customer relationships.

(c) **Delivery details**. Where these are different from customer/order details, these help the representatives identify new contacts and new sites/establishments.

(d) **Profitability (by product/by customer)**. It is important that the sales force put their energy into spending time with their most profitable customers and building relations with them accordingly.

(e) **Complaints**. Having an understanding of the nature of complaints can help sales and marketing people communicate with the customers more effectively. It may be a question of explaining the functioning of the product differently or changing the customers' expectation and perceptions.

(f) **Stock levels**. Knowing that there is stock that needs to be shifted quickly or that a particular item will need two weeks' notice can help the sales staff seem more professional and interested in their customers.

(g) **Debtor information**. A representative could have spent a lot of time building up a good relationship only to have the time wasted by a letter going out from the accounts department threatening to withdraw credit facilities. It would be preferable to discuss such matters with the sales manager and in certain instances ask the manager or representative to discuss it directly with the customer (or at least know that it may not be a good time to call!).

3.7 The **basis of good relationships** with customers is having the **right amount of information** about one's own business and the customers' business. Much of that information is available in-house and it is important that sales and marketing staff are given such data and also that they communicate back to other departments any intelligence acquired (impending bankruptcy or an imminent large order for example) so that the appropriate steps can be taken by other departments.

4 PUBLISHED STATISTICS

4.1 It is with **external** data that the problems of volume and multiplicity of sources becomes a problem. The best approach, particularly in completely unknown areas, is to start with general information and then 'telescope' on to more specific data on industries and then individual companies or markets.

Directories

4.2 Examples (of business directories) include the following (although there are many others).

- Kompass Register (Kompass)
- Who owns Whom (Dun and Bradstreet)
- Key British Enterprises (Dun and Bradstreet)

As mentioned above, these directories can make a good starting point. The information provided is usually on industries and markets, manufacturers (size, location), products, sales and profits.

Computerised databases

4.3 These include the following.

- ACORN (consumption indices by class of neighbourhood)
- PRESTEL (British Telecom)
- TEXTLINE (abstracts and articles from approximately 80 newspapers)
- Marketing Surveys Index (CIM)
- MRS Yearbook (Market Research Agencies and their specialisms)
- TGI and other syndicated omnibus surveys

4.4 Webb (1992) also lists European databases.

- European Kompass Online
- Financial Times Company Information
- Hoppenstedt Austria/Germany/Netherlands
- Jordanwatch
- PTS Prompt
- Reuters Textline

4.5 With computer databases, it is usual for the researcher's computer to be connected to the database computer by modem. These databases are not cheap to use, but it is usually much less expensive than collecting the information oneself. A trained operator should be used to begin with, to avoid expensive waste of the resources.

Associations

4.6 There are associations in almost every field of business and leisure activity. All these bodies collect and publish data for their members which can be of great interest to other users. Examples of such bodies include the Road Haulage Association (RHA), the British Association of Ski Instructors and the Institute of Chartered Accountants in England and Wales.

Government agencies

4.7 There is a wealth of published statistics which can be used in marketing research. There are two prime sources - government and non-government.

4.8 The government is a major source of economic information and information about industry and population trends. Examples of government publications are as follows.

(a) The **Annual Abstract of Statistics** and its monthly equivalent, the **Monthly Digest of Statistics**. These contain data about manufacturing output, housing, population etc.

(b) The **Digest of UK Energy Statistics** (published annually).

(c) **Housing and Construction Statistics** (published quarterly).

(d) **Financial Statistics** (monthly).

(e) **Economic Trends** (monthly).

(f) **Census of Population**. The Office for National Statistics publishes continuous datasets including the **National Food Survey**, the **Household Survey** and the **Family Expenditure Survey**.

(g) **Census of Production** (annual). This has been described as 'one of the most important sources of desk research for industrial marketers'. It provides data about production by firms in each industry in the UK.

(h) **Department of Employment Gazette** (monthly) gives details of employment in the UK.

(i) **British Business**, published weekly by the Department of Trade and Industry, gives data on industrial and commercial trends at home and overseas.

(j) **Business Monitor** (published by the Business Statistics Office), gives detailed information about various industries.

(k) **Social Trends** (annually).

4.9 Official statistics are also published by other government bodies such as the European Union, the United Nations and local authorities.

4.10 Non-government sources of information include the following.

(a) Companies and other organisations specialising in the provision of economic and financial data (eg the *Financial Times* Business Information Service, the Data Research Institute, Reuters and the Extel Group)

(b) Directories and yearbooks, such as Kompass or Kelly's Directory

(c) Professional institutions (eg Chartered Institute of Marketing, Industrial Marketing Research Association, British Institute of Management, Institute of Practitioners in Advertising)

(d) Specialist libraries, such as the City Business Library in London, collect published information from a wide variety of sources

(e) Trade associations, trade unions and Chambers of Commerce

(f) Trade journals

(g) Commercial organisations such as banks and TV networks

(h) Market research agencies

Action Programme 2

Most industries are served by one or more trade journals which can provide invaluable information on new developments in the industry, articles about competitors' products, details of industry costs and prices and so on.

Find out to what trade journals your organisation subscribes. Look through a number of them and note the type of information they contain and assess how that information may be used by both you and other members of your organisation.

Environmental scanning

4.11 **Environmental scanning** is a grand term for the process of **keeping one's eyes and ears open to what is going on generally in the market place**, especially with respect to competitors, and more widely in the technological, social, economic and political environment. Much of the data will be qualitative but they would be systematically logged and backed up by quantitative data if possible.

4.12 The result of environmental scanning is market intelligence. Its sources are:

(a) business and financial newspapers, especially the *Financial Times* and the *Wall Street Journal*;

(b) general business magazines, such as the *Economist* and *Business Week*;

(c) trade journals, such as *Campaign*;

(d) academic journals, such as *Harvard Business Review*;

(e) attending conferences, exhibitions, courses and trade fairs;

(f) making use of salesforce feedback;

(g) developing and making use of a network of personal contacts in the trade; and, most importantly

(h) watching competitors.

Exam tip

Scan some of the above publications for relevant articles and use your own work experience to provide examples to use in your exam.

Action Programme 3

Here is a small selection of headlines from *The Daily Telegraph* (August 8, 1995)

(a) Two tube strikes a week being planned by unions
(b) Inquiries pour in for jobs at Siemens
(c) Protesters halt royal tree felling
(d) Film comeback for Mickey Mouse at 67

In each case what sort of organisations should take note of the articles as part of their environmental scanning for marketing threats and opportunities?

4.13 With regard to watching competitors, a **competitor intelligence system** needs to be set up to cope with a vast amount of data from:

- financial statements;
- common customers and suppliers;
- inspection of a competitor's products;
- the competitor's former employees;
- job advertisements.

In other words there is a combination of published data and 'field data', which need to be compiled (eg clipping services, standard monthly reports on competitors' activities), catalogued, for easy access, and analysed (eg summarised, ranked by reliability, extrapolating data from financial reports).

4.14 The object of what is usually an informal but constant process is to ensure that the organisation is not caught by surprise by developments which could have and should have been picked up. The organisation needs to be able to adapt always to changing circumstances.

> **Exam tip**
> What information does your organisation hold on its competitors? How does it obtain that information? What does it use it for? Get used to thinking about practical application of textbook theory!

Other published sources

4.15 This group includes all other publications, including the following.

(a) Some **digests** and **pocket books**

- Lifestyle Pocket Book (annual by the Advertising Association)
- Retail Pocket Book (annual by Nielsen)
- A to Z of UK Marketing Data (Euromonitor)
- UK in figures (annual, free from Office for National Statistics)

(b) Some important periodicals (often available in the public libraries)

- Economist (general)
- Campaign (advertising)
- ADMAP (advertising)
- Mintel (consumer market reports)
- Retail Business (consumer market reports)
- BRAD (all media selling advertising space in the UK including TV, radio, newspapers and magazines)

4.16 Since this heading can include all newspapers, journals and so on, it would be wise to use an expert librarian as a guide to the 'way in' to this information. Webb (1992) also suggests hard copy directories of abstracts including the following.

- Business Periodicals Index
- ANBAR Management Abstracts
- Research Index
- ABI/Inform

> **Action Programme 4**
>
> As stated previously, this section has only given an indication of where to find secondary data and what type of information is available. This week, go to your nearest large library and look through all the 'sources' of secondary data you can find.

5 MARKET RESEARCH AGENCIES

5.1 The sources of secondary data we have looked at so far have generally been **free** because they are **in the public domain**. Inexpensiveness is an advantage which can be offset by the fact that the information is unspecific and needs considerable analysis before being useable.

5.2 A middle step between adapting secondary data and commissioning primary research is the **purchase of data collected by market research companies** or business publishing houses. The data tend to be expensive but less costly than primary research.

5.3 There are a great many commercial sources of secondary data, and a number of guides to these sources are available.

- *The Source Book*, Key Note Publications
- *Guide to Official Statistics*, HMSO
- *Published Data of European Markets*, Industrial Aids Ltd
- *Compendium of Marketing Information Sources*, Euromonitor
- *Market-Search*, British Overseas Trade Board

5.4 Commonly used sources of data on particular industries and markets are:

- Key Note Publications;
- *Retail Business*, Economist Intelligence Unit;
- Mintel publications;
- *Market Research GB*, Euromonitor.

Consumer panels

5.5 A form of continuous research which result in secondary data often bought in by marketers is that generated by **consumer panels**. These constitute a representative sample of individuals and households whose buying activity in a defined area is monitored either continuously (every day, with results aggregated) or at regular intervals, *over a period of time*. There are panels set up to monitor purchases of groceries, consumer durables, cars, baby products and many others.

5.6 Most consumer panels consisting of a **representative cross-section of consumers** who have agreed to give information about their attitudes or buying habits (through personal visits or postal questionnaires) at regular intervals of time. Consumer panels with personal visits are called **home audit panels**.

(a) It is **difficult** to select a panel which is a **representative** sample. The panel must be representative of:

(i) all the customers in the target market;

(ii) the decision making units who will make the purchase decision (eg male as well as female partners).

(b) Panel members **tend to become sophisticated** in interviewing techniques and responses and so the panel becomes 'corrupt' (but Superpanel overcomes this to some extent).

(c) It is **difficult to maintain a stable personnel**; turnover of members may be high and this will affect results as new members are enlisted.

5.7 Consumer panels generate a vast amount of data which need to be sorted if they are to be digestible. Analyses available include:

(a) **standard trend analysis**, showing how the market and its major brands have fared since the last analysis, grossed up to reflect the entire UK population or a particular region;

(b) **special analyses** depending on industrial preferences. Common ones are:

(i) source of purchase analysis;

(ii) frequency of purchase analysis;

(iii) **demographic analysis** (in terms of household age, number of children, ACORN classification etc); and

(iv) tracking of individuals, to show their degree of brand loyalty, how and when they change brands etc.

Retail panels

5.8 **Trade audits** are carried out among panels of wholesalers and retailers, and the term 'retail audits' refers to panels of retailers only. A research firm sends 'auditors' to selected outlets at regular intervals to count stock and deliveries, thus enabling an estimate of throughput to be made. Sometimes it is possible to do a universal audit of all retail outlets. EPOS makes the process both easier and more universal.

5.9 The audits provide details of the following.

(a) Retail sales for selected products and brands, sales by different type of retail outlet, market shares and brand shares.

(b) Retail stocks of products and brands (enabling a firm subscribing to the audit to compare stocks of its own goods with those of competitors).

(c) Selling prices in retail outlets, including information about discounts.

The Nielsen Retail Index

5.10 Nielsen was the first market research organisation to establish continuous retail tracking operations in the UK. The Nielsen Index is not an index in the statistical sense (the ratio of a current value to a past value expressed as a percentage), but refers instead to a **range of continuous sales and distribution measurements**, embracing ten separate product fields.

- Grocery
- Health and beauty
- Confectionery
- Home improvements
- Cash and carry outlets
- Sportswear
- Liquor
- Toys
- Tobacco
- Electrical

5.11 These indexes together measure a large number of sales and distribution variables for over 600 different product categories and over 120,000 brands and associated brand variants.

5.12 Data are collected from the **major multiples** (like Tesco and Sainsbury) through their EPOS systems. For other types of shop where EPOS data are not available, a monthly audit of stocks is undertaken and, using data from deliveries, the level of what sales must have been since the last audit is determined. It is essential to take account of non-EPOS retail units otherwise the survey would generate misleading data.

5.13 Increasingly, **Nielsen clients receive their data electronically** on databases, Nielsen having developed a range of data management and analysis software. A Nielsen service called Inf*Act Workstation offers a powerful yet flexible personal, computer-based decision support system.

AGB's superpanel

5.14 AGB's Superpanel consists of 8,500 households, covering the **purchases of some 28,000 individuals** aged between 5 and 79, who are resident in **domestic households** across Great Britain which are equipped with telephones.

5.15 Data collection is through **personal data terminals** equipped with a laser light pen. The terminal is designed to resemble a digital phone and is kept in a modem linked to the domestic power supply and the telephone socket. Data capture is via overnight polling (which means that AGB's central computer dials each panel number in turn and accesses the data stored in the modem).

5.16 All that is required from informants is that when they unpack their shopping, they pass the laser light pen over the barcode for each item, and also enter standardised data about the date, shop(s) visited, prices paid and so on. The process incorporates procedures for entering details of products either without barcodes or which have a bar-code that is difficult to read.

5.17 Recruitment to the AGB Superpanel uses a multi-stage procedure. A large sample of households are screened to identify those in each sampling point eligible for the service and with known demographics. For this purpose, AGB uses personal home interviews, some 200,000 annually, within 270 parliamentary constituencies (about half the total number).

5.18 The households with the relevant target demographics are then selected and the 'housewife' (who may be male or female) for each household is contacted by phone. If the initial contact proves positive, the household as a whole is briefed and the equipment installed.

Taylor Nelson's Omnimas

5.19 Taylor Nelson claims Omnimas to be one of the largest single **random omnibus surveys** in the world, with some **2,100 adults being interviewed face-to-face** every week.

5.20 A random sampling approach is employed, using the **electoral registers** from 233 parliamentary constituencies selected in proportion to size within each of the ten standard regions of the UK.

5.21 **Each interviewer has a minimum of 13 interviews** to do a week. Because the only quota set is that the interviewer should obtain either six men and seven women, or vice versa, there is a control on sex, but everything else depends on the randomness of the sample.

5.22 The Omnimas questionnaire is divided into three sections.

(a) **A continuous section**, including questions asked on every survey and inserted on behalf of a particular client

(b) An **ad-hoc section** of questions included on a one-off basis

(c) A **classification section** that includes all the demographic questions

5.23 Given an average completion time of 25 minutes per respondent and the 20-30 seconds needed to administer an average question, the total number of Omnimas questions will not be more than about 60-70. Most questions are fixed-choice, with a predetermined number of possible responses, but some clients require open-ended questions and the Omnimas approach allows for a few of these to be included.

BMRB's Target Group Index (TGI)

5.24 TGI's purpose is to increase the efficiency of marketing operations by identifying and describing **target groups** of consumers and their **exposure to the media** (newspapers, magazines, television and radio) and the extent to which they see or hear other media.

5.25 In design, the TGI is a regular interval survey and is also 'single source', in that it covers both **product usage data** and **media exposure data**.

5.26 Respondents are questioned on a number of areas; **purchase behaviour and media use are cross-tabulated** to enable more accurate media audience targeting.

- Their use of 400 different products covering 3,500 brands
- Their readership of over 170 magazines and newspapers
- Cinema attendance
- ITV television watching
- Listening patterns for commercial radio stations
- Their lifestyles, based on nearly 200 attitude questions

5.27 The major **product fields** covered are foods, household goods, medicaments, toiletries and cosmetics, drink, confectionery, tobacco, motoring, clothing, leisure, holidays, financial services and consumer durables. It is worth noting that respondents are only asked about the use, ownership and consumption of the products identified, not about purchases made or prices paid.

5.28 The **lifestyle questions** are in the form of Likert-type attitude statements with which people are asked to agree or disagree on a five-point scale from 'definitely agree' to 'definitely disagree'. These attitude statements cover the main areas of food, drink, shopping, diet/health, personal appearance, DIY, holidays, finance, travel, media, motivation/self-perception, plus questions on some specific products and attitudes to sponsorship.

5.29 Each questionnaire runs to more than 90 pages and can take four hours to complete. However, the document is totally pre-coded and adapted for optical mark reading, with respondents being able to indicate their replies by pencil strokes. There are three versions of the questionnaire, for men, for housewives, and for other women.

5.30 TGI results supply enormous amounts of information, both within categories and cross-tabulated against other relevant categories. There are about 25,000 responses per annum.

(a) **Total numbers of product users** for each demographic category

(b) **Percentages of product users** in each demographic category

(c) Information on **heavy/medium/light** and **non-users** for each product or product category

(d) For **brands and product fields** with more than one million claimed users, consumption can be **cross-tabulated** against a range of **demographic variables** including sex, age, social class, area, number of children, and media usage

(e) Brand usage tables, listing the following.

    (i)   **Solus users** - users of the product group who use the brand exclusively

    (ii)   **Most-often users** - those who prefer it, but use another brand as well

    (iii)   **Minor users** - whose who do not discriminate between brands

5.31 TGI appears in 34 volumes, published annually in July and August, but subscribers have **on-line access** to datasets for which they have subscribed, and they can analyse the data on their own PCs.

6 BENEFITS, RISKS AND DANGERS OF RELIANCE ON SECONDARY DATA

6.1 When considering the quality of the secondary data it is a good idea to consider the following characteristics of it:

(a) the **producers** of the data (they may have an axe to grind; trade associations may not include data which runs counter to the interest of its members);

(b) the **reason for the data** being collected in the first place;

(c) the **collection method** (random samples with a poor response rate are particularly questionable);

(d) how **old** the data is (government statistics and information based on them are often relatively dated, though information technology has speeded up the process);

(e) **how parameters were defined**. For instance, the definition of family used by some researchers could well be very different to that used by others.

Advantages and disadvantages of secondary data

6.2 The **advantages** arising from the use of secondary data include the following.

(a) Secondary data may solve the problem without the need for any primary research: **time and money is thereby saved**.

(b) Cost savings can be substantial because secondary data sources are a great deal **cheaper** than those for primary research.

(c) Secondary data, while not necessarily fulfilling all the needs of the business, can be of great use by:

    (i)   **setting the parameters**, defining a hypothesis, highlighting variables, in other words, helping to focus on the central problem;

    (ii)   **providing guidance**, by showing past methods of research and so on, for primary data collection;

    (iii)   **helping to assimilate the primary research** with past research, highlighting trends and the like;

    (iv)   **defining sampling parameter**, (target populations, variables and so on).

6.3 There are, of course, plenty of **disadvantages** to the use of secondary data.

(a) **Relevance**. The data may not be relevant to the research objectives in terms of the data content itself, classifications used or units of measurement.

(b) **Cost**. Although secondary data is usually cheaper than primary data, some specialist reports can cost large amounts of money. A cost-benefit analysis will determine whether such secondary data should be used or whether primary research would be more economical.

(c) **Availability**. Secondary data may not exist in the specific product or market area.

(d) **Bias**. The secondary data may be biased, depending on who originally carried it out and for what purpose. Attempts should be made to obtain the most original source of the data, to assess it for such bias.

(e) **Accuracy**. The accuracy of the data should be questioned. Weiers (1988) suggests the following checklist.

(i) Was the sample representative?

(ii) Was the questionnaire or other measurement instrument(s) properly constructed?

(iii) Were possible biases in response or in non-response corrected and accounted for?

(iv) Was the data properly analysed using appropriate statistical techniques?

(v) Was a sufficiently large sample used?

(vi) Does the report include the raw data?

(vii) To what degree were the field-workers supervised?

In addition, was any raw data omitted from the final report, and why?

(f) **Sufficiency**. Even after fulfilling all the above criteria, the secondary data may be insufficient and primary research would therefore be necessary.

Action Programme 5

How can secondary data help when a firm is considering an international advertising campaign?

6.4 The golden rule when using secondary data is **use only meaningful data**. It is obviously sensible to begin with internal sources and a firm with a good management information system should be able to provide a great deal of data. External information should be consulted in order of ease and speed of access: directories, catalogues and indexes before books, abstracts and periodicals (Stoll and Stewart, 1984). A good librarian should be a great help.

6.5 It is worth remembering Peter Jackson's comment (in *Desk Research*).

'All that is published is not necessarily accurate. It may even be quite untrue. However, print conveys authority and there is a common tendency to take published data, uncritically, at face value. Computer databases possibly legitimise dubious data to an even greater degree. The thorough researcher should therefore attempt, wherever possible, to evaluate the accuracy and reliability of secondary data.'

Marketing at Work

'Teenagers Europe is the first multi-country, single-source survey of teenage product use, media consumption and attitudes. Questionnaires were completed by 11- to 19- year-old groups in Britain, France, Germany and Italy. They covered topics ranging from TV viewing to fast-food chains, from sportswear purchasing to views on key social and political issues.

The survey yields a mass of information which is comparable across all four countries, some of which confirms existing hypotheses and some of which surprises.

In terms of market size, the survey base represents a teenage (11 to 19) population of 27 million (64 per cent of the teenage population of the EU). This group has a total disposable income of about £24.8 billion.

The average weekly income differs significantly from country to country. British teenagers, for example, enjoy an income more than twice that of their French counterparts.

But while income levels differ, patterns of expenditure show marked similarity. Clothes are the top priority for teenagers in all countries with the exception of Britain, where most is spent on going out. Music is important in terms of spending and it is worth noting that 60 per cent of teenagers agree with the statement that they "couldn't live without music".

Personal appearance is equally important to teenagers in all four countries – nearly half agree that they like keeping up with the latest fashions, and some two-thirds feel that they take a lot of care with the way they look. Shopping habits confirm this. About a fifth of Italian and British teenagers go shopping for clothes at least 26 times a year. Germans are less keen: 40 per cent go clothes shopping less than six times a year, and they are also more likely to agree that "shopping for clothes is boring".

Teenagers Europe shows that "pester power" varies markedly across the four countries. The toiletries market is a good example. It is not the kind of product that teenagers would necessarily expect to buy for themselves. But they do have views on the brands they prefer. Just under half of Britain's teenagers use spot cream, a slightly higher proportion than in the other three countries. Of these, three-quarters decide what brand to use themselves, in Britain and Germany while just over half the teenagers in France and Italy make that decision, with a third leaving it entirely to their parents. Similar patterns can be seen across other markets.

The strategic value of the survey's information on product and brand use is greatly enhanced by the media consumption data. Some of the most revealing statistics in this area relate to TV viewing and computer use. British teenagers watch TV for more than four hours every day – more than any other country surveyed.

This figure is probably helped by the fact that three-quarters of British teenage TV viewers have a set in their bedroom, well ahead of Germany and Italy, and more than twice the proportion measured in France.

Computer use is also more widespread in Britain – nine out of ten teenagers use one, compared with less than 60 per cent of German teenagers. A sixth of the British sample use them to access the Internet – a market currently growing faster in Britain than elsewhere in Europe. Perhaps reassuringly, about half of the teenagers across the four countries agree that they "really enjoy reading books". Given the extensive consumption of broadcast media and the relative consistency of expenditure patterns across the four countries, does the study reveal evidence of pan-European branding at work?

There are some impressive examples: over 70 per cent of all teenagers drink Coke; and more than six in ten have visited McDonald's in the past three months. But there are some surprises too: ten per cent of respondents claim to use Clearasil spot treatments – a market of nearly 3 million loyal users across the four countries surveyed. Impulse deodorant shows strongly, as does Sensodyne toothpaste, despite not being the top brand in the UK.

The research also opens up a further dimension for planners, with the inclusion of 160 attitude statements. Six clusters of teenagers have been identified and it may yet prove possible to characterise the elusive "Euro-teenage" – and to reach that audience through his or her favourite media.'

Marketing Week, 11 December 1997

Chapter roundup

- The collection of secondary data is often referred to as desk research, since it does not involve the collection of raw data from the market direct. Desk research includes using library sources, the organisation's information system, databases and internal reports.

- Environmental scanning is an informal process resulting in the possession of market intelligence. Sources include newspapers, journals and attending conferences.

- Useful statistics are published by government and non-government sources.

- Data and reports can be bought in from marketing research organisations. Often these are the result of continuous research using consumer and retail panels.

- Secondary sources of data are of limited use because of the scope for compounding errors arising from why and how the data were collected in the first place, who collected them and how long ago.

- Customer and competitor intelligence are vital tools in any organisation's marketing strategy.

- Customer intelligence depends on understanding customer priorities, segmenting customers into differing expectation groups, and designing appropriate methods for the systematic acquisition of customer feedback.

- Relying on customer complaints as a source of evidence for measuring customer satisfaction is extremely dangerous.

- Securing information about actual and potential competitors can be achieved through diligent attention to secondary data.

- A competitor information system may use data acquired from various sources, plus market signals transmitted by competitors themselves.

- Secondary data can be immensely cost-effective, but have to be used with care.

- There are several well-known sources of secondary data supplying market intelligence on a continuous basis.

Quick quiz

1   What activities are involved in desk research? (see para 1.2)

2   Newson-Smith says that secondary data can perform four roles: what are they? (2.3)

3   What are the principal sources of internal secondary data for an organisation? (3.1, 3.2)

4   Provide five examples of computerised databases. (4.4)

5   What are the principal sources of government information in the field of secondary data? (4.8)

6   What is a consumer panel? What are their limitations? (5.5)

7   What are the disadvantages of secondary data? (6.3)

Action Programme Review

1   The limitations of desk research are as follows.

   (a)   The data gathered is by definition not specific to the matter under analysis. It was gathered and prepared for another purpose and so is unlikely to be ideal.

   (b)   Because it was gathered for another purpose, the data are likely to require a fair amount of adaptation and analysis before they can be used.

   (c)   The data gathered are historical and may be some time out of date.

3   Here are some suggestions. You may have other better ideas.

    (a)   Coach firms, car park owners, environmental groups, regional competitors of organisations likely to be adversely affected in London.

    (b)   Competitors at Siemens, recruitment consultants.

    (c)   Land developers, environmental groups.

    (d)   Makers of teeshirts, watches, toys, nostalgia-related goods.

It is a good idea to get into the habit of playing this game whenever you read a newspaper. One day you will spot a golden opportunity for your organisation that all competitors will miss.

5   Secondary data sources can be used to investigate the advertising regulations in different countries. In certain countries there may be restrictions on advertising directed at children, on advertising tobacco or alcohol. Some countries may insist on pre-broadcast screening and so on. The secondary data could also provide information on the advertising authorities in each country (if any).

Part E
Customer dynamics and the future

17 *Trends in customer behaviour and expectations*

Chapter Topic List	Syllabus reference
1 Setting the scene	5.1
2 The future of customer service	5.1
3 Ecological, environmental and ethical issues	5.1
4 Demographic and social trends	5.1
5 Labour market issues	5.1

Learning Outcomes

- After completing this chapter you will be able to comprehend the directions for customer dynamics in the foreseeable future and identify related marketing opportunities. This final section of the text examines developing trends in customer behaviour.

Examples of Marketing at Work

- Rank Xerox and Milliken
- US car manufacturers and Japan
- Robert Maxwell
- The Cooperative Bank
- Environmentally-friendly/ethically-sound products
- The Corvair, Perrier, Unilever and fish oil
- Shell's business principles

1 SETTING THE SCENE

1.1 In today's competitive conditions, customer care and customer service are significant opportunities for competitive advantage and therefore profitability and organisational survival. Within a concern for customers can be included **everything an organisation does to win, satisfy and retain customers, profitably and more thoroughly than the competition.** All the research suggests, moreover, that only organisations with a suitably holistic approach - ie ones which successfully integrate their external customer orientation with their internal processes and systems - become market leaders in this critical activity.

1.2 The four broad criteria against which organisations should measure themselves are as follows.

- Customer focus
- Operational excellence
- Success in engaging the hearts and minds of employees
- Leadership, vision and values from the top down.

Customer focus

1.3 As we have seen elsewhere in this book, 'best practice' companies seek answers to these questions.

(a) Who are our customers?
(b) What are their needs and expectations?
(c) How are we regarded compared to the competition?
(d) What will our customers want next?

Operational excellence

1.4 Operational excellence means delivering the right products (or services) and being easy to do business with. It is now generally accepted that quality, by itself, is not sufficient to win customers. After all, many purchasers may not understand the complexities of the product they are buying (especially if it is sophisticated, like a PC), but any customer can assess the quality of a relationship and the organisation's eagerness to be helpful.

Engaging the hearts and minds of employees

1.5 This implies an organisation-wide understanding that everything depends on people. The greater the effort devoted to developing, training, motivating, recognising, rewarding, empowering and selecting people, the more success will be achieved in the customer service field.

Leadership, vision and values

1.6 Best practice organisations have leaders wholly committed to promoting a culture of customer care, an environment in which people are encouraged to serve the needs of individual customers.

Marketing at Work

(a) **Rank Xerox**

Here are the characteristics of Rank Xerox, in terms of their customer-facing strategies and goals.

(i) The company has a **clear and shared vision**, rooted in the customer. Customer satisfaction is the number one goal (even before profitability).

(ii) **Top management is visibly committed to change**. Managers are expected to act as positive role-models and are assessed as such by their staff.

(iii) **Employee commitment and involvement** is the company's number two goal: Rank Xerox has systems in place to share the vision, the purpose of change, and to secure employee engagement.

(iv) **Rewards, recognition and remuneration** reflect a strategic focus on the customer: management pay in particular is linked to improvements in customer satisfaction (measured through independent attitude surveys).

(v)   **Activities within the organisation are justified only by the extent to which they add value for customers.**

(vi)   **IT concentrates only on the key processes which deliver value for customers**.

(b)   **Milliken**

Milliken is a manufacturer of contract carpeting and tennis-ball fabric; despite its relatively small size and unglamorous product fields, it has won the European Quality Award (1993) and the US Baldridge Award (1989); it is quoted approvingly in books by Tom Peters and Richard Schonberger. Some of the key features of its approach are summarised here.

(i)   It does not believe that quality belongs to managers. Prominent in Milliken plants are notices indicating that any 'associate' (Milliken staff are not called 'employees') can, and indeed must, stop the production line in cases of quality difficulties.

(ii)   Milliken has a suggestion scheme known as OFI (Opportunities for Improvement). The European contribution rate is over 20,000 OFI suggestions annually, or 25 per person per year, of which 85% are implemented. OFIs are not huge improvements bought for money; they are countless small suggestions born out of a habit, now ingrained, of assuming that continuous improvement is natural. In the words of Helen Cheers, a telemarketing associate, 'We don't spend all our lives thinking about quality, because it is a way of life'.

(iii)   Spending on education and training has trebled in the past decade, the target being 40 hours of training per year per associate.

(iv)   There is an almost complete absence of hierarchy. The structure is moving towards self-managed teams, responsible for their own quality, maintenance and other targets.

(v)   One of the major lessons from the Milliken experience is that **quality works** - when, that it, it is carefully and consistently used as a means to the end of customer satisfaction and long-term profitable survival.

(vi)   However, the company does recognise that it is engaged on a never-ending journey. As MD Clive Jeanes has said, 'Customers may be delighted with something initially. But six months later they take it for granted and then they demand it. **Delight is a treadmill you can't get off'**.

2   THE FUTURE OF CUSTOMER SERVICE

2.1   The 1998 Bain report, *The Future of Customer Service*, makes it clear that customer service demands have increased dramatically over the past five years. According to their results, customers now:

(a)   **Demand more access time** - often 24 hour service, seven days a week;

(b)   **Are less willing to wait** - in one organisation, the average time callers are prepared to wait on hold before they hang up has fallen in just two years from 130 seconds to 30 seconds;

(c)   **Demand faster responses** - customers now expect the person who answers the phone to be able to deal with their request or query, there and then. It doesn't matter whether the person works directly for the respondent organisation or for a call centre - the same expectations operate.

(d)   **Want more information** - they want it delivered directly, and they are less willing to wait to receive something in the post.

(e)   **Have less patience with broken promises** - in Bain's example, should roadside recovery be promised in 30 minutes, customers ring if the engineer hasn't arrived in 25. If the water is off for 10 minutes longer than customers were told it would be, customers phone to complain - yet, as Bain points out, it was only a little while ago that water companies started to tell people how long the cut-off was likely to be.

(f)   **Complain more and more, and are more aggressive in their telephone manner** - UK customers are no longer frightened to complain, and are quicker to demand to speak to the manager, to demand compensation, and to threaten legal action, reference to their MP, or contact with any one of a number of television consumer protection programmes.

> ### Exam tip
> These are the trends in customer behaviour outlined by the senior examiner:
> * enhancement of expectations
> * intolerance of poor service
> * increased willingness to complain
> * concerns about ecological and environmental issues

2.2 It is clear, too, that these trends are continuing. Sir John Egan's answer to the question, 'What does the customer want?', delivered at a meeting of the Marketing Council's Pan-Company Marketing Advisory Session (on 8 March 1996):

> It's quite clear: very high quality and very low cost. And next year - they are absolutely insatiable - they want even higher quality and even lower cost. So if you can't deliver continuous improvement, cost-effective processes, you will not satisfy your customer. To deliver cost-effective processes, you have to get everybody in the company involved, with some system of empowerment, otherwise people give the shop away and don't deliver cost-effective processes. These three things seem to be consistently present in all of these quality companies that we looked at.

2.3 Sir John Egan may be able to point to some highly successful organisations that have revealed the significance of focusing on the external customer, and have also exploited the necessary connection between treating the external customer well and treating people inside the organisation properly. But there are **still plenty of organisations that can get away with poor customer service, indifferent complaints management, slow responses, self-defeating and defeated employees** who are asked to **treat customers like gold** but are themselves **treated like dirt**.

2.4 In a 1993 survey of 1,000 people, MORI found that the groups most commonly classified as **top service providers** were typically those which could be described as displaying a bedside manner: doctors, chemists, nurses, supermarkets and dentists; whereas those at the **bottom of the list** were public transport, banks, local authorities, motorway services and garages. It may be no accident that:

(a) the **'good' service providers** (and some of them were by no means brilliant) were chiefly those invigorated by pro-service attitudes, empathy, and an 'other-focus'; some of them, too, operated in an environment characterised by strong, innovative and imaginative competition;

(b) the **'poor' service providers** were organisations which were wither monopolies (local authorities, motor services) or where the degree of competition was relatively sluggish (banks and garages - remember that this survey was done in 1993, and much has changed, especially in the field of financial services, since that time: even so, despite the invasion of new competitors, the competitive context for financial services remains strongly regulated). It is worth recalling that there is no recorded case in history where a monopolistic (or oligopolistic) organisation has been customer-focused.

2.5 The same MORI study concluded that only 17 per cent of customers with a grouse would actually register a complaint; this figure has undoubtedly increased over the years, and will continue to do so, but it still represents a **striking increase over the proportions willing to complain a decade earlier**.

2.6 Other survey results generate findings which in some respects conflict with MORI's material. In 1995, the Grass Roots Group published its own commentary (*The Front Line Survey, Management Today*, 1995), derived from visits from more than 100 trained 'mystery shoppers' into a total of 2,500 assorted retail outlets. Their task was to **assess service levels** according to a variety of parameters - like time spent waiting for attention, the knowledgeableness of the assistant, whether eye-contact was made, and so forth.

2.7 On average, according to Grass Roots, the retailers scored 82 out of a possible 100 when judged by these semi-objective criteria. But a **wide gulf existed between the best and worst categories**. The top spot, surprisingly, was taken by the privatised electricity showrooms, and the High Street electrical retailers also showed up well; by contrast, McDonalds and Burger King, often regarded as models of cheerful efficiency, barely scraped into the upper half of the table.

2.8 The **stores were black spots**. 'The main problem shoppers experienced was in getting staff to acknowledge their presence,' says the report. Some criticism was very specific: 'The truth is that you do not get served at M&S, you get efficiently processed.' Music shops were particularly economical with smiles and eye contact; newsagents scored 'below average on knowledgeability, helpfulness and friendliness.'

2.9 Interestingly and perhaps not surprisingly, some of the organisations mentioned by name did not like what they read, and **found ingenious ways of rejecting adverse conclusions**. WH Smith claimed that the Grass Roots study 'flies in the face of our own research' because 'we [have] completely changed the focus of the business. [Beginning in March 1994] we took out a layer of management and regarded people to put everyone in touch with the customer.' The key question remains: **Do customers notice the difference?** If they don't, then internal re-organisations are pointless. Even if the customers do notice, do they think the company is addressing the key issues (from the customer's point of view)? Again, if the answer is 'no', then the organisation has got it wrong. The lesson, surely, is that customer perceptions are the only form of evaluation which matters.

2.10 Also in 1995, the *Daily Telegraph* published the results of a NOP poll of just under 1,000 adults from a cross-section of telephone-owning households. In general, customer service was thought to have improved compared with five years earlier, but **three out of four respondents** (well above the 17 per cent of complainants produced by MORI earlier the same year) said they **had cause to make complaints** to organisations in the previous 12 months.

2.11 The principal **reasons for such complaints** were:

- Failing to do something when promised
- Inefficiency
- Rudeness
- Delays
- Failing to keep the customer informed of changes
- Inflexibility

2.12 By contrast, the **most important aspects of customer service** were seen to be:

- Efficiency/professionalism
- Knowledge of products and expertise
- Friendly service
- Politeness
- Value for money

- Reliability
- Speed
- Ease of access
- Flexibility
- Empowerment to solve problems

2.13 So, if organisations were in any doubt about what constitutes good service, consumers themselves were clear on the priorities. They are unimpressed by smiles and civility which are not backed up by expertise, efficiency and professionalism.

2.14 The NOP results endorse findings generally produced elsewhere, namely, that customers today are no longer willing to remain white-knuckled but tight-lipped when they encounter bad service experiences. They are **increasingly likely to take direct action**.

(a) Half the survey sample had boycotted companies after poor service.

(b) 40% of the sample had bad-mouthed organisations with poor service to friends, relatives and colleagues.

(c) 23% were so incensed by poor service that they walked out or cancelled in mid-order.

2.15 The industries or suppliers with the **best reputation** for customer service were BT, doctors, banks, airlines, police, electricity suppliers, travel agents and airports; **at the other extreme**, those receiving critical attention included local authorities, the Inland Revenue, solicitors, rail services, computer services, and (last of all!) recruitment consultancies.

Marketing at Work

As an illustration of this argument, take the story told by Joseph Pine II in his 1993 book, *Mass Customisation - the New Frontier in Business Competition*. As Pine notes, US President George Bush visited Japan in January 1992 in order to promote American exports to Asia Pacific generally and Japan in particular; he was accompanied by various luminaries from the automobile industry, who had complained constantly about what they argued were the **barriers preventing their cars from being sold** effectively in Japan.

In reality, the Japanese drive on the left, so the steering wheel is found on the right. Japanese car companies have always produced right-hand steering for their domestic consumption, and left-side steering for their US exports. This had proved too much for Detroit's production systems, and so the American car manufacturers had persisted in trying to sell left-hand drive cars in Japan. Not surprisingly, their efforts had not proved outstandingly successful - and they were anxious, like failures everywhere, to attribute their problems to every cause other than the causes within their own jurisdiction. Thus Ford's then CEO claimed:

> You've got a market of 7.8 million units in Japan and imports total 2.9%. That says something about the Japanese market. All the manufacturers in the world can't be that bad. The cars we sell from the US have left-hand drive. But would right-hand drive really make a big difference?

As Pine wryly observes, if a company can't (or won't) even get such basics right as the positioning of the steering wheel, what hope have they of meeting the customer's expectations in other areas? He concludes, convincingly enough, that the attitude of the automobile manufacturers, in approaching the Japanese market, essentially reflects a sales rather than a marketing orientation. In a sales-oriented world, the job of the company (and its sales people) is not to figure out what the customer wants (or might want if it were put in front of him), but rather to sell the customer what the company has already built (and wants to continue to build). To support this perspective, Pine cites the triumphant claim of a general sales manager when he retired from one of the large auto makers:

> If I've accomplished nothing else in my years here, I have succeeded in stamping out special orders.

Some readers may be old enough to recall similar behaviour on the part of the oil companies when it was first suggested that they might manufacture unleaded petrol. For a long while it was argued that such petrol was a physical impossibility, that the extra costs would be prohibitive, that there was no demand, that unleaded petrol would damage engines, and so forth. Only when customer (and legislative) pressures became irresistible did these obstacles prove to be illusory, mythical, special pleading. Now virtually all petrol is unleaded, and from 1999 it will be illegal to sell any leaded variants. How ironic!

---

3   ECOLOGICAL, ENVIRONMENTAL AND ETHICAL ISSUES

The economics of green issues

3.1   **Not long ago** issues concerning the use of natural resources and concern for the environment, both natural (land, water, forests etc) and human (urban decay, overuse of roads) were regarded as fringe and slightly crackpot. **Companies certainly perceived no advantage in concerning themselves with green issues**, and carried on producing and selling with regard purely to profitability.

3.2   In a fairly short time things have changed.

(a)   It has become apparent that **natural resources are being depleted**, the natural environment is suffering and the bad old days of pollution and non-replacement of natural resources cannot continue - for example, the effects of deforestation and depletion of the ozone layer are **obvious to all**.

(b)   Companies with a marketing focus **listen** to their customers - and are being told that a large proportion of customers are concerned about the environment and want products which are **environment-friendly**.

3.3   Far from being an act of altruism then, **green marketing is a perfectly logical strategic plan**: give the customer what he/she wants. Indeed, many customers are prepared to pay more for products which are green; this can be described as a **'green premium'** for the fact that, when resources are scarce (eg wood from forests that are being replaced), demand exceeds supply and the price rises. It is also a transparent marketing ploy!

3.4   Some words of caution are appropriate. First, concern for green issues is chiefly a **middle-class phenomenon** and is much less apparent in the C2/D socio-economic segments. There are several possible explanations.

(a)   The people in these segments may simply reflect **more inner-directed priorities** and values, ie they are less concerned about the environment.

(b)   They have **more limited incomes**, and are thus less inclined to pay the 'green premium'.

3.5   The second note of caution concerns the discrepancy between **what people say** they will do and **what they actually do** when confronted with a purchasing choice. Attitude surveys have shown a widespread preference for 'organic' fruit and vegetables, for instance; but the proportion of people actually buying organic fruit and vegetables is much, much smaller. As some might say, it is one thing to be 'politically correct'; it is quite another actually to do something about it!

The product life cycle and green issues

3.6   The product life cycle suggests that products at different stages in their life cycle have different financial and marketing characteristics. The profitability and sales of a product can be expected to change over time. The product life cycle is an attempt to recognise distinct stages in a product's sales history.

BPP PUBLISHING

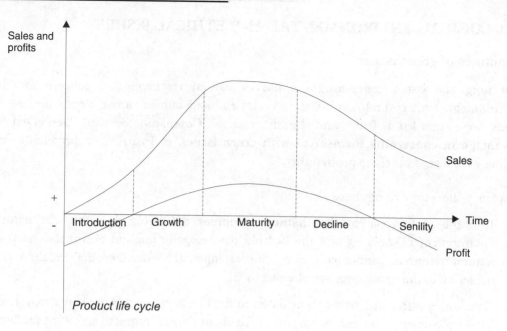

Product life cycle

3.7 It is quite possible to use environmental factors in the PLC, particularly in the following phases.

(a) **Introduction and launch.** When the product is being designed, considerations of its **environmental impact** are important.

(i) Does it use recycled materials (eg recycled paper)?

(ii) Can it be recycled once the consumer has finished with it? (Some German companies are designed recyclable cars.)

(b) **Growth and maturity**

Is the manufacturing process energy-efficient? Just as there are economies of scale in manufacture, so too there might be an optimum production level to minimise the environmental impact.

(c) **Maturity and decline**

It is here that the decisions might be hardest. Financial and marketing considerations might suggest that the life cycle of a product be extended, to milk as much profit from it as possible. However, it may be the case that **new technology** gives a firm the opportunity to provide the customer with the same benefit for a lower environmental cost. Different materials might be employed (eg carbon fibre instead of steel for car manufacture). In this case, the firm might decide to kill off the product early on environmental grounds.

3.8 This is also relevant to the **international trade product life cycle** which suggests that the product life cycle is timed differently in countries with different stages of economic development. Countries have different stages of economic development and environmental priority is sometimes less important than economic growth. To what extent does a firm *insist* on imposing the most up to date environmental standards on overseas operations? Also, should a firm reduce the sales of cheap but polluting products with perhaps more expensive ones?

Ethical standards

3.9 Social attitudes, such as a belief in the merits of education, progress through science and technology, and fair competition, are significant for marketers. Other beliefs which have either gained strength or been eroded in recent years include the following.

(a) There is a growing belief in **preserving and improving the quality of life by reducing working hours,** reversing the spread of pollution, developing leisure activities etc. We have seen that pressures on organisations to consider the environment are particularly strong because most environmental damage is irreversible and some is fatal to humans and wildlife.

(b) Many pressure groups have been organised in recent years to **protect social minorities and under-privileged groups**. Legislation has been passed in an attempt to prevent racial discrimination and discrimination against women and disabled people.

3.10 **'Ethics'** is a code of moral principles that people follow with respect to what is right or wrong. Ethical principles are not necessarily enforced by law, although the law incorporates moral judgements (murder is 'wrong' ethically, and is also punishable legally).

3.11 The ethical environment refers to justice, respect for the law and a moral code. The **conduct of an organisation,** its management and employees will be **measured against ethical standards** by the customers, suppliers and other members of the public with whom they deal.

Ethical problems facing marketers

3.12 Marketers have a duty (in most enterprises) to market for **profitability**. At the same time, modern ethical standards impose a duty to **guard, preserve and enhance the value of the enterprise** for the good of all touched by it, including the general public. Large organisations tend to be more often held to account over this than small ones.

3.13 The types of ethical problem a marketer may meet with in practice are very numerous. A few of them are as follows.

(a) In the area of **products and production,** companies have responsibility to ensure that the public and their own employees are **protected from danger**. Attempts to increase profitability by cutting costs may lead to dangerous working conditions or to inadequate safety standards in products.

(b) Ethical issues also arise in the area of **corporate governance and finance**.

Marketing at Work

An example is provided by the various Maxwell scandals and some accusations that companies are over zealous in their use of creative accounting techniques.

(c) Another ethical problem concerns **payments by companies to officials** (particularly officials in foreign countries) who have power to help or hinder the payers' operations.

(d) A difficult area for marketers concerns the extent to which an organisation's activities may appear to give support to **undesirable political policies**. The boycotting of goods and services from South Africa, when it was run by the apartheid regime, is an example. It can also be an opportunity for new product development: many unit trusts are now successfully marketed as being supportive of only ideologically sound regimes.

BPP PUBLISHING

(e) Business ethics are also relevant to **competitive behaviour**. This is because a market can only be 'free' if competition is, in some basic respects, *fair*. There is a distinction between competing aggressively and competing unethically.

Ethics and competitive advantage

3.14 There are a number of ways in which ethics impact upon an organisation's desire to maintain a competitive advantage.

Product differentiation

3.15 If an organisation is able to differentiate its products from those of its competitors it is likely to have a competitive edge over those competitors. One way in which products can be differentiated is on ethical grounds.

Marketing at Work

The Cooperative Bank's competitive advantage is based around their decision to stop dealing with customers deemed to be involved in 'unethical' activities. The bank severed its ties with twelve customers, including two fox hunting associations and a company that tests its products on animals, in the first twelve months of running the policy.

Segmentation

3.16 Other organisations wishing to use ethics to their advantage have focused on small segments of customers who are particularly concerned with ethical issues.

Marketing at Work

The majority of supermarket chains now produce free range eggs, as well as eggs from birds kept in unspecified conditions, in an attempt to appeal to those of their customers concerned with animal welfare. Unbleached toilet tissue and toilet tissue made from recycled paper is now widely available and aimed at those concerned about deforestation and the effects of harmful chemicals on the environment.

Lowering waste and pollution

3.17 By reducing waste and controlling the emission of pollutants, organisations cannot only save themselves money (for example, insurance premiums are likely to be lower if pollution emission is controlled) but can find a competitive advantage over organisations with less ethical policies.

The effect of unethical behaviour

3.18 In a competitive environment, in the face of intensifying competition and diminishing profit margins, organisations can face pressure to use **materials and components of a lower quality** in an attempt to reduce costs. An ethical problem therefore arises if customers are **not told about changes to product quality**.

Marketing at Work

(a) A prime example of such an ethical problem occurred in 1959 with the launch by General Motors of their Chevrolet Corvair.

'The Corvair gave American consumers an affordable sports car, but one which unfortunately had a significant design flaw which, in some circumstances, caused steering difficulties and led to accidents, several of which proved fatal. Although evidence of the problem existed by the early 1960s, the company resisted taking the action that was necessary to correct the fault, viz the installation of a $15 stabilising bar, until 1964. In 1965 a shareholder requested that the cars that had been made between 1960 and 1963 should be recalled for the necessary part to be refitted. However General Motors refused to act, apparently because of the cost, which was estimated at $25 million.'

Professor Gilligan, *Marketing Success*, August 1996

(b) There have been several, more positive responses in recent years to such problems.

When traces of a carcinogen were found in bottles of Perrier water in 1990, the company made an immediate and very public response: 160 million bottles of the water were withdrawn worldwide. The cause of the problem was quickly identified, quality control measures were improved and the public were given very firm reassurances of the safety of Perrier. It is felt to be the speed of the response and the degree of social responsibility demonstrated by the company which have maintained both levels of public confidence and sales of Perrier.

Johnson & Johnson acted similarly in relation to its Tylenol brand of pain relief and Heinz responded quickly and positively when its babyfoods were tampered with.

(c) Unilever announced in April 1996 that it was to cease sourcing fish oil derived from industrial fishing in the North Sea because the practice damages the environment and threatens stocks of cod and haddock. This will cut up to £10m off net profits as Unilever switches to imported soya or palm oil. However, the reason given was to protect Unilever in the long term, particularly in its cod and haddock frozen food business.

Fish oil is used in margarine, shampoo and cosmetics and is derived from low value food such as sprat. These are the staple food of cod and haddock, whose stocks are threatened by overfishing but also by a lack of food.

Unilever has pledged by 2005 that all its fish products will come from sustainable fishing grounds. This policy is ecologically sound, as well as being commercially right.

3.19 Other organisations have not dealt with ethical problems so well. One example of the damage that can be done when an organisation **makes mistakes, refuses to admit that it has done so** and **continues to deny liability** is an asbestos producer which chose to ignore or suppress evidence of the links between asbestos and an asbestos-related, incurable cancer of the chest so that its employees continued to work, oblivious to the dangers. The damage to the organisation's reputation was made worse because there appeared to have been a deliberate concealment of information which, if it had been available, might have led employees to act differently.

Customers' concerns for ethics

3.20 Increasingly customers are interested in the values displayed by the companies with which they do business. They expect organisations to have clearly expressed values which tie in with their own ethical concerns and they will take their custom to such organisations, which include Marks &Spencer, Bodyshop and the Co-operative Bank.

Action Programme 1

Are you influenced by the ethical stance taken by organisations? Do you shop for cruelty-free cosmetics? Would you prefer to do business with an organisation that does not exploit, for example, child labour?

Marketing at Work

The business principles of Shell International, the oil company, were first drawn up 20 years ago to address the issue of taking and offering bribes. The revised principles were published in 1997 and include references to human rights (as a result of criticism of Shell over its operations in Nigeria following the execution of Ken Saro-Wiwa, the Ogoni minority rights activist).

Shell's action reflects a growing interest in ethics among UK and European companies. This interest has arisen partly from stakeholder debate, partly by environmental concerns and partly because some companies believe that ethical values are central to good business.

It has been estimated that between 7 and 15 per cent of FTSE companies are experimenting with or examining the idea of social audits so that they can ensure their business practices are fully aligned with their principles or ethical codes. A social audit has been described as an external-facing exercise designed to enable an organisation to account for its actions whereas as an ethical audit is more of an internal management information tool.

The Body Shop and the Co-operative Bank have helped pioneer ethical and social audits in the UK, while Ben and Jerry's, the premium ice cream manufacturer, and Johnson & Johnson, the pharmaceuticals company, are held up as examples of ethical companies in the US. But the ethical movement is spreading into other big companies. British Telecommunications recently embarked on a full-scale social audit and Grand Metropolitan is also piloting the idea.

Social audits must take account of constantly changing mores and be sensitive to cultural differences in different countries. For example, five years ago Nike would not have considered children in Bangladesh to be significant stakeholders in their business but they are today because customers in the UK and the USA insist that their welfare is important. *'A Moral Stance', Financial Times*, September 1997

4 DEMOGRAPHIC AND SOCIAL TRENDS

Class consciousness

4.1 We have already looked at how class is defined and how it impacts on marketing. But **what is the future of 'class'**? There are some reasons to suppose that some of the class barriers are declining.

(a) Occupation is less a guide to political allegiance than before.

(b) The population in work has enjoyed rising living standards.

(c) Property ownership, and the ownership of shares (whether directly or through pension funds) is also held to erode class barriers.

4.2 On the other hand there are reasons to suggest that class is still strong in the UK.

(a) Since 1979 there has been increased **income inequality**. The rich have got richer both in absolute and relative terms. Some commentators, perhaps drawing too much on US experience, suggest an **underclass** is developing, possessing only a marginal relationship with work.

(b) **Background** still affects people's life chances.

The demographic profile of the UK

4.3 Many important facts about a country's demographic profile are collected by government to aid planning. We saw earlier in the text that every ten years, the UK government conducts a census. Originally this was undertaken as a population count alone, but recently additional information about the population has been requested.

4.4 The UK government publishes various statistics every year, as a result of its various data collection exercises. Two examples are the *Annual Abstract of Statistics* and *Social Trends*.

Both contain population data, although *Social Trends* goes into more detail about people's habits. Although *Social Trends* is published annually, some of the information it contains is, invariably, a projection. Below is a summary of the main changes shown by the data available in the 1998 edition of *Social Trends*.

Population size

4.5 The population of the UK as a whole has grown significantly since the turn of the century, but this growth is expected to level off. The increase is projected to continue, but slowly. The population of the world as a whole (eg Asia and India) is growing much faster. England and Wales constituted 88% of the total population of the UK in 1996 compared to 85% in 1901.

Gender distribution

4.6 There is a slightly greater number of women than men in the population. Women generally have a longer life expectancy than men. If age is taken into account, however, there are more males below the age of 65 than females.

Age structure

4.7 The age structure of the population is of particular concern to planners and business organisations. In 1951, 10% of the population were over 65. This will rise to nearly 20% by 2021.

Family

4.8 Trends in the UK family are as follows.

(a) More and more people live alone, accounting for 27% of all households in 1996/7 (compared to 14% in 1961).

(b) Married couples with one or two dependent children comprised 30% of households in 1961 compared with 21% in 1996/7. (The percentage of households with 3 or more dependent children fell from eight to five.) However about 71% of people live in 'families' (defined as couples with or without children, and/or lone parent families).

The declining role of the state

4.9 Since World War II, the state in the UK has taken the responsibility for most social provision in relation to:

(a) health care;
(b) education; and
(c) social provision and pensions.

4.10 The state has been withdrawing, however, from many areas of life, and government since 1979 have been keen for individuals to make their own provision.

(a) **Private medicine** has increased. It is unlikely, in the UK, that private health will take over from the NHS: after all, consumers may not see the need to pay twice, unless NHS standards fall too far.

(b) There has always been a flourishing **private education sector** in the UK. The attractiveness of private education is determined by the alternative: if the state sector provides a suitable standard, then private education will be a minority pursuit.

However school fees, largely driven by teachers' salaries, rise higher than the rate of inflation, and this limits the attractiveness of private education. The boarding option is increasingly unpopular, as families tend to stick together in the middle and lower classes, where many of the newer recruits to private education are found, as opposed to the upper classes, where the market has traditionally been. Many UK public schools are actively marketing themselves *abroad* (eg to Russia's new rich, or to the Far East) for students.

(c) There has been some privatisation of social provisions, most significantly in **pensions provision**, where personal pensions have been actively encouraged.

(d) Some **social services** (eg nursing care of the elderly) will be provided by private firms, either:

(i) directly employed by individuals; or
(ii) subcontracted by local authorities.

5 LABOUR MARKET ISSUES

5.1 The changing marketplace for organisations has had powerful implications for the nature of the labour market and work itself. Some commentators have argued that the substance of paid work is shifting in fundamental ways; others highlight the scale and scope of technological change, the forces of globalisation, the pattern of corporate restructuring, all contributing to a dramatic transformation in the forms of paid and unpaid work, and the boundaries between work, leisure and family life.

5.2 In the UK, the structure of the labour market is remarkably complex. Sources of labour vary enormously, in terms of quality, quantity and productivity. Some regions suffer from variations in the balance between vacancies and the availability of suitably qualified applicants; virtually the whole of the labour market has experienced strains arising from disequilibrium between pay and rewards, employee representation, advancement opportunities, hours of work and levels of security. Shifts in the sectoral distribution of paid employment have coincided with an increase in female participation rates in paid, predominantly part-time employment, and the decline of full-time manual job opportunities for men. These developments suggest important - and as yet not fully emergent - implications not only for the performance of the paid workforce, but also for the division of labour in the domestic household, the provision of child care facilities, the informal ('black') economy and the use of paid domestic labour.

5.3 Constant high-profile instances of corporate re-organisations, downsizing, outsourcing, acquisitions and mergers, some of them involving global switching of resources and facilities, are likely to reinforce arguments about the declining opportunities for secure careers and 'jobs for life'. As some occupations disappear into obsolescence, others rise in their place.

5.4 In their 1998 report, *Occupations in the Future* (*The Independent*, 28 May 1998), the consultancy Business Strategies concedes that, 'It's very difficult to predict the jobs of the future and those which will no longer be needed, but management and information technology skills look like the best combination.'

They point out: 'Back in 1981 there were nearly six million people employed in manufacturing and only two and a half million in financial and business services. The two are now equal, at a little over four million.' However, the public sector and service industries will be major and growing sources of employment, contrasted with the kinds of jobs which are already in decline:

Estate agents - as people buy homes on-line.

Banking - staff are being replaced by computers, and more customers use telephone banking.

Supermarket checkout staff - consumers will order goods electronically to be delivered to their door.

Chapter roundup

- There is likely to be continued enhancement of customer expectations in terms of: product/service quality (beyond functionality); organisational service standards and response times; and restitution processes (the 'aspirational customer').

- Customers now demonstrate intolerance of broken promises and impatience with delays and they transfer performance achievements experienced in one sector into expectations about performance delivery in another (the 'demanding customer').

- Customers have increasing opportunities to complain and willingness to do so, supplemented by legal enhancements to consumer power and the availability of media outlets (the 'litigious, complaining and powerful customer').

- Customers have concerns about ecological and environmental issues, about product/service ingredients and about ethical issues such as poor employment conditions in supplier organisations.

Quick quiz

1. What four broad criteria should organisations measure themselves against? (1.2)

2. List six customer service demands that have emerged in recent years. (2.1)

3. What are the principal reasons for complaints? (2.11)

4. What are the most important aspects of customer service? (2.12)

5. How altruistic is 'green marketing'? (3.3)

6. List five types of ethical problems a marketer might face. (3.13)

7. In what four respects is the demographic profile changing? (4.5 - 4.8)

18 *Market trends with customer-facing implications*

Chapter Topic List	Syllabus reference
1 Setting the scene	5.2
2 The global marketplace	5.2
3 Globalisation: the case of retailing	5.2
4 Customer loyalty and the lifetime customer	5.2
5 Electronic commerce	5.2
6 The future for manufacturing	5.2

Learning Outcomes

- After studying this chapter you will have an understanding of the future of customer service. You will comprehend the directions for customer dynamics in the foreseeable future, and be able to identify related marketing opportunities.

Key Concepts Introduced

- Ethnocentrism
- Polycentrism
- Geocentrism
- Customer loyalty

Examples of Marketing at Work

- Globalisation
- Euro-products
- Levi-Strauss
- Marks and Spencer
- Wal-Mart and Tesco
- Tesco
- The Hullachan Pro
- The Cambridge Local Guide
- R S Components

1   SETTING THE SCENE

1.1   This chapter explores some of the trends influencing the market place and customer perceptions. These include globalisation, customer expectations and the building of a lifetime relationship, and electronic commerce.

2   THE GLOBAL MARKETPLACE

2.1   Prompted by ever-increasing competition and constant attacks on costs, markets, profitability and resources, more and more organisations are redefining themselves to operate on a **global scale**, thus spreading their costs and revenues across the world.

Marketing at Work

In the words of Percy Barnevik of ABB (quoted in the *Financial Times,* 7 November 1997), 'Globalisation is a long-lasting competitive advantage. If we build a new gas turbine, in 18 months our competitors also have one. But building a global company is not so easy to copy.' The significance of globalisation is emphasised by Jean-Marc Espalious of the French hotel group, Accor, who claims that there is no future for purely national hotel chains, except in very specific niche markets: 'National chains cannot optimise their operations. They cannot invest enough money.'

2.2   Operating successfully on a global scale means **re-thinking very aspect of the organisation's activities**: sourcing, production, brand management, distribution, finance, governance, performance management, executive development, customer relations. Nearly always, the global company will create **international brands** - even firms that in the past would not have thought of introducing strong end-user brands (like Intel) now see the necessity for doing so. Nonetheless, international brands have to be promoted through decentralised structures: as Peter Brabeck of Nestle points out

> 'Marketing cannot be a head office activity. Giving life to our brands, making them relevant to our consumers, is the responsibility of local management.'

2.3   The resultant **tension between central and local management** is a key feature of the challenge in creating a global company; indeed, the 21st century's biggest management challenge is the obligation to combine worldwide reach with the flexibility of a local competitor. Given that customers are increasingly fickle, spontaneous and unpredictable, so **responsiveness** is now expected from businesses which have hitherto remained immune to such pressures.

Exam tip

Going global is not the only possible approach to the 21st century business challenge: indeed, it isn't even a credible option for many organisations. For them, it is necessary to build a corporate strategy around the defence of a home market. But you must still be aware of the consequences of globalisation: keeping up with market trends across the world, seeking out cheap components and advanced technology from wherever they are available, learning from innovations in other markets, and keeping one step ahead of customer expectations.

Service sector

2.4   Globalisation is connected to the increasing '**weightlessness**' of the UK economy. The idea of weightlessness refers to the fact that as economies mature, an increasing proportion of their gross domestic product becomes devoted to **service-sector activities**. In Britain, manufacturing accounts for about one-fifth of all economic activity, whereas the services sector accounts for approximately two-thirds. Services growth has been responsible for the bulk of all economic growth in the UK over the past 25 years, and a similar pattern has occurred in the USA, where the share of services in total output has increased from 63 per cent in the mid-1970s to 70 per cent at the close of this decade.

2.5   Of course, the concept of weightlessness includes not only such relatively low-level activities as hairdressing, gardening and the stocking of supermarket shelves, but also financial services, telecoms and most IT, notably computer software. Some services can easily be exported, such as on-line information and financial services. Some manufacturing products cannot in themselves be sold abroad (British electrical plugs, for example).

2.6   If a bank wishes to shift its foreign exchange dealing from London to Frankfurt, it can do so simply by taking a few of its dealers to Germany: this is far more straightforward than shutting down a factory and moving production overseas. IT activity is almost totally independent of any particular geographical location: it is stateless as well as weightless.

The global consumer

2.7   In practice, is there such a person as the **'global consumer'**? Or even a Euro consumer? This will only happen where cultures converge, and there are good reasons to suppose why this will not be so.

Marketing at Work

The *Guardian* (26 August 1994) reported the failure of several 'Euro-products'. Most spectacularly, MTV (the American music channel) promoted MTV-Europe, a pan-European channel. This failed in the UK, and has been replaced by a strategy of market segmentation.

'So now MTV are trying a completely different approach. The launch of VH-1 is a bid to attract more mature British viewers who are lukewarm about MTV Europe's exuberant 24 hour output, heavily weighted to technodance music and eclectic Europop, which goes down a storm from Amsterdam to Ankara. However, MTV Europe boss Bill Roedy admits it is the first step in a new policy of tailoring its output more closely to national markets. MTV has screened national advertising on its pan-European service for two years.

Some brands transcend any barriers: Euro-youth drinks Coke and wears Levis. But our Continental neighbours have different tastes in music and television. Britain, in particular, has a strong and very distinctive pop and rock music tradition and its sensibilities vary accordingly. MTV hopes that VH-1 will reflect these.'

2.8   Ideally, firms would prefer to offer a global product like Coke - the same product, with the same pricing policy using the same promotional methods and through the same distribution channels in all its markets.

2.9   Complete **global standardisation** would greatly increase the profitability of a company's products and simplify the task of international marketing. The extent to which standardisation is possible is controversial in marketing. Theodore Levitt wrote:

'The global corporation operates with resolute constancy, at low relative cost, as if the entire world (or major regions of it) were a single entity; it sells the same things in the same way everywhere.'

2.10 At the other end of the spectrum, it has been argued that **adaptability** is the key ingredient for global success.

Marketing at Work

The experience of Levi-Strauss is one of the latest instances of the trend towards mass customisation, the process in which the economies of scale associated with mass production are combined with a 'personal' service which makes individual customers feel valued.

Customers at the Levi shops in London and Sheffield can try on prototypes from a stock of more than 300 pairs of jeans, and then fine-tune the measurements to provide a perfect fit. The details are recorded on computer, together with the shopper's name and address; the finished product is shipped direct to the customer or back to the store for collection.

There is a price premium (£19 in 1997), but shoppers can re-order garments using a barcode sewn inside the jeans.

2.11 A firm's approach to this decision depends to a large extent on its attitude towards internationalisation and its level of involvement in international marketing. There are broadly three types of approach in this context.

Key Concepts

Ethnocentrism. Overseas operations are viewed as being secondary to domestic operations and are often simply a means of disposing of surpluses. Any plans for overseas markets are developed at home with very little systematic market research overseas. There is little or no modification of any aspects of the mix with no real attention to customer needs. This is the first step into international marketing and involves a centralised strategy.

Polycentrism. Subsidiaries are established, each operating independently with its own plans, objectives and marketing policies on a country by country basis. Adaptation will be at its most extreme with this approach. Polycentrism can be viewed as an evolutionary step and involves a decentralised strategy.

Geocentrism. The organisation views the entire world as a market with standardisation where possible and adaptation where necessary. It is the final evolutionary stage for the multinational organisation and involves an integrated marketing strategy.

2.12 There are **strong forces in the business environment** drawing companies towards **global marketing strategies,** the most important of which are as follows.

(a) **Demographic, cultural and economic convergence** among consumer markets and increasing homogeneity in the needs of industrial customers worldwide.

(b) Increased need for **investment and research** to ensure long term competitiveness, longer lead times involved in bringing products to market and the growing return needed for this process.

(c) The growing importance of **economies of scale** (purchasing, manufacturing, distribution).

(d) Changes in **regional economic cooperation** resulting in freer movement of goods and capital.

(e) The impact of **technology** on manufacturing, transportation and distribution.

(f) The deregulation of national markets, in areas such as air transport, financial services, telecommunications and power generation.

Global brands or not?

2.13 The debate continues to rage about **whether there are, or can be, genuinely global brands.** Of course, there are global companies, and some of these have become world leaders through the strengths of their brands - and the brand **is** the company, so to speak, for organisations like Coca-Cola, McDonalds, Walt Disney, Sony, Body Shop and Mercedes-Benz.

2.14 Other companies - like PepsiCo, Danone and Nestle - powerful corporate brands in their own right - have created a **global identity through particular products**, like Doritos tortilla chips, Evian mineral water and Nescafc instant coffee. A well-established brand name can broaden a company's ambitions, allowing it to introduce new products or move into new markets: in this way, for example, Walt Disney has stretched its brand well beyond films to cover books, clothing, toys, games and holidays; Ribena is now linked to many other drinks

BPP PUBLISHING

than the blackcurrant juice of its birth; Guinness produces a limited range of books and clothing.

2.15   Most of the world's famous brands are in **consumer goods and services**; but branding is becoming important in supplying businesses, as corporate clients seek the assurance of a global brand for their IT services, audit and legal support.

2.16   While in some fields the brand (or at least the brand name) may be global, and evoke global recognition, in other cases it **makes sense to retain local brands** which have strong appeal in their markets. Frito-Lay, PepsiCo's snack food division, has adopted this strategy for its potato crisp business, which has grown by acquiring companies with established brands. Lay's is the group's global brand, used when entering new markets; increasingly it is supplanting weak local brands (eg in Canada, where Hostess was converted to Lay's in early 1998), but where the existing brand has strong equity (as in the UK, where Walkers crisps is the market leader), then Frito-Lay remains in the background.

2.17   In other words, Frito-Lay **does not seek uniformity for the sake of it,** and will defer to the preferences of its customers, especially whether they have **strong nationalistic tendencies** and may rebel if they believe they are purchasing further evidence (as they may see it) of US marketing hegemony.

2.18   Most large companies with diverse consumer products follow similarly diverse branding strategies. Nestle, for example, has **multiple layers of branding**: its dried milk is always sold under the company name and Nescafe is obviously part of the Nestle organisation. On the other hand, the group's Buitoni Italian food products makes no mention of the ultimate owner: 'Consumers outside Italy see it as a quintessentially Italian family brand; they don't want to be reminded that it belongs to a giant Swiss conglomerate,' says Raymond Perrier, brand evaluation director for brand consultancy Interbrand (quoted in the *Financial Times*, 14 March 1998).

2.19   Even where global branding makes sense, organisations **cannot afford to ignore local preferences** in the same way that Disney once did when it opened its Paris operation, refusing to sell wine and paying no attention at all to French national holidays (whilst rubbing salt into the situation through earnest celebration of all US holidays). McDonalds serves wine and salads with its burgers in France; for India, where beef products are unacceptable, it has created the Maharaja Mac made from mutton.

Exam tip

Doubtless the issues around globalisation will continue to be debated vigorously because in practice they reflect **two opposing perspectives** on the way the world is going.

On the one side are the pressures of **technology and business strategy**, promoting globalisation because of its opportunities for scale economies and market domination.

On the other hand, **consumers stubbornly exert their individuality**, often reacting violently (either metaphorically or even literally) against what they perceive to be the arrogance of global players.

There is no right or wrong answer!

2.20   As some observers have pointed out, too, the emergence of the global village is accompanied, paradoxically, by individual affinity to more localised and differentiated communities. Young urban professionals in London have more in common with their counterparts in Singapore than with middle-class families in Berkshire; the latter have more in common with people living in the affluent suburbs of Sydney. The challenge for marketers, as for organisations generally, is to **become global whilst remaining local**: to achieve the commercial advantages from a world-wide identity whilst tailoring their products and services to the needs of the individual and his/her immediate sector.

3 GLOBALISATION: THE CASE OF RETAILING

3.1 The trends towards **globalisation** have generally been led by the manufacturing sector, but retailing companies have pursued similar strategies in the past few years. Their experience supplies some salutary lessons for marketing in general and for the marketing/customer interface in particular.

Marketing at Work

From the UK, Marks & Spencer has established footholds in most major countries; Tesco operates in six overseas markets, including South Korea; fast-growing clothes chains like Gap, Hennes (from Sweden) and Zara (from Spain) are opening branches in new countries every few weeks.

3.2 Despite this enthusiasm, most retailers find it hard to make a success of the transition from national to multinational: their profits are invariably much higher in their home market than in any others they choose to enter. Indeed, the French company Carrefour, with operating margins of more than six per cent in France, still loses money in much of Asia, Latin America and other parts of Europe, despite having embarked upon foreign expansion more than 30 years ago.

3.3 Part of the explanation is to be found in the **reasons for going overseas** in the first place. They include:

- The small size of the company's **domestic market** - especially if located in, say, Sweden.

- **Slow growth** in the domestic market, encouraging a search for opportunities elsewhere.

- A desire to escape from the rigours of **planning laws** in the domestic country.

- Perceived opportunities to exploit **economies of scale** and spread the rising costs of marketing and technology.

- In Europe in particular, internationalisation should help companies cope with the **single currency**.

3.4 Without a significant operation to begin with, new entrants into a foreign country will find it difficult to justify the expense of setting up a large **distribution network** and installing the latest technology. Moreover, **cross-border scale economies** are particularly elusive in food retailing: almost all food retailers over-estimate the scope for savings from aggregating lots of local orders for a product into a single worldwide contract. Few deals manage to produce even one or two per cent of sales in savings.

3.5 Global sourcing conflicts with the need to cater for local tastes and for the preferences of local customers. Local taste crucially affects the way retailers sell their goods, too.

Marketing at Work

In 1996 *Wal-Mart* set up efficient, clean supercentres in Indonesia, only to find that Indonesians preferred Matahari, the shabbier shop next door, which reminded shoppers of a street market where they could haggle and buy the freshest fruit and vegetables. By 1998, Wal-Mart had admitted defeat and withdrew from Indonesia.

Similarly, *Boots* found that the number of visitors to its Thai shops soared after it started playing pop music videos at full volume: previously, customers had found the shops too quiet.

The staff at the checkout in the *Boots* store, Tokyo, stand up all the time because research has shown that Japanese shoppers find it offensive to pay money to seated staff.

3.6   It is clear that for such obstacles to be overcome, multinational retailers need a fanatical attention to detail, and a willingness to comply unquestioningly with **customer preferences** at the point of sale.

Marketing at Work

Initially, when Marks & Spencer opened in Paris (their first trip outside the UK), their shop did not include cubicles for trying on clothes. Parisian shoppers refused to accept the alternative, namely, that unwanted items could be returned or exchanged without argument - after all, many of these shoppers had long distances to travel before a return/exchange service could be activated. Unlike the UK, where branches of Marks & Spencer may be found in any decent-sized town, the company (at the time) had only one site in all of France. M&S found that their female customers were undressing in the aisles in order to test-drive the clothing that appealed to them: once that began to happen, M&S conceded defeat and installed changing rooms.

3.7   One way of learning about local customer tastes is to join a **local partner** (indeed, in some countries this is required by law). But even this does not work if the entry company ignores the information supplied by the supposedly joint-venture colleague. In Brazil, Wal-Mart paid no attention to the knowledge possessed by its partner, Lojas Americanas, and failed to notice that most Brazilian families shop at the weekends. Wal-Mart built car parks and store aisles that were too small to accommodate the weekend rush.

3.8   Multinational retailers do have some advantages: the greatest is probably **know-how**, reflected in a sophisticated understanding of **supply chains** and the use of IT for activities like inventory control.

3.9   The leaders so far are the category killers with a strong focus, products with universal appeal, and their own brands. Examples include: Gap (khakis and white shirts) and IKEA (furniture) - both combine large volumes with higher margins, and control over design, distribution and sourcing.

3.10   Some Internet retailers may turn out ultimately to be winners, though **maintaining a global brand** can turn out to be cripplingly expensive. The international failures of Laura Ashley, Body Shop and Toys 'R' Us show what can happen if expansion abroad is not carefully managed.

3.11   Strong brands are necessary if consumers are to trust them with their personal details or buy their higher-margin products and services. Tesco and 7-Eleven in Japan have successfully used information from loyalty cards to adapt their stores, products and services to local tastes, and to move into services such as banking and bill payments. Trusted retail brands have great power: a 1999 survey by CLK, a market-research group, shows that a third of the 1000 British adults surveyed said they would buy a house from an estate agent with a supermarket brand; 15 per cent would buy a supermarket-branded car.

4   CUSTOMER LOYALTY AND THE LIFETIME CUSTOMER

4.1   Successful companies focus first on selling more, and more often, to their existing customers, rather than finding new ones. The cost of selling to existing customers is minimal, whilst finding new customers is an expensive business.

4.2   As we have seen, a loyal customer is one who buys more, more regularly.

> ## Key Concept
> Remember the definition of **customer loyalty** as **voluntary re-purchasing and referral**.

Over a period of 10 or 20 years, the value of these sales can mount up to a large sum - even in the case of a small customer. Consider, for example, someone who purchases £100 of food and non-food items each week from a supermarket in the UK. If they are 20 years old, they have a life expectancy of a further 60 years. Even if they spend no more, their total value to the supermarket is at least £300,000 - and that takes no account of inflation or of increased expenditure as the customer acquires a family. Nor does it take any account of the likelihood that the satisfied customer will recommend that supermarket to others.

4.3   Given these sorts of calculations, it seems absurd that supermarkets and similar organisations (like financial services, airlines, and so forth) would worry about **profitability per transaction**. If they do, they stand to lose not only all future business from that customer, but also the possibility of favourable referrals.

4.4   On the other hand, **some customers are more worth retaining** than others. Some customers may not justify retention because the costs of servicing them are excessive and in effect erode all possibility of profit.

4.5   **Calculating the lifetime value of the customer.** This can be done by working through the following three steps.

(a)   **For each customer (individual or segment) roughly estimate the annual gross profit which they generate.** This can be done by multiplying the annual sales to that customer (or segment) by the gross profit margin for the type of product or service which they buy. The resultant figure may need to be adjusted for any special costs which apply to doing business with that customer.

(b)   **Work out your customer retention rate, ie the percentage of customers retained each year.** Increasing the retention rate should be an important strategic goal, because a small improvement can have a dramatic effect on the company's profitability.

(c)   **The 'lifetime value' of the customer is the annual gross profit multiplied by the average time a customer stays with you.**

4.6   This 'lifetime value' is useful in three ways:

(a)   It enables the organisation to select a list of **premium customers** for its loyalty programme.

(b)   It gives the company an idea of how much time and money to invest in **basic customer care** (for all customers) and the **customer loyalty programme** (for premium customers).

(c)   It helps the company to work out which segment of the market is the   most profitable, so that other premium customers can be targeted in the future.

4.7   **Basic customer care.** The first step in building genuine customer loyalty is to achieve a high standard of service for all customers: companies need to be better than their competitors in this field, otherwise they will lose customers. The following ingredients are indispensable in a thorough-going programme of customer care.

(a) **The customer should be at the centre of everything which the company does.** For example, customers may be consulted about product development plans, and a senior manager should be given key accountability for the customer care programme as a whole.

(b) **All the points at which the customer has direct contact with the business ('critical incidents') should be identified.** Standards for speed, courtesy and decision-making should be specified and then published to both internal and external customers.

(c) **All staff should be trained in basic communication skills and in customer service generally.** This embraces such dimensions as politeness, friendliness, altruism, empathy, and the ability to concentrate on the customer's needs.

(d) **All employees should be trained in the effective handling of complaints.** The six steps are: apologise, show sympathy, listen, establish the facts, agree what you will do, then do it. This approach can turn the complainer into a committed customer.

(e) **Organisations must constantly consider ways in which customers might be saved time, money and aggravation throughout their whole interaction.** Such innovations could include:

- Using reliable suppliers and keeping adequate stock levels.

- Setting up production processes which ensure no defects ('right first time'), rather than relying on inspection of the finished product.

- If anything goes wrong or might go wrong, let the customer know immediately - don't try to keep the information concealed.

(f) **Customers like a personalised service.** This can be done through giving each customer an 'account manager' eg in a local hairdresser's salon, customers may be offered appointments with 'their' hair stylist - where this happens, customer loyalty automatically increases.

(g) **To create a sensation of customer delight, the company should develop ways to make the service experience memorable.** For example, on a very hot day a stationery company gave its delivery driver a box of ice creams; the driver gave an ice cream to everyone who had ordered stationery.

4.8 **Two-way communication systems with customers.** Organisations who initiate a dialogue with their customers typically find that customers will approach them when they need the type of products which the organisation supplies.

4.9 Customers should be divided into three groups for communication purposes, with different types of communication for each.

(a) **Potential customers:** the aim is to build up interest and possibly make a sale.

(b) **Customers who have made one purchase:** the aim is to increase the frequency of their buying and sell them other products or services.

(c) **Premium customers who have made more than one purchase already:** the aim is to turn them into 'advocates' who recommend the company's products to their contacts.

4.10 **Special treatment for the premium (lifetime) customers.** These people are enormously valuable and it is generally worth pampering them and making them feel special. Here are some possibilities, many of them costing little or nothing:

- Such customers can be given direct telephone numbers.
- Restrictions on minimum order quantities can be waived.

- They may receive first options on opportunities like discounted stock clearances.
- Premium customers may be invited to special events or may receive special gifts.

4.11 **Added-value schemes** may promote loyalty, but it should be remembered that in reality they are nothing more than sales promotion initiatives - and the reaction of customers has little to do with loyalty. Such schemes may offer a cumulative or retrospective discount (ie money back), forward discounts (off next purchases), or straightforward rewards.

Marketing at Work

Sainsburys rewarded their shoppers with British Airways discount points. It was an attractive offer - if you planned to buy an airline ticket.

Tesco offered customers a 'Clubcard' incorporating a personalised letter every 13 weeks with their bonus points statement, shopping vouchers, and money-off coupons. The vouchers were even over-printed with the customer's name. Tesco customers appreciate the 'personal' component and go straight back to Tesco to spend more money.

---

5   ELECTRONIC COMMERCE

5.1 A report from Andersen Consulting (*Financial Times*, 9 September 1998) points to huge differences between the US and European attitudes towards electronic commerce. Although 82% of the 300 European executives interviewed recognise the strategic importance of e-commerce, only 39% are doing anything about it.

5.2 The excuse given by most of them was the **lack of a 'framework for commercial regulation'** for e-commerce. More than 80% wanted governments to create a common 'international framework' of regulations.

5.3 So, whereas US industrialists are working hard to keep government regulation out of e-commerce, European businesses want to bring governments in so that rules can be created. The contrast could hardly be more extreme.

5.4 The point being missed is that e-commerce is **not a distinct marketplace** in itself: rather, internet technology has created **new tools** that businesses can use, if they choose, to broaden their markets. E-commerce brings big changes, creating opportunities for some, threats for others; it may affect commerce in ways akin to the discovery of **new trade routes** or the invention of **faster modes of transportation** - broadening trade horizons and creating, in some fields, truly global markets, products and services.

5.5 It is unlikely that the Internet can remain totally free of political intervention and some measure of control; on the other hand, Europeans cannot expect that e-commerce will become cosily regulated.

5.6 The Internet is affecting all businesses in similar ways. Every industry is now part of a global network, with all companies in the industry equally contactable. **Information**, once valuable, is now a **commodity**. These two forces in themselves have powerful consequences: many businesses that survived merely because they were conveniently located, or because they provided information that was hard to find, must increasingly seek other sources of competitive differentiation.

5.7 On the other hand, **some organisations have benefited enormously from Internet growth**: in 1996, Forrester Research calculated that PCs, pornography and CDs - 'boy-toys' -

BPP
PUBLISHING

and gift items such as flowers made up a little over half of all online consumer revenues. In May 1997, *The Economist's* survey of electronic commerce listed the following industries which are especially affected, for good or ill.

(a) **Financial services**

As *The Economist* points out, this is a classic example of how the Internet can open up an existing infrastructure - the financial markets' computerised information needs - to all comers, and thus transform an industry. Now that investors can get advice and market information from many (free) sources, they are less willing to pay a premium just to trade. The result is the appearance of discount online brokers; Forrester estimates that assets worth $111 billion are already managed online, and the figure will rise to $474 billion by 2000. The downside is that discount broking will become a commodity service, surviving (in *The Economist's* phrase) on razor-thin margins, and depend on economies of scale - unless the companies involved can find some other way to add value, increase their margins, and differentiate themselves from their competitors.

(b) **Sex**

Forrester Research estimates that erotic material accounted for sales of $52m on the Internet in 1996, one-tenth of all retail business on the Web. Typical consumers, says *The Economist*, are 'avid, savvy and well-wired young men,' skilled in teasing out the best material at the lowest price from the thousands of sex sites on-line. Porn purveyors, in a highly competitive environment, must promote their products enthusiastically with video clips, customisable service (there's that **customisation** word again) and even live video conferencing.

(c) **Travel**

Although most travellers prefer to use travel agents in order to manoeuvre themselves around opaque ticket prices, schedules and flight availability, especially since using an agent costs them no more, the emergence of the Internet has **given airlines an opportunity to cut out the middle man**. They do this in two ways. First, some airlines sell seats direct through their own web sites; second, companies like Northwest and Continental have reduced the commission they pay to online travel agencies on the grounds that much of the work is done by customers themselves. Yet online purchases still make up only about 1% of total airline ticket sales, and Forrester Research estimates that the figure will gradually creep up to no more than about 1.5%. As long as airlines are legally prevented from offering online bookers a price advantage, then most independent travellers (some of them, doubtless, driven by sheer inertia and force of habit) will continue to use agencies.

(d) **Retailing**

The most obvious advantages of **online shops** are that their **costs are lower** and they are **less constrained for space** than their physical counterparts. Yet only about a third of online retailers make money. Not only must they cope with deeply ingrained suspicions about online purchasing, but many of them appear to have entered the Internet half-heartedly. Their product ranges often consist of only a limited selection from the goods which they sell through their catalogues or shops; many items are hard to find, slow to download, and hard to see on-screen, according to *The Economist*.

(e) **Music**

In principle, because the recording industry is controlled by only a few companies, they have the power to stifle Internet competition. Most of the online CD retailers are still losing money.

(f) **Books**

Stimulated by the apparent success of Amazon.com, two of the USA's largest booksellers - Barnes & Noble, and Borders - have gone online, along with some international competitors. Optimists think that online book sales will reach 8% of the market by 2000.

(g) **Cars**

In the USA, customers of Auto-by-Tel, the leading Internet car-buying service, simply tell the service what kind of car they want, and wait for nearby dealerships to make their best offer. *The Economist* says that customers report prices up to 10% lower than the best face-to-face haggling efforts could achieve, without stepping into a dealership until it is time to pay and pick up the car. It costs the dealer only about $25 to respond to an Auto-by-Tel lead, instead of hundreds of dollars to advertise and sell a car in the conventional way. In 1996, two million of the 15.1 million cars sold in America were sold through the Internet; Chrysler believes that by the turn of the century it will sell around 25% of its production online.

(h) **Advertising and marketing**

The Internet, unlike any other advertising medium, is **completely customisable for each consumer**; it enables companies to target potentially interested people and communicate interactively with them. Using the Internet it is easy to know which advertising works; just count the 'click-throughs'.

Electronic commerce: the implications and the experience

5.8 For an established company, one of the principal challenges of electronic business is **the extent to which its existing value chain is made redundant**, and whether its competitive advantage is eroded, or even fatally wounded. Successful companies usually have competitive advantages in a few parts of the value chain; electronic commerce may mean that these advantages disappear.

5.9 Philips Evans and Thomas Wurster, of Boston Consulting Group, point out that, 'Where once a sales force, a system of branches, a printing press, a chain of stores or a delivery fleet served as **formidable barriers to entry** because they took years and heavy investment to build, in this new world they **could suddenly become expensive liabilities**. New competitors on the Internet will be able to come from nowhere to steal your customers.' Thus a bank may find its branch network threatened by the growth of online banking.

5.10 The potential threat is obvious. The conundrum for bankers is to assess the likely extent of the damage. How many customers will be lost? **Does the branch network retain important advantages in customer acquisition and retention?** Quite possibly, customers find it reassuring to know that their bank does have branches and real people whom they can visit and talk to if necessary, just as they find it pleasant to visit a bookshop.

5.11 On the other hand, **customer profiles are changing.** Those who are uncomfortable with online transactions will eventually be replaced by others who have been computer-literate more or less from birth. In addition, even if only a minority of customers were to switch from traditional banks to electronic banking, the numbers may still be sufficient to **affect product/service pricing.** In other words, the arrival of cheaper electronic transaction availability will gradually force service providers (like banks) to re-price the whole range of their activities, even for those customers who still transact their business by conventional means. Some effort is being made to avoid this by organisations which operate both retail and electronic arms, since they work hard to make sure that the retail customers (typically paying higher prices) either **do not know** that they could incur lower costs by switching, or **do not care**. Such customers may not be driven purely by price considerations, of course; they can often be persuaded that their retail status involves the delivery of superior value for which, of course, a price has to be paid.

5.12 Activities like customer acquisition and customer service are already encountering threats from electronic commerce. Even more profound challenges are emerging, however, when the whole value chain is undermined through the introduction of entirely new delivery systems.

5.13 In an article in *The Financial Times* (Value Chain: Exposed links in the established chain', 14 October 1998), Peter Martin discusses the specific case of **electricity supply**. Until recently, electricity was generated, transmitted and distributed by vertically integrated monopolies. Changes in regulation have meant that these monopolies are now split into separate generation, transmission and distribution companies; the next change - which, significantly, could not have occurred without the possibilities implied through electronic commerce - is the further split between distribution and supply. This means that one company may own the cables over which electricity travels, whilst another supplies the electricity to customers, having bought it in the first place from the generators.

5.14 As Martin points out, in this sort of operation, 'the **traditional strengths** of an electricity utility - reliability, technological depth, physical presence - may be **less important than skill in managing customer relationships and spot-marketing trading**.'

5.15 The bifurcation of the electricity market is only one example of a development which (to repeat the point) is **crucially dependent on the presence of highly sophisticated electronic communication and data-management systems**, but what it also shows is the degree to which traditional value chains are being modified or even turned upside down. What could happen, in the final analysis, is that the competitive advantage will ultimately migrate to companies that have particularly strong customer relationships. Already, trusted retailers like Tesco, Marks & Spencer and Sainsbury in the UK are extending their brands into other industries, like energy supply or financial services.

5.16 Their logic is impressive. **Electronic commerce has eliminated many of the competitive advantages enjoyed by existing competitors**. Retailers can buy the ingredients they need, and rely on their brand names to help them create competitive advantage. Indeed, in an ironic twist of fortune, the major financial services companies of today may end up being little more than marginally-profitable sub-contractors to the key players (like Tesco) of tomorrow. In Martin's phrase, 'The value added will migrate to the businesses that control the customer relationships.'

5.17 On the other hand, it may be that in practice most businesses do not enjoy the relationships with their customers that they think they do. Just because a customer makes **frequent use** of a supplier - whether a retail supermarket or a bank's retail branch - does not mean that the customer is necessarily **loyal or committed**: it is equally plausible to argue that transaction frequency is a product of **necessity rather than desire**. If so, then the temptation to go elsewhere is always present and may occasionally be activated. It is for this reason that many banks, in particular, are somewhat disenchanted about the return they are securing from their vast investments in customer databases.

5.18 Another issue concerns the degree to which customers are prepared to **reply on a single supplier** (albeit a trusted one) for a range of apparently unrelated products and services. Many are **reluctant** to do so in case it makes them excessively **dependent**; others are reluctant because of some vague unease about the consequences of **quasi-monopolistic power**. With this in mind, John Hagel of McKinsey envisages the creation of 'infomediaries', businesses that make money by 'capturing customer information and developing detailed profiles of individual customers for use by selected third-party vendors.' This emphasises yet again how current value chains are jeopardised through electronic commerce and its market consequences.

Marketing at Work

The Tesco experience with financial services

Tesco Personal Finance (TPF) began operations in 1997. In its first year it accumulated 700,000 customers and more than £700 million in deposits; it became profitable in 1999. For comparative purposes, it is worth noting that it took five years (between 1988 and 1993) for First Direct to become profitable; however, First Direct did not have the advantage of directly-available retail outlets, nor the opportunity to attract large numbers of potential customers virtually without incurring any advertising costs whatsoever, nor the benefit of a ready-made brand name.

Indeed, the principal advantage for the supermarkets, when entering financial services, is that they have low overheads and 'warm' customer bases - shoppers who do not need to be solicited, who do not need to respond to media advertising, and who do not have to be cold-called. The low costs have enabled the supermarkets to offer competitive interest and loan rates, although Tesco is still dependent on its alliance partner (Royal Bank of Scotland) for technical expertise in risk pricing for loans, for back office functions, and for call centre services. The added value from Tesco is, of course, the brand name itself - which attracts customers who would not respond at all to any invitations from the Royal Bank of Scotland - plus its skills with merchandising, customer acquisition and product design. As TPF matures, it is likely that the reliance on the Royal Bank of Scotland will be reduced and the alliance may ultimately disappear altogether.

It is wrong to assume that TPF's advantages stem principally from sophisticated digital or Internet-based technologies, especially since these are broadly available to all competitors. The key differentiator is the reputation of the brand, which may explain why TPF exclusively targets its activities towards existing Tesco customers, rather than towards financial-services customers more generally. Nor does TPF set out to develop 'relationships' with its customers: it is content simply to offer them a range of products, at competitive prices, and let them get on with it.

Perhaps foolishly and certainly short-sightedly, the traditional banks still see supermarkets as a nuisance rather than as a threat. They rely for their profits on customer inertia; they acknowledge that companies like TPF may do well with simple products (like deposits) but will struggle once they enter more complicated arenas like mortgage supply, pension schemes and credit card management. Moreover, the benevolent image of the supermarket could easily be undermined once its financial-services operation starts to refuse loans, withdraw credit cards, or foreclose on mortgages.

Electronic commerce and the concept of 'core competencies'

5.19 Electronic commerce has significant implications for the concept of **'core competency'**, which has been a central issue in strategic management for some years. Core competencies may be identifiable and measurable if the external environment remains reasonably static, or if it is subject only to rhythmic and incremental adaptation; but if the environment begins to fluctuate alarmingly then a core competency one minute may become a **core liability** in the twinkling of an eye.

5.20 For many organisations, its brands reflect a core competency - and, moreover, one which is not easily replicable. However, for this purpose brands fall into two categories: those that tell you the product is reliable and trustworthy, or those that appeal to your tastes.

   (a) If the brand is attractive because it reflects **customer preferences,** then so long as the preference remains then the brand is a genuine core competency.

   (b) So far as reliability is concerned, however, there are two problems.

(i)   The first is that with most products, **reliability (and quality) may now be taken for granted**. Not for nothing do people only take about twelve minutes to decide which washing machine to buy: because they expect all of them to work, ie to meet minimal functionality obligations - then they will simply differentiate according to price, to appearance, to availability and to shape: only a very small proportion of their purchasing choice will be influenced by the brand name itself.

(ii)   The second problem is that when it comes to performance and reliability, **customers can increasingly collect information for themselves** by searching the world wide web. This can be advantageous for new entrants into the competitive marketplace, though it may also be a liability if their offerings are a mite unsatisfactory. It is particularly important for new entrants to ensure that their first customers are pleased with what they get, so that positive rumours begin to spread. The position is further complicated by the fact that new entrants inevitably have a very small market share, so opinions about their product reliability can be shaped through the feedback from a very small number of customers (bearing in mind, too, that it is the dissatisfied customers who are more likely to make a noise).

5.21   If it appears that brands are more vulnerable than initially might be seen to be the case, then it may be more effectively argued that **any organisation's core competency is likely to be found somewhere in the middle of its activities**: somewhere between procurement (conventionally the first phase in the value chain) and marketing/sales. After all, when procuring raw materials, the company is operating in an open market. At the other end, sales/marketing activities are visible to competitors. **The episodes in between** these two extremes are concealed and harder to replicate: maybe, for this reason alone, these **intermediate activities** present more opportunities for 'core competency' acquisition and development.

5.22   Arguably, in fact, the organisation's core competency may turn out to be, in many instances, an **inhibitor for commercial success** rather than a source of strategic advantage. This is especially true for companies who think that their core competency depends upon the possession of information which other people do not have: oddly enough, their core competency may prove to be of more of a competitive benefit if it were to be **shared** than if it continues to be withheld. Thus Philips made audio cassette and compact disc technology freely available; Pilkingtons gave away the secrets of float glass; the Silicon Valley companies shared their technological breakthroughs and flourished (whereas the Route 128 companies, like Wang and Digital Equipment, tried to own and control their core competences, and failed). Giving a core competency away may sound crazy, but it does make **competitive innovation** less likely.

5.23   The general line of thinking summarised here is pursued at much greater length by Larry Downes and Chunka Mui (*Unleashing the Killer APP*, Harvard Business School Press, 1998) with particular reference to **digital information**. Increasing the number of people using it costs nothing, but adds exponentially to its value: this is why crucial pieces of Internet software, like the Netscape browser, have been provided free of charge.

5.24   It is still necessary for organisations to retain and develop their own internal skills, however. If they do not, then there is no rationale for their continued existence - and this is the scenario facing those companies which have outsourced so far. So long as IT, for example, is nothing more than an enabling function, then it can legitimately be left to subcontractors: but **IT is becoming increasingly pervasive - a determinant not only of how companies do things, but also of what they do.**

Marketing at Work

The Hullachan Pro

Hullachan is a Glasgow-based company which designs, manufactures and sells Highland and Irish dance shoes. Since opening its website, Hullachan now achieves 75 per cent of its sales through the Internet and exports to North America, Australasia and Ireland. All its overseas distributors were appointed as a result of approaches potential partners made to Hullachan after viewing its product offerings through the web; the company receives over 1000 EMails a week, which it promises to answer within 12 hours; of these, over 700 are customer enquiries which are converted to the distributors. Since January 1998 Hullachan has achieved a 60 per cent success rate with people confirming sales after looking at the site.

New problems and new products can be identified and addressed. Products are offered for testing to volunteers around the world and their feedback collected. Hullachan's owner, Craig Coussins, is currently investigating the possibility of equipping trade customers with Sony Viewcams so that product solutions can be presented visually.

The Cambridge Local Guide

AdHoc, specialising in the Internet production of town/city guides, has produced the most complete local guide to the city of Cambridge available: it complements a printed version, but is far more interactive. It generates around 10,000 visitors a month, plus high repeat usage because of the site's 'sticky content' which ensnares site visitors and reduces the likelihood that they will immediately (within a few seconds) click to something else. The Cambridge site gives much faster access to what's on at the local cinema than the recorded information facility provided by the cinema itself. It is this ease of access and updated content which encourages surfers to return and to become loyal users.

The Cambridge case illustrates the increasing obligation to create websites which entice people to stay, return, and tell their friends: all it takes to enable them to move is a single click, if they don't like what they see (it's not like walking out of a shop and going elsewhere, which requires real energy and takes much more time). The battle for website customer loyalty is important for several reasons: first, sites can extract higher advertising revenue if they can prove that users remain and return; second, users spend much longer with the marketing message, leading to a far higher proportion of conversions from 'just looking'.

RS Components

RS Components has spent £2.5 million on developing an Internet site which currently accounts for less than 1 per cent of its sales. However, it is in a high-margin business: in 1998, it delivered pre-tax profits of £118m on sales of £662m. The company stocks some 130,000 different electronic components and its customers - typically engineers and small tradesmen - want quick delivery of small amounts of stock (average order size is around £80). According to the RS CEO, 'Our customers after a solution to their immediate supply problems. They want availability, reliability, quality and technical support. Price comes about fifth on their list of priorities.'

Prior to creation of the website, it was calculated that the cost of completing an order to RS from placement to payment of the invoice was £60. This has fallen now to £10, and has produced savings of £100,000 a year. More important is the quality of information that has been acquired about each customer: RS currently deploys 10 customer categories, but ultimately expects to create a category for each individual customer. Interestingly, the CEO believes that in the future, 'Customer loyalty will go out of the window and will be replaced by customer retention: it is about how can we best deliver, service and fulfil our customers.'

6 THE FUTURE FOR MANUFACTURING

6.1 To satisfy customers, manufacturers of the immediate future will require a fundamental shift in organisational cultures. To create value for customers, manufacturers, in other words, must eliminate **traditional boundaries** between customers and **integrate** more closely with them.

6.2 The new state of manufacturing - where companies are expanding into new markets, confronting new competitors, coping with new technology - means that power and presence today does not guarantee power and presence tomorrow. New wealth from manufacturing is being created more by **adaptability, value-added** services and **speed of execution** than by sheer quantity of capital or machinery.

Fierce **global competition** and increasing demand for **customised products** and services, coupled with shortened product life cycles in most manufacturing industries, suggest that many of today's leaders will not necessarily be around for much longer.

6.3 To combat ever-shrinking product life cycles, for example, many companies are trying to 'pull' ideas from their customers rather than merely 'push' products into the market.

6.4 Differentiation in the era of the virtual customer will require **superior marketing and customer service**. Most manufacturers do not yet possess these capabilities. A global manufacturing study by Deloitte Consulting in 1998, involving 900 executives in 35 countries, suggests that many continue to focus on product quality and neglect the integration of manufacturing with marketing and sales. While manufacturers say they recognise the importance of superior service, they have not kept pace with rising customer expectations and tight delivery deadlines dictated by complex manufacturing systems.

6.5 Gaining customer loyalty is as important as 'getting the order'. Although market leaders in manufacturing have the advantage of greater brand awareness, established customer relationships and broad product lines, they suffer from weaknesses in the arenas of market and customer research.

6.6 To create a customer-centric organisation, **process re-engineering** is important for many manufacturers. However, this is not true for manufacturing companies in North America: they are focusing instead on IT (data warehousing, customer-integrated data and ecommerce) in order to improve marketing, sales and service. They are using these tools to capture and manage critical customer information across functions and geographies.

6.7 To succeed in the next few years, manufacturers will focus on **service-related attributes**, such as

- on-time delivery,
- customer-perceived product quality,
- prompt handling of customer complaints,
- fast response deliveries
- building superior customer relationships.

6.8 For customers, **on-time delivery** has never been more important. Their advanced production and control scheduling systems, lean manufacturing and inventory reduction practices make delivery reliability critical. This, with the growing use of direct Internet sales, especially in high technology and consumer product industries, will only heighten the pressure for product availability on demand.

Chapter roundup

- Prompted by ever-increasing competition and constant attacks on costs, markets, profitability and resources, more and more organisations are redefining themselves to operate on a global scale, thus spreading their costs and revenues across the world.

- The world economy has been characterised by the rapid growth of service sector activities.

- The existence of a 'global consumer' is tied to the concepts of global standardisation and adaptability.

- The debate continues to rage about whether there are, or can be, genuinely global brands.

- The reasons for marketing overseas include the small size of the domestic market and perceived opportunities to exploit economies of scale.

- Calculating the lifetime value of a customer can be done by roughly estimating the annual gross profit that they generate, working out customer retention rate and multiplying them together.

- Customers can be divided into three groups for communication purposes.

  o potential customers
  o customers who have made one purchase
  o premium customers who have made more than one purchase

- Electronic commerce can broaden trade horizons and create wider markets for products and services.

- The Internet is affecting all businesses in similar ways. Every industry is now part of a global network, with all companies in the industry equally contactable. Information, once valuable, is now a commodity.

- Electronic commerce has eliminated many of the competitive advantages enjoyed by existing competitors and will affect the value chain by making some parts of it redundant, and creating entirely new delivery systems.

- To satisfy customers, manufacturers of the immediate future will require a fundamental shift in organisational cultures. To create value for customers, manufacturers, in other words, must eliminate traditional boundaries between customers and integrate more closely with them.

Quick quiz

1 What is the concept of 'weightlessness' when applied to an economy? (see para 2.4)

2 What are the three approaches to international marketing? (2.11)

3 Give some examples of global brands. (2.13)

4 What replaces the Big Mac in India, and why? (2.19)

5 What can new entrants into a foreign country find expensive to set up? (3.4)

6 How can a global operator find out about local tastes? (3.7)

7 What is a loyal customer? (4.2)

8 Give some key elements of a customer care programme. (4.7)

9 Name some industries that have been particularly affected by electronic commerce. (5.7)

10 Why is on-time delivery increasingly important for customers? (6.8)

Illustrative questions and suggested answers

These past questions from CIM papers have been selected for this question bank by the senior examiner because they are of precisely the type which may appear in future *Marketing Customer Interface* exams. The Indicative Content has five principal sections: (1) Overview, Concepts and Background; (2) Managing the Marketing/Customer Interface; (3) Customer Dynamics; (4) Investigating Customer Dynamics; and (5) Customer Dynamics and the Future. Candidates must prepare themselves across the comprehensive range of the subject-matter, and should diligently practise some typical examination issues or questions, such as those involving electronic commerce, the increasing demands of customers, the need to integrate internal service practices with external customer orientation, and so forth. Virtually all the questions in the examination will contain a mixture of description (i.e., reproducing previously-internalised information), evaluation (i.e., critique and analysis), and situational application. It is not possible to pass the examination by merely reproducing facts and knowledge; conversely, however, generous credit will be given for the inclusion of up-to-date examples and illustrations.

For more comment from the examiner on the approaches to be adopted when answering the questions, see pages (xiii) to (xv) at the front of the text.

PART A

QUESTION 1

The Retail Distribution Revolution (*from The Selling Environment, December 1996*)

Retailers have grown into some of the world's largest companies, rivalling or exceeding manufacturers in terms of global stretch. Wal-Mart, a discount chain that has become the world's top retailer (see table below), has bigger sales than its competitors and many of its main suppliers. Its turnover of $67 billion in the year to 31st January 1994 was the fourth largest of any American company. It is Procter & Gamble's largest single customer, buying as much as the household-products giant sells to the whole of Japan.

The retail elite

The world's top retailers, by sales

	Main type of trade	Home country	Sales 1993 $bn	Number of stores 1993
Wal-Mart	Discount	United States	68.0	2,540
Metro Int	Diversified	Germany	48.4	2,750
Kmart	Discount	United States	34.6	4,274
Sears, Roebuck	Department	United States	29.6	1,817
Tengelmann	Supermarket	Germany	29.5	6,796
Rewe Zentrale	Supermarket	Germany	27.2	8,497
Ito-Yokado	Diversified	Japan	26.0	12,462

Source: Management Horizons

The distribution chain used to be controlled by manufacturers and wholesalers. The retailer's role was to buy goods from a range offered by the wholesaler or other intermediaries, and sell them on to the consumer. The main competitive advantage lay in merchandising - the skill in choosing the assortment of goods for sale in the store. There was a second potential advantage - closeness to the customer - but its only use, if any, was to beat rival retailers. For it was manufacturers who decided what goods were available, and in most countries at which price they could be sold to the public.

Information technology, mainly through the use of computer systems such as EPOS (electronic point of sale), EDI (electronic data interchange), smart cards and the Internet, has enabled retailers to transform the way they do business.

Is it time that the distribution system be turned upside down? The traditional supply chain, powered by manufacturer 'push', is becoming a demand chain, driven by consumer 'pull'. Could the next big development be the rise of genuine consumer power? We all know that consumers are sovereign, but so far they have operated a peculiar kind of dominion. They've been able to exercise choice - enough to make or break a company's fortunes. But that choice has been very limited and highly influenced by external forces. If retailer and consumer purchasing habits are shifting, new channels may have to be cut.

Source: The Economist - adaptation of a survey (March 1995)

Required

(a)   In relation to **two** of the following technological changes,

- EDI
- Smart cards
- Touchscreen technology
- Home shopping

comment on their significance for:

(i)   a retailer   **(10 marks)**

(ii)   a consumer **or** manufacturer (as appropriate)   **(10 marks)**

(b)   Drawing on your understanding of the retailing environment, suggest reasons why the power is shifting from seller to buyer.   **(10 marks)**

(c)   What recommendations would you make to a traditional retailer to retain competitive advantage in the future?   **(10 marks)**

                                                                                                          (40 marks total)

PART B

QUESTION 2 (*from Effective Management for Marketing, June 1998*)

In a recent industry wide survey your firm was rated lower than your main competitors, in terms of a number of key customer service and satisfaction areas. Your own analysis confirms that average customer spend and repeat purchase levels are also lower than the market leaders. As marketing manager, you are to prepare a report to the management team detailing how you propose improving this situation.   **(20 marks)**

QUESTION 3 (*from Effective Management for Marketing, December 1997*)

You are part of the marketing research team who has recently completed a mystery shopping exercise designed to evaluate the levels of customer service, at eighty stores nationally. Ten stores have been identified has having standards significantly below the others. Produce a report for the company outlining your proposals for identifying the underlying cause of the problems in these stores and suggesting possible strategies for improving customer service.   **(20 marks)**

QUESTION 4 (*from The Selling Environment, June 1997*)

You are the sales director of a financial services organisation, whose selling efforts have traditionally been directed at expanding sales through a constant stream of new customers.

Prepare a memorandum for discussion at your next board meeting on customer loyalty programmes. Your paper should cover the following:

(a)   The value of customer retention.   **(4 marks)**

(b)   The information needed before implementing a loyalty programme.   **(12 marks)**

(c)   An appropriate loyalty scheme.   **(4 marks)**

                                                                                                          (20 marks)

QUESTION 5 (*from Planning and Control, June 1997*)

Your company is about to launch a new computer software package into the airline and hotel reservations market. Prepare a report for your marketing director identifying the information needed to develop customer profiles and how these profiles might then be used to develop the segmentation, targeting and positioning strategy.   **(20 marks)**

QUESTION 6 (*from Effective Management for Marketing, June 1997*)

At a meeting of marketing team members it is identified that the marketing function has a poor image within the organisation. Few people understand the role and function of the marketing team, and it is wrongly assumed by many to be simply a promotional activity. Prepare a paper for presentation at the next team meeting proposing a course of action to improve the marketing of marketing within the organisation.**(20 marks)**

QUESTION 7 (*from Planning and Control, June 1998*)

Making reference to examples, discuss how either the Internet or developments in database management are changing managers' thinking on the marketing strategy and how customers might be managed.   **(20 marks)**

QUESTION 8 (*from Marketing Communications Strategy, June 1997*)

Evaluate the ways in which the rapid growth of the Internet is changing the way businesses communicate with their customers, suppliers and within their own organisations.   **(20 marks)**

QUESTION 9 (*from Effective Management for Marketing, June 1997*)

You are working with a national charity as a consultant. Increased competition for donations has forced the organisation to review its culture and philosophy. It is now recognised that it has been very operationally focused and needs to become much more customer focused, which in the case of a charity means centred around the needs of its supporters, both individual and business.

Required

Prepare a report for presentation to the governing body of the charity reviewing briefly the benefits of a more supporter focused culture and detailing the ways in which such a transformation could be achieved.**(20 marks)**

QUESTION 10 (*from The Selling Environment, December 1996*)

As sales director of a production orientated organisation, you would like to recommend an organisational structure to achieve maximum customer orientation. Prepare a brief for discussion at the next board meeting, highlighting the advantages and disadvantages of such a change.   **(20 marks)**

Suggested answers

The suggested answers we have included here represent responses to questions of precisely the type which may appear in future *Marketing Customer Interface* examinations. In each case, the senior examiner has written a short preface explaining why the question is significant and what approaches he would expect candidates to adopt.

PART A

1

> *The senior examiner says*: The references to Wal-Mart in the question are particularly poignant in view of the company's acquisition of Asda in mid-1999. However, the main thrust of the quotation is contained within its final paragraph's references to the possibility of 'genuine consumer power', and students would be well advised to examine again the senior examiner's commentary about some of the trends in the field of customer dynamics: greater expectations, greater willingness to complain, enhanced enthusiasm about fighting dirty (ie collective action, use of the media, litigation), greater preparedness to move to alternative suppliers, and so forth.
>
> One or two aspects of the question, given its 1996 provenance, now seem slightly antiquated and there is only a passing reference to the Internet. In 1990, there were no companies or commercial operations on the Internet; by 1995, there were around 5,000 companies with a strong Web presence; at the start of 1999, the number had grown to more than half a million. By 2000 it is expected that there will be more than 2.5 million businesses operating with websites (admittedly not all of them transactional), and at the present rate of growth, it is possible that the number of businesses online will exceed the number of people on earth by the year 2010, and the online economy may dominate all global commerce by 2015.
>
> The final part of the question could yield very imaginative responses, involving both customer relationships and internal process-and-people systems. The wording of the question itself does not specify the field in which the retailer may be operating, nor the retailer's size, so answers in practice should cover all the more likely alternatives. Thus, if small retailers cannot compete on price, they can compete on customer value and relationship marketing: the danger these days is that large retailers can more easily do the same, especially as the information gleaned from so-called 'loyalty' cards enables such retailers to target their product/service offerings very specifically to very tightly-defined segments.

PART B

2

> *The senior examiner says*: Generous credit will always be given in the marking scheme for those responses which adhere to the requirement for producing material in the form of a (businesslike) report. More substantively, however, the senior examiner would expect to see the report contain references to mechanisms for enhancing organisational performance so far as both its external and its internal customers are concerned. Many sources have demonstrated that customer perceptions of service cannot be achieved without a proper concentration on internal customer service and the promotion of a customer mentality among all employees. Three of these sources are referred to below.
>
> - The International Service Study, headed by Professor Chris Voss from the London Business School, shows that customer service achievement (as measured in the only way that matters, by customer perceptions) is strongly correlated with the presence of customer-service practices within the organisation. If the practices do not exist, and people spend much of their time with corporate in-fighting, then it is very unlikely that customers will receive good service. According to Voss and his colleagues, critical factors inside the organisation include leadership from the top, empowerment of people, the existence of appropriate performance measures, a strong sense of market acuity, and the inclusion of customer service as a key feature of the organisation's scorecard.

- Chris Daffy, in *Once a Customer, Always a Customer (1997)*, uses a three-phase framework incorporating 'vision and values', 'internal people things' and 'external customer things'. So far as 'internal people things' are concerned, the inputs of recruitment, training and trust are linked to the outputs of teamwork, commitment, performance and continuity; similarly, with 'external customer things', partnership leads to loyalty, referrals and retention.

- Reichheld's celebrated article for the *Harvard Business Review* on 'the loyalty effect' shows that there is a 'virtuous circle' linking both customer focus and internal mechanisms. High levels of external service quality produce customer satisfaction which in turn leads to customer loyalty and profitable growth (because the cost of servicing current customers is much lower than the cost of acquiring new ones). Profitable growth makes it easier for the organisation to devote resources for internal service quality, and internal service quality is correlated with employee satisfaction, in turn generating employee retention. With employee retention (and profitability) we are back at the beginning of the cycle, because employees who have progressed far along the learning curve are more likely to deliver external service quality. As Reichheld points out, however, the 'virtuous circle' can easily become a downward-facing 'doom loop' as each of the ingredients begins to fail.

To: Senior management team
From: Marketing manager
Subject: Improvement of customer service and customer satisfaction

(a) Current situation

You are aware that in a recent industry-wide survey our company had a rating for customer service and satisfaction lower than our major competitors. This will obviously have serious implications for our future market share, and urgently needs addressing.

First of all, we need to understand what our problems really are. This means carrying out an audit in various ways.

(i) Customers

The key to customer retention is satisfied customers. First of all we need to find out if and why they are dissatisfied. This can be done in a number of ways, customer satisfaction questionnaires, personal interviews with major customers and analysis of internal records for customer sales history etc.

I recommend a mixture of all three ways because external questionnaires can prove unreliable unless questions are carefully thought out, and it would need presenting to customers in a positive light, not as a reaction to our apparent poor service.

All large customers should receive visits from the management team to discuss our performance, with medium sized customers visited by senior field sales staff. The interviews need to identify not only the reasons for dissatisfaction, but also customer needs and service expectations.

(ii) Working practices

An audit is also required of our processes from initial customer enquiry to order fulfilment. This will help identify main delays and barriers to speeding up our whole process.

(iii) Staff

The audit also needs to evaluate the staffing levels and abilities at each stage in the processes for (ii). Many companies put much more staffing and effort into customer acquisition departments, but limit customer service and customer retention departments.

(iv) Internal attitudes

We must understand how far our company attitudes and priorities match those of the customers identified in the customer audit, and whether we are addressing customer priorities. This applies both at management and staff levels, particular for negative attitudes to satisfying customers.

(v) Competitors

We should benchmark our service against competitors, and also seek to identify best practice from similar companies. This can be achieved by talking to their customers, our internal staff who have worked for competitors, observing competitors in action or posing as potential customers.

401

(b) **Proposed strategy**

The audit will help us develop main objectives for an improved customer service programme.

(i) **Main objectives.** These should be:

(1) To develop a genuine 'customer first' belief in all departments

(2) To ensure and prioritise customer needs, and match our company priorities to these needs

(3) To provide an urgent and effective programme of training and development to all staff involved in customer service

(4) To alter company structures to give greater authority to staff at the customer interface

(5) To provide an overall action programme which will make our service match the best of our competitors in customer satisfaction and retention rates within 12 months

(ii) Action to achieve the objectives would be as follows.

(1) **Resources**

Recent studies show that it costs about five times as much to generate a new customers than to keep an existing one. This means that we must allocate enough resources. This will involve resources for new staff, re-allocation of staff from other areas, training and development, and any new technology limited to service, customer database and distribution.

(2) **Responsibilities**

Senior management staff must understand that everybody is responsible for customer service. However, we should appoint or reallocate a member of senior management with specific responsibility to implement the improvement programme.

The senior manager can appoint a team from different departments with responsibilities for their own departmental programmes. The audit will identify particular action points, and these can be addressed in the department concerned. The interdepartmental team will also look at overall process improvements and be given responsibility to drive through any changes.

It is also vital that we involve all relevant staff in workshops, suggestion schemes etc, and promote the positive impact on improving customer service for the whole company.

(3) **Training and development**

It is important that both management and staff are involved in customer service training programmes. The recommendation is that our Chief Executive address managers and staff directly, describing how we want our products and services perceived by customers.

Individual and group training programmes can be developed from individual appraisals and team assessments. It is also vital that 'customer first' attitudes are continuously developed during the programmes. This is helped by explaining what customer service means to each service area, and how it can be delivered. The message has to be that we only get ahead by meeting customer needs better than the competition.

(4) **Working practices**

We need to ensure our processes are focused on customer priorities, and that all customer contact interfaces are 'customer friendly'. The audit should have identified reasons for losing orders and customers, and also reasons why customers place orders with certain suppliers. We can then focus on delivering service on the order-winning factors, and correcting the order-losing factors.

(5) **Structure**

We cannot implement improved customer service programmes without improving authority levels at the customer interface. Staff who deal with customers must have higher authority to make decisions, correct complaints and instruct other departments to take necessary actions to meet service requirements.

Our overall structure needs evaluation to ensure it is market orientated.

(c) **Monitoring and control**

Once the action programmes are initiated, these need to be monitored and modified as necessary.

(i) **Targets**

We need to set both quantitative and qualitative measures of success. Quantitative measures will include percentage of orders fulfilled by customer required date, percentage of delivery promises kept, reduction in customer complaints, reduction in lost orders and customers, etc. Qualitative measures will include customer and employee feedback, comments in complaints areas, customer satisfaction levels from questionnaires.

(ii) **Incentives**

The incentive and bonus programme should change to be paid on achievement of customer service targets. This will involve a culture change away from such incentives as commission on sales targets, which can discourage customer service activities. All staff must understand that increased customer service means increased sales.

(iii) **Feedback**

We need record systems for providing feedback from both customers and employees. Records will include details of service performance, regular purchase and preferences, as well as personal details. An efficient customer database is a prerequisite of developing a customer loyalty programme. Customer satisfaction surveys can also be used for feedback, and a further audit carried out of customer attitudes after six months.

3

The senior examiner says: The theme for this question is similar to that already addressed in question 2 above. On the other hand, on this occasion the senior examiner would expect students to recommend a fact-gathering exercise which would highlight all significant differences between the poorly performing stores and a similar number of above average units. Although some may argue that low levels of achievement could be derived from the presence of unusually tolerant customers, or the inability to recruit appropriate people from the local labour market, it is much more likely that that the causes will home in on the leadership behaviour of the store manager in terms of role-modelling, creating and disseminating an inspirational vision, recruiting and selecting staff with a positive balance of customer facing attributes, and so forth.

REPORT

To: Customer service manager
From: Researcher
Date: 12 December 1997
Re: Stores with poor customer service

1   Poor customer service

1.1   The mystery shopping exercise is a fact and has revealed low levels of service. It is no good for the stores to say that the poor level of service was a 'one-off'. Such one-off experiences are still moments of truth for the customer. If disappointed even on one occasion they will leave with a bad impression, and pass on their opinions about the stores to their friends.

1.2   The market research also identifies the scope of the problem. Service levels are significantly worse and so must be investigated.

2   Identifying the causes

2.1   Present the findings of the survey to the store management. They might be able to give some explanations or excuses. They might cite high staff turnover. This may reflect the catchment area of the recruits, but it is just as likely to reflect the quality of management.

2.2   Managers may say that customer service levels are impossible to achieve. However there is the example of the better stores to show that good customer service is possible.

2.3   Staff can also be shown the results of the survey. They may have their own ideas as to how things can be done better, but may be afraid to say so for fear of offending the management team. Staff may not be interested, anyhow, if they are demotivated or not committed to the company or its customers.

2.4 Identify the type of service failure.

(a) With mass services, such as banks for example, the quality of service depends a great deal on the efficiency and effectiveness of the systems underlying the service. Perhaps there are systems or procedural failures at the stores, for example in stock control or invoicing, which can be rectified.

(b) With personal services, the quality of service depends far more on the individual giving the service. In a store, factors such as staff's product knowledge can influence levels of customer service.

(c) The firm should identify whether service failures are technical (eg whether the right goods are sold at the right prices) or functional (eg appearance and manner of service personnel).

2.5 Consider why the better performing stores are performing well, and also the performance of competitors.

2.6 Once the nature of the problem has been identified, then measures can be taken to improve service.

3 Improving service quality

3.1 Outside help. A radical step, but if the service failures are result of bad management, then new management can be brought in, if only for the short term, to repair the situation, and to give some on the job management training to those who remain.

3.2 Change recruitment practices. Perhaps the wrong people are being recruited. Managers can be trained in how to recruit effectively.

3.3 Institute and follow up training programmes in areas relevant to customer service. This is especially relevant for personal services, when a friendly and professional manner is appreciated by customers. Training programmes should be focused on the problems found. Good service should be illustrated by using 'real-life' examples, particularly from the stores that are performing well, as these will be most relevant to the employees being trained.

3.4 Review systems and procedures where these are lowering standards of customer services. Introduce new procedures, if they are needed.

3.5 Consider ways of motivating staff, by reviewing the culture of each store. Culture is very hard to change, but a more open culture can encourage better communication. even a store bonus scheme might help.

4 Conclusion

4.1 The service standards desired are perfectly possible to achieve. A variety of measures relating to the processes and people elements of the services marketing mix can be employed to improve matters.

4

> *The senior examiner says*: The subject of customer 'loyalty' has already appeared in the *Understanding Customers* paper on more than one occasion. A moment's intelligent reflection should reveal that customer loyalty and customer retention are not necessarily different interpretations of the same phenomenon. The organisation may retain its customers for all kinds of reasons which have nothing to do with loyalty: they may not be able to switch to alternative suppliers (in the UK, citizens continue to pay council tax to their municipal authorities, but this does not mean that they would not switch to another organisation, or withhold payment altogether, if they had the chance); they may remain out of sheer inertia, as many do so far as their bank accounts are concerned; they may remain because they know that they are getting a very good deal (eg they pay no charges to their bank, so long as their account is in credit) even though, by the same token, they regard the bank with contempt; they may remain because what they are spending is a very small proportion of their total disposable income; they may remain because going somewhere else would involve them in substantial set-up costs (they may have to buy new computer software, for example). Finally, customers may continue to purchase from a given organisation because they are incentivised through a 'loyalty' card. Let us be clear: the use of 'loyalty' cards is not a measure of customer loyalty. If loyalty means anything, is must surely imply voluntary, profitable repurchasing and referral: it is voluntary because it is undertaken without any bribes being involved; it is profitable because the supplier earns a surplus from the transaction; and it must include recommendation to others.

5

> *The senior examiner says*: Customer profiling as an exercise in segmentation is a very important part of *The Marketing Customer Interface* indicative content. This question gives students the opportunity to demonstrate their grasp of segmentation as a philosophy plus their ability to apply segmentation concepts to a briefly-outlined scenario.

To: Marketing Director
From: Marketing Manager
Date: June 1997
Subject: Report Identifying Customer Information Required

This report aims to identify the information needed to develop customer profiles and how these profiles might then be used to develop the segmentation, targeting and positioning strategy.

Who are our Customers?

Our key customers are likely to be Airlines, Travel Agencies and any business involved in booking holidays and flights. Within those markets there are several people who will be *using* the systems. They are also our customers, so they will likely to affect the choice of software bought. The airlines and hotels are also likely to exert pressure on the choice of software bought in terms of how the information is presented to them and software compatibility.

Organisational buying has distinct characteristics (Kotler, 1994).

(a)   Organisations buy goods and services to satisfy a variety of goals: making profits, reducing costs, meeting employee needs, and meeting social and legal obligations.

(b)   More persons are typically involved in organisational buying decisions, especially in procuring major items. The decision group often will have different job titles and apply different criteria to the purchase decision.

(c)   There may be formalised structures and policies that they must follow.

Although no two companies are likely to buy in the same way, it is possible that there is enough similarity in the way that buyers of the DMU approach the task to be of strategic significance.

Information Required

The kinds of customer profiling information that we would be interested in compiling would be as follows.

(a) **Demographic**	(b) **Operating variables**	(c) **Purchasing approaches**
• Industry • Company • Location	• Technology • User status • Customer capabilities	• Buying criteria • Buying policies • Current relationships

(d) **Situational factors**	(e) **Personal characteristics**
• Urgency • Size of order • Applications	• Loyalty • Attitudes to risk

This information will give us alternative variables for segmenting our market. For example, we could concentrate on companies which buy large orders (situational factor), companies that use a specific operating system (operating variable) or segments which combine a number of similar characteristics in different areas.

Targeting

Once we have segmented the markets we need to assess the attractiveness of each of the segments. These need to be assessed in terms the following.

- Measurability
- Accessibility
- Substance
- Meaning

In choosing which segments to target, of course our overriding aim is going to be **profitability**. This is influenced by competitive activity as illustrated by Porter.

Through developing our customer profiles, in the first instance we will have an extremely good information base on which to make these decisions for example the number of purchases they make, the length of time they take over decision making, geographical spread etc.

Positioning

Once we have made the decisions on how to segment and which segments we are going to target we can position our product and company in the best possible position to meet the different needs of the segment

From the customer profiling, it may be the case that a segment emerges which uses a specific kind of technology at the moment; we can present our products unique compatibility as being a USP. This would be extremely attractive to those companies and we know that no other software is available to do this so easily.

Conclusion

It is only through such detailed customer profiling that we can identify and target the most lucrative segments. Using the information that we have complied about them, we know what their needs are and can present them with the best/most appropriate solution/package.

The time and expense involved in the initial profiling stage will be offset with the efficiency in which we will be able to target the most lucrative markets and present our software package in the most attractive manner.

6

Introduction

The problem we have faced in recent years is that marketing's role is perceived to be very limited. We need to find out marketing is viewed in this way and develop a strategy to improve perceptions.

Audit of perceptions

We need specific information about how marketing is perceived, and in particular we need to ensure we obtain feedback:

(a)   from senior management since they influence decisions about the resources available to marketing and their decisions affect our priorities;

(b)   from the various operational departments, as their individual needs will differ.

We can obtain feedback by:

(a)   one-to-one contact with senior or influential individuals;
(b)   a marketing needs survey asking about what support operational staff require.

Developing a strategy

Having obtained feedback we should then be in a position to decide the specific objectives we should be seeking to achieve within the overall aim of improving the perception of marketing within the business.

Key elements in developing a strategy for marketing will include:

(a)   deciding the extent of marketing's involvement with the operational departments. We should consider whether the aim should be to offer increased support facilities or whether to take a more interventionist approach, setting standards or implementing quality checks on marketing activities undertaken by operational departments;

(b)   deciding how different departments or staff should be targeted;

(c)   deciding how operational departments can be involved in the work of the marketing department.

Members of the marketing department must be involved in developing the strategy. Involvement is particularly important as department members are likely to be given increased individual responsibility for enhancing the department's image.

Tasks

Various methods can be used to enhance the image of marketing.

(a)   Encouraging operational departments to make suggestions and give feedback can enhance their involvement in the marketing process.

(b)   Members of the marketing team can enhance their understanding by contact with the user departments. An example of this is a newly privatised water authority, which had staff working with plumbers and sewer repair teams to find out what their jobs entailed. This sort of shadowing can work in the other direction- an example is operational staff attending marketing presentations.

(c)   Another way of linking marketing in with operational staff is to make individual members of the marketing department responsible for contacts with particular operational departments or senior staff.

(d)   Similarly we could develop a network of marketing contacts within operational departments. We can keep in touch with these contacts on a regular basis and invite them for seminars or training in marketing techniques. The idea will be to build up links from whom we can obtain informed comment and criticism, and who will act as 'champions' of the marketing department.

(e)   Other means of increasing marketing visibility include a newsletter, highlighting the variety of activities marketing undertake.

Controls

The process of change needs to be monitored if it is to be fully effective. Ways of monitoring whether the image of marketing is perceived to have changed include requesting the opinions of senior operational management, the volume of contacts between operational departments and marketing (how much is the marketing department being used) and targets relevant to specific activities(for example, response times for requests for information).

7

The senior examiner says: Given the forecasts about the spread of electronic commerce over the foreseeable future, then questions on this subject must feature prominently in *The Marketing Customer Interface*. As things stand (in 1999), today's websites are not addressing the real potential of the Internet economy. Look-to-buy ratios are very low – similar to direct mail yields – with 2.7 buyers for every 100 website visitors; where websites offer transaction facilities, the orders being taken are generally for low-consideration products, and most purchases completed over the Internet are for easy-to-buy, strongly branded products. By contrast, on-line completion rates for complex products like mortgages and other financial services are less than one in 20. Today's e-commerce sites cater largely for self-motivated, self-directed technology optimists who can integrate content and transactions from multiple source to buy successfully on-line.

According to Forrester Research, a US consultancy, companies entering the realm of electronic commerce must engage in 'guided selling', which is defined as 'consultative online sales processes that enable buyers to efficiently define needs and make decisions in a self-service environment.' To realise guided selling, websites must fulfil three imperatives:

- *Build objectives and create alternatives* – in other words, help buyers to construct and refine their objectives, and then match products to these objectives. Sellers must build and maintain rich profiles of buyers, to understand how to interact effectively with them and tailor what is offered.

- *Assist with decisions* – by allowing buyers to create, and see, their own solutions; by offering independent and authoritative proof (from new sources, product demonstrations, on-line decision support tools or the brokering of contacts between uncertain buyers and customer references via chatlines or e-mail); and by equipping buyers with analysis tools.

- *Manage and measure the process* – to guide rudderless buyers, sites must suggest next steps, and attempt to engage potential buyers who wander away. It is important that the commercial website has a high degree of 'stickiness', ie it captures the Internet browser: otherwise the browser can simply click forward to the next 'shop'.

Again based on 1999 data, two-thirds of all online transactions are abandoned because of inadequate customer support. Despite these hiccups, on the other hand, the vast majority of company directors and senior executives are convinced that the Internet will reshape both business strategy and the marketplace.

The benefits of the Internet as a marketing medium have been much hyped, with hundreds of companies leaping on the bandwagon as essentially an act of faith. But has the Web delivered on all its promises? Keeler (1995) states that the marketing uses of the Internet are fivefold.

(a)   Sending messages via e-mail thereby eradicating location issues.

(b)   Transferring files thus quickly and cheaply connecting customers and suppliers.

(c)   Monitoring news and opinion thus very useful for marketing research.

(d)   Searching and browsing.

(e)   Posting, hosting and presenting information which facilitates brand building and sales generation.

Effects on marketing strategy

Companies operating through the Internet are likely to build databases of customers who have visited or used their site as the basis for further activity. Both approaches lead to the development of a more direct relationship being built with the individual customer over time. The areas of marketing strategy the Internet is likely to effect are:

(a) **Markets:** markets can be exploited that are not related to geographic nearness or physical contact (ie face to face activity). Customers' needs can be serviced remotely using the new technologies. However, investment would be needed in the IT infrastructure of an organisation. The cost of a web-site can range from a few thousand pounds to many hundred of thousands. Rank Xerox's web-site reinforces the company's brand values, as it documents its history of innovation but it also leads the user on a sales journey that aims to stimulate and capture a response. Over £2m has been generated from sales leads in one year.

(b) **Brands.** In the service sector the Internet may allow customers access to service providers anywhere in the world, where previously the customer has been restricted to local providers. This could lead to the globalisation of service brands. (For instance why study an MBA at your local university when you could study via the Internet at a major international business school?)

(c) **Products.** A whole new generation of information based products/services can be developed. Feedback from customers can facilitate more tailor-made offerings.

(d) **Promotion.** The Internet creates a new approach to promotion, as it creates a new mass communication medium for marketers to use and one which promotes far greater two-way communication. It allows customers to 'enter' an advert, providing involvement and direct response.

(e) **Distribution channels**. The Internet enables an organisation to operate in the world market from a small and centralised base. It could change the whole nature of distribution in the service sector in particular as a result.

(f) **Service**. The internet can deliver economies via providing service 24 hours a day, seven days a week, without prohibitive cost implications.

Managing Customers

The Internet allows for a customer relationship to be built without direct face-to-face contact. In order to do this successfully, companies will need to develop sophisticated databases that allow companies to develop tailor made products and offers for customer groupings within their database. It also helps in securing their loyalty through the greater convenience it delivers. For example, Marketing Business (June 1997) provides an interesting case study. Transport company *TNT Express Worldwide* is in fierce competition with its rivals. It hopes that its new web site will encourage its customers to ship parcels with it again and again. Central to the site is a facility that delivers improved customer service - Web Tracker. While tracking parcels from a web site is not new TNT wanted to make it easier. So instead of having to cut and paste individual parcel consignment numbers into Web tracker, TNT engineered its site to accept up to 500 consignment numbers at one time and users didn't have to enter date or destination details either. Customers like it - 5% of TNT parcels are now tracked on-line - and a number are working to integrate Web Tracker into their Intranets.

Conclusions

Use of the Internet in marketing is here to stay. Like all developments the extreme positive and negative forecasts are likely to be exaggerated. Whilst it offers new ways of reaching your customer, servicing them and encouraging their loyalty there are a number of pitfalls which O'Commor and Galvin (1997) highlight.

- Poor targeting capabilities
- Cost
- Incompatible marketing messages
- Immaturity of the medium and its users
- Communication speed

That stated the Internet should certainly be on every marketing manager's agenda.

The senior examiner says: The theme for this question focuses on the way that the Internet may influence communications between suppliers and customers, and within organisations.

Research carried out in 1999 by Rubic Inc, in the USA ('Evaluating the 'Sticky' Factor of E-commerce Sites') has found that the majority of websites fail to communicate effectively with their (new or existing) customers. Only 40% have a strategy of personalisation for their e-mail messages to customers; when customers respond to follow-up offers, only one quarter of websites recognise the fact that it is a repeat purchaser; 40% of e-mail product queries go unanswered despite promises of replies within two days. If this evidence is accurate, there is clearly plenty of work to be done. There is also much to be done within organisations, too, where processes often continue to be dominated by inter-departmental rivalries rather than customer-focused action.

What is the Internet?

The Internet is a world-wide network of computer networks. These are linked together so that users can search for and access data and information provided by others, linked through the different networks.

The World Wide Web is the multimedia element which provides facilities such as full-colour, graphics, sound and video. Web sites are points within the network created by members who wish to provide an information point for searchers to visit and benefit by the provision of information and/or by entering into a transaction.

Current uses and development issues

There are an increasing number of interactive uses that the Internet can be used for:

(a)   Communication (information provision)
(b)   Product development
(c)   Facilitating transactions
(d)   Fostering dialogue and relationships with different stakeholders

The attributes of the Internet that allow for these uses also need to be considered.

(a)   High speed of interaction
(b)   Low cost provision and maintenance
(c)   Ability to provide mass customisation
(d)   Global reach and wide search facilities
(e)   Instant dialogue
(f)   Multi-directional communications (eg: to suppliers, customers and regulators)
(g)   High level of user control
(h)   Customer (Visitor) driven
(i)   Moderate level of credibility

Use with customers

The use of the Internet by organisations with their customers has in the initial years been focussed upon the business-to-business sector rather than consumer end users. Those customers that have used the Internet do so primarily in search of entertainment and information. Web sites have become increasingly sophisticated and are a useful means of meeting the needs of customers and organisations.

Businesses can communicate more cost-effectively with their customers and provide a wide range of facilities. The volume of customer traffic that can be handled is far larger and quicker than through traditional means. Sales literature, product designs and innovations, ideas, price lists, complaints, sales promotions such as competitions, and orders and sales can all be undertaken over the Internet. The objectives are essentially two-fold. The first is to generate the first steps of a relationship (or maintain one already established). The second is the collection of customer profile information to be added to the database. Names, addresses and other demographic and psychographic data can be collected without any human intervention and/or the associated costs.

The execution of financial transactions over the Internet has been a deterrent due to the fear of fraud and misappropriation of funds. More secure systems and protection devices are now becoming available and this will spur the growth of purchasing activities over the Internet in the future.

A further development is to integrate the Internet with other elements of the marketing and promotional mix. For example the Tesco and Sainsbury's initiatives to develop home shopping have met with limited success but further investment will generate new shopping patterns and purchasing behaviours.

Use with suppliers

The use of the Internet with suppliers will provide a more dynamic form of communication exchange. Problem identification, the formation of solutions and constant dialogue opportunities will enable suppliers to forge closer relationships in the marketing channel.

Marketing communications opportunities will arise where, for example, new products can be presented to suppliers much more quickly, sales literature and product specification data can be relayed instantly and, in some cases, advertising materials presented more effectively.

Sales order processing and lead management systems are already providing marketing channel members (and end-user customers) with greater efficiency and speed of information retrieval. Suppliers also benefit from being able to contribute to product modifications and fault-finding processes can be speeded up. Perhaps one of the more exciting opportunities the Internet provides is greater customisation - more tailored products for specific customers.

Use within organisations: intranets

Internally the greatest advance is the development of intranets. The provision of internal, password-protected communication networks allows for the rapid dissemination of corporate and marketing information. For global organisations this represents a tremendous step forward as an intranet can overcome time barriers and allow for the transmission of materials to all parts of a company instantaneously. It provides a wealth of information for members to keep themselves informed of company news.

The development and interest in *internal marketing* has been assisted by this new form of internal communications. The involvement of staff and the motivational opportunities afforded by intranet technology enable employees and management to work more closely together.

Future of the Internet

The future of the Internet is bounded only by imagination and technological advances. Essentially there will be greater interactive opportunities which will enable a range of stakeholders to interact with organisations as a community to provide information, education, entertainment, products, services and financial transactions quickly, efficiently and so release more time for leisure and recreational activities.

9

> *The senior examiner says*: This question concerns itself with a cultural transformation towards customer focus in a charity. The topic is suitable relevant to a major section of the indicative content for *The Marketing Customer Interface*.

To: Governing Body, National Charity
From: Consultant
Date: August 1999
Subject: Refocusing the charity

Advantages of a supporter focused culture

Switching to a more supporter focused culture is essential for the charity's future. 'Competition' from other charities is increasing and in particular other charities are becoming more skilled at targeting supporters who are likely to be responsive.

Once the refocus has taken place, the charity should be able to maintain its income by attracting new supporters and also keeping existing supporters. It is particularly important then to try to build relationships with supporters, since guaranteed regular income from long-term supporters can help the charity plan ahead. Additionally retaining the support of active supporters, who assist in the charity's activities, will mean that fundraising activities do not decrease, and also the charity can continue to carry out its charitable objectives.

The change process has a number of important elements.

Research supporters' wishes

The charity needs to understand who its supporters are and why they have chosen to support the charity. This means the charity requires a detailed analysis of the profile of its existing supporters, and needs to consider how to strengthen relationships with them through regular communication and more active involvement in the charity's activities. In particular the charity should differentiate between supporters whose support is purely financial, and supporters who wish to play an active role in the charity's affairs. The latter may be attracted by opportunities to participate more effectively and training in better management or fundraising skills can help them do this.

Communication with supporters may be by means of questionnaire or letters. Seminars may be organised for supporters who participate actively in the charity's work, similar to the seminars organised for full-time staff (see below).

Involvement of senior management

The magnitude of the proposed changes mean that senior management must be actively involved in promoting change, in explaining the need for and implications of the changes to staff and to supporters.

Involvement of staff

The benefits of the new culture must be sold to the charity's staff, and awareness is needed of the problems of doing so. Staff may resist change for the following reasons.

(a) There may be a feeling that the motivation for change is suspect, that as a result of the change the charity is becoming 'too commercial' and hence losing its integrity.

(b) Staff may not realise how vital it is for the charity to change, and may prefer to avoid the disruption change involves.

(c) Change may be perceived as inconvenient or damaging the standing of staff.

Consultation with and involvement of staff will therefore be vital, to convince them that the proposals for change will take into account their knowledge and experience. It is recommended that seminars be run, demonstrating why change is necessary, what will be expected of staff and the benefits to staff and the charity. The seminars should also be an effective means of soliciting the views of staff. In addition the board should try and identify who is likely to support the changes and who is likely to oppose them and perhaps tailor the initial communication process with staff appropriately.

Consideration should also be given to changing the charity's system of internal communication so that staff are kept regularly informed about the changes that are needed and the staff most affected by particular changes are informed early on.

Training of staff

Staff will need appropriate training in whatever new skills are necessary to mean that they are more focused on the charity's supporters. This should include communication skills training for staff dealing directly with supporters.

As noted above, increased training may also be given to supporters who actively participate in the charity's activities.

Re-organisation of activities

Re-organisation will involve changes in the staffing structure of the charity, and also changes in which supporters are organised. Increased delegation of decision-making to volunteers may be appropriate. However because the time of volunteers is likely to be limited, full-time staff may be more involved than before in supporting and providing necessary backup or expertise to supplement volunteer activity.

Timetable

Activity	Timescale
Consult supporters	0-2 months
Consult staff	2-4 months
Draft re-organisation plan	5 months
Consult supporters and staff on re-organisation plan	5-6 months
Supporter and staff training	7-9 months
Implement re-organisation plan	9-12 months

10

The senior examiner says: The theme for this question once again involves cultural transformation, and students will be expected to show that they are sufficiently familiar with the organisational and structural dimensions of a customer-focused, customer-service company.

Specimen paper and marking guide

Certificate in Marketing

8.35 The Marketing Customer Interface

3 Hours Duration

This examination is in two sections.

Part A is compulsory and worth 40% of total marks.

Part B has **SIX** questions, select **THREE**. Each answer will be worth 20% of the total marks.

DO NOT repeat the question in your answer but show clearly the number of the question attempted.

Rough working should be included and ruled through after use.

DO NOT OPEN THIS PAPER UNTIL YOU ARE READY TO START UNDER EXAMINATION CONDITIONS

PART A

The PleasureFood Restaurant Group

As the name of the company suggests, the PleasureFood Group operates a collection of fast-food restaurants located principally in town and city centres, shopping malls, leisure complexes and airports. The Group has expanded from a single café/bar opened by the PleasureFood company's owner about 30 years ago; it now has 75 units, some run directly by PleasureFood's personnel, and some operated by franchisees.

The PleasureFood strategy has been founded on organic growth, but it is now contemplating more rapid expansion, if promising lines of development can be found. Some of the major alternatives include: diversification into food 'manufacturing', industrial catering (ie restaurants inside office buildings for corporate employees), the creation of branded food products for sale through supermarkets, and entry into overseas markets.

Each of the PleasureFood restaurants is built to a common standard and is intended to provide identical meals and service. Head Office supplies detailed instructions about every aspect of the PleasureFood operation, including portion control, cleanliness and hygiene, the appearance of the staff, the words and phrases used when communicating with customers, and price/product standardisation.

Currently, PleasureFood's principal customer segments are teenagers, shoppers, and families with children. It has around 30 per cent of its chosen market place, its major competitors being McDonalds, Burger King, and a couple of the major pizza companies; the remainder of the competition is occupied by very small, local companies.

The PleasureFood group is a well-managed and successful company. It is in good shape financially. However, the Board consists entirely of people who have spent their careers with PleasureFood, and Board meetings are dominated by the presence of the company's owner.

Question 1

You are a consultant who has been engaged by PleasureFood's Marketing Director in order to offer the company some guidance about the optimal direction which it should pursue in the future. Produce a report initially aimed at the Marketing Director but ultimately intended for distribution to the Board, in which you respond to each of the issues raised by the Marketing Director in her brief, as follows.

(a)   Given the fact that the PleasureFood Group has never established a customer database, and has never systematically investigated customer perceptions about its products and service, how could it cost-effectively acquire such a database and also secure definitive information about customer satisfaction?   **(10 marks)**

(b)   What are the major trends in customer segmentation and customer dynamics which could affect the PleasureFood Group's business in the foreseeable future?   **(10 marks)**

(c)   Assuming that one of the options facing the PleasureFood Group is expansion into overseas markets, what are the factors which should be evaluated before such an option is actively pursued?   **(10 marks)**

(d)   How could the PleasureFood Group create competitive advantages for itself against the major threat presented by McDonalds?   **(10 marks)**

Total marks = 40

Note. It is permissible to make assumptions by adding to the case details supplied above, provided the essence of the case study is neither changed nor undermined in any way by what is added. You may assume that the PleasureFood Group is located in the UK or in any other country of your choice.

PART B - Answer THREE questions only

Question 2

Critically examine the accuracy of each of the following statements which are often to be found in marketing literature:

(a)   'The customer is king (or queen)'

(b)   'The customer is always right'

In what circumstances is it possible that these propositions could be successfully challenged? How accurate are they, for example, when applied to

(1)   the concept of the 'internal customer' and

(2)   the 'customers' of a monopoly such as a water utility, municipal authority or taxation-funded central government department?

(20 marks)

Question 3

What does the term 'customer-centric' mean when applied to the structure of an organisation engaged in **either** financial services OR retailing? Having produced your answer, discuss the features of any organisation known to you which in your judgement is **not** customer-centric, and outline what changes would need to be introduced if the organisation in question were to seek to become genuinely customer-centric.

(20 marks)

Question 4

Debates continue to rage about whether mass customisation is

(a)   a marketing opportunity,

(b)   a threat,

(c)   a passing fad, or

(d)   an illusion.

Imagine that you work for a car manufacturer: write a report to your Marketing Manager in which you comment on each of the four interpretations offered above, in the context of the motor industry, and offer a reasoned assessment of the benefits and risks associated with mass customisation so far as your own company is concerned.

(20 marks)

Question 5

You are the newly-recruited marketing officer for either an international airline, a newspaper publisher, or a holiday package-tour business.

Produce a memo for your company's marketing department in which you explore

(a)   The future for electronic commerce in general terms;

(b)   The implications so far as your own organisation is concerned; and

(c)   A reasoned set of actions which you believe your company should take in order to capitalise on the opportunity or prepare itself for the threats.

(20 marks)

Question 6

It has been widely argued that, in the future, manufacturing companies will find it virtually impossible to remain profitable through reliance on manufacturing alone; as a result, they will be forced, whether they like it or not, to achieve competitive superiority (if they can) in such arenas as customer service and relationship marketing. Why might it be thought that profitability from manufacturing alone is so problematic? In what specific ways can manufacturing companies ensure their continued success through customer service and relationship marketing? Illustrate your answer with relevant examples.

(20 marks)

Question 7

'Customers are being more aspirational, more demanding, more litigious and more ethical, all at the same time,' you hear someone say at a marketing conference. What do these claims mean, and what evidence could you produce to support them? Assuming that the speaker's predictions are correct, what are the implications of these developments so far as effective consumer marketing is concerned?

(20 marks)

SPECIMEN QUESTION PAPER: OUTLINE MARKING GUIDE

Introduction

Scripts will be assessed against the five competencies explored in the Tutors Guidance Notes, namely:

- Breadth of familiarity with the subject-matter
- Depth of comprehension and understanding
- Demonstration of a businesslike perspective
- Application capability
- Packaging skills

The precise balance between these five will depend on the priorities within any given question. No specific mark allocation will be made available for 'packaging skills', but it may be assumed that it could influence about 10 per cent of the assessment (ie 2 marks out of 20 for Part B, 4 marks out of 40 for Part A).

PART A

As the question wording itself specifies, 10 marks may be awarded for each of the substantive ingredients within the case-study report. The four separate totals, when added together, may be supplemented by up to a further 4 marks for adherence to the requirement for a business report.

PART B

Question 2

Critical examination of the two statements supplied (10 marks) plus a further 10 marks for comments on their accuracy when applied to 'internal' customers and the 'customers' of a monopoly.

Question 3

Ten marks for exploration of the term 'customer-centric' in relation to structure, leadership, recruitment, reward systems, values, processes geared around customer types or categories, and so forth; a further 10 marks for references to an organisation which is not customer-centric and what it might do to transform itself.

Question 4

Commentary on the four interpretations of mass customisation (10 marks) plus the remaining 10 marks for an assessment of the benefits and risks within the car manufacturer.

Question 5

The future for electronic commerce in general terms (10 marks) plus 10 marks for the specific implications and suggested action programme.

Question 6

Examination of the reasons why profitability from manufacturing alone could be problematic (10 marks), plus 10 marks for the ways in which manufacturing companies can survive through customer service and relationship marketing. Credit will particularly be given for the inclusion of examples, eg GE's use of microchips and satellite communications for product maintenance.

Question 7

Discussion of the claim that customers are more aspirational, more litigious and more ethical, plus supply of supporting evidence (10 marks), with a further 10 marks for the implications in the field of consumer marketing.

RELATIONSHIP TO THE INDICATIVE CONTENT

PART A

1   Overview, Concepts and Background, *especially 1.2, 1.3*

2   Managing the Marketing/Customer Interface, *especially 2.1, 2.3 and 2.4*

3   Customer Dynamics, *especially 3.2*

4   Investigating Customer Dynamics, *passim*

5   Customer Dynamics and the Future, *passim*

PART B

Question 2

1   Overview, Concepts and Background, *especially 1.1*

2   Managing the Marketing/Customer Interface, *especially 2.2*

3   Customer Dynamics, *especially 3.1*

Question 3

1   Overview, Concepts and Background, *especially 1.4*

2   Managing the Marketing/Customer Interface, *passim*

Question 4

1   Overview, Concepts and Background, *especially 1.2, 1.3*

2   Managing the Marketing/Customer Interface, *especially 2.4*

3   Customer Dynamics, *passim*

5   Customer Dynamics and the Future, *especially 5.1*

Question 5

1   Overview, Concepts and Background, *especially 1.2*

2   Managing the Marketing/Customer Interface, *passim*

3   Customer Dynamics, *passim*

5   Customer Dynamics and the Future, *passim*

Question 6

1   Overview, Concepts and Background, *especially 1.2, 1.3*

2   Managing the Marketing/Customer Interface, *especially 2.1, 2.3 and 2.4*

3   Customer Dynamics, *especially 3.4*

5   Customer Dynamics and the Future, *passim*

Question 7

1   Overview, Concepts and Background, *especially 1.2*

2   Managing the Marketing/Customer Interface, *especially 2.4*

3   Customer Dynamics, *passim*

4   Investigating Customer Dynamics, *passim*

5   Customer Dynamics and the Future, *especially 5.1*

List of key concepts and index

BPP
PUBLISHING

BPP
PUBLISHING

CIM Order

To BPP Publishing Ltd, Aldine Place, London W12 8AA

Tel: 020 8740 2211. Fax: 020 8740 1184

Mr/Mrs/Ms (Full name) _____

Daytime delivery address _____

Postcode _____

Daytime Tel _____

Date of exam (month/year) _____

	6/99 Texts	9/99 Kits	9/99 Tapes	Specimen paper (When available)
CERTIFICATE				
1 Marketing Environment	£16.95 ☐	£7.95 ☐	£12.95 ☐	☐
2 Customer Communications in Marketing	£16.95 ☐	£7.95 ☐	£12.95 ☐	☐
3 Marketing in Practice	£16.95 ☐	£7.95 ☐	£12.95 ☐	☐
4 Marketing Fundamentals	£16.95 ☐	£7.95 ☐	£12.95 ☐	☐
ADVANCED CERTIFICATE				
5 The Marketing Customer Interface	£16.95 ☐	£7.95 ☐	£12.95 ☐	☐
6 Management Information for Marketing Decisions	£16.95 ☐	£7.95 ☐	£12.95 ☐	☐
7 Effective Management for Marketing	£16.95 ☐	£7.95 ☐	£12.95 ☐	☐
8 Marketing Operations	£16.95 ☐	£7.95 ☐	£12.95 ☐	☐
DIPLOMA				
9 Integrated Marketing Communications	£17.95 ☐	£8.95 ☐	£12.95 ☐	☐
10 International Marketing Strategy	£17.95 ☐	£8.95 ☐	£12.95 ☐	☐
11 Strategic Marketing Management: Planning and Control	£17.95 ☐	£8.95 ☐	£12.95 ☐	☐
12 Strategic Marketing Management: Analysis and Decision (9/99)	£24.95 ☐			☐
SUBTOTAL				£ ☐

POSTAGE & PACKING

Study Texts

	First	Each extra
UK	£3.00	£2.00 £ ☐
Europe*	£5.00	£4.00 £ ☐
Rest of world	£20.00	£10.00 £ ☐

Kits/Passcards/Success Tapes

	First	Each extra
UK	£2.00	£1.00 £ ☐
Europe*	£2.50	£1.00 £ ☐
Rest of world	£15.00	£8.00 £ ☐

Grand Total (Cheques to *BPP Publishing*) I enclose

a cheque for (incl. Postage) £ ☐

Or charge to Access/Visa/Switch

Card Number ☐☐☐☐☐☐☐☐☐☐☐☐☐

Expiry date ☐☐☐☐   Start Date _____

Issue Number (Switch Only) _____

Signature _____

We aim to deliver to all UK addresses inside 5 working days. Orders to all EU addresses should be delivered within 6 working days.
All other orders to overseas addresses should be delivered within 8 working days.
* Europe includes the Republic of Ireland and the Channel Islands.

REVIEW FORM & FREE PRIZE DRAW

All original review forms from the entire BPP range, completed with genuine comments, will be entered into one of two draws on 31 January 2000 and 31 July 2000. The names on the first four forms picked out on each occasion will be sent a cheque for £50.

Name: _____   **Address:** _____

_____

_____

How have you used this Text?
(Tick one box only)

☐ Home study (book only)

☐ On a course: college _____

☐ With 'correspondence' package

☐ Other _____

Why did you decide to purchase this Text?
(Tick one box only)

☐ Have used companion Kit

☐ Have used BPP Texts in the past

☐ Recommendation by friend/colleague

☐ Recommendation by a lecturer at college

☐ Saw advertising

☐ Other _____

During the past six months do you recall seeing/receiving any of the following?
(Tick as many boxes as are relevant)

☐ Our advertisement in the *Marketing Success*

☐ Our advertisement in *Marketing Business*

☐ Our brochure with a letter through the post

☐ Our brochure with *Marketing Business*

Which (if any) aspects of our advertising do you find useful?
(Tick as many boxes as are relevant)

☐ Prices and publication dates of new editions

☐ Information on Text content

☐ Facility to order books off-the-page

☐ None of the above

Have you used the companion Practice & Revision Kit for this subject?   ☐ Yes   ☐ No

Your ratings, comments and suggestions would be appreciated on the following areas.

	Very useful	Useful	Not useful
Introductory section (How to use this text, study checklist, etc)	☐	☐	☐
Setting the Scene	☐	☐	☐
Syllabus coverage	☐	☐	☐
Action Programmes and Marketing at Work examples	☐	☐	☐
Chapter roundups	☐	☐	☐
Quick quizzes	☐	☐	☐
Illustrative questions	☐	☐	☐
Content of suggested answers	☐	☐	☐
Index	☐	☐	☐
Structure and presentation	☐	☐	☐

	Excellent	Good	Adequate	Poor
Overall opinion of this Text	☐	☐	☐	☐

Do you intend to continue using BPP Study Texts/Kits?   ☐ Yes   ☐ No

Please note any further comments and suggestions/errors on the reverse of this page.

Please return to: Kate Machattie, BPP Publishing Ltd, FREEPOST, London, W12 8BR

REVIEW FORM & FREE PRIZE DRAW (continued)

Please note any further comments and suggestions/errors below.

FREE PRIZE DRAW RULES

1   Closing date for 31 January 2000 draw is 31 December 1999. Closing date for 31 July 2000 draw is 30 June 2000.

2   Restricted to entries with UK and Eire addresses only. BPP employees, their families and business associates are excluded.

3   No purchase necessary. Entry forms are available upon request from BPP Publishing. No more than one entry per title, per person. Draw restricted to persons aged 16 and over.

4   Winners will be notified by post and receive their cheques not later than 6 weeks after the relevant draw date. Lists of winners will be published in BPP's *focus* newsletter following the relevant draw.

5   The decision of the promoter in all matters is final and binding. No correspondence will be entered into.